KU-573-450

SUPPLEMENTARY VOLUME LXXX
2006

THE ARISTOTELIAN SOCIETY

THE SYMPOSIA READ AT THE
JOINT SESSION OF THE
ARISTOTELIAN SOCIETY
AND THE MIND ASSOCIATION
AT THE UNIVERSITY OF SOUTHAMPTON
JULY 2006

PUBLISHED BY
The Aristotelian Society
2006

First published 2006 by
The Aristotelian Society

ISBN 0 907111 54 8
ISSN 0309-7013

THE ARISTOTELIAN SOCIETY PUBLICATIONS

PROCEEDINGS: as a journal, three times a year, and as a bound volume annually in June.

SUPPLEMENTARY VOLUME: annually in June. This records the papers read at the annual Joint Session of the Aristotelian Society and the Mind Association.

BOOK SERIES (in co-operation with Blackwell Publishers): The Society has editorial responsibility for these books, which are published by Blackwells. They are available at less than half price to members of the Society. Currently available:

Barry Taylor	*Modes of Occurrence: Verbs, Adverbs and Events* (1985)
Jonathan Westphal	*Colour: Some Philosophical Problems from Wittgenstein* (1987)
Tim Maudlin	*Quantum Non-Locality and Relativity: Metaphysical Intimations of Modern Physics* (1994)
John Martin Fischer	*The Metaphysics of Free Will* (1994)
S. Lovibond & S. Williams (eds)	*Essays for David Wiggins: Identity, Truth and Value* (1996)
J. Corbi and J. Prades	*Minds, Causes and Mechanisms* (2000)
Tom Sorell	*Moral Theory and Anomaly* (2000)

LINES OF THOUGHT SERIES: These books are published by Oxford University Press, which offers them to members of the Society at a 25% discount. Already published:

Jerry A. Fodor	*Hume Variations* (2003)
David O. Brink	*Perfectionism and the Common Good: Themes in the Philosophy of T. H. Green* (2003)
Mark Eli Kalderan	*Moral Fictionalism* (2005)
Jason Stanley	*Knowledge and Practical Interests* (2005)

ORDERS for past *Proceedings* and *Supplementary Volumes*: Single issues from the current and previous two volumes are available at the current single issue price from Blackwell Publishers Journals. Earlier issues may be obtained from Swets & Zeitlinger, Back Sets, Heereweg 347, PO Box 810, 2160 Lisse, The Netherlands. Email: backsets@swets.nl

All institutional enquiries should be addressed to the Distributors.

OTHER ENQUIRIES should be addressed to the Editor.

Printed in England by
4word Ltd
Unit 15 Bakers Park
Cater Road
Bristol BS13 7TT

Journals Subscriptions Department
Marston Book Services
PO Box 87, Oxford OX2 0DT
Tel (01865) 791155
Fax (01865) 791927

Editor:
Mark Eli Kalderan
Department of Philosophy
University College London
Gower Street
London WC1E 6BT

Assistant Editor:
David Harris
Department or Philosophy
University College London
Gower Street
London WC1E 6BT

Please check in most recent volume for current addresses

CONTENTS

PROGRAMME

JOINT SESSION OF THE ARISTOTELIAN SOCIETY AND THE MIND ASSOCIATION UNIVERSITY OF SOUTHAMPTON, 7–9 JULY 2006

Friday 7 July	5.00 pm	The Inaugural Address: Timothy Williamson *'Conceptual Truth'* Chair: Aaron Ridley
Saturday 8 July	9.00 am	Andy Clark and Naomi Eilan *Sensorimotor Skills and Perception* Chair: Barry Smith
	11.00 am	Sally Haslanger and Jennifer Saul *Philosophical Analysis and Social Kinds* Chair: Miranda Fricker
	2.00 pm	Graduate Papers
	4.30 pm	Submitted Papers—Open Sessions
	8.00 pm	John Hawthorne and Scott Sturgeon *Disjunctivism* Chair: Matt Soteriou
Sunday 9 July	9.00 am	Tom Hurka and John Tasioulas *Games and the Good* Chair: Brad Hooker
	11.00 am	Lloyd Humberstone and Herman Cappelen *Sufficiency and Excess* Chair: Peter Milne
	11.00 am	Ken Gemes and Christopher Janaway *Nietzsche on Free Will and Autonomy* Chair: Peter Poellner
	2.00 pm	Submitted Papers—Open Sessions
	4.30 pm	Submitted Papers—Open Sessions

The Inaugural Address

'CONCEPTUAL TRUTH'

by Timothy Williamson

ABSTRACT The paper criticizes epistemological conceptions of analytic or conceptual truth, on which assent to such truths is a necessary condition of understanding them. The critique involves no Quinean scepticism about meaning. Rather, even granted that a paradigmatic candidate for analyticity is synonymy with a logical truth, both the former and the latter can be intelligibly doubted by linguistically competent deviant logicians, who, although mistaken, still constitute counterexamples to the claim that assent is necessary for understanding. There are no analytic or conceptual truths in the epistemological sense. The critique is extended to purportedly analytic inference rules. An alternative account is sketched on which understanding a word is a matter of participation in a linguistic practice, while synonymy and concept identity consist in sameness of truth-conditional semantic properties. Although there are philosophical questions about concepts, the idea that philosophical questions in general are conceptual questions generates only an illusion of insight into philosophical methodology.

I

How do we know that vixens are female foxes? Such questions tend to receive short shrift. We are told that it is a *conceptual truth* that vixens are female foxes, or that it is *conceptually impossible* for something to be a vixen without being a female fox, or that being a vixen has *conceptual connections* to being female and being a fox. In unfashionable terminology, 'Vixens are female foxes' is said to be *analytic*. What, if anything, do such responses mean? How, if at all, do they answer the original question?

Since it is a boring triviality that vixens are female foxes, one might wonder how much those questions matter. Yet human reasoning is riddled with steps like those from 'vixen' to 'female' and 'fox'. Many are equally trivial, but more significant steps of reasoning have been assimilated to the trivial ones: for example, basic inferences in deductive logic, characteristic moves in philosophical argument, and fundamental inferences involving theoretical terms in natural science have all been treated as somehow built into the concepts or the meanings of the words at issue, and as backed by conceptual or analytic truths with a status not fundamentally different from that of 'Vixens are female foxes'. Until we are clear about the epistemology of the simple, unimportant cases, we are poorly placed to judge the aptness of assimilating the more complex, important cases to them, and whether doing so renders the latter epistemologically unproblematic. Some mathematicians use the rule of thumb that one should not try to solve a problem when one cannot yet solve a simpler problem of the same form. Applying the rule to questions of conceptual truth, let us start with 'Every vixen is a female fox'.[1]

A common view is that analytic or conceptual truths are epistemologically unproblematic because whatever cognitive work is necessary for understanding them is somehow already sufficient for knowing them to be true. Thus principles like this are implicitly or explicitly proposed:

UKt Necessarily, whoever grasps the thought that every vixen is a female fox knows that every vixen is a female fox.

Some clarifications are in order. To grasp a thought is to entertain it, irrespective of what specific attitude such as belief, disbelief or wonder one takes towards it. Since a thought in UKt is the candidate bearer of *conceptual* truth, we should presumably take it as composed of concepts in something like the way in which a sentence is composed of words. Thus a thought is not a set of possible worlds, which has no such structure. Nor is a thought a Russellian proposition, composed out of the objects, properties and relations which it is about; a thought about Vienna contains a concept of Vienna, not Vienna itself. If a proposition is a Fregean thought, the sense of a sentence, composed of the senses of its constituent expressions, then thoughts may be propositions. But if propositions are sets of possible worlds, Russellian propositions, or something else of that worldly kind, then thoughts are not propositions, although they may express propositions. For example, if it is a conceptual truth that Hesperus is Hesperus, but no conceptual truth that Hesperus is Phosphorus, then the thought

1. Of course, it is not always clear in advance which problem is simpler. Sometimes it is easier to find a proof by mathematical induction of a stronger hypothesis than of a weaker one.

that Hesperus is Hesperus is not the thought that Hesperus is Phosphorus, even though the Russellian proposition that Hesperus is Hesperus is the Russellian proposition that Hesperus is Phosphorus, and the set of possible worlds in which Hesperus is Hesperus is the set of possible worlds in which Hesperus is Phosphorus.[2,3] If propositions are not thoughts, questions of conceptual truth, conceptual necessity and conceptual connections do not arise at the level of propositions, but only at that of thoughts. Consequently, there is a terminological awkwardness if propositional attitude constructions in English (such as 'knows that every vixen is a female fox') ascribe relations to propositions rather than thoughts, for then UKt is not formulated at the level at which questions of conceptual truth arise. However, we can finesse the issue by reading UKt in that case as concerning only grasping and knowing which relate to the proposition that every vixen is a female fox under the guise of the thought which the sentence 'Every vixen is a female fox' expresses in the present context. For defenders of conceptual truth, such a reading should not be too artificial. Analogous qualifications will be in force throughout this paper. Thus the theorist of thought can allow that one may know that Hesperus is Hesperus without thereby knowing that Hesperus is Phosphorus, and that knowing that $0 = 0$ does not automatically count as knowing that every vixen is a female fox.[4]

A linguistic analogue of UKt is:

UKl Necessarily, whoever understands the sentence 'Every vixen is a female fox' recognizes it as true.

2. Add the condition 'if Hesperus exists' if needed.
3. Attempts are sometimes made to distinguish the Russellian proposition that Hesperus is Hesperus from the Russellian proposition that Hesperus is Phosphorus by treating the proper names as abbreviations of (rigidified) definite descriptions. Those who favour such attempts may wish to identify thoughts with Russellian propositions. Attempts are also sometimes made to distinguish the set of possible worlds in which Hesperus is Hesperus from the set of possible worlds in which Hesperus is Phosphorus by considering the worlds as live epistemic ('indicative') possibilities rather than as metaphysical ('counterfactual') possibilities, so that the sets are 'primary intensions' rather than 'secondary intensions' (see Chalmers 2002). Those who favour the latter attempts can make finer-grained distinctions by identifying thoughts with complexes composed quasi-sententially out of primary intensions as the atomic constituents rather than simply with primary intensions themselves.
4. For accounts of propositional attitude ascriptions on which UKt needs such fine-tuning see Stalnaker 1984 and 1999 and Salmon 1986.

Recognition as true here is assent to the sentence on the basis of knowledge of the truth which it expresses. For example, you recognize the sentence 'Every vixen is a female fox' as true because you know that it means that every vixen is a female fox and that every vixen *is* a female fox. The explicit metalinguistic thought that the sentence is true is not required. Thus recognition is factive, because knowledge is: one can recognize a sentence as true only if it is true. Of course, the sentence 'Every vixen is a female fox' in UKl must be taken with its actual present meaning in English, since UKl would trivially fail if we allowed understandings of 'Every vixen is a female fox' with a counterfactual meaning, such as that every viscount is a female fox. In charity too, we can and should read UKt and UKl so that a native speaker of English who has never explicitly addressed the question whether every vixen is a female fox does not thereby constitute a counterexample. Call principles such as UKt and UKl 'understanding/knowledge links'.

In effect, understanding/knowledge links say that the epistemological problem is automatically solved for the thoughts or sentences in question; but they do not say *how* it is solved. An account of that might start with some weak consequences of such links. For UKt and UKl entail UBt and UBl respectively:

UBt Necessarily, whoever grasps the thought that every vixen is a female fox believes that every vixen is a female fox.

UBl Necessarily, whoever understands the sentence 'Every vixen is a female fox' assents to it.

For, we may assume, knowledge entails belief and recognition as true entails assent, but not vice versa. Unlike knowledge and recognition, belief and assent are not factive. Call principles such as UBt and UBl 'understanding/belief' links. One might regard UBt and UBl as more or less bedrock or constitutive constraints on, respectively, possession of the concepts which make up the thought that every vixen is a female fox and understanding of the words and modes of combination which make up the sentence 'Every vixen is a female fox'. On this view, belief is simply part of what it takes to grasp the thought, and assent is simply part of what it takes to understand the sentence. In the terminology of Carnap (1947, p. 222), the sentence is a meaning postulate. Similar conceptions remain in the background of much contemporary discussion.

Since belief does not entail knowledge and assent does not entail recognition as true, the respective paths back from UBt and UBl to UKt and UKl must be less direct. Nevertheless, attempts have been made to explain understanding/knowledge links by appeal to understanding/belief links. On such a view, an understanding/belief link for a thought or sentence somehow constrains it to have a content or meaning on which it is true: accordingly, UBt makes the thought that every vixen is a female fox true and UBl makes the sentence 'Every vixen is a female fox' true. Thus the understanding/belief link would somehow generate an understanding/truth link, so that the belief would be formed in a reliable way. That reliability might itself be regarded as epistemically transparent or otherwise special enough to generate, somehow or other, an understanding/knowledge link. In some such way, the constitutive conditions for grasping the thought or understanding the sentence are supposed to explain the knowledge in question. If such an epistemological schema is realized, the thought, for instance that every vixen is a female fox, will deserve the title of 'conceptual truth', and the corresponding sentence will deserve to be called 'analytic'.[5]

For philosophers of an internalist bent, the key epistemological notion is justification rather than knowledge. They will focus on understanding/justification links:

UJBt Necessarily, whoever grasps the thought that every vixen is a female fox is justified in believing that every vixen is a female fox.

UJBl Necessarily, whoever understands the sentence 'Every vixen is a female fox' is justified in assenting to it.

5. For a recent example of a programme of something like the envisaged kind see Boghossian 1997 and 2003. The careful qualifications there make little difference to the arguments below. Williamson 2003 replies to Boghossian 2003; the present paper takes its arguments further. The theory of concept possession developed in Peacocke 1992 and modified in many subsequent publications is related to understanding/belief links. More generally, programmes which go under titles such as 'conceptual role semantics', 'inferentialism', 'use theories of meaning', and the like, tend to rely on assumptions of the kind at issue. The focus of this paper is not on some few thinkers in particular; it aims to make explicit and criticize a conception on which many contemporary philosophers still rely, often tacitly, at various points in their work.

Some rationalists may regard such links as characteristic of a priori intuition. Whether they try to derive them from understanding/belief links, and whether they endorse the preceding story about understanding/truth and understanding/knowledge links, are further questions.

It is often allowed that understanding/belief links can fail to generate understanding/truth links, and thereby fail to generate understanding/knowledge links, if the beliefs built into understanding by the former links embody substantive commitments about the world, for the world may be unkind. Perhaps the understanding of some theoretical terms in science embodies theories not satisfied by any things in nature at all, as some say of 'phlogiston'. The beliefs built into understanding may even turn out to be inconsistent, as some say of 'true', adverting to the threat which the Liar paradox poses to disquotational principles about truth. Once the error has come to light, such beliefs cease to be justified, if they ever were, and the understanding/justification links fail, although versions watered down with a '*ceteris paribus*' clause might survive. We should reject the beliefs together with the concepts and meanings in which they are embedded. Of course, where understanding/truth links fail there is no analytic or conceptual *truth*. Nevertheless, the idea of concepts or meanings which embody errors or confusions itself depends on something like understanding/belief links.

Such failures of the understanding/truth links may be treated as pathological cases. Thus understanding/belief links may still be held to generate understanding/truth links in non-pathological cases, and thereby indirectly to explain understanding/knowledge links. Others will treat the failure of understanding/belief links to generate understanding/truth links as more general, and reject the understanding/knowledge links altogether. For example, some naturalists hold that many assumptions built into ordinary concepts or the meanings of ordinary words are simply the prejudices of folk theory: even when the assumptions are in fact true, merely possessing the concepts or understanding the words does not enable one to know that they are true. But someone who rejects a folk concept or part of folk language on the grounds that it embeds a false theory still seems to presuppose something like an understanding/belief link, for without such links there is no embedding: one could keep the understanding and drop the beliefs.[6]

The foregoing remarks, however sketchy and programmatic, serve to indicate a familiar cluster of vague ideas. The cluster has been under a cloud since Quine argued in 'Two Dogmas of Empiricism' that 'a boundary between analytic and synthetic statements simply has not been drawn' (1953, p. 37). But without a strong independent desire to believe Quine's conclusions, it is hard to find his arguments compelling. They require verificationist or reductionist assumptions about meaning which we lack good reason to accept. One of his targets, the idea of synonymy, is alive and well, both in semantics as a branch of linguistics and in the philosophy of language, which suggests that his arguments, if they proved anything, would prove too much. Although the idea of analyticity has never quite regained the central position in analytic philosophy which it occupied before 'Two Dogmas', the reason for that may be less Quine's critique than Kripke's clarification of the differences between analyticity, apriority and metaphysical necessity. Kripke did not deny the existence of a boundary between the analytic and the synthetic; he merely distinguished it from other boundaries, between the a priori and the a posteriori and between the necessary and the contingent (1980, p. 39). In effect, he showed that the analytic/synthetic distinction could not do the work proper to those other distinctions, contrary to what had been expected of it in the heyday of the 'linguistic turn'.[7] Often under the less provocative guise of 'conceptual truth' or 'conceptual necessity', analyticity plays a reduced but still substantive role in contemporary philosophy.

There is little reason to doubt that if we try to sort statements as 'analytic' or 'synthetic' in the manner of chicken-sexers, we can generally achieve a rough consensus. Of course, borderline cases will occur, but so they do for almost every distinction worth making: perfect precision is an unreasonable demand. The issue is what theoretical significance, if any, attaches to the rough

6. In effect, Horwich (1998, pp. 131–53) allows understanding/belief links for which the understanding/truth links fail.
7. For some criticisms of the linguistic turn which complement the considerations of this paper, see Williamson 2004a.

boundary thus drawn. As indicated above, much of the putative significance of the analytic/synthetic distinction is epistemological. That epistemological significance depends on something like understanding/belief links.

This paper gives reasons to reject understanding/belief links. *A fortiori*, those are reasons to reject understanding/knowledge links too. Similar considerations defeat understanding/justification links. Those putative links depend on a misapprehension of what it is to possess a concept or to understand a word. When we strip out the verificationism and scepticism about meaning from Quine's arguments, epistemological insights remain. The arguments of this paper involve no Quinean scepticism about meaning. Rather, they rely on our rough working conceptions of meaning and understanding—for example, when applying UBl—in order to reach the conclusion that no truths are analytic in the epistemological sense.

Section II argues that anything like an understanding/belief link fails for some elementary logical truths. Section III generalizes the argument to other truths which are often called 'analytic' or 'conceptual'. If analyticity or conceptual truth requires anything like an understanding/belief link, then there is no analyticity or conceptual truth.[8] The final section begins to sketch an alternative account of understanding, on which no such links are needed.

8. This paper is not directly concerned with conceptions of analyticity as truth in virtue of meaning, although it does show that such conceptions lack the epistemological payoff which might be hoped from them. They are, in any case, less influential in contemporary philosophy. It is widely acknowledged that 'Vixens are female foxes' is true not simply because it means that vixens are female foxes but because it means that vixens are female foxes and vixens *are* female foxes, just as 'Vixens are hunted' is true not simply because it means that vixens are hunted but because it means that vixens are hunted and vixens *are* hunted. Of course, it is necessary that every sentence which means that vixens are female foxes is true, and merely contingent whether every sentence which means that vixens are hunted is true, but that does not show that 'Vixens are female foxes' is true in virtue of meaning in any interesting sense, even given that the sentence means that vixen are female foxes, in the absence of an independently established connection between meaning and necessity—just as the corresponding point with 'always the case' in place of 'necessary' does not show that 'Vixens are female foxes' is true in virtue of meaning, since there is no independently established connection of the right kind between meaning and time. It is necessary that every sentence which means that 97 is prime is true, but that does not show that '97 is prime' is true in virtue of meaning, even given that it means that 97 is prime. Similarly, that a sentence is synonymous with a logical truth does not show that it is true in virtue of meaning in the absence of an independent argument that logical truths are true in virtue of meaning.

II

Here is an elementary logical truth:

(1) Every vixen is a vixen.

Few quantified logical truths are simpler than (1), in either syntactic complexity or the number of steps needed to derive them in a standard system of natural deduction rules.[9]

One might be tempted to endorse understanding/belief links for (1):

UBt* Necessarily, whoever grasps the thought that every vixen is a vixen believes that every vixen is a vixen.
UBl* Necessarily, whoever understands the sentence 'Every vixen is a vixen' assents to it.

On the pattern of Section I, UBt* and UBl* might be exploited in an attempt to derive corresponding understanding/knowledge links for (1):

UKt* Necessarily, whoever grasps the thought that every vixen is a vixen knows that every vixen is a vixen.
UKl* Necessarily, whoever understands the sentence 'Every vixen is a vixen' recognizes it as true.

But are UBt* and UBl*, let alone UKt* and UKl*, even true? Consider two native speakers of English, Peter and Stephen.

Peter's first step in evaluating (1) is to notice that it seems to presuppose:

(2) There is at least one vixen.

On reflection, Peter comes to the considered view that the presupposition is a logical entailment. He regards the truth of

9. Parenthetical numerals such as '(1)' are taken throughout to refer to sentences rather than to the thoughts which those sentences express. On a standard formalization of (1) as $\forall x\,(Vx \rightarrow Vx)$, one proves it by starting from an instance of the rule of assumption, $Vx \vdash Vx$, applying the standard introduction rule for '$\rightarrow$', conditional proof, to discharge the premiss, giving $\vdash Vx \rightarrow Vx$, followed by the standard introduction rule for '$\forall$', universal generalization, to reach $\vdash \forall x\,(Vx \rightarrow Vx)$ (no logical truth can be derived by the usual quantifier and structural rules alone, since none of them permits the discharge of all assumptions). A formalization of (1) closer to the English original uses a binary quantifier: $\vdash$ (EVERYx (Vx; Vx)) is derivable from $Vx \vdash Vx$ in a single step by an appropriate introduction rule for 'EVERY'.

'There is at least one F' as a necessary condition for the truth of 'Every F is a G' quite generally, and the falsity of 'There is at least one F' as a sufficient condition for the falsity of 'Every F is a G'; he takes universal quantification to be existentially committing. More formally, he holds that 'Every F is a G' is true if and only if (i) there is a value of the variable 'x' for which 'x is an F' is true, and (ii) there is no value of the variable 'x' for which 'x is an F' is true while 'x is a G' is not, and that 'Every F is a G' is false if and only if it is not true. Peter also has the weird belief that (2) is false. For he spends far too much time surfing the Internet, and once came across a site devoted to propagating the view that there are no foxes, and therefore no vixens, and never have been: all the apparent evidence to the contrary has been planted by a secret international agency; for sinister purposes best known to itself, it produces elaborate fox-hallucinations. Being a sucker for conspiracy theories, Peter accepted this one. Since he denies (2) and regards it as a logical consequence of (1), he also denies (1), and so does not assent to (1).[10]

Stephen has no time for Peter's pet theories. What worries him is vagueness. He believes that borderline cases for vague terms constitute truth-value gaps. Like many truth-value gap theorists (such as Soames 1999), he generalizes classical two-valued semantics by treating the gap as a third value ('undefined') and using Kleene's three-valued 'strong tables' (1952, p. 334). On Stephen's view, for 'Every F is a G' to be true is for the conditional 'x is an $F \rightarrow x$ is a G' to be true for every value of the variable 'x'; for 'Every F is a G' to be false is for 'x is an $F \rightarrow x$ is a G' to be false for some value of 'x'. On his semantics, for the conditional sentence with '$\rightarrow$' to be true is for either its antecedent to be false or its consequent to be true, and for it to be false is for its antecedent to be true and its consequent false. Stephen also believes that some clearly female evolutionary ancestors of foxes are borderline cases for 'fox' and therefore for 'vixen'. Consequently, for such an animal as the value of 'x', 'x is a vixen' is neither true nor false, so the conditional 'x is a vixen

10. Alternatively, one can imagine that Peter thinks that foxes were only recently hunted to extinction, but that his presentist conception of time implies that (2) is true only if there is now at least one vixen. Yet another alternative is that Peter is a metaphysician who denies (2) on the grounds that putative macroscopic objects such as foxes do not exist, because if they did they would have vague boundaries, and nothing can have vague boundaries (compare Horgan 1998).

$\rightarrow x$ is a vixen' is also neither true nor false, by the strong Kleene table for '$\rightarrow$'. Hence 'Every vixen is a vixen' is not true; it is also not false, because the conditional is not false for any value of 'x'. Thus Stephen treats (1) as a truth-value gap. Of course, his initial reaction when presented with (1) is not to go through this explicit metalinguistic reasoning; he just says 'What about borderline cases?' But his refusal to assent to (1) as true is firm.[11]

Let us assume that Peter and Stephen are wrong about (1), at least on its standard reading: it is in fact a logical truth. It is true however we interpret its only non-logical syntactically atomic constituent, 'vixen', given classical logic and two-valued semantics. If not, we can change the example, describing new characters who are deviant with respect to some sentence which really is a logical truth. Peter and Stephen do not assent to (1). Thus, according to UBl*, Peter and Stephen do not understand (1) (with its standard English meaning). If so, they presumably fail to understand at least one of its constituent words or modes of combination. Is that the impression which one would have in conversing with them?

Both Peter and Stephen treat 'vixen' as synonymous with 'female fox'. Stephen's popular but mistaken theory of vagueness does not prevent him from understanding 'female', 'fox', or their mode of combination. Even Peter's conspiracy theory, however silly, involves no semantic deviation, just as religious fanatics who assert that there were never any dinosaurs do exactly that: they use the words 'There were never any dinosaurs' to assert that there were never any dinosaurs. Their problem is not that they fail to understand the word 'dinosaur', but that they have silly beliefs about prehistory. Peter, like Stephen, understands the word 'vixen'.

The best candidate for a word or mode of composition in (1) which Peter and Stephen fail to understand is the word 'every'. Is it a good enough candidate? Peter's not uncommon conception of the existential commitments of universal quantification makes little difference in practice, for when sentences of the form 'Every

11. Note that while Peter assents to the conditional 'If there are vixens, then every vixen is a vixen', Stephen does not, because it has a true antecedent and an undefined consequent, and is therefore itself undefined on the Kleene semantics. Given the qualifications in Boghossian 2003, this makes Stephen more problematic than Peter for Boghossian's programme.

F is a *G*' occur in conversation, 'There is an *F*' tends to be common ground amongst the participants anyway; it is a pragmatic presupposition in the sense of Stalnaker 1999. Pragmatically, Peter adjusts his conversation to a society which obstinately retains its belief in the existence of foxes much as members of many other small sects with unpopular beliefs have learned to adjust to an unenlightened world. Stephen's deviation is less localized than Peter's, because his Kleene-inspired semantics turns many universal generalizations with empirical predicates into truth-value gaps. In practice, however, he often manages to ignore the problem by focusing on a small domain of contextually relevant objects amongst which there are no borderline cases for the noun or complex phrase which complements 'every'. Occasionally he cannot avoid the problem and sounds pedantic, as many academics do, but that hardly constitutes a failure to understand the words at issue. When Peter and Stephen are challenged on their logical deviations, they defend themselves fluently. In fact, both have published widely read articles on the issues in leading refereed journals of philosophy, in English. They appear to be like most philosophers, thoroughly competent in their native language, a bit odd in some of their views.

Someone might insist that Peter and Stephen appear to be using the word 'every' in its standard sense because they are really using it in senses very similar to, but not exactly the same as, the standard one. Indeed, it may be argued, their non-standard senses were explained above, since in each case a semantics for the relevant fragment of English was sketched on which (1) is not true, whereas by hypothesis, (1) is true on the standard semantics of English. However, matters are not so simple. Peter and Stephen are emphatic that they intend their words to be understood as words of our common language, with their standard English senses. They use 'every' and the other words in (1) as words of that public language. Each of them believes that his semantic theory is correct for English as spoken by others, not just by himself, and that if it turned out to be (heaven forbid!) incorrect for English as spoken by others, it would equally turn out to be incorrect for English as spoken by himself. Giving an incorrect theory of the meaning of a word is not the same as using the word with an idiosyncratic sense. Peter and Stephen's semantic beliefs about their own uses of 'every' may be false, even if they sometimes rely on those beliefs in conscious processes of truth evaluation. Indeed, we may assume that Peter and Stephen do not regard the elaborate articulations of truth conditions and falsity conditions for 'Every *F* is a *G*' above as capturing the way in which they or other English speakers conceptualize the meaning of 'every', which they regard as a semantically unstructured determiner for which a homophonic statement of meaning would be more faithful. For them, the more elaborate articulations are simply convenient records of important logical facts about 'every'. We may further assume that only in tricky cases do they resort to their non-standard semantic theories in evaluating non-metalinguistic claims such as (1) expresses. Their non-metalinguistic unorthodoxy as to when every *F* is a *G* is not ultimately derived by semantic descent from metalinguistic unorthodoxy as to when 'Every *F* is a *G*' is true; rather, the metalinguistic unorthodoxy is ultimately derived by semantic ascent from the non-metalinguistic unorthodoxy.

Peter and Stephen learned English in the normal way. They acquired their non-standard views as adults. At least before that, nothing in their use of English suggested semantic deviation. Surely they understood (1) and its constituent words and modes of construction with their ordinary meanings then. But the process by which they acquired their eccentricities did not involve forgetting their previous semantic understanding. For example, on their present understanding of (1), they have no difficulty in remembering why they used to assent to it. They were young and foolish then, with a tendency to accept claims on the basis of insufficient reflection. By ordinary standards, Peter and Stephen understand (1) perfectly well. Although their rejection of (1) might on first acquaintance give an observer a defeasible reason to deny that they understood it, any such reason is defeated by closer observation of them. They genuinely doubt that every vixen is a vixen. Peter and Stephen are not marginal cases of understanding: their linguistic competence is far more secure than that of young children or native speakers of other languages who are in the process of learning English. If some participants in a debate have an imperfect linguistic understanding of one of the key words with which it is conducted, they need to have its meaning explained to them before the debate can properly continue. But to stop our logical debate with Peter and Stephen in order to explain to them what the word 'every' means in English would be irrelevant and gratuitously patronizing. The understanding which they lack is logical, not semantic. Their attitudes to (1) manifest only some deviant patterns of belief. Since there clearly could have been, and perhaps are, people such as Peter and Stephen, we have counterexamples to UBl*.

It would be pointless to try to save UBl* by restricting it to rational agents. By ordinary standards, Peter and Stephen are rational agents. Although they fall short of some high standards of rationality, so do most humans. Understanding/belief links which do not apply to most humans will be of limited epistemological interest. The picture was that we can exclude those who appear to reject putatively conceptual truths from the discussion on the grounds that they lack the relevant concepts; but we cannot exclude humans who reject such truths from the discussion on those grounds if the connection between rejecting them and lacking the concepts holds only for superhumans, not for humans.

The foregoing considerations suggest a different possibility. Peter and Stephen once assented to (1). Perhaps they still have a disposition to assent to (1), masked by their later theorizing, and use 'every' and other words and modes of construction with the same senses as the rest of us because they have the same underlying inferential dispositions as the rest of us.[12] At some deep level, they have a disposition to accept (1) as true. That disposition is prevented from manifesting itself by conscious reflection at an overlying level of theory construction, just as someone's pet views about grammar might interfere with their performance in speech while having no effect on the syntactic competence which they possess in virtue of their underlying language module. UBt* and UBl* might therefore be watered down as follows:

UDBt* Necessarily, whoever grasps the thought that every vixen is a vixen has a disposition to believe that every vixen is a vixen.

UDBl* Necessarily, whoever understands the sentence 'Every vixen is a vixen' has a disposition to assent to it.

Having a disposition to believe a proposition does not entail believing it; having a disposition to assent to a sentence does not

12. See Martin 1994 and Martin and Heil 1998 for relevant discussion.

entail assenting to it. Thus UDBt* and UDBl* are consistent with the denials of UBt* and UBl*. In particular, perhaps Peter and Stephen grasp the thought that every vixen is a vixen and understand the sentence 'Every vixen is a vixen', and have the dispositions to believe that every vixen is a vixen and to assent to 'Every vixen is a vixen', although as it happens they do not believe that every vixen is a vixen or assent to 'Every vixen is a vixen'.

The dispositional story might be used as the basis for an answer to the question 'How do we know that every vixen is a vixen?' similar to that sketched in Section I. On such a view, a link between understanding and a disposition to believe a thought somehow constrains the belief to have a content on which it is true, and a link between understanding and a disposition to assent to a sentence likewise somehow constrains the sentence to have a meaning on which it is true: accordingly, UDBt* makes the thought that every vixen is a vixen true and UDBl* makes the sentence 'Every vixen is a vixen' true. Thus even the understanding/disposition-to-believe link would generate an understanding/truth link, so that the disposition to believe would be reliably truth-directed. That reliability might itself be regarded as epistemically transparent or otherwise special enough to generate, somehow or other, a corresponding understanding/disposition-to-know link:

UDKt* Necessarily, whoever grasps the thought that every vixen is a vixen has a disposition to know that every vixen is a vixen.

UDKl* Necessarily, whoever understands the sentence 'Every vixen is a vixen' has a disposition to recognize it as true.

But are UDBt* and UDBl*, let alone UDKt* and UDKl*, even true?

There are two salient ways of filling out the dispositional story: the *personal level* account and the *sub-personal level* account. On the personal level account, the postulated dispositions require counterfactual conditionals to the effect that the person would be brought round to appropriate propositional attitudes by sufficient conscious reflection, exposure to further arguments or the like. On this view, Peter and Stephen would believe that every vixen is a vixen and accept 'Every vixen is a vixen' as true if only they thought about it more or talked to more experts. By contrast, on the sub-personal level account, the postulated dispositions can be grounded in the structure of the person's unconscious logic module or the like, even if the personal-level counterfactual conditionals are false. On this view, the default outcome of Peter and Stephen's underlying competence is belief that every vixen is a vixen and assent to 'Every vixen is a vixen', even if that default is irreversibly overridden by stable dispositions to the contrary from other sources.

An analogous contrast arises in the case of syntax. To take a standard example, native speakers of English tend to reject (3) at first sight as ill-formed:

(3) The horse raced past the barn fell.

They want to insert 'and' between 'barn' and 'fell'. But they tend to change their minds about (3) when asked to consider the result of inserting 'which was' between 'horse' and 'raced' instead: they realize that the original string was well-formed after all; 'the horse' can be the object rather than the subject of 'raced'. Conversely, native speakers often unreflectively accept ill-formed strings as well-formed, for example when a verb in the plural is separated from its subject in the singular by a long intervening string which includes a noun in the plural, but can be brought to acknowledge their mistake, for example when a draft of a paper is corrected. On a personal level account, such conscious reflective judgements, actual or counterfactual, are necessary for well-formedness. On the contrasting sub-personal level account, such judgements play a merely evidential role: what constitutes well-formedness is the structure of the syntactic component of the unconscious language module, even if the person's conscious reflective judgement is irreversibly contrary as a result of extraneous factors, such as their dogmatic commitment to a pet theory of syntax.

The personal level account fails to shield UBtd* and UBld* from the counterexamples of Peter and Stephen. For, by hypothesis, their refusal to accept (1) as true is stable under conscious reflection, exposure to further arguments and the like. We may assume that as they became comfortable with their deviant theories they gradually ceased to feel even an initial inclination to assent to (1), although they still remember what it was like to feel such an inclination.

They assimilate the change to one in which education gradually eradicates the tendency to make a particular false assumption. On the personal level account, they are *not* disposed to accept (1) as true. Perhaps that makes them irrationally obstinate, but not more so than most philosophers and many other people. Such a degree of obstinacy in defence of a favourite view is frequently combined with possession of the concepts and understanding of the words and modes of construction at issue.

The sub-personal level account has more room for manoeuvre in defence of UDBt* and UDBl*. For it can insist that even though Peter and Stephen's personal refusal to accept (1) as true is stable under conscious reflection, exposure to further arguments, and so on, they still retain a disposition to accept (1) as true in virtue of features of their unconscious logic module. This view requires the postulated module to have a structurally distinct existence, for if it consisted only in acquired habits of reasoning, Peter and Stephen's earlier habits would eventually be erased by their later ones, and the disposition to accept (1) as true would disappear. Moreover, the module must include a component for deductive reasoning, since that is the kind of reasoning relevant to (1). After all, if the grounds for accepting (1) as true were merely inductive—that we have never observed a vixen which was not a vixen—then some people who understood (1) could reasonably refuse to accept it as true on the grounds that they had observed too few vixens to be in a position to judge. A prima facie attractive conjecture is that the deductive component of the reasoning module would comprise basic rules for natural language connectives similar to the introduction and elimination rules in a Gentzen-style system of natural deduction. But do humans have an unconscious logic module of the required sort?

One might suppose the primary adaptive value of a cognitive module to be its capacity to perform a specific type of useful information processing quickly and reliably enough for the purposes of action in a changing environment. Its design can exploit special features of the type of task to which it is dedicated, in order to achieve efficiencies which would be impossible for a general purpose central processing unit. A diversion through higher mental processes, in particular through consciousness, would be slower and less reliable. Thus one might expect unconscious modular deductive reasoning to pay its way by the speed and reliability of its results, just as modules for vision and natural language processing appear to do. Naturally, performance would tail off as the complexity of problems increased, but there should be good performance over a worthwhile range of non-trivial problems. Is that prediction borne out?

Evidence from empirical psychology, amassed over several decades, suggests that most humans are strikingly bad at even elementary deductive reasoning, a finding which should come as no surprise to those who have taught introductory logic. For example, in the combined results of over 65 large-scale experiments by different researchers on simple conditional reasoning, although 97% (not 100%!) of subjects endorsed *modus ponens* (if *p* then *q*; *p*; therefore *q*), only 72% endorsed *modus tollens* (if *p* then *q*; not-*q*; therefore not-*p*), while as many as 63% endorsed the fallacy of affirming the consequent (if *p* then *q*; *q*; therefore *p*) and 55% endorsed the fallacy of denying the antecedent (if *p* then *q*; not-*p*; therefore not-*q*). When the antecedent is negative, affirming the consequent overtakes *modus tollens* in popularity.[13] In some cases, when a further premiss of the form 'If *r* then *q*' is added to *modus ponens*, only a minority endorses the inference (Byrne 1989). Similar phenomena arise for elementary syllogistic reasoning.

Performance greatly improves when the conditional premiss in a reasoning task has a realistic, deontic content, such as 'If you use a second-class stamp, then you must leave the envelope unsealed' (Wason and Shapiro 1971, Manktelow and Over 1987). In general, the real-life credibility or otherwise of premisses and conclusion strongly influences judgements of validity and invalidity.

For simple problems in formal deductive reasoning, when the specific subject matter provides no helpful clues, success is significantly correlated with intelligence, in whatever sense it is measured by IQ tests, SAT scores or the like (Stanovich and West 2000). For some simple tasks, success is rare except amongst those with the intelligence of able undergraduates (Newstead et al. 2004). Contrast this with the efficient success which humans typically show in judging whether short strings of words constitute well-formed sentences of their native language, for example. There is little sign of anything like a module for formal deductive reasoning.

13. See Schroyens and Schaeken 2003; the percentages are as summarized in Oaksford 2005, p. 427.

A widespread, although not universal, view amongst psychologists of reasoning is that humans have two reasoning systems. In the terminology of Stanovich and West, System 1 is associative, holistic, automatic, relatively undemanding of cognitive capacity, relatively fast, and acquired through biology, exposure and personal experience; its construal of reasoning tasks is highly sensitive to personal, conversational and social context. System 2 is rule-based, analytic, controlled, demanding of cognitive capacity, relatively slow, and acquired by cultural and formal tuition; its construal of reasoning tasks is rather insensitive to personal, conversational and social context.[14] System 1 lacks the formal rules which enable deductive reasoning to succeed in the absence of helpful clues from the content of premisses and conclusion. It is defeasible and only moderately reliable, but it performs an important role in tasks of the kind for which it presumably evolved, such as integrating new information from perception or testimony with our standing beliefs. System 1 is not a system for formal deductive reasoning. A suitably educated, highly intelligent person can achieve success in formal deductive reasoning by means of System 2, but its structure is not that of an unconscious, sealed-off module.

We can apply this picture to Peter and Stephen. With respect to System 1, they do not deviate from the human norm. They are slightly unusual with respect to System 2, but it is in any case much more sensitive than System 1 to specific features of the individual's intelligence and education. But neither high intelligence nor a good education is needed for understanding simple sentences such as (1). Any putative System 2 differences at issue between Peter or Stephen and average speakers of English are entirely consistent with Peter and Stephen's competence in their native language. If Peter and Stephen do have any underlying disposition to accept (1) as true, it concerns their System 1. But System 1 is only distantly related to the truth conditions of sentences, for its overall performance in assessing whether arguments are truth-preserving is very poor. Many System 1 judgements of such matters have to be overruled by System 2. An underlying System 1 disposition to accept (1) as true would therefore be quite insufficient to generate

14. See Stanovich and West 2000, p. 659, where a list is also provided of earlier authors who have proposed similar views.

an understanding/truth link of the sort needed to advance from an understanding/disposition-to-believe link such as UDBl* to an understanding/disposition-to-know link such as UDKl*. Nor is a System 1 disposition to accept (1) needed to understand it, since a normal System 1 is disposed to give wildly fallacious results in many simple cases. Thus the sub-personal level account fails to deliver a disposition to recognize (1) as true.

The two-systems picture has not been conclusively established; it may well need revision. Nevertheless, it throws into relief the empirical assumptions on which the sub-personal level account depends, and their clash with much current thinking in the psychology of reasoning. If the two-systems picture is right to even a first approximation, the sub-personal level account is in trouble.

One might wonder how System 1, or any other system, could evaluate deductive arguments without use of something like formal rules for reasoning with logical constants in natural language, even if their effect is almost swamped by associations, heuristics and other pragmatic factors (perhaps as in Braine and O'Brien 1991). But there are alternatives. In particular, one of the main current psychological theories of deductive reasoning is the *mental models* approach. Two of its leading proponents write:

> The evidence suggests that it [the reasoning mechanism] is *not* equipped with logical rules of inference, which it sometimes uses correctly and sometimes misuses, misapplies or forgets. This analogy with grammar, which has seduced so many theorists, is a mistake. The reasoning mechanism constructs a mental model of the premises, formulates a putative conclusion, and tests its validity by searching for alternative models in which it is false. The search is constrained by the meta-principle that the conclusion is valid only if there are no such models, but it is not governed by any systematic or comprehensive principles. (Johnson-Laird and Byrne 1993, p. 178)

Thus subjects may erroneously classify an invalid argument as valid, because the unrepresentative sample of models which they have examined includes no counter-model, and they wrongly treat the sample as representative. They may erroneously classify a valid argument as invalid, because although the representative sample of models which they have examined includes no counter-model, they do not treat the sample as representative. Background beliefs about the specific subject matter of an argument influence its classification, because they focus attention on some mental models rather than others. Johnson-Laird and Byrne argue that their theory gives the best fit to the empirical data.

On the mental models approach, the nearest one normally comes to employing deductive rules of inference is in the procedures for evaluating sentences (premisses or conclusions) with respect to a given model, itself conceived as a mental representation.[15] But that process does not involve deductive reasoning in a natural language. Nor need it involve anything like natural deduction rules, in or out of a natural language. For example, in the case of conditionals, it need not involve *modus ponens* or conditional proof (standard proofs of formalizations of (1) use the latter rule). More generally, it might involve something closer to an imaginative analogue of the processes which issue in complex perceptual judgements such as 'Everybody over there is wearing a hat'. Not all such universally quantified conclusions are reached by deduction from further premisses. One might employ this argument:

> *A* is wearing a hat.
> *B* is wearing a hat.
> *C* is wearing a hat.
> Everybody over there is *A*, *B* or *C*.
> ———————————————
> Everybody over there is wearing a hat.

But of course, the final premiss is itself a universally quantified perceptual judgement. To suppose that it too was reached as the conclusion of a deductive argument is merely to embark on a futile regress.

Although the mental models theory does not apply to all human reasoning—for example, to the kind which some humans learn to carry out in logic classes—it may apply to a considerable proportion of it. In any case, the theory is a salutary reminder that reasoning with the usual logical constants need not be formal deductive reasoning, and that the empirical evidence suggests that in humans it usually is not.

15. Mental models need not be visualized (ibid., p. 182). Johnson-Laird and Byrne also claim that human reasoning is a semantic rather than a syntactic process (ibid., p. 180), but the significance of this claim is not entirely clear, since they treat reasoning as a manipulation of representations.

To summarize: The case for treating rejection of (1) as a failure to manifest linguistic competence depends on the status of (1) as an elementary truth of deductive logic. But human deductive competence is far more sensitive than linguistic competence to high intelligence and advanced education. Deductive competence is a reflective skill, often painfully acquired and under one's personal control. It is not insulated from one's conscious theorizing. Thus deductive proficiency is not a precondition of linguistic competence. One can understand (1) as a sentence of English without assenting or being disposed to assent to it.

So far, the argument of this section has been mainly at the level of language rather than of thought. It has been directed primarily against UBl* and UDBl*, and therefore against UKl* and UDKl*, rather than against UBt* and UDBt*, and therefore against UKt* and UDKt*. Could a theorist of thought admit that Peter and Stephen understand (1) as a sentence of English without assenting or being disposed to assent to it, but nevertheless insist that they do so by means of different concepts from those which ordinary speakers of English employ? The suggestion might be that Peter and Stephen do not grasp the thought that every vixen is a vixen, that is, the thought which *we* express with (1); instead, they grasp only some other thought which *they* express with (1). Thus they would not be counterexamples to UBt* and UDBt*, even though they are acknowledged as counterexamples to UBl* and UDBt*. Might there be consequent hope for UKt* or UDKt*, although not for UKl* or UDKl*, after all?

Perhaps the envisaged theorist of thought treats (1) as indexical, expressing different propositions (thoughts) in different contexts. Many semanticists would accept that (1) is context-sensitive, for example because 'every' ranges over different domains of quantification in different contexts, but that form of context-sensitivity is only marginally relevant to the present concerns.[16] Such a theorist of thought is proposing that (1) is context-sensitive in an unexpected way, because what proposition it expresses depends on the identity of the speaker, more specifically, on the speaker's theoretical proclivities. For the sake of argument, let us allow for such context-sensitivity. Consider UBt* and

16. Some restricted domains of quantifications contain no vixens, so Peter's concern becomes less far-fetched.

UDBt* as uttered in Peter or Stephen's context. Thus we may think of the following argument as uttered by Peter or Stephen:

> Given what has already been conceded, I understand the English sentence (1). As uttered in this context, it expresses the thought that every vixen is a vixen. Indeed, I know that (1) expresses the thought that every vixen is a vixen. Consequently, in the sense relevant to UBt* and UDBt*, I grasp the thought that every vixen is a vixen; I entertain it in doubting that every vixen is a vixen. Thus I satisfy the antecedent of UBt* and UDBt*. But I do not satisfy the consequents; I neither believe that every vixen is a vixen nor in any relevant sense am disposed to believe it. For I know that (1) expresses that thought, and I firmly reject (1), nor am I inclined to accept any other sentence which expresses that thought. Thus I counterexemplify UBt* and UDBt*, just as much as I do UBl* and UDBl*.

We should accept the argument. It relies on none of Peter or Stephen's idiosyncratic views as premisses; it merely requires to be uttered by a speaker with those views in order to express the relevant thoughts, according to the form of context-sensitivity which the envisaged theorist of thought postulates. In particular, we should not object that Peter believes that every vixen is a vixen under the guise of the sentence 'If there is at least one vixen then every vixen is a vixen', for that sentence expresses a thought more complex than the thought (1) expresses; similarly for other candidate guises significantly different from (1). Thus the postulation does not save UBt* or UDBt* as schemata, since both have false instances in contexts of utterances such as Peter or Stephen's.

The theorist of thought's postulation of a special form of context-sensitivity in (1) is in any case implausible. Why should the meanings of the everyday words and modes of construction in (1) make special provision for Peter or Stephen's abstruse theoretical speculations? For the theorist of thought's claim is *not* that they use (1) with an idiosyncratic meaning other than the one it usually has in English; it has already been conceded that they use (1) with its ordinary meaning in English. Rather, the claim is that, in virtue of its ordinary meaning in English, when (1) is used by a theoretically unorthodox speaker such as

Peter or Stephen it expresses a thought other than the one it expresses as used by a theoretically orthodox speaker. That is not just unlikely in itself; it distorts the way in which Peter and Stephen hold themselves responsible to the meaning of (1) in the public language. They do not try to defend their rejection of (1) by appealing to the special context in which they are speaking; each of them acknowledges that if other speakers are correct in accepting (1) then he is incorrect in rejecting it. Part of the point of a natural language is to articulate and negotiate or resolve divergences of viewpoint. That point would be undermined by a mechanism of context-sensitivity which automatically made speakers talk past each other in case of such divergence. Peter and Stephen doubt that every vixen is a vixen. That is, they doubt exactly what we affirm. The hypothesis of a special form of context-sensitivity in (1) is to be rejected.

A theorist of thought might reply that although the sentence (1) does not *express* different thoughts as used by different speakers of English, it is nevertheless *associated with* different thoughts in the minds of different speakers. Of course, in a loose sense any normal speaker of English associates (1) with many different thoughts, for example those corresponding to all the inferences they are disposed to make from (1). 'Associated' in the proposal should therefore be read as something like 'associated most directly'. The suggestion is that Peter and Stephen do not associate (1) with the thought that every vixen is a vixen, the thought we associate (1) with; they associate (1) with some other thought, even if the two thoughts determine the same Russellian proposition. One could simply use the word 'thought' subject to the stipulation that the inferential differences between Peter, Stephen and us *constitute* differences between the thoughts we associate (1) with. But what would be the point of such a stipulation? As seen above, the linguistic understanding of (1) we share with Peter and Stephen already suffices for them and us to articulate our disagreements in rational discourse; we are not merely talking past one another. In its small way, (1) determines a piece of the common intellectual heritage of mankind, something we share with Peter and Stephen in our very capacity to disagree with respect to it. To insist that the thought we associate (1) with nevertheless differs from the thoughts Peter and Stephen associate (1) with is to undermine Frege's requirement of the publicity of senses and, in particular, thoughts. Moreover, if Peter and Stephen associate (1) with different thoughts from ours, should we not understand them better by translating their idiolects non-homophonically into ours? Presumably we should seek sentences other than (1) which we associate with the very thoughts they associate (1) with, or at least sentences we associate with thoughts more similar to the thoughts they associate (1) with than is the thought we associate (1) with, and translate their dissent from (1) in their mouths as dissent from those other sentences in our mouths. But the use of such a translation scheme would be intellectually disreputable, just because it would involve a refusal to acknowledge the full challenge which Peter and Stephen have issued to (1) in our mouths, not just in theirs. However mistaken their challenge, it is real. They are quite explicit that they are challenging our thought that every vixen is a vixen, and that we should not apply any non-homophonic translation scheme when interpreting their dissent from (1). To insist on applying such a non-homophonic translation scheme to them in the teeth of their protests would be to treat them less than fully seriously as human beings, like patients in need of old-fashioned psychiatric treatment, whose words are merely symptoms. The claim that Peter and Stephen associate (1) with different thoughts from ours repackages our disagreement with them in a way which makes it sound less threatening than it really is. It misleadingly bundles together logical and semantic differences, without any genuine unification of the two categories. To call the logical disagreement a difference in associated 'thoughts' is an advertising trick. Since a homophonic reading of (1) in the mouths of Peter and Stephen is more faithful to their intentions than is any non-homophonic reading, they associate (1) with the same thought as we do in any relevant sense of 'thought'.

Naturally, when Peter dissents from 'Every *F* is a *G*', we may decide in the light of his logical unorthodoxy to store only the information that either not every *F* is a *G* or there are no *F*s. But this is not a non-homophonic *translation*, any more than it is when someone notorious for exaggeration says 'At least six thousand people went on the march', and we decide to store only the information that at least one thousand people went on the march. By 'six thousand' the speaker did not mean what we mean by 'one thousand'. If exactly one thousand people went on the march he spoke falsely, not truly, for he was speaking English. Since we do not fully trust him, when he asserted one thing we stored only something weaker. Similarly, since we do not fully trust Peter, we store something weaker than he asserts. If there were no *F*s, he spoke falsely, not truly, for he was speaking English. Our lack of trust in Peter and Stephen's logical proclivities is entirely consistent with reading their utterances homophonically.

Peter and Stephen are counterexamples to UBt* and UDBt* as uttered by us, just as they are to UBt* and UDBt* as uttered by them. *A fortiori*, UKt* and UDKt* fail in both contexts too. At both the level of thought and the level of language, one can understand (1) without recognizing it as true or even having a disposition to do so.

A further watering-down of the epistemological claims might be proposed. For one might regard Peter and Stephen as wilfully and perversely turning their backs on knowledge which is available to them: although they do not know and are not even disposed to know, their understanding puts them *in a position* to know. It offers them the knowledge, but they may refuse to accept it. On this view, UKt* and UDKt* should be replaced by UPKt*, and UKl* and UDKl* by UPKl*:

UPKt* Necessarily, whoever grasps the thought that every vixen is a vixen is in a position to know that every vixen is a vixen.

UPKl* Necessarily, whoever understands the sentence 'Every vixen is a vixen' is in a position to recognize it as true.

The intended point of the phrase 'in a position to' here is that the knowledge is readily available, not merely that some non-observational psychological route of unspecified complexity leads ultimately to the knowledge in question, for the latter reading makes UPKt* and UPKl* too weak to be of much interest.

But do Peter and Stephen really satisfy UPKt* and UPKl*? The mere existence of an a priori argument for (1) in their language does not put *them* in a position to recognize (1) as true, for they cannot appreciate the argument's force. From the theoretical positions into which they have got themselves, they cannot give (1) more than insincere or superficial verbal assent. Psychologically, they are now incapable of simply walking away from their theoretical commitments. Although sustained psychological and social pressure might cause a change of view, it does not follow that they are *presently* in a position to recognize (1) as true. Such pressure might in any case convince Peter and Stephen that every vixen is a vixen by a causal route too insensitive to truth for the belief to constitute knowledge. They have blinded themselves, but the upshot is still that they cannot see. Although they can still grasp the content of (1), they have lost their insight into its truth. Even UPKt* and UPKl* miss this point. One can grasp the thought that every vixen is a vixen without being in a position to know that every vixen is a vixen, and one can understand the sentence 'Every vixen is a vixen' without being in a position to recognize it as true.

Do at least the understanding/justification links survive for (1)? Consider the analogues of UJBt and UJBl:

UJBt* Necessarily, whoever grasps the thought that every vixen is a vixen is justified in believing that every vixen is a vixen.

UJBl* Necessarily, whoever understands the sentence 'Every vixen is a vixen' is justified in assenting to it.

Do Peter and Stephen satisfy UJBt* and UJBl*? That is, are they justified in believing that every vixen is a vixen (even though they do not in fact believe that every vixen is a vixen), and are they justified in assenting to (1) (even though they do not in fact assent to it)? They are justified at most in a weak sense, for, as just argued, they are not in a position to know that every vixen is a vixen, nor are they in a position to recognize (1) as true. Moreover, they have reflected on the matter as carefully as they can, and come to a considered rejection of (1). Of course, their problem is not that they lack empirical evidence for (1). Nevertheless, if they were to accept (1) as true, and believe that every vixen is a vixen, they would be acting in a way which looks deeply irrational to them. From an external perspective, we may note that (1) has probability one on their evidence, simply because it is a logical truth, and therefore deserves to be believed. But justification rather than knowledge is the central epistemological question only for internalist theories: they try to concentrate on factors which are available from the subject's own point of view. From thc point of view of Peter or Stephen, the logical truth of (1) is not available, given their deep theoretical orientation. To exclude such matters of theoretical orientation from the subject's point of view by insisting that logical truths are always available from that point of view is to give up much of the spirit of internalism, if not the letter, and in a way which threatens to undermine the motivation for what is left. Thus UJBt* and UJBl* are unlikely to survive in a form which makes them a satisfying substitute for UKt* and UKl* or even for UPKt* and UPKl*.[17] In any case, the concern of this paper is primarily with knowledge. For unless a radical form of scepticism holds, *we* know that every vixen is a vixen, even though Peter and Stephen do not.

III

It is time to apply the lessons of Section II to a supposed paradigm of analyticity, such as the sentence used in Section I:

(4) Every vixen is a female fox.

Given that 'vixen' is synonymous with 'female fox', (4) results from substituting synonyms for synonyms in the logical truth (1). Thus (4) is what is sometimes called 'Frege-analytic', without itself being a logical truth.[18] In Section II we saw that the understanding/belief links fail for (1), even in watered-down versions, and therefore do not explain our knowledge that every vixen is a vixen. If the understanding/belief links do no better for (4), then our knowledge that every vixen is a female fox also cannot be explained along the lines of the programme sketched in Section I.[19]

One might argue that the understanding/belief links for (4) reduce to those for (1), because (1) and (4) express the very same thought; thus UBt and UBl are equivalent to UBt* and

17. See Williamson forthcoming for a critique of an internalist conception of justification.
18. The term 'Frege-analytic' is taken from Boghossian 1997; in this connection he refers to §3 of Frege 1950, without insisting on the historical accuracy of attributing exactly this notion of analyticity to Frege. Quine considers this notion of analyticity (amongst others) in 'Two Dogmas'.
19. Quine 1966, p. 111, notes that so-called truths by definition (compare (4)) depend on prior logical truths (compare (1)).

UBl* respectively. Consequently, since Peter and Stephen are counterexamples to UBt* and UBl*, they are automatically counterexamples to UBt and UBl too.

At the level of thought, the argument is simply that, necessarily, one grasps the thought that every vixen is a vixen if and only if one grasps the thought that every vixen is a female fox (because it is the very same thought) and one believes that every vixen is a vixen if and only if one believes that every vixen is a female fox (because it is the very same belief). Thus the antecedent and consequent of UBt are necessarily equivalent to the antecedent and consequent of UBt* respectively, so UBt is equivalent to UBt*.

At the level of language, the argument must be slightly more complicated, because (1) and (4) are distinct sentences even if they express the same thought. More specifically, the antecedent of UBl* does not entail the antecedent of UBl. Someone can understand (1) without understanding (4): consider, for instance, a native speaker of another language who is learning English; she has mastered the construction 'Every . . . is a ---', and understands the word 'vixen' through being taught it as a synonym for a word of her native language, but has not yet encountered the words 'female' and 'fox'. Nor do the consequents of UBl* and UBl entail each other. Someone who understands neither (1) nor (4) can assent to one of them without assenting to the other, on the testimony of someone else who tells her that the former is true without telling her that the latter is true. Nevertheless, one might try arguing for the equivalence of UBl and UBl* themselves as follows.

Suppose that UBl* holds. Consider a possible situation in which someone understands (4); thus she understands the expressions 'vixen' and 'female fox', because they are constituents of (4); therefore, since those expressions are synonymous, she treats them as intersubstitutable *salva veritate* in non-quotational contexts which she understands; since 'female fox' occurs in (4) in a non-quotational context which she understands in virtue of understanding (4), and (1) is the result of substituting 'vixen' for 'female fox' in (4), she assents to (1) if and only if she assents to (4); but she also understands (1), because it is composed entirely out of words ('vixen') and modes of construction ('Every . . . is a ---') which she understands in virtue of understanding (4); therefore, by UBl*, she assents to (1); consequently, she assents to (4). Therefore UBl holds. Thus UBl* entails UBl. Conversely, suppose that UBl holds. Consider a possible situation *S* in which someone understands (1). Thus she understands the word 'vixen' and the construction 'Every ... is a ---'. She may not understand (4), because she may not understand 'female' or 'fox'. However, we can consider another situation *Sf* like *S* except that, in *Sf*, she understands 'female', 'fox' and 'female fox'. In *Sf* she still understands the word 'vixen' and the construction 'Every ... is a ---'. Moreover, since the words 'female' and 'fox' do not occur in (1), in *Sf* she assents to (1) if and only if in *S* she assents to (1). In *Sf*, since 'vixen' and 'female fox' are synonymous expressions which she understands, she treats them as intersubstitutable *salva veritate* in non-quotational contexts which she understands; since 'female fox' occurs in (4) in a non-quotational context which she understands, and (1) is the result of substituting 'vixen' for 'female fox' in (4), she assents to (1) if and only if she assents to (4); but she understands (4), because it is composed entirely out of words and modes of construction which she understands; therefore, by UBl, she assents to (4); consequently, she assents to (1)—in *Sf*. But, as already noted, she assents to (1) in *Sf* if and only if she assents to (1) in *S*, the original situation. Hence, in *S*, she assents to (1). Therefore UBl* holds. Thus UBl entails UBl*. So the understanding/belief links for (1) and (4) are equivalent at the level of language too.

The preceding arguments for the equivalence of UBt and UBl with UBt* and UBl* rely on controversial assumptions. Burge 1978 has built on a point of Mates 1952 to argue that synonyms cannot always be substituted for synonyms *salva veritate* in belief ascriptions. Thus someone (not Peter or Stephen) under the misapprehension that the term 'vixen' also applies to immature male foxes may believe that every vixen is a vixen without believing that every vixen is a female fox. Burge argues powerfully against attempts to reconstrue such beliefs as metalinguistic. If his interpretation of such examples is right, the argument above for the equivalence of UBt and UBt* rests on a false premiss.

Can one reply that whoever believes that every vixen is a vixen *ipso facto* believes that every vixen is a female fox, even if they understand (4) without assenting to it? But if they understand (4), they know that it means that every vixen is a female fox, and presumably therefore that it is true if and only if every vixen is a female fox; if they believe that every vixen is a female fox, why do they not conclude that (4) is true, and accept it as such? The question is not unanswerable. Even good logicians may be unable to draw valid inferences when the same proposition is presented to them under different guises, for example by the sentences (1) and (4).[20]

Whether or not one accepts Burge's view of attitude ascriptions, one may argue that a subject can understand two synonymous expressions without knowing them to be synonymous.[21] A subject may assent to (1) while dissenting from (4) and still count as having attained at least a minimal level of understanding of all the relevant words and modes of construction, enough to use them to express non-metalinguistic propositional attitudes. If so, the argument above for the equivalence of UBl and UBl* rests on a false premiss.

Fortunately, we need not resolve those disputes for present purposes; we can remain agnostic over the cogency of the objections to the arguments for the equivalence of UBt and UBl with UBt* and UBl* respectively. For we can deploy Peter and Stephen directly as counterexamples to UBt and UBl themselves, as well as to UBt* and UBl*, without settling the general question of equivalence. They *do* use 'vixen' and 'female fox' interchangeably, at least in non-quotational contexts which they understand. Even if 'vixen' and 'female fox' were equivalent by explicit stipulative definition, that would be no objection to the present argument. Peter and Stephen's unorthodoxy concerns general issues of logic, not what it is to be a vixen. By the argument of Section II, they understand (1); but their understanding of (4) is as good as their understanding of (1); therefore, they understand (4). They manifestly refuse assent to (4), just as they manifestly refuse assent to (1). Thus they are counterexamples to UBl. Similarly, by the argument of Section II, they grasp the thought that every vixen is a vixen; but their grasp of the thought that every vixen is a female fox is as good as their grasp of the thought that every vixen is a vixen (whether or not it is strictly the same thought); therefore, they grasp the thought

20. See Kripke 1979 and Horwich 1998, pp. 100–1.

21. This contradicts Dummett's claim that 'It is an undeniable feature of the notion of meaning—obscure as that notion is—that meaning is *transparent* in the sense that, if someone attaches a meaning to each of two words, he must know whether these meanings are the same' (1978, p. 131). A direct argument against Dummett's claim is from pairs of synonymous natural kind terms such as 'furze' and 'gorse' (Kripke 1979). For more theoretical considerations see Williamson 2000, pp. 94–106.

that every vixen is a female fox. By the argument of Section II again, they do not believe that every vixen is a vixen; but they are no more inclined to believe that every vixen is a female fox than they are to believe that every vixen is a vixen (whether or not is strictly the same belief); therefore, they do not believe that every vixen is a female fox. Thus Peter and Stephen are counterexamples to UBt too. Crudely: (1) is at least as obvious a truth as (4). So if the understanding/belief links fail for (1), they will not hold for (4).

Since Peter and Stephen are counterexamples to the understanding/belief links for (4), *a fortiori* they are counterexamples to the corresponding understanding/knowledge links, UKt and UKl. Moreover, the attempt to replace the understanding/knowledge links for (4) by understanding/disposition-to-know links analogous to UDKt* and UDKl*, or by understanding/position-to-know links analogous to UPKt* and UPKl*, faces obstacles exactly analogous to those considered in Section II. A fallback to understanding/justification links for (4) is equally unhelpful, just as it was for (1).

The underlying style of argument is quite general; it does not depend on any special feature of (1) or (4) as a candidate for links of the kinds at issue. Of course, which forms of logical unorthodoxy are relevant depends on the form of the given candidate for analytic or conceptual truth. But with a little ingenuity one can always find or invent some relevant forms of logical unorthodoxy. Often, when the understanding/belief links are shown to fail for some candidate conceptual truth by reference to some form of logical unorthodoxy, there is a natural alternative candidate conceptual truth, a watered-down sentence for which the understanding/belief links cannot be shown to fail by reference to that form of logical unorthodoxy. A different form of logical unorthodoxy is needed to show that the new candidate fails: but there will be such a different form.

The attempt to base the epistemology of obvious truths such as (1) and (4) on preconditions for understanding them, as envisaged in Section I, rests on a false conception of understanding. For even the simplest candidates for analyticity or conceptual truth, understanding is consistent with considered rejection.[22]

22. For a similar conclusion concerning lexical competence in a shared language see Marconi 1997, p. 56.

Someone might accept the conclusion so far with respect to analytic or conceptual *truth* but resist its generalization to the analytic *validity* of inference rules ('conceptual connections'). For in treating 'vixen' and 'female fox' as intersubstitutable *salva veritate* in non-quotational contexts, do not Peter and Stephen accept the inference from '*a* is a vixen' to '*a* is a female fox' (and its converse)? Thus they do not counterexemplify a putative link between understanding the words and accepting the inference. However, the preceding considerations destabilize such a conception of analytic inference rules without analytic truths in at least two ways.

First, the preceding considerations show that if Peter and Stephen accept the inference from '*a* is a vixen' to '*a* is a female fox', then they must reject other inference rules more central to logic. Stephen must reject the rule of conditional proof, the standard introduction rule for the material conditional '→', since it would take him to the conclusion '*a* is a vixen → *a* is a female fox', which he rejects as a truth-value gap when '*a*' denotes a borderline case for 'vixen' and 'female fox'. Consequently, Stephen counterexemplifies the putative understanding/acceptance link for the rule of conditional proof. Unlike Stephen, Peter accepts that singular conditional, but he must reject the rule of universal generalization, the standard introduction rule for the universal quantifier, since it would take him on to the conclusion (4) itself, which he rejects. Consequently, Peter counterexemplifies the putative understanding/acceptance link for the rule of universal generalization. Thus the proposed conception of analytic inference rules without analytic truths omits logically central inference rules.

Second, once Stephen applies his logical unorthodoxy to his metalanguage, his original acceptance of the inference from '*a* is a vixen' to '*a* is a female fox' is undermined. For in order to accept it as valid once he reflects on the question, he must accept that it is truth-preserving. More specifically, he must assent to the conditional '"*a* is a vixen" is true → "*a* is a female fox" is true'. But just as both '*a* is a vixen' and '*a* is a female fox' are borderline in some cases, so both '"*a* is a vixen" is true' and '"*a* is a female fox" is true' are borderline in some cases: the latter cases are the same as the former if a disquotational principle holds for 'true', but even if Stephen doubts the disquotational principle, he acknowledges that there are cases of the latter kind, in view of higher-order vagueness. Thus he cannot reflectively endorse the inference from '*a* is a vixen' to '*a* is a female fox', even though in practice he uses 'vixen' and 'female fox' interchangeably. This result may be the basis for a philosophical objection to Stephen's views, but for reasons already seen it does not show that he lacks understanding of the relevant words or grasp of the relevant concepts. Thus Stephen counterexemplifies the understanding/acceptance link even for the inference for which it was originally proposed. Thus the envisaged conception of analytically valid inference rules ultimately fares no better than did the conception of analytic truths.[23,24]

IV

Old theories tend to survive refutation in the absence of new theories to take their place. Despite all the evidence against the existence of understanding/belief links, it can be hard to resist the idea that there *must* be such links, otherwise the distinction between understanding and not understanding would dissolve: speakers who all understood the same term might have nothing substantive in common to constitute its shared meaning. For example, in the case of moral vocabulary, which he treats as representative, Frank Jackson writes:

> Genuine moral disagreement, as opposed to mere talking past one another, requires a background of shared moral opinion to fix a common, or near enough common, set of meanings for our moral terms. We can think of the rather general principles that we share as the commonplaces or platitudes or constitutive principles that make up the core we need to share in order to count as speaking a common moral language. (1998, p. 132)[25]

23. Strictly speaking, Stephen cannot even accept the circular argument from '*a* is a vixen' to itself as valid, since the same argument shows that he must reject the conditional ' "*a* is a vixen" is true → "*a* is a vixen" is true' in some cases.

24. Whether a similar metalogical problem affects Peter depends on the exact form of the generalization. On his view, 'Every argument of the form "*a* is a vixen, therefore *a* is a female fox" with a true premiss has a true conclusion' has a false existential commitment (because there is no argument of the form '*a* is a vixen, therefore *a* is a female fox' with a true premiss) but 'Every argument of the form "*a* is a vixen, therefore *a* is a female fox" is truth-preserving' does not (because there is an argument of the form '*a* is a vixen, therefore *a* is a female fox').

25. Jackson's application of the Ramsey-Carnap-Lewis method for defining theoretical terms to moral vocabulary (and more generally in his programme of conceptual analysis) requires not merely some agreed role for moral terms but an

Jackson's only argument for these claims is failure to see an alternative. But there is an alternative.

What binds together uses of a word by different agents or at different times into a common practice of using that word with a given meaning? This is an instance of a more general type of question: what binds together different events into the history of a single complex object, whether it be a stone, a tree, a table, a person, a society, a tradition, or a word? In brief, what makes a unity out of diversity? Rarely is the answer to such questions the mutual similarity of the constituents. Almost never is it some invariant feature, shared by all the constituents and somehow prior to the complex whole itself—an indivisible soul or bare particular. Rather, it is the complex interrelations of the constituents, above all, their causal interrelations. Although we should not expect a precise non-circular statement of necessary and sufficient conditions for the unity in terms of those complex interrelations, we have at least a vague idea of what it takes. The similarity of the constituents is neither necessary nor sufficient; different constituents can play different but complementary roles in constituting the unity: both events in the head and events in the heart help constitute the life of a person. The claim that a shared understanding of a word requires a shared stock of platitudes depends on the assumption that uses of a word by different agents or at different times can be bound together into a common practice of using that word with a given meaning only by an invariant core of beliefs. But that assumption amounts to one of the crudest and least plausible answers to the question of what makes a unity out of diversity. In effect, it assumes that what animates a word is a soul of doctrine.

That different speakers can make asymmetric contributions to binding together different uses of a word into a common practice of using it with a given meaning was one of Putnam's best insights. After describing the role of scientific experts in fixing

agreed role specific enough to be uniquely instantiated: this further assumption is criticized at Williamson 2001, pp. 629–30. Jackson's reply on this point (2001, p. 656) reiterates something like the assumption in the quoted passage. He further misunderstands the objection by falsely supposing that the claim that we can mean the same by a word and disagree radically about its application restricts the disagreement to what occupies the roles, rather than the roles themselves, however one imagines the latter as demarcated. For criticism of the Ramsey-Carnap-Lewis method as applied in Boghossian 2003 see Williamson 2003.

the reference of natural kind terms, he makes this conjecture:

> HYPOTHESIS OF THE UNIVERSALITY OF THE DIVISION OF LINGUISTIC LABOR: Every linguistic community exemplifies the sort of division of linguistic labor just described: that is, possesses at least some terms whose associated 'criteria' are known only to a subset of the speakers who acquire the terms, and whose use by the other speakers depends upon a structured cooperation between them and the speakers in the relevant subsets. (1975, p. 228)

Even if Putnam oversimplified the relation between natural kind terms in natural language and scientific theory, a more refined account will still respect the division of linguistic labour, for distinctions between levels of expertise are observable even within the pre-scientific use of natural kind terms.

Putnam's insight is relevant far beyond the class of natural kind terms, as Burge observed (1986). Even where we cannot sensibly divide the linguistic community into experts and non-experts, the picture of a natural language as a cluster of causally interrelated but constitutively independent idiolects is still wrong, because it ignores the way in which individual speakers defer to the linguistic community as a whole. They use a word as a word of a public language, allowing its reference in their mouths to be fixed by its use over the whole community.[26] Such verbal interactions between speakers can hold a linguistic practice together even in the absence of a common creed which they are all required to endorse.

Evidently, much of the practical value of a language consists in its capacity to facilitate communication between agents in epistemically asymmetric positions, when the speaker or writer knows about things about which the hearer or reader is ignorant, perhaps mistaken. Although disagreement is naturally easier to negotiate and usually more fruitful against a background of extensive agreement, it does not follow that any particular agreement is needed for disagreement to be expressed in given words. A practical constraint on useful communication should not be confused with a necessary condition for literal understanding. Moreover, the practical constraint is holistic;

26. If the term is indexical, what is fixed by use over the whole community is not the content but the character in the sense of Kaplan 1989. For the bearing of this on communication in a vague language, see Williamson 1999, pp. 512–14.

agreement on any given point can be traded in for agreement on others. The same applies to principles of charity as putatively constitutive conditions on correct interpretation: imputed disagreement on any given point can be compensated for by imputed agreement on others.[27]

It is far easier and more rewarding to discuss the existence of true contradictions with a dialetheist such as Graham Priest than intelligent design with a Christian fundamentalist or Holocaust denial with a neo-Nazi.[28] The difficulty of engaging in fruitful debate with fundamentalists or neo-Nazis cannot plausibly be attributed to some failure of linguistic understanding on their part (or ours); it arises from their wilful disrespect for the evidence. Such difficulty as there is in engaging in fruitful debate with dialetheists provides no significant reason to attribute to them (or us) a failure of linguistic understanding. Competence with the English language no more requires acceptance of some law of non-contradiction or any other logical law than it requires acceptance of the theory of evolution or the historical reality of the Holocaust.

We cannot anticipate all our disagreements in advance. What strike us today as the best candidates for analytic or conceptual truth some innovative thinker may call into question tomorrow for intelligible reasons. Even when we hold fast to our original belief, we can usually find ways of engaging rationally with the doubter. If a language imposes conditions of understanding which exclude such a doubt in advance, as it were in ignorance of its grounds, it needlessly limits its speakers' capacity to articulate and benefit from critical reflection on their ways of thinking. Such conditions are dysfunctional, and natural languages do not impose them.[29]

There is of course a distinction between understanding a word and not understanding it. One can lack understanding of a word

27. Davidson famously endorses a holistic principle of charity while rejecting the analytic/synthetic distinction (for example, 2001, pp. 144–9). For an argument that charity should maximize imputed knowledge rather than imputed truth, see Williamson 2004b, pp. 131–47.
28. For examples of rational debate for and against a law of non-contradiction see Priest, Beall and Armour-Garb 2004.
29. W. B. Gallie's intriguing account of the positive function of 'essentially contested concepts' is relevant here; his examples are 'the concepts of a religion, of art, of science, of democracy and of social justice' (1964, p. 168).

through lack of causal interaction with the social practice of using that word, or through interaction too superficial to permit sufficiently fluent engagement in the practice. But sufficiently fluent engagement in the practice can take many forms, which have no single core of agreement.[30]

If we accept such an account of linguistic understanding, what should we say about grasp of concepts? There is no quick generalization from the former to the latter. Different uses of the same word must be causally related, at least indirectly.[31] Creatures who are causally unrelated to us cannot have a word numerically identical with our word 'set'; at best they can have a word exactly like our word in its general syntactic, semantic and phonetic properties. By contrast, on the usual view, they can have a concept numerically identical with our concept *set*. If different uses of the very same concept need not be bound together by causal ties, what does bind them together? Are links between the possession of concepts and belief needed here?

Similar questions arise at the linguistic level once we consider the relation of synonymy, since uses of distinct but synonymous words need not be causally related, even indirectly. Fortunately, the tradition of truth-conditional semantics is richly provided with resources for an account of synonymy, if we take it seriously as a branch of linguistics and put aside Quinean reservations. Synonymous expressions do not simply have the same extension in the actual world. With respect to each context of utterance, they have the same intension, that is, the same extension with respect to each circumstance of evaluation; equivalently, they have the same character in the sense of Kaplan 1989. Adapting Carnap's notion of intensional isomorphism (1947, p. 56), we may further insist that synonymous complex expressions can be mapped onto each other in ways that preserve both constituent structure and the character of corresponding constituents; thus '0 = 0' and '1 = 1' come out non-synonymous. We can even distinguish pairs of simple expressions such as 'and' and 'but', which make the same contribution to the truth conditions of sentences in which they occur, by requiring synonymous

30. Someone who understands a word without being disposed to utter it (perhaps because they find it obscene or unpronounceable) can still count as sufficiently engaged in the practice of using it.
31. On the metaphysics of words see Kaplan 1990.

expressions to have their conventional implicatures satisfied with respect to the same contexts of utterances and circumstances of evaluation. Such a fine-grained conception of synonymy makes no appeal to analyticity in the form of supposed understanding/belief links.

A criterion of synonymy along the envisaged lines does not distinguish between rigid non-indexical semantically simple terms without conventional implicatures. For instance, it does not distinguish 'Cicero' from 'Tully' or 'furze' from 'gorse' in meaning. But that is the right result, for 'Cicero' is synonymous with 'Tully' and 'furze' is synonymous with 'gorse', even if not all rational speakers with a minimal understanding of the relevant words recognize the synonymies. Some such speakers assent to 'All furze is furze' while refusing assent to 'All furze is gorse'. To insist that 'furze' and 'gorse' must therefore differ in meaning is, implausibly, to make the individuation of meanings as fine-grained as the individuation of words, and thereby in the end to lose the point that causally unrelated words can be synonymous.[32] We do better to stick with a criterion of synonymy along the lines of the previous paragraph.

Given that linguistic meanings can be individuated without appeal to supposed understanding/belief links, there is no reason to expect the individuation of concepts to appeal to such links. Attempts to argue for the existence of analytic or conceptual truths in the epistemological sense from the need to individuate linguistic meanings or concepts are hopeless.

Although we can make some sense of the analytic/synthetic distinction in epistemological terms, nothing falls on the analytic side: in this sense, there are no conceptual truths, conceptual necessities or conceptual connections. Thus philosophical questions had better not be conceptual questions, if that means questions whose answers are conceptual truths. Of course, philosophers can legitimately ask questions *about* concepts, as was done here, but with equal legitimacy they can ask questions about minds or bodies, space or time, numbers or sets, properties or relations. Reflection on how we can know the answers to

32. Consider a community *C* which uses a word *W* with a meaning *M* and a hitherto causally unrelated community *C** which uses a word *W** with the very same meaning *M*. If *C* and *C** encounter each other, each may come to understand the other's words without realizing that *W* and *W** are synonymous. Kripke 1979 highlights such cases.

philosophical questions is liable to induce epistemological panic, and make us run to conceptual truth. The refuge is illusory. Don't panic.[33]

References

Boghossian, P. A. 1997: 'Analyticity'. In R. Hale and C. Wright (eds), *A Companion to the Philosophy of Language*. Oxford: Blackwell.
——— 2003. 'Blind Reasoning'. *Proceedings of the Aristotelian Society Supplementary Volume*, 77, pp. 225–48.
Braine, M. D. and D. P. O'Brien 1991: 'A Theory of *if*: A Lexical Entry, Reasoning Program, and Pragmatic Principles'. *Psychological Review*, 98, pp. 182–203.
Burge, T. 1978: 'Belief and Synonymy'. *Journal of Philosophy*, 75, pp. 119–38.
——— 1986: 'Intellectual Norms and Foundations of Mind'. *Journal of Philosophy*, 83, pp. 697–720.
Byrne, R. M. J. 1989: 'Suppressing Valid Inferences with Conditionals'. *Cognition*, 31, pp. 1–21.
Carnap, R. 1947: *Meaning and Necessity: A Study in Semantics and Modal Logic*. Chicago: University of Chicago Press.
Chalmers, D. J. 2002: 'Does Conceivability Entail Possibility?' In T. Szabó Gendler and J. Hawthorne (eds), *Conceivability and Possibility*. Oxford: Clarendon Press.
Davidson, D. 2001: *Subjective, Intersubjective, Objective*. Oxford: Clarendon Press.
Dummett, M. A. E. 1978: *Truth and Other Enigmas*. London: Duckworth.
Frege, G. 1950: *The Foundations of Arithmetic*. Trans. J. L. Austin. Oxford: Blackwell.
Gallie, W. B. 1964: *Philosophy and the Historical Understanding*. London: Chatto and Windus.
Horgan, T. 1998: 'The Transvaluationist Conception of Vagueness'. *The Monist*, 81, pp. 313–30.
Horwich, P. 1998: *Meaning*. Oxford: Clarendon Press.
Jackson, F. 1998: *From Metaphysics to Ethics: A Defence of Conceptual Analysis*. Oxford: Clarendon Press.
——— 2001: 'Responses'. *Philosophy and Phenomenological Research*, 62, pp. 653–64.
Johnson-Laird, P. N. and R. M. J. Byrne 1993: 'Models and Deductive Rationality'. In K. Manktelow and D. Over (eds), *Rationality: Psychological and Philosophical Perspectives*. London: Routledge.
Kaplan, D. 1989: 'Demonstratives: An Essay on the Semantics, Logic, Metaphysics, and Epistemology of Demonstratives and Other Indexicals'. In J. Almog, J. Perry and H. Wettstein (eds), *Themes from Kaplan*. Oxford: Oxford University Press.
——— 1990: 'Words'. *Proceedings of the Aristotelian Society Supplementary Volume*, 64, pp. 93–119.
Kleene, S. C. 1952: *Introduction to Metamathematics*. Amsterdam: North-Holland.
Kripke, S. 1979: 'A Puzzle About Belief'. In A. Margalit (ed.), *Meaning and Use*. Dordrecht: Reidel.
——— 1980: *Naming and Necessity*. Oxford: Blackwell.
Manktelow, K. I. and D. E. Over 1987: 'Reasoning and Rationality'. *Mind and Language*, 2, pp. 199–219.
Marconi, D. 1997: *Lexical Competence*. Cambridge, MA: MIT Press.

33. Some of the material in this paper was presented in Oxford, and some derives from the 2005 Jack Smart Lecture at ANU, the 2005 Blackwell/Brown Lectures at Brown University and at a lecture at the University of Munich; I am grateful to the audiences on all these occasions for discussion, and to Brian Leftow, Ofra Magidor and Oliver Pooley for written comments.

Martin, C. B. 1994: 'Dispositions and Conditionals'. *Philosophical Quarterly*, 44, pp. 1–8.
——— and J. Heil 1998: 'Rules and Powers'. *Philosophical Perspectives*, 12, pp. 283–312.
Mates, B. 1952: 'Synonymity'. In L. Linsky (ed.), *Semantics and the Philosophy of Language*. Urbana, IL: University of Illinois Press.
Newstead, S. E., S. J. Handley, C. Harley, H. Wright, and D. Farrelly 2004: 'Individual Differences in Deductive Reasoning'. *Quarterly Journal of Experimental Psychology*, 57A, pp. 33–60.
Oaksford, M. 2005: 'Reasoning'. In N. Braisby and M. Gellatly (eds), *Cognitive Psychology*. Oxford: Oxford University Press.
Peacocke, C. 1992: *A Study of Concepts*. Cambridge, MA: MIT Press.
Priest, G., JC Beall and B. Armour-Garb (eds) 2004: *The Law of Non-Contradiction: New Philosophical Essays*. Oxford: Clarendon Press.
Putnam, H. 1975: *Mind, Language and Reality: Philosophical Papers, Volume 2*. Cambridge: Cambridge University Press.
Quine, W. V. O. 1953: *From a Logical Point of View*. Cambridge, MA: Harvard University Press.
——— 1966: *The Ways of Paradox and Other Essays*. New York: Random House.
Salmon, N: *Frege's Puzzle*. Cambridge, MA: MIT Press.
Schroyens, W. and W. Schaeken 2003: 'A Critique of Oaksford, Chater, and Larkin's (2000) Conditional Probability Model of Conditional Reasoning'. *Journal of Experimental Psychology: Learning, Memory and Cognition*, 29, pp. 140–9.
Soames, S. 1999: *Understanding Truth*. Oxford: Oxford University Press.
Stalnaker, R. C. 1984: *Inquiry*. Cambridge, MA: MIT Press.
——— 1999: *Context and Content*. Oxford: Oxford University Press.
Stanovich, K. E. and R. F. West 2000: 'Individual Differences in Reasoning: Implications for the Rationality Debate?' *Behavioral and Brain Sciences*, 23, pp. 645–65.
Wason, P. C. and D. Shapiro 1971: 'Natural and Contrived Experience in a Reasoning Problem'. *Quarterly Journal of Experimental Psychology*, 23, pp. 63–71.
Williamson, T. 1999: 'Schiffer on the Epistemic Theory of Vagueness'. *Philosophical Perspectives*, 13, pp. 505–17.
——— 2000: *Knowledge and its Limits*. Oxford: Oxford University Press.
——— 2001: 'Ethics, Supervenience and Ramsey Sentences'. *Philosophy and Phenomenological Research*, 62, pp. 625–30.
——— 2003. 'Understanding and Inference'. *Proceedings of the Aristotelian Society Supplementary Volume*, 77, pp. 249–93.
——— 2004a: 'Past the Linguistic Turn?' In B. Leiter (ed.), *The Future for Philosophy*. Oxford: Clarendon Press.
——— 2004b. 'Philosophical "Intuitions" and Scepticism About Judgement'. *Dialectica*, 58, pp. 109–53.
——— forthcoming: 'On Being Justified in One's Head'. In J. Greco, A. Mele and M. Timmons (eds), *Rationality and the Good*. Oxford: Oxford University Press.

SENSORIMOTOR SKILLS AND PERCEPTION

by Andy Clark and Naomi Eilan

I—Andy Clark

COGNITIVE COMPLEXITY AND THE SENSORIMOTOR FRONTIER

ABSTRACT What is the relation between perceptual experience and the suite of sensorimotor skills that enable us to act in the very world we perceive? The relation, according to 'sensorimotor models' (O'Regan and Noë 2001, Noë 2004) is tight indeed. Perceptual experience, on these accounts, is *enacted* via skilled sensorimotor activity, and gains its content and character courtesy of our knowledge of the relations between (typically) movement and sensory stimulation. I shall argue that this formulation is *too* extreme, and that it fails to accommodate the substantial firewalls, dis-integrations, and special-purpose streamings that form the massed strata of human cognition. In particular, such strong sensorimotor models threaten to obscure the computationally potent *insensitivity* of key information-processing events to the full subtleties of embodied cycles of sensing and moving.

I

The Painter and the Perceiver. Seeing, according to Noë 2004, is like painting. Painting is an ongoing process in which the eye probes the scene, then flicks back to the canvas, then back to the scene, and so on, in a dense cycle of active exploration and partial, iterated cognitive uptake. It is this cycle of situated, world-engaging activity that constitutes the act of painting. Seeing (and more generally, perceiving) is likewise constituted (Noë claims) by a process of active exploration in which the sense organs repeatedly probe the world, delivering partial and restricted information on a need-to-know basis. It is this cycle, of situated, world-engaging, whole animal activity, that is the locus, on Noë's account, of genuine cognitive interest, at least for perceptual experience.

An important implication of this, according to Noë, is that appeals to internal representations (if such there be) cannot tell the whole story, either for painting or for seeing:

> The causally sufficient substrate of the production of the picture is surely not the internal states of the painter, but rather the dynamic pattern of engagement among the painter, the scene and the canvass. Why not say the same thing about seeing? Seeing, on this approach, would depend on brain, body and world. (Noë 2004, p. 223)

In the case of seeing (and perceiving in general) a theoretical construct peculiarly well-suited to this dynamic target is the notion of sensorimotor dependencies (aka sensorimotor contingencies—see O'Regan and Noë 2001). Sensorimotor dependencies are relations between movement or change and sensory stimulation. Such relations may be of many kinds (see below) but what they all have in common is that they concern a kind of loop or cycle linking real-world objects and properties with systematically changing patterns of sensory stimulation. These changing patterns of sensory stimulation may be caused by the movements of the subject (this is the central case), as when we use head and eye movements to scan a visual scene. Or they may be caused by movements of the object itself, or be due to other elements in the environmental frame (such as changes in illumination or light source). In addition, some features of these various kinds of changing pattern will be due to properties of the objects themselves (for example, the self-similarity of a straight horizontal line along its length, giving rise to an unchanging pattern of retinal stimulation as the eye tracks along the line (see O'Regan and Noë 2001, p. 942), while others will be due to the idiosyncrasies of the human visual apparatus (for instance, the same straight line projected onto the retina distorts dramatically as the eye moves up and down, due to the curvature of the eyeball (op. cit., p. 941)).

Usually, many kinds of sensorimotor dependence (some, as we have just seen, much more truly sensorimotor than others) are in play when we see an object. It is our implicit knowledge of these sensorimotor dependencies that explains, according to the strong sensorimotor model, both the contents and the character (visual, tactile, auditory, etc.) of our perceptual experiences. This stress on knowledge of (or expectations concerning) sensorimotor dependencies is meant as an alternative to standard appeals to qualia conceived as intrinsic, 'sensational' properties of experience. Instead of appreciating such mysterious intrinsic qualities in experience, it is suggested, we *enact* (that is, by acting bring into being) perceptual experience.[1] In the case of shape and spatial properties, for example:

> [T]he enactive view denies that we represent spatial properties in perception by correlating them with kinds of sensation. There is no *sensation* of roundness or distance, whether tactile, visual or otherwise. When we experience something as a cube in perception, we do so because we recognize that its appearance varies (or would vary) as a result of movement, that it exhibits a specific sensorimotor profile. (Noë 2004, pp. 101–2)

Noë's account, taken as a whole, has at least three apparent virtues, some key aspects of which I shall be seeking (as far as possible) to preserve.

First, and most importantly, there is the emphasis on skills rather than on qualia as traditionally conceived.[2] Skill-based accounts (see also Pettit 2003, Clark 2000, Matthen 2005, and of course Dennett 1991) offer a powerful antidote to the venom of zombie thought experiments.[3] In particular, the strong sensorimotor account would—if all worked out according to plan—ensure that sameness of world-engaging sensorimotor skills and discriminatory capacities implied sameness of perceptual experience. More demonstrably, the emphasis on world-engaging loops and knowledge of sensorimotor dependencies affords an elegant and compelling account of a range of real-world phenomena involving sensory substitution and neural re-wiring.

The classic example here is Tactile-Visual Sensory Substitution (TVSS; see Bach-y-Rita and Kercel 2002 for a recent review). Equally impressive, though perhaps less well known, is the

1. This general claim most strongly characterizes the work of O'Regan and Noë 2001 and Noë 2004. Historically, the view has roots that span science (especially ecological psychology; see Gibson 1979) and several influential philosophical traditions (ranging from Husserl 1907, Heidegger [1927] 1961 and Merleau-Ponty [1945] 1962, to Ryle [1949] 1990, MacKay 1967, and on to the original enactive approach of Varela, Thompson and Rosch 1991). It is also consistent with (but goes far beyond) the project of understanding mind and cognition in ways that are heavily 'action-oriented' (Clark 1997) and that stress the importance of body, action, and the canny use of environmental structure (for example, Hurley 1998, Ballard et al. 1997, Hutchins 1995, Churchland, Ramachandran and Sejnowski 1994, Thelen and Smith 1994)).

2. For an excellent (though itself sceptical) account of the traditional conception of qualia, see Pettit 2003.

3. For Noë's own take on such thought experiments, see, for example, Noë 2004, p. 124.

auditory-visual substitution system (discussed in some detail in O'Regan and Noë 2001), known as The Voice (see Meijer 1992). In this system, visual inputs to a head-mounted camera are systematically translated into audible patterns. Objects high in the visual field yield high-pitch sounds, while low ones yield low-pitch sounds. Lateral location is indicated by the balance of stereo sound, brightness by loudness of sound, and so on. Crucially, as you move the camera around, the sound changes, and over time subjects begin to learn the signature patterns (the sensorimotor dependencies) characteristic of different objects. In the original versions, subjects learnt to distinguish plants from statues, crosses from circles, and such like.

The overall effect, though powerful, fell short of creating a truly visual experience. But the claim of sensorimotor dependency theory is bold and clear: to whatever extent it is *possible* to recreate the same body of sensorimotor dependencies using an alternative route, you will recreate the full content and character of the original perceptual experience. This explains, according to O'Regan and Noë, why some of Bach-y-Rita's subjects report, for example, feeling as if they were *seeing* a looming ball when fitted with a TVSS system. By stressing similarities and differences in the profile of sensorimotor dependencies, Noë-style accounts neatly explain both the sense in which such systems create quasi-visual experiences and the ways in which the experiences thus generated (currently) fall short of those supported by the original routes. For example, there is a clear sensorimotor signature for a looming object whose invariant characteristics are as well captured by patterns of sound or tactile stimulation as they are by the (more typical) patterns of retinal stimulation. Very fine-grained colour information, by contrast, is currently not well captured by these kinds of substitution system. In each case, however, what is at issue is not the presence or absence of mysterious, ineffable qualia, but simply the presence or absence of distinctive loops linking real-world objects and properties to changing patterns of sensory stimulation.

The same story explains, we are told, the remarkable results concerning the rewiring of visual inputs to auditory cortex in young ferrets (Sur et al. 1999). Here, 'auditory' cortical areas become (thanks to the early re-wiring) involved in the kinds of sensorimotor loop characteristic of vision, and appear to support fully normal visual capacities in the modified ferret:

> Appropriately embedded in a 'visual' sensorimotor dynamic, neural activity in 'auditory' cortex in young ferrets takes on 'visual' functions. (Noë 2004. p. 227)

In short, appeals to the shape of a space of signature sensorimotor dependencies here replaces appeal either to the intrinsic properties of sensations (qualia) or to their more hard-nosed (but arguably equally unexplanatory) cousins, the putative special properties of specific neural regions.

The sensorimotor account is thus meant to be successful in cases 'where neural accounts alone are explanatorily afloat' (Noë 2004, p. 226). What does the work is simply 'the way neural systems subserve the activity of the embodied and embedded animal' (op. cit.). For Noë, then, experience is

> not caused by and realized in the brain, although it depends causally on the brain. Experience is realized in the active life of the skilful animal. (Noë 2004, p. 226)

I shall argue that neural accounts need not be seen as quite so 'explanatorily afloat' even if we agree (as I think we should) that *certain* bodies of skill provide the key to understanding perceptual experience.

Second (in the list of possible virtues) is the sensorimotor model's recognition of the importance, power and scope of what (in the artificial neural network community) is known as prediction learning. Prediction learning is an ecologically plausible form of supervised learning. In supervised learning, an agent is provided with detailed feedback concerning the desired output for a given input. Since such training seems to require a well-informed, continually present teacher, its ecological plausibility, for most real-world learning situations, looks doubtful. In some cases, however, the world itself provides, at the very next time-step, precisely the training information we need. Such is the case if, for example, the task (typically, as presented to a Simple Recurrent Neural Net; see, for example, Elman 1995) is to predict the next sensory input itself, whether it be the next word in a sentence or the next 'frame' in an evolving visual scene. Such prediction, for a mobile embodied agent, often requires a double input, namely information concerning the current sensory state and information (for instance, in the form of efferent copy) concerning any motion command currently in play. Given these items of information, a prediction can be made concerning the likely next sensory state. Such a prediction, in the visual case, will thus need to take into account both features of the scene and any motions of the agent, and can immediately be tested against the actual sensory stimulations duly delivered by the world.

Prediction learning has shown itself to be a valuable tool for the extraction of a number of important regularities, such as those characteristic of grammatical sentences, of shape, and of object-permanence. In a sense, Noë and his collaborators are extending this proven paradigm to attempt to account for the full spectrum of perceptual experience, whose contents and character are said to be sensitively dependent upon acquired expectations (implicit knowledge) concerning the ways sensory stimulation will morph and evolve with movement and other kinds of input-altering change. This is, it seems to me, precisely the kind of knowledge that would be embodied in the weights and connections of a neural network trained using a prediction learning regime.

Prediction learning is computationally potent, demonstrably possible, and almost certainly biologically actual. The standard models are, however (as we just saw), resolutely sub-personal, with the predictions defined over sensory patterns that obtain outwith any conscious awareness. On Noë's account, however, a critically important sub-class of cases are defined over *consciously experienced perspectival properties* ('P-properties'; see Noë 2004, p. 83) of objects. These are depicted as objective but relational properties: properties belonging to a perceiver-object pair situated in some larger environment:

> That a plate has a given P-shape is a fact about the plate's shape, one determined by the plate's relation to the location of a perceiver, and to the ambient light. (Noë 2004, p. 83)

Importantly, P-properties are *also* depicted as 'looks of things, their visual appearances' (op. cit., p. 84), and thus as able to participate in *phenomenologically salient* bouts of prediction learning. Thus:

> To see a circular plate from an angle, for example, is to see something with an elliptical P-shape, and it is to understand how that perspectival shape would vary as a function of one's (possible or actual) movements... (Noë 2004, p. 84)

But whilst agreeing that prediction learning is a powerful *knowledge-extraction tool*, especially in the perceptual arena, I am not convinced that mature perceptual experience is then constituted by[4] the running of (what might be thought of as) the prediction software itself. That is to say, I am not convinced that appeal to predictions (or expectations) concerning the next sensory stimulation directly and exhaustively explains (sub-personally) or even characterizes (personally) perceptual experience.

We shall return to these issues in subsequent sections. For the moment, it is useful simply to distinguish three different questions that may be asked:

(1) What kinds of unconscious know-how drive or power our fluid sensorimotor engagements with the world?
(2) What do we implicitly know about how our conscious perceptual experience will vary during with movement or change?
(3) What determines the content and character of our conscious perceptual experience itself?

These questions are all different, but the strong sensorimotor model tends to offer the same kind of answer (one that invokes implicit knowledge of sensorimotor dependencies) to them all. I shall argue, however, that while the appeal to knowledge of sensorimotor dependencies might well be crucial to answering the first (as when an agent deploys 'emulator circuitry' to anticipate sensory input and hence drive smooth reaching, etc.[5]), it is by no means obvious what role it should play in the other two. Probably we do (regarding question (2)) have *expectations* concerning the ways conscious experience will alter as we move etc., but it is not obvious that these expectations are crucial to the experience itself. Indeed (and moving on to question (3)) there is considerable evidence that perceptual experience is linked to specific forms of neural processing that are systematically insensitive to much of the fine detail of the sensorimotor loops themselves, thus casting doubt on the strong sensorimotor response to both these questions.

4. Noë uses 'constituted by' to mean something like 'realized by', and that is the sense intended here.
5. For one worked-out account of this, see Clark and Grush 1999.

The third and final virtue I want (very briefly) to mention is rather general, but both important and surprisingly delicate. It is that the sensorimotor model is well poised to accommodate *narcissistic experience in an objective world.* Talk of cognitive agents that, by their own activity, 'bring forth their worlds' can seem mysterious, if not mystical (see Clark and Mandik 2002 for some discussion). But, by linking the contents and character of perceptual experience rather directly to acquired expectations concerning patterns of sensorimotor dependence, the enactive framework is able to do justice both to the notion of an objective, mind-independent reality and to the sense in which the world as perceived is the world of a specific type of embodied agent. Such a (perceived) world is characterized by a suite of distinctive sensorimotor dependencies, whose nature sensitively determines the way the world is experienced through the senses.

According to this account, differently embodied beings will not be able to directly experience our perceptual world, not because it is populated by its own mysterious qualia but because they lack the requisite 'sensorimotor tuning' (Noë 2004, p. 156). It is a virtue of the sensorimotor model that it allows us to address this thorny topic in a straightforward manner. But it is a vice (or so I shall later suggest) that in doing so it implies that differently embodied beings *necessarily* inhabit different 'perceptual worlds'.

In general, then, I shall argue that in several domains the strong sensorimotor model takes us one step too far. By stressing skills, abilities and expectations, such accounts begin to offer a genuine alternative to traditional qualia-based approaches to perception and perceptual experience. But by focusing so much attention upon the sensorimotor frontier, they deprive us of the resources needed to construct a more nuanced and multi-layered model of perceptual experience, and risk obscuring some of the true complexity of our own cognitive condition.

II

Sensorimotor (Hyper) Sensitivity. Strong sensorimotor models suffer, it seems to me, from a form of sensorimotor hypersensitivity. Such models, or so I shall argue, are hypersensitive to the very fine details of bodily form and dynamics and, as a result, are prematurely committed on a variety of prima facie open (empirical) questions concerning the tightness of the relation between perceptual experience and embodied action.

To begin to bring this rather general concern into focus, consider first the matter of what Clark and Toribio (2001) dub 'sensorimotor chauvinism'. A sensorimotor chauvinist, as we use the term, is someone who holds, without compelling reason, that absolute sameness of perceptual experience requires absolute sameness of fine-grained sensorimotor profile. Noë (2004) is clear enough about this commitment. For example, in a discussion of the extent to which TVSS systems support 'similarity of experience' (to normal vision) Noë asserts that:

> Tactile vision is vision-like to the extent that there exists a sensorimotor isomorphism between vision and tactile vision. But tactile vision is unlike vision precisely to the extent that this sensorimotor isomorphism fails to obtain. It will fail to obtain, in general, whenever the two candidate realizing systems differ ... in their ability to subserve patterns of sensorimotor dependence. (Noë 2004, p. 27)

Expanding on this idea, Noë adds that:

> Only a vibrator array with something like the functional multiplicity of the retina could support genuine (full-fledged, normal) vision. To make tactile vision more fully visual, then, we need to make the physical system on which it depends more like the human visual system. (Noë op. cit., pp. 27–8)

Despite the superficially liberal appeal, in these quotes, to 'functional multiplicity', the required identity (for precise sameness of experience) actually reaches far down into the structure of the physical apparatus itself, and demands very fine-grained similarities of body and gross sensory equipment. O'Regan and Noë are more explicit:

> For two systems to have the same knowledge of sensorimotor contingencies *all the way down* they will have to have bodies that are identical *all the way down* (at least in relevant respects). For only bodies that are alike in low-level detail can be functionally alike in the relevant ways. (O'Regan and Noë 2001, p. 1015)

While later on in Noë's single-author treatment he asserts that:

> Creatures with bodies like ours would have systems that are visual in the way ours are. Indeed, *only such systems can participate in the identical range of sensorimotor interactions that we participate in.* (Noë 2004, p. 159, my italics)

The position is thus that while some coarse-grained isomorphisms may be sufficient to begin to render the experience of a differently embodied being visual, the full glory of normal human visual experience depends upon a gross sensorimotor profile that very sensitively tracks the fine details of human embodiment (including, we saw, such matters as the precise curve of the eyeball).[6] Of course, even such a strong view need not be (as Noë (2004, p. 28) rightly points out) chauvinistic *if* the requirement of full sensorimotor isomorphism (for identity of experience) flows from a compelling theoretical model.

But does it? The claim in question (let's call it the claim of Fine-Grained Sensorimotor Dependence) is that every difference in fine-grained patterns of sensorimotor dependence will potentially impact any associated perceptual experience. Notice that this consequence does not in any way follow from the fact (if it is a fact) that prediction learning plays a key role in the *acquisition* of certain kinds of perceptual knowledge and understanding. For the upshot of such learning might well be forms of understanding that are systematically insensitive to some changes in sensory stimulation, while exaggerating others.

Notice also that the patterns of sensorimotor dependence in question cannot *themselves* be patterns in experiential space (in the space of appearances) on pain of triviality. For of course, every difference in experience implies some difference in experience. But if we step outside the phenomenological arena, then the claim (of Fine-Grained Sensorimotor Dependence) looks to involve the premature settling of what should be an open empirical question.

Thus suppose, to imagine a concrete case, that certain patterns of sensorimotor dependence concern the relations between movement and retinal stimulation. And suppose that some very small difference in embodiment makes a very small difference to such patterns. It is surely an open empirical question whether every difference in respect of such stimulation *makes a difference* to the content and character of any conscious perceptual experience

6. Thus we read that '... it turns out that there is good reason to believe that the sensorimotor dependencies are themselves determined by low-level details of the physical systems on which our sensory systems depend. The eye and the visual parts of the brain form a most subtle instrument indeed, and thanks to this instrument, sensory stimulation varies in response to movement in precise ways. To see as we do, you must have a sensory organ and a body like ours' (Noë 2004, p. 112).

that ensues. And the same will be true wherever in the processing story we choose to focus, even if we opt for patterns of cortical rather than retinal stimulation.

Systematic insensitivities might, in fact, serve some functional purpose. It is easy to imagine design and engineering considerations that would favour various kinds of buffering, filtering, and re-coding of perceptual inputs such that the contents and character of conscious perceptual experience might be determined at some considerable remove from the fine-grained details of sensorimotor loops. As we shall later see, there is some reason to believe that human perceptual experience is indeed determined at just such a remove, and that it involves tweaked and optimized representations that do not march sensitively in step with the flow of gross sensory stimulation.

It might be objected that the kind of hypersensitivity I am contesting is simply the price one pays for appealing to embodied skills as an alternative to traditional appeals to qualia. But this is not so. For the skills to which such deflationary accounts (among which I count the strong sensorimotor theory) appeal may *themselves* be coarse- or fine-grained, and may thus involve activities and capacities that are systematically insensitive to some of the goings-on at the sensorimotor frontier. For example, they may focus on what Matthen (2005) (and see also Pettit 2003) calls 'epistemic' skills: skills of sifting, sorting, classifying, selecting, choosing, re-identifying and comparing. These skills (which must, in any deflationary context, be said to constitute, rather than to call upon, perceptual experience) may depend on modes of processing and forms of internal representation that ultimately float free of the full spectrum of fine sensorimotor detail. Nor, finally, need the appeal to skills (rather than qualia) force us to abandon the notion of a distinctive personal level at which a cognitive agent has access to (some) information. That is to say, it should not force us to abandon the notion of that which is in some important sense *manifest* (see Pettit 2003) to the agent concerned.

I suspect that in his (admirable) eagerness to avoid the qualia trap, Noë has been led to define appearances rather too directly in terms of objective relations between objects and perceivers, with the result that whatever impacts this objective relation (more precisely, whatever impacts the way this relation unfolds during sensorimotor activity) is said to impact (if only very subtly) how things look to the agent. Other ways of unpacking a skill-based account need not, as we'll see, buy into this kind of picture. But before exploring such a possibility, it helps to introduce a missing layer of complexity in (at least some versions of) the strong sensorimotor model itself.

III

What Reaching Teaches. The complexity in question concerns the role of reason and planning in (what might be thought of as) the architecture of perceptual experience. According to O'Regan and Noë we are conscious of a specific visually presented state of affairs only when our practical knowledge about the ways movement will yield sensory change is actively invoked in the service of reason, planning and judgement. In such cases we do not merely exercise our mastery of sensorimotor contingencies, for we do this even when we are unaware of our own actions, as when returning a fast tennis serve or absent-mindedly driving along a familiar road. Rather, conscious awareness enters the scene when we make use of *that very same* knowledge of sensorimotor contingencies 'for the purposes of thought and planning' (O'Regan and Noë 2001, p. 944). On this account to consciously see is

> to explore one's environment in a way that is mediated by one's mastery of sensorimotor contingencies, and to be making use of this mastery in one's planning, reasoning and speech behavior. (O'Regan and Noë op. cit., p. 944)

The point of adding such a requirement is clear. Very often, when we exercise our implicit knowledge of patterns of sensorimotor dependence, no corresponding perceptual awareness ensues. To explain the difference, O'Regan and Noë invoke use in reason, planning and speech behaviour as a kind of spotlight that allows some (but not all) of our active knowledge of sensorimotor contingencies to condition perceptual awareness.[7]

7. Interestingly, this requirement (which is made much of by O'Regan and Noë) is nowhere in evidence in Noë's 2004 solo treatment. What we find there is just the bare idea of the active use of specific bodies of knowledge concerning sensorimotor dependencies in the guidance of behaviour. Noë (personal communication) picks this issue out as one where his views are in a state of flux. The guiding thought, he writes, is that 'being conscious of a feature is actively probing it—it's reaching out

There is, however, another possibility hereabouts, one that has significant empirical support and that is ultimately (or so I shall argue) at odds with the strong sensorimotor model. This is the possibility (Milner and Goodale 1995, Clark 2001, Jacob and Jeannerod 2003) that the contents of conscious perceptual experience are determined by the activation of a distinctive body of internal representations operating quasi-autonomously from the realm of direct sensorimotor engagement. Such representations are perceptual but are geared towards (and optimized for) the specific needs of reasoning and planning rather than those of fluent physical engagement. These representations are conditioned by a stream of inputs that do indeed originate at the sensors, but this stream proceeds in large part in parallel to the processing stream dedicated to the fluid control of online, fine-tuned, sensorimotor engagement, and is systematically insensitive to much of the lower-level detail.

These 'dual-stream' models appear to differ from strong sensorimotor models in at least two crucial respects. First, they depict visual experience as depending on a suite of representations optimized for reasoning and planning, whereas strong sensorimotor models depict visual experience as occurring when (possibly very fine-grained) sensorimotor knowledge is either simply *active*, or more plausibly when it is *put into contact with*, or *used for the purposes of*, reasoning and planning. Second, these models looks to be fully compatible with the idea (rejected outright by the strong sensorimotor model) that conscious visual experience might often (and perhaps always) depend on specific local aspects of internal representational activity rather than on whole-animal sensorimotor loops.

A major part of the empirical impetus for the dual-stream story comes from Milner and Goodale, who suggest (1995) that conscious visual awareness reflects information-processing activity in a specific visual processing stream geared towards enduring object properties, explicit recognition, and semantic recall. This

and making contact with it, as it were'. But such active probing surely characterizes the intelligent saccades of the driver's eyes even when the driver is attending to other matters and not consciously experiencing the details of the road. Alternatively, if active probing means something like 'probing in the context of attentive problem-solving', then we are back to the full-strength role for reason and planning assigned by O'Regan and Noë.

stream—the ventral stream—is also in charge whenever real-world objects are unavailable, and governs our attempts to mime actions on imagined or recalled objects. Actual object-based motor engagements, by contrast, are depicted as the province of a semi-autonomous processing stream—the dorsal stream—that guides fluent motor action in the here and now. Milner and Goodale thus contrast capacities of visually-guided action and capacities of conscious visual perception, suggesting that these come apart in a variety of unexpected and revealing ways.

In support of this hypothesis, Milner and Goodale invoke a rich body of data concerning patients with damage to areas in either the dorsal or ventral streams. The best known of these is the patient DF who suffers from ventral stream lesions and cannot visually identify objects or visually discriminate shapes. Nonetheless, she is able to pick up these very same objects—that she cannot visually identify—using fluent, well-oriented precision grips. Others, by contrast, suffer dorsal stream lesions and

> have little trouble seeing [i.e., identifying objects in a visual scene] but a lot of trouble reaching for objects they can see. It is as though they cannot use the spatial information inherent in any visual scene. (Gazzaniga 1998, p. 109)

Milner and Goodale also cite performance data from normal human subjects using experimental paradigms such as Aglioti et al.'s ingenious use of the Tichener Circles illusion. In the standard illusion, subjects misjudge the relative size of two circles each surrounded by a ring of larger or smaller circles. Aglioti et al. (1995) set up a physical version of the illusion using thin poker chips as the discs, and then asked subjects to 'pick up the target disc on the left if the two discs appeared equal in size and to pick up the one on the right if they appeared different in size' (Milner and Goodale 1995, p. 167). The surprising upshot was that even when subjects were unaware of—but clearly subject to—the illusion, their motor control systems produced a precisely fitted grip with a finger-thumb aperture perfectly suited to the *actual* (non-illusory) size of the disc. This aperture was not arrived at by touching and adjusting, but was instead the direct result of the visual input. Yet—to repeat—it reflected not the illusory disc size given in the subject's visual experience, but the actual size. In short:

> Grip size was determined entirely by the true size of the target disc [and] the very act by means of which subjects indicated their susceptibility to the visual illusion (that is, picking up one of two target circles) was itself uninfluenced by the illusion. (Milner and Goodale 1995, p. 168)

This was, indeed, a somewhat startling result, again suggesting[8] that the processing underlying visual awareness may be operating quite independently of that underlying the visual control of action.

Finally, Milner and Goodale invoke a number of computational conjectures concerning the inability of a single encoding to efficiently support both visual form recognition and visuomotor action. I shall not further rehearse these bodies of evidence here (see Clark 1999, 2001, Jacob and Jeannerod 2003). Notice, however, that it seems very likely that prediction learning will play a big role in the development and exercise of the kinds of skill that best characterize the (putatively non-conscious) dorsal stream. For smooth visuomotor action (such as reaching and grasping without jagged movements or unwanted oscillations) looks to require the ability to predict the next sensory input in advance of its actual (too late) arrival at the sensory peripheries, and this kind of prediction (see Clark and Grush 1999) certainly requires implicit knowledge of sensorimotor dependencies.

At this point it will be useful to locate the dual visual systems hypothesis in a wider framework. This framework depicts *conscious* visual perception as making available—at the personal level—forms of encoding and representation optimized for (or simply specialized for) their role in reasoning, choice and action-selection rather than for their role in actual sensorimotor engagement. Thus in the Titchener Circles experiment, the conscious visual representations would be specialized (just as Milner and Goodale suggest) to guide the choice of *which* disc to pick up, and the choice of what *kind* of grip to deploy (one apt for picking up and not for, say, throwing). The conscious illusion (of one circle's being larger than another) may then be best explained by the visual system's delivering a representation

8. There has been much discussion, pro and con, of this example in the recent literature. For a good overview (whose conclusion is that a weakened form of dual-stream model is probably correct) see Jacob and Jeannerod 2003. For further discussion of these complexities, see Clark 2001.

enhanced in the light of information about relative size, a trick that is effective for reasoning and choice in most ecologically realistic situations, but that would be damaging (resulting in a mass of failed or botched encounters) were it replicated by fine sensorimotor control systems.

This general model of the functional role of conscious awareness is found in (among others) the work of Koch (2004) who speaks of 'summaries' apt to aid frontal regions in the selection of one among a set of possible types of action or response. It is also suggested by Campbell's (2002) 'targets' view of consciousness, and (in the treatment closest to the present account) in Jacob and Jeannerod's (2003) delicately nuanced version of the dual visual streams view.[9]

Common to all these views is the image of conscious perceptual experience as reflecting the content of representations whose special cognitive role is to enable the deliberate selection of targets for action and of types of action, and to support a range of 'epistemic skills' such as sorting, sifting, comparing and the like (see Pettit 2003, Matthen 2005). Representations optimized for such purposes need not, and typically do not, reflect the full intricacies of our actual ongoing sensorimotor engagements with the world. Instead, they are geared, tweaked and nuanced so as to inform reason, selection, comparison and choice. They thus reflect only the very broad outlines of a space of possible targets and possible *kinds* of sensorimotor engagement. And though they must be sensitive to sensory input, they need not (indeed, must not) be sensitive to every nuance in the ongoing mass of sensory stimulation. The representations that ultimately determine visual experience are quite distinct, this alternative account insists, from those that support the sensorimotor loops by means of which we successfully engage the very world we perceive. They are, nonetheless, still distinctively visual, in so far as they represent the special kinds of information gathered (in normal agents) by (part of) the visual pathway: features such as rough spatial location, colour, shape, and so on. TVSS systems, on this account, aim to make the same kinds of information available by means of superficially different sets of signals, and will succeed to whatever extent this turns out to be

9. It also seems implicit in Matthen's (2005) account of the class of 'descriptive sensory systems'.

possible (which will in turn depend both on the nature and extent of neural plasticity and on the ability, of these alternate input devices, to make the same bodies of information available, and at roughly the same time-scale: for this take on TVSS, see Bach y Rita and Kercel 2003).

Noë (2004, p. 19) claims that these dual visual systems ideas are 'at best orthogonal to the basic claims of the enactive approach'. The reason given (see also op. cit., p. 11) is that the enactive approach makes no claims about what conscious visual perception is *for*, and hence remains neutral on the topic of vision-for-action versus vision-for-conscious-perception. More positively, O'Regan and Noë (2001, p. 969) claim that, with a few provisos, there is actually a good fit between the strong sensorimotor model and the dual visual systems ideas, since the requirement (for conscious experience) that sensorimotor knowledge be active in the service of reason and planning predicts the kinds of dissociation found in the literature.

I think it should be clear, however, that such direct attempts at reconciliation cannot succeed. For what is at issue is not simply the evidence of (substantial) dissociation but the best *functional and architectural explanation* of that evidence. And the best functional and architectural explanation, according to Milner, Goodale and others, is that conscious perceptual experience reflects the activation of representations that have less to do with the fine details of world-engaging sensorimotor loops, and more to do with the need to assign inputs to categories, types, and relative locations, so as better to sift, sort, select, identify, compare, recall, imagine and reason.

The contrast between the two views emerges in, for example, O'Regan and Noë's surprising description of DF as a case of 'partial awareness' in which 'she is unable to describe what she sees but is otherwise able to use it for the purpose of guiding action' (op. cit., p. 969). DF, recall, is able to use visually presented information for some purposes, for example, to post a letter into a slot, even though she claims not to visually experience the shape, colour or orientation of the slot. O'Regan and Noë depict this as a case of 'partial awareness', since visual information is still playing an action-guiding role in the overall organism–environment loop. But this surely conflates visual awareness with the use of visual information, precisely the knot that Milner and Goodale were trying to untie. For this reason Goodale (2001) rejects O'Regan and Noë's account of DF, pointing out that she 'shows almost perfect visuomotor control in the absence of any evidence that she actually "sees" the form of the object she is grasping'.

Here, I suspect, the enactive framework is trying to wag the empirical dog. For the enactive framework is, as we saw, pre-committed to linking the perceptual facts to facts about whole animal embedded, embodied activity. Perception, including conscious perception, is thus said to be 'a kind of skilful activity on the part of the animal as a whole' (Noe 2004, p. 2; and see Varela, Thompson and Rosch 1991).[10] But this pre-commitment works against taking truly seriously the evidence for deep dissociations between vision-for-action and vision-for-perception.

In contrast with this 'whole animal' view, dual stream models are open to the possibility that specific perceptual capacities and experiences depend upon (and can be brought about by) the activity of specific aspects of neural circuitry. In the case of conscious visual experience, such models embrace the idea that processing in the ventral stream plays a special role in the construction of conscious experience, and that there is serious functional decomposition (coupled with dense online integration; see Jacob and Jeannerod 2003) between systems for conscious experience and systems for fluent, fine-tuned visuomotor action.

Such models retain the important emphasis on skills rather than qualia. But they do so while recognizing the very large extent to which the human agent is a *fragmented bag of embodied skills*, only some of which are potentially relevant to the contents and character of perceptual experience. In particular, these will be skills geared rather directly towards reasoning and planning, such as abilities of sifting, sorting, classifying, selecting, choosing, re-identifying, imagining, recalling and comparing. This special focus opens up a significant buffer zone between the fine details of movement and of motion-dependent sensory input and the rather more specialized skill base that determines the contents

10. As an aside, this same broad commitment, to the constitutive role of whole organism activity, probably leads to other oddities, such as Noë's later suggestion that a concert pianist, in losing his arms, would thereby (instantly, as what appears to be a matter of conceptual necessity) lose his know-how since 'the knowledge was, precisely, arm-dependent' (Noë 2004, p. 121).

and character of perceptual experience. What counts (for perceptual experience) is then this suite of epistemic skills, *however they happen to be supported by cycles of low-level sensorimotor pick-up*. And there is, as far as I can see, no compelling reason to believe that *these* kinds of epistemic skills need to march in tight lockstep with a being's full sensorimotor profile. Indeed, they may depend on representational forms that are deliberately (that is to say, productively) insensitive to many fine details of bodily orientation and sensory stimulation. If this is correct, then the perceptual experience of differently embodied animals could in principle be identical (not merely similar) to our own.

I'd like to end by addressing (however inadequately) what is perhaps the very largest issue hereabouts, namely the role of actual world-engaging loops in the construction of perceptual experience. For it is here that the greatest care is needed if we are to preserve what is most important in the sensorimotor account. Thus consider, to take one final example, the claim (Noë 2004, p. 67) that 'experiential content is itself virtual'. The idea here, in keeping with the general emphasis on sensorimotor contact with the world, is that experience presents all the detail in a visual scene as present, but virtually so, rather like 'the way that a web site's content is present on your desktop' (op. cit., p. 50). In the latter case, it can seem just as if, to use Noë's own example, you have the entire contents of the online version of the *New York Times* encoded on your hard drive. But of course, this is not so. Rather, information is accessed from the distant site on a kind of just-in-time, need-to-know basis. Similarly, according to Noë, we perceptually experience the visual scene as rich in detail. But this experience, while not illusory (*pace* the Grand Illusion idea popularized by Dennett and others: see Noë 2004, pp. 50–67) is rooted not in the presence of a rich neurally encoded representation of all that detail, but in our skill-based access to the requisite detail as and when needed:

> The detail is present—the perceptual world is present—in the sense that we have a special kind of access to the detail, an access controlled by patterns of sensorimotor dependence with which we are familiar. (Noë 2004, p. 67)

This stress on access is correct and, I think, profoundly important.

But what *exactly* is the role of the actual sensorimotor loops by means of which such access is provided? How, that is to say, should we conceive the role of the *specific routines* by means of which we thus engage the world, retrieving more visual information as and when needed?

One radical possibility is that these specific sensorimotor loops are now part of the supervenience base for the present experience of richness. Another, only slightly less radical, possibility is that our implicit knowledge of these specific sensorimotor loops is part of the supervenience base for the present experience of richness. But still another possibility is that the present experience of richness is simply a present experience of the easy accessibility of certain kinds of information as and when needed, and that the specific world-engaging loops provide merely the contingent means to this end. The supervenience base for the perceptual experience of richness, on this model, would not include the routines that actually retrieve such information. Indeed, the very same experience of perceptual richness looks compatible with the running (behind the scenes, as it were) of a wide variety of quite different retrieval routines.

The deepest question raised by the strong sensorimotor model, is surely this: to what extent does the 'how' of information pick-up (the specific details of some sensorimotor retrieval routine) matter *for perceptual experience itself*? My own suspicion, which I have tried to make plausible in the present treatment, is that such details may be merely the contingent means by which a certain higher-level, overarching functional organization is achieved. The kind of functional story required will vary from case to case, but will typically be pitched at some remove from the full details of our active sensorimotor repertoire.

IV

The Heideggerian Theatre. In sum, none of the considerations adduced by the strong sensorimotor theorist seem to support the radical conclusion that qualitative experience is 'not caused by and realized in the brain' (Noë 2004, p. 226). What does seem to be true is that intentionally-driven cycles of world-engaging organism–environment activity are the typical means by which neural circuitry becomes recruited so as to be poised to control certain key kinds of action. It is this achieved poise, rather than anything more specific to the neural circuitry itself, that then does the real explanatory work. Thus the fans of skill-based approaches (and I count myself among them) believe that the right kinds of action-enabling poise (of, I want to say, some active inner state) quite literally constitute the presence of perceptual experience of various kinds. The considerations concerning ventral stream processing suggest, however, that the relevant kinds of action-enabling poise[11] are not tied to the fine detail of specific bodily equipment or motions. Instead, what matters is poise is for the control of a special class of more epistemically pregnant actions, such as those (highlighted by Dennett, Matthen and Pettit) of sifting, sorting, comparing and discriminating.

Suppose we then push the question: what is it about the active neural patterns that makes them yield or support the very experiences that they do? The best answer, just as the skill-based story insisted, looks to be: because they are such as to enable the kinds of activities they do. If that is so, there may simply be no answer to the bald (hard) question, 'Why does this pattern of neural pattern yield this experience?' Rather, the neural pattern, in bodily and worldly context, is such as to support a signature set of epistemic abilities, and it is these alone that explain (by constituting) the phenomenal content. The correct conclusion is that neural activity alone indeed suffices, as far as we can currently tell, to *support* any given perceptual experience, but that no explanation of the *link* between the neural activity and the experience can afford to ignore the shape of the space of enabled actions (of that special epistemic class) on pain of eventually identifying an unexplanatory disjunction instead of an explanatorily pregnant correlation.[12]

Strong sensorimotor models of perceptual experience do us a service by foregrounding embodied skills and eschewing appeals

11. It remains possible that more neglected elements of experience, ones other than those concerning the typical qualia suspects such as shape, colour, texture, and so on, may depend more directly on dorsal stream activity. Thus Matthen (2005, p. 301) argues that the 'feeling of presence' may depend on dorsal stream activity even if the other more descriptive elements do not.

12. For an argument of this kind, but without the stress on a special class of epistemic actions, see Hurley forthcoming.

to qualia as traditionally conceived. But they fail to do justice to the many firewalls, fragmentations and divisions of cognitive labour that characterize our engagements with the world our senses reveal. Strong sensorimotor models, despite (or perhaps because of) their emphasis on whole animal world-engaging activity, paper over this complex motley by casting everything prematurely in the single currency of known patterns of fine sensorimotor dependence. By trying to distil all that matters about human perceptual experience from the homogeneous mash of expectations concerning sensorimotor dependencies, such models are congenitally blind to the computationally potent *insensitivity* of key information-processing events to the full subtleties of embodied cycles of sensing and moving. In place of this common sensorimotor currency we need to consider a more complex picture that displays a cognitive economy replete with special-purpose streamings and with multiple, quasi-independent forms of internal (and external) representation and processing. To embrace such complexity is not to downplay the role of the body, but to reveal it aright. The body matters because it is the *common locus* of many (though by no means all) of these diverse epistemic currents and influences, and because it is their common, and often conflicted, object of proximal control. The body is (dare I say it?) the Heideggerian Theatre: the one place where it all comes together, or as together as it comes at all.

References

Aglioti, S., M. Goodale and J. F. X. DeSouza 1995: 'Size Contrast Illusions Deceive the Eye But Not the Hand'. *Curr. Biol.*, 5, pp. 679–85.

Bach y Rita, P. and S. W. Kercel 2003: 'Sensory Substitution and the Human–Machine Interface'. *Trends in Cognitive Sciences*, 7:12, pp. 541–6.

Ballard, D. H., M. M. Hayhoe, P. K. Pook and R. P. N. Rao 1997: 'Deictic Codes for the Embodiment of Cognition'. *Behavioral and Brain Sciences*, 20, 4, pp. 723–67.

Bridgeman, B., S. Lewis, G., Heit and M. Nagle 1979: 'Relation Between Cognitive and Motor-oriented Systems of Visual Position Perception'. *Journal of Experimental Psychology* (*Human Perception*), 5, pp. 692–700.

Campbell, J. 2002: *Reference and Consciousness*. Oxford: Oxford University Press.

Churchland, P., V. Ramachandran and T. Sejnowski 1994: 'A Critique of Pure Vision'. In C. Koch and J. Davis (eds), *Large-Scale Neuronal Theories of the Brain*. Cambridge, MA: MIT Press, pp. 23–61.

Clark, A. 1997: *Being There: Putting Brain, Body and World Together Again*. Cambridge, MA: MIT Press.

——— 1999: 'Visual Awareness and Visuomotor Action'. *Journal Of Consciousness Studies*, 6, 11–12, pp. 1–18.

——— 2000: 'A Case Where Access Implies Qualia?' *Analysis*, 60:265, pp. 30–8.
——— 2001: 'Visual Experience and Motor Action: Are The Bonds Too Tight?' *Philosophical Review*, 110:4, pp. 495–519.
——— and R. Grush 1999: 'Towards a Cognitive Robotics'. *Adaptive Behavior*, 7:1, pp. 5–16.
——— and P. Mandik 2002: 'Selective Representing and World-Making'. *Minds and Machines*, 12, pp. 383–95.
——— and J. Toribio 2001: 'Sensorimotor Chauvinism?: Commentary on O'Regan, J. K., and Noë, A., "A sensorimotor approach to vision and visual consciousness"'. *Behavioral and Brain Sciences*, 24:5, pp. 979–80.
Dennett, D. 1991: *Consciousness Explained.* Boston, MA: Little, Brown.
Elman, J. 1995: 'Language as a Dynamical System'. In R. Port and T. van Gelder (eds), *Mind as Motion.* Cambridge, MA: MIT Press.
Gazzaniga, M. 1998: *The Mind's Past.* Berkeley, CA: University of California Press.
Gibson, J. J. 1979: *The Ecological Approach to Visual Perception.* New York: Houghton-Mifflin.
Goodale, M. 2001: 'Real Action in a Virtual World: Commentary on O'Regan and Noë'. *Behavioral and Brain Sciences*, 24:5, pp. 984–5.
Heidegger, M. [1927] 1961: *Being and Time*. London: Harper and Row.
Hurley, S. 1998: *Consciousness in Action.* Cambridge, MA: Harvard University Press.
——— forthcoming: 'The Varieties of Externalism'. In M. Aydede and P. Robbins (eds), *The Cambridge Handbook of Situated Cognition.* Cambridge: Cambridge University Press.
Husserl, E. 1907: *Thing and Space.* Trans. R. Rojcewicz. Boston, MA: Kluwer.
Hutchins, E. 1995: *Cognition in the Wild.* Cambridge, MA: MIT Press.
Jacob, P. and M. Jeannerod 2003: *Ways of Seeing: The Scope and Limits of Visual Cognition.* Oxford: Oxford University Press.
Koch, C. 2004: *The Quest for Consciousness.* New York: Roberts and Co.
MacKay, D. 1967: 'Ways of Looking at Perception'. In W. Wathen-Dunn (ed.), *Models for the Perception of Speech and Visual Form.* Cambridge, MA: MIT Press, pp. 25–43.
Matthen, M. 2005: *Seeing, Doing and Knowing*. Oxford: Oxford University Press.
Meijer, P. B. L. 1992: 'An Experimental System for Auditory Image Representations'. *IEEE Transactions on Biomedical Engineering*, 39:2, pp. 112–21.
Merleau-Ponty, M. [1945] 1962: *The Phenomenology of Perception.* Trans. Colin Smith. London: Routledge.
Milner, A. and M. Goodale 1995: *The Visual Brain in Action.* Oxford: Oxford University Press.
Noë, A. 2004: *Action in Perception*. Cambridge, MA: MIT Press.
O'Regan, J. K. 1992: 'Solving the "Real" Mysteries of Visual Perception: The World as an Outside Memory'. *Canadian Journal of Psychology*, 46:3, pp. 461–88.
——— and A. Noë 2001: 'A Sensorimotor Approach to Vision and Visual Consciousness'. *Behavioral and Brain Sciences*, 24:5, pp. 939–73.
Pettit, P. 2003: 'Looks as Powers'. *Philosophical Issues*, 13, pp. 221–52.
Ryle, G. [1949] 1990: *The Concept of Mind.* London: Penguin.
Sur, M., A. Angelucci and J. Sharma 1999: 'Rewiring Cortex: The Role of Patterned Activity in Development and Plasticity of Neocortical Circuits'. *Journal of Neurobiology*, 41:1, pp. 33–43.
Thelen, E. and L. Smith 1994: *A Dynamic Systems Approach To The Development Of Cognition And Action.* Cambridge, MA: MIT Press.
Varela, F., E. Thompson and E. Rosch 1991: *The Embodied Mind.* Cambridge, MA: MIT Press.

SENSORIMOTOR SKILLS AND PERCEPTION

by Andy Clark and Naomi Eilan

II—Naomi Eilan

ON THE ROLE OF PERCEPTUAL CONSCIOUSNESS IN EXPLAINING THE GOALS AND MECHANISMS OF VISION: A CONVERGENCE ON ATTENTION?

ABSTRACT The strong sensorimotor account of perception gives self-induced movements two constitutive roles in explaining visual consciousness. The first says that self-induced movements are vehicles of visual awareness, and for this reason consciousness 'does not happen in the brain only'. The second says that the phenomenal nature of visual experiences is consists in the action-directing content of vision. In response I suggest, first, that the sense in which visual awareness is active should be explained by appeal to the role of attention in visual consciousness, rather than self-induced movements; and second, that the sense in which perceptual consciousness does not happen in the brain only should be explained by appeal to the relational nature of perceptual consciousness, appeal to which also shows why links with action cannot exhaust phenomenal content.

I

Introduction. The strong sensorimotor account of perception gives self-induced movements two constitutive roles in explaining the nature of perceptual consciousness. The claims it makes in this connection concern perception in general, but I will focus throughout on the case of vision. The first says that self-induced movements are vehicles of visual awareness. The second says that the phenomenal nature of visual experiences is to be explained in terms of the action- directing content of vision.

These claims about the role of self-induced movement are particularizations of several more general claims about the nature of visual experience, which include the following:

1. There is an internal connection between the explanation we should give of the mechanism of vision and the account

we should give of its content. And both are essential for getting the phenomenology right.

2. There is something essentially temporally extended and in this sense non-representational about vision.
3. There is something essentially physically extended and in this sense non-representational about vision. ('Consciousness does not happen (only) in the brain.')
4. There is something essentially active about vision.

A distinctive feature of Andy Clark's critique of the strong sensorimotor approach, here and in other places, is (a) to suggest that there are interesting, very important insights in the generalized claims, but (b) to question whether the appeal to self-induced movements is the correct way of doing justice to all of them. I think he is exactly right on both scores, though it may be that I take (b) further than he would want to.

Claims 2–4 above can be read both as claims about the mechanisms involved in vision and as claims about its content. Clark has focused mostly, though not exclusively, on mechanism issues. The question he raises is whether we can capture what is right in claims 2–4, considered as claims about the mechanisms of vision, by appeal to the role of self-induced movement in delivering information about the environment. I return to some of the issues he raises in the second half of the paper. Before that I raise the question of whether appeal to action-directing content can capture what is right about claim 3 in characterizing the content of visual experience. Rather than do this directly, I focus on the role of vision in providing for objective knowledge of the environment. I suggest that taking this role seriously requires treating consciousness as a two-term relation between subject and presented intrinsic properties of external objects (so visual experience is in some sense physically extended). The particular reasons I give for this also explain why the appeal to action-direction cannot be the right characterization of the content of experience.

How, if the claims I will be making about content are right, do they link up with claim 1, which says that there is interdependence between claims about mechanisms and claims about content; and that exploring these is essential to a correct account of phenomenology? It goes without saying that I will only begin to scratch the surface of this issue: I do so by raising and beginning to address the following, more specific, questions. First, is there a single concept we can and should appeal to in explaining the nature of perception, the correct account of which requires endorsing claims 2–4? Second, does this concept justify the central contention made in claim 1? Third, given this concept, what exactly should we say about the relation between content and mechanism specifically with respect to temporal and physical extension of consciousness?

In 'Visual Awareness and Visuomotor Action' (1999) Clark suggests that what is right about claims 2 and 4, considered as claims about mechanism, should be absorbed by claims about the role of attention in vision. In *Reference and Consciousness*, John Campbell suggests that we should appeal to the nature of attention in explaining the sense in which visual experience presents us directly with intrinsic properties of the environment (Campbell 2002). The proposal I will be pursuing is that the concept of attention, for a combination of reasons adduced by Campbell and Clark, is the place to do justice to what is right in claims 2–4, considered as claims about both content and the mechanism of vision. A particular consequence, though, of the way I pursue this is that the appeal to action seems to drop out altogether from an explanation of the truth of any of the claims listed above. And this is a point at which there may be a genuine difference between the approach to consciousness I am sketching here and the approach advocated by Clark.

II

On the Very Idea of Giving Consciousness an Explanatory Role. (1) What are goals of vision? (2) How are these goals achieved? (3) Does our concept of perceptual consciousness have a role in answering (1) and (2)? My question is the third, but, naturally, how one goes about addressing it is deeply dependent, in various and difficult ways, on how one answers the others.

Roughly put, there are two ways of delivering an a priori negative answer to the third question about the role of consciousness. The first is to give an account of the goals of vision and of how they are achieved, on the one hand, and of the nature of perceptual consciousness, on the other, which are not only completely independent of each other, but which are also such that, given these definitions, it is not possible for consciousness to have a role in addressing either of the first two questions. For example, suppose you say that the goal of vision is, solely, to control environmentally directed action. And suppose you say this is achieved by means of a combination of computations and physical activity. And now suppose you say that experiential consciousness consists in the occurrence of sensations or sensational properties which are (a) essentially non-physical and (b) such that their intrinsic nature has no internal connection at all with action. (a) rules out sensations, and hence consciousness, from having any causal role in the process of vision; (b) rules them out from having any role in explaining the goals of vision.

The second way of depriving appeal to experiential consciousness of any explanatory force is reductive. The reduction can go either way, but the most common, and the one that will be our main concern, is this. You first give a wholly consciousness-independent answer to the goals and means questions, and then go on to define experiential consciousness in these terms. For example, you might give the same answers as above to the goals and means questions and then simply say (a) that whenever the means to achieving the goals of vision are enacted you have conscious experience; and (b) that the phenomenal properties of the experience just are the properties of the perception in virtue of which the goal of vision is achieved. In particular, you may identify the phenomenal properties with the action-directing content of the perceptual information. On this kind of reductive approach, you might say that there is a sense in which consciousness has an explanatory role in achieving the goals of vision, but this is only because you have defined being conscious in terms of these wholly independently defined and explained skills. But the concept of consciousness is not doing any independent explanatory work in controlling your account of these means, and this is, in part, because it is playing no *independent* role in identifying the goals of vision.

If our concept of experiential consciousness does have a role in explaining the goal of vision and/or the way this goal is achieved, then in saying what it is we need to avoid both kinds of accounts of what such consciousness consists in. On one view, what makes the problem of consciousness hard is that it is not possible to do this. The options just are dualism, reductionism or the position labelled 'mysterianism' on which our current understanding of consciousness is constitutively such as to prevent us from going beyond these options.

An alternative account of what makes the problem of consciousness hard is not that it is impossible to do so, but very difficult. For what is required, if we are to avoid the two ways of depriving consciousness of an explanatory role, is an account of what consciousness consists in which is both, in some sense, independent of empirical theories about the mechanisms involved in visual information processing and, at the same time, so as to have causal relevance to them, such that they can impose a genuine constraint. And this is not an easy thing to get right.

If I have understood the general sprit of Clark's approach to consciousness, we share the second approach to the difficulty here. On this view, our everyday concept of perception does give consciousness a genuinely explanatory role—what is difficult is getting right, on a theoretical level, the mixture of empirical and a priori components in this concept, in virtue of which it can have this role. Put in very general terms, the complaint against the strong sensorimotor theory is that it does not pull off the feat of getting the mixture right. One of Clark's main complaints is that commitment to an a priori theory about the nature of phenomenal consciousness, namely that it should be equated with its action-directing content is made to 'wag the empirical dog', in the face of strong converging evidence (to which I soon return) that this content is often instantiated independently of consciousness. What I have been rehearsing is the complement of this complaint. The reductive account outlined above is where the strong sensorimotor theory ends up. This is in part because it does not provide sufficiently robust a priori constraints on the notion of perceptual consciousness. The central proposal I will be pursuing in the next two sections is that getting the right kind of independence here requires focus on the role of vision in making knowledge of the objective environment possible.

III

On the Goals of Vision. 'What does it mean to see? The plain man's answer (and Aristotle's too) would be to know what is where by looking' (Marr 1982). This is the first sentence of David Marr's introduction to *Vision*. As he later develops this idea, the distinctive goal of human vision is to deliver objective representations of the environment (he focuses especially on three-dimensional shapes), which can be used as the basis for expressions of such knowledge. This is contrasted with, for example, the goal of fly vision, which is to deliver sufficient information to allow it to perform a few key actions needed for survival. And it is also contrasted with a different conception of the goal of human vision, on which the goal is to deliver sense-data, which can be used as the basis for inference about the nature of the external world that caused them.

As I will be interpreting it, this is at least partly a claim about the content of vision. The eventual upshot of information processing by the visual system is content that represents shapes, say, in a way that is independent of any peculiarities of the viewing subject, including her dispositions to act in various ways in response to the information. The information is non-egocentric in this sense.

An extreme reading of this characterization—which is definitely not Marr's own—of the goal of human vision, in contrast to that of the fly's, is that the delivery of such objective representations is the sole aim of human vision, in the following sense. When visual information is in fact used to guide action, this is only subsequent to its delivery of objective representations of the kind needed for knowledge. There is no independent vision-to-action channel.

An equally extreme converse claim, which is one way of reading the main idea behind the strong sensorimotor approach, is to say that the goal of vision is solely and exclusively to deliver information that can be used in the direction of actions. The content of the information is in this sense egocentric, cashed out exhaustively in terms of the significance for the subject of actions she can or will perform in response to the information. Here too, there is a contrast with the claim that the goal is to deliver sensations—the two approaches have this much in common. But what about objective knowledge on this approach? This tends not to get discussed much, but there are two ways of reading what does get said. On the first, we are capable of objective knowledge, but getting there involves starting again, so to speak, introducing concepts and ways of reasoning that are wholly independent from the egocentric content of perceptions. On the other, we cannot, even in thought, get beyond the contents delivered by perception. Our spatial thinking is egocentric through and through. O'Regan and Noe's approving quotation of Poincaré's reductive account of the nature of our spatial thinking in their paper on the sensorimotor approach suggests the latter reading (O'Regan and Noe 2001). Although this idea does, indeed, hover in the background, it is clear we are here going beyond architectural empirical claims. For the analogy with the extreme reading of Marr to go through we need the first reading, and that is the only one we will be focusing on.

Over the past two decades it has become increasingly clear that neither extreme view can be true. Converging evidence from anatomical studies of the brain, double dissociations among neuropsychological patients and particular kinds of insensitivity of action to perceptual illusions have made it clear that we need to think of vision as having two distinct functions, whose implementations are to a large extent, though not always and exhaustively, independent of each other. Much of this work, examples of which are given in Clark's paper in this volume, is summarized in Milner and Goodale's *The Visual Brain In Action*, and has given rise to what is often labelled 'the dual visual system' hypothesis. As they summarize the different functions of the two streams, the first (ventrally based) is designed for the deliverance of stable properties of objects to be used in recognition, reasoning and semantic recall (that is, naming). The province of the second, dorsal, stream, in contrast, is said to be the ongoing fine-tuning of motor responses to stimulation.

Note that so far the distinction has been made without any appeal to consciousness. One of Milner and Goodale's innovations was to introduce phenomenal perceptual consciousness into the distinction between the two streams and to identify the ventral stream with consciousness. The basis for this was empirical: patients whose ventral stream was damaged but whose dorsal stream was intact, in a way that enabled them to direct fine-tuned actions towards the environment, reported an absence of any experience, whereas patients with grave impairments in action due to dorsal stream damage gave full and accurate descriptions of their experiences.

Suppose we accept this evidence. The first point to note is that it is problem-raising rather than immediately or obviously problem-solving. This is made espccially vivid if we think of a story such as Marr's, at least in some of its details, as giving an account of the information processing that happens in the ventral stream. As he presents it, this is a matter of applying algorithms to formal mathematical descriptions of structures, beginning with descriptions of the structure of light intensity distributions on the retinal array and ending up with formal descriptions of three-dimensional shapes. On the face of it, this has no connection at all with the way, on the basis of reflection, we think of what it is like to see, either with respect to the process of seeing or with respect to what seeing delivers.

Two kinds of responses are common at this point. One is to introduce a kind of causal hypothesis to the effect that this information processing produces, in addition to formal descriptions, an array of sensations, the nature of which explains everything we want to say about what it is like to see. Information processing falls out as completely irrelevant to anything we want to say about phenomenology; and phenomenology becomes wholly irrelevant to anything we want to say about information processing. Another is to try to identify conscious seeing with particular stages in the visual information-processing story (see, for example, Tye 1995). Rather than examine these two responses, both of which, as noted, a priori deprive consciousness of any explanatory role, I want now to turn to an attempt to give consciousness a role in explaining the goals of vision. I return to the process problem in the following section.

IV

The Problem of Structural Knowledge and Phenomenal Externalism. There is a striking analogy and also a very important disanalogy between the way Marr presents the computational problems our brains need to solve when arriving at a representation of the external world and Russell's explanation in the *Analysis of Matter* of the problems subjects of experience need to solve when arriving at a representation of the external world. The analogy turns on the idea that in both cases the task is conceived of as one of arriving at representations of the external world from a structural description of what is given, the distribution of light intensities on the retinal image in Marr's case and a sensory array in Russell's. The major and decisive difference is that Marr helps himself to both general and specific substantive assumptions about the objective nature of the represented external world in constraining the computations that take us from structural descriptions of the image to representation of specific three dimensional shapes, for example; whereas the point for Russell is that we cannot help ourselves to any such assumptions. Our knowledge of the external world is exhausted by the structural descriptions of the sensations plus an assumption of a general isomorphism between the structure of the world and the structure of sensations (this assumption is the basic idea behind the causal theory of perception he endorses). The suggestion I want to pursue is that a particular account of perceptual consciousness is needed to ground the extra assumptions about the nature of the objective world that Marr helps himself to in explaining the goals of human vision.

First, a few words about Russell. The aim of the *Analysis of Matter* is (a) to show that scientific knowledge is indeed knowledge of a mind-independent external world, in contrast to earlier claims of his that the external world is a logical construction out of sense-data, but (b) to argue that this knowledge is purely structural. The central idea is this. We have direct and immediate acquaintance only with mind-dependent sensations, where this gives us knowledge of their intrinsic character. It is, however, reasonable to assume the truth of a causal theory of perception, where this, in turn, gives us the right to assume the existence of a structural isomorphism between the abstract structure of our sensational fields and the structure of the external world. As he puts it, 'Thus, from the structure of our perceptions we can infer a great deal as to the structure of the physical world, but not as to its intrinsic character' (Russell [1927] 1992, p. 400). At most what can be known is the logical form or structure, that is, the second- or higher-order properties and relations of events in the external world. And, as he sums it up, 'The only legitimate attitude about the physical world seems to be one of complete agnosticism about all but its mathematical properties' (p. 270). He also suggests that a correct interpretation of scientific theorizing at the time would render its deliverances in purely structural terms.

The main complaint against this claim was first made by M. H. A. Newman a year after the publication of the *Analysis of Matter* in his 1928 *Mind* paper entitled 'Mr. Russell's "Causal Theory of Perception"'. It was revived by Demopoulos and Friedman (1985) and subsequently much discussed in the philosophy of science under the heading of 'structural realism'. The charge was that purely structural propositions are devoid of empirical content, they are trivially true, given certain theorems of set theory. To give them empirical content they need to be anchored to particular actual relations in the external world. But for this kind of anchoring to occur we need to go beyond purely structural claims. As Newman saw it (and Demopulous and Friedman endorse his conclusion), the only way to make structural claims latch onto particular properties is by treating them as mediated by ways of referring to these properties that deliver access to their intrinsic character. And if this is right, the conclusion we need to draw from the argument is that our knowledge of the external world cannot be purely structural. Either, we have no empirical knowledge of it or it must include knowledge of intrinsic properties.

In slightly more detail: Newman begins by noting that Russell's view, that we have no knowledge of the *physical* relations over and above their formal (that is, structural) features, amounts to the claim that the only kinds of statement we can make about the external world take the following form: '*There* is a relation *R* such that the structure of the external world with reference to *R* is *W*' (Newman 1928, p. 144). He then urges us to consider the logical theorem that '[For] any aggregate *A*, a system of relations between its members can be found having any assigned structure compatible with the cardinal number of *A*' (p. 140). According to this theorem, the mere number of members in an aggregate entails that there are systems of relations definable over those members having a specified structure. If this is all that is being asserted by the existential claim, the claim is trivial in the sense of true a priori, and devoid of empirical content. The only way to avoid trivialization, according to Newman, is by specifying the particular relation(s) that generate(s) a given structure. That is, if we specify *R*, instead of just saying 'There is a relation *R* that has a certain structure *W*', the fact that *R* has structure *W* is no longer trivial.

How do such relations get specified? Newman made two assumptions. The first was that only a form of indexical expression mediated by acquaintance with intrinsic properties would do the trick, where, as Russell put it, the result was immediate presence of the intrinsic property to the subject. The second assumption, and here he went along with Russell, at least for the sake of the argument, was that such presence was only possible when the referent of the indexical was a sensation or sensational property. Given the latter assumption, this threatened to undermine Russell's claim that he had done away with logical constructionism, because if these two assumptions are right then, ultimately, the meanings of all terms are cashed in terms of properties of mind-dependent entities.

The obvious immediate alternative, if we want to insist that we can and do have knowledge of a mind-independent world, is to anchor the meanings of our basic terms to external intrinsic properties via a relation analogous to acquaintance, a relation that makes these properties immediately present to us. And, roughly put, the suggestion is that this is the role of perceptual consciousness, to deliver the kind of access to external intrinsic properties that is needed for grounding the empirical status of our representations of the external world. This is the position I am labelling 'phenomenal externalism'.

Now, the idea that perceptual consciousness presents us directly with such intrinsic properties is one of the mainstays of naïve realism, on which perception is conceived of as a two-term relation between subjects and objects, and thereby their properties. Very roughly, on this picture, the phenomenal properties of an experience are determined not by the intrinsic properties of sensations we are acquainted with, but by the intrinsic qualities of objects we are presented with. However, the version of this idea that is most closely related to the problematic as we have set it up is John Campbell's idea that the role of perceptual consciousness is to provide us with access to the categorical properties of objects, for example shape, where this is contrasted with the claim that all we have access to are dispositional characterizations of such properties. His specific suggestion is that it is conscious attention (the cognitive but extensional replacement for Russell's acquaintance) that has the role of putting us in touch with these categorical properties (see Campbell 2002, Chs 1 and 12). This is the claim that links up with issues of mechanism, and I return to it soon. But let us first look at some immediate consequences of accepting the basic Newman point for other issues. There are several, on various levels of generality, and for convenience I lay them out in list form.

1. The Empirical Status of Cognitive Science. All cognitive scientists, including adherents of the sensorimotor approach, help themselves to an objective world in theorizing about our perception of it, and also help themselves to the assumption that in some way visual processes latch onto particular objects and to their properties. I think that if queried about the nature of the connection the general response would be as follows. The relation between objects and the brain is purely causal, by which I mean wholly non-cognitive. Cognition sets in only when the brain gets going on the sensory input. A much-discussed consequence of this is that if phenomenology is to be found anywhere it will be found only once the mind/brain enters into the picture.

One consequence of taking the Newman point seriously is that this cannot be a resting point. The problem cognitive scientists face is the same that any science faces—grounding the empirical content of their claims. If Newman is right then ultimately, as scientists, they will need to ground their own claims about the external world to which our visual systems connect us by appeal to their own consciousness of these mind-independent properties. The problem of consciousness begins at home.

2. Phenomenal Externalism and 'The Hard Problem'. On a prevailing view, what we can say a priori about phenomenal consciousness stems from what we can say about experiences on the basis of introspection, where introspection is conceived of as a way of accessing experiences which explicitly brackets off any assumptions about the nature and existence of the external world (otherwise it would not be a wholly a priori way of knowing about experience). Phenomenal properties just are those properties of experience we access using this method. If this is the picture of what we know a priori about phenomenal consciousness, and of what phenomenal properties are, then it does indeed follow that it would be entirely illegitimate to appeal to what we know a priori about phenomenal consciousness to impose any constraint on the empirical workings of vision. The only way forward, if we do want to link phenomenal properties to these workings, is wholly reductive, which means eschewing the authority of what we know a priori.

If we take the Newman point seriously, though, then whatever else we say about introspection, it cannot be a source of wholly a priori knowledge about phenomenal properties, because when we introspect, what we are describing are external mind-independent properties; and we need to think of consciousness in this way if we are to ground the empirical status of any claims we make. One thing this means, of course, is that there is no danger of any illegitimate imposition of a priori constraints on empirical theorizing when we do appeal to introspection to constrain our accounts. But as importantly, in my view, it means that if there are a priori constraints on our concept of experiential consciousness, which are a source of independent constraints on what we say about the empirical mechanisms, relative to which we resist a purely reductive account, they will not stem from claims about the nature of introspection as a source of knowledge about them. In effect, what I have been suggesting is that the a priori constraints come from a consideration of what is required for knowledge of the environment. The proposal is: If knowledge is possible, this is how we must think of consciousness. Taking this on involves either denying that we need to think of consciousness in this way or denying that we do have knowledge through perception of the environment. The a priori constraints here come from considerations of what empirical knowledge is and what it requires. Of course, the correctness of the a priori arguments depends on there actually being mechanisms that are correctly described as yielding such knowledge. This is where we begin to turn to attention, and I come back to that soon.

3. The Spatial Extension of Consciousness. A recurring slogan in the embodied/embedded approach to perception and cognition in general is that the 'mind isn't in the brain'. (This was claim 3 at the beginning of the paper.) The external world plays a crucial part. However, as Clark has repeatedly emphasized, the external world here tends to be the body rather than objects perceived, and it comes in as a part of the explanation of the mechanism of vision. The first methodological suggestion I want to make to adherents of this approach is that they need to take seriously the extension of externalism to the determination of the phenomenal qualities of experience, and hence its content, at least for the reason just outlined. To do so is to say that it comes in as a consequence of explaining how perception can yield empirical objective knowledge. The question is whether there are any good reasons for rejecting this that would not at the same time undermine the kinds of claim they make against views to the effect that the location of consciousness must be the brain.

The second question they need to consider is this. Suppose that as a consequence of the kinds of arguments just rehearsed we do extend the location of conscious experience to include the object perceived. If we think that the ontological kind to which perceptual experiences belong are processes (for reasons I return to in the next section) then the process we are talking about here is one that is individuated essentially by the objects of consciousness and the embodied subjects who are doing the perceiving. The question then is: Is there any role that self-induced movement or actions more generally can play in doing justice to the sense in which conscious experiences are spatially extended? If it doesn't come from consideration of content (see the next point) it will have to come from a consideration of the mechanisms. If Clark and others are right about the relevant mechanisms being attentional (see the next section) then appeal to actual movement drops out all together.

4. Action-direction and the Phenomenal Character of Experience. On some versions of the strong sensorimotor approach, the subject's knowledge of the structure of sensorimotor dependencies is what determines phenomenal character. In particular, in accounting for the phenomenology of what it is like to see a particular shape we need to appeal exclusively to the subject's knowledge of the structure of the sensorimotor contingencies associated with this shape. There are two ways of reading this idea. On one, the knowledge is purely structural, all the way through. To say this is to deny that there is something like immediate awareness of intrinsic properties. Aside from phenomenal implausibility, to say this is to deny the Newman point. Of course, this is possible; but to do so is to go well beyond the kinds of consideration appealed to by the sensorimotor approach, and to engage in fundamental metaphysical questions about the nature of the world (is it purely structural?) and our access to it. A second way of reading the structural claim is to treat the content of the knowledge as not purely structural, but as structural only relative to seen properties, and as including acquaintance-mediated references to spatial properties of the body or the body in action. On this view, our basic understanding of objective spatial properties is rooted in our immediate awareness of the body and its parts. Again, this is a possible claim, though there is nothing immediately appealing about it, either on empirical grounds or on conceptual ones. In particular, if we are allowed immediate awareness of mind-independent physical properties of our bodies (through proprioception?), why should the same not be possible for non-proprioceptive perception of other objects?

5. Attention and Objective Knowledge. Coming back now to Marr: recall his approving endorsement of Aristotle: the role of vision is to deliver objective knowledge of the environment. The question he asks is: How is this possible given the direct physical input to the brain, a distribution of light intensities on the retina? If what we have been saying is along the right lines, then there is a further question to be asked: how is it possible for purely formal descriptions to yield such knowledge? And the answer is that only something like immediate conscious awareness of intrinsic properties could do this. This is what anchors the realist status of these descriptions. To say this, though, is only to raise another problem. Consciousness of these properties cannot be magic. There must be a causal story to tell, both about what this immediate consciousness is and of how it serves to control the information-processing story we tell. Campbell's specific proposal is that conscious attention to objects sets the target for further information processing. Taken at face value, the claim is that the kind of information processing that delivers objective information, the kind people identify with the working of the ventral stream, gets going in the form it does once conscious attention sets the target for such processing. This is the point at which we begin to move over to claims about the mechanism of vision, and to one of the major metaphors that informs the embodied/embedded cognitive approach, including the strong sensorimotor one, the idea that there is something essentially active about the process. And these are the issues to which we now turn.

V

The Mechanism of Vision: Time, Perceptual Consciousness and Attention. Here are some questions we might ask about the mechanisms of vision:

a. Are they essentially representational?
b. Are they active or passive?
c. Where do they occur?

As Clark notes, the strong sensorimotor approach tends to appeal to self-induced movement (as at least a partial answer to the third question) to deliver the following answers to the first two questions: (a) They are not representational at all; (b) They are essentially active.

I have said what there is the space here to say about the third question; so from now on I will focus exclusively on the first two. It seems to me that one of the most interesting general suggestions implicit in the sensorimotor approach is the suggestion that we should appeal to the sense in which perception is active to explain the sense in which it is temporally extended and in this sense non-representational. The question I want to focus on is: Is appeal to self-induced movement the right way to do justice to this intuition? And the suggestion I want to elaborate is Clark's to the effect that what is right here should be absorbed by appeal to the role of attention. I begin with the question of what it means to say the process is not, at least in part, representational, and use some distinctions drawn in this context to link up with activity and attention.

VI

Are Perceptual Processes Essentially Representational? What does this question mean? I take my point of departure from two passages, the first quoted in Soteriou's 'Content and the Stream of Consciousness' (2005), and the second quoted in Clark's 'Time and Mind' (1998a).

> Even when experience does not change in type or content it still changes in another respect: it is constantly renewed; a new sector of itself is then and there taking place. This is because experiences are events or processes, and each momentary new element of any given experience is a further happening or

> occurrence (by contrast with (say) the steady continuation through time of one's knowing that 9 and 5 make 14). (O'Shaughnessy 2000, p. 42)

> The heart of the problem is time. *Cognitive processes and their context unfold continuously and simultaneously in real time.* Computational models specify a discrete sequence of static internal states in arbitrary 'step' time (t1, t2, etc.). Imposing the latter onto the former is like wearing shoes on your hands. You can do it, but gloves fit a whole lot better. (Van Gelder and Port 1995, p. 2; italics in original)

Van Gelder is interested in the correct characterization of the vehicles of perception, O'Shaughnessy in the phenomenology of perceptual experience. In both quotations we have a hint of a contrast each thinks is essential for getting right what is involved in vision—between treating mental entities, of any kind, as essentially processive, on the one hand, and characterizing them exclusively in terms of their representational content (O'Shaughnessy) and vehicles (Van Gelder), on the other. I am not going to begin to do justice to the fascinating issues raised by both Soteriou's and Clark's treatment of this issue. Rather, I focus on the question of the connection if any between claims about vehicles, content and phenomenology here. In particular, I want to suggest that we need to appeal to the insights underpinning each of these claims to justify the other's claim that vision is essentially processive.

Let us say that the vehicles of a cognitive process (event or state) are essentially representational if we can give an exhaustive account of their nature, *qua* vehicles, by appeal to their syntactic role in instantiating the semantic or representational content(s) we use to individuate the cognitive process (state or event). Now, as Clark puts it, the essential idea behind the cognitive dynamicists' claim here is that there are, essentially, non-syntactic stages in the process of vision. Why and in what sense should this, if true, introduce a sense in which vision, say, is essentially temporal in a way a purely syntactic process is not, as the quotation from Van Gelder maintains? I suggest that the answer is to be found in Soteriou's development of Geach's point that thoughts, characterized in terms of their content, have no temporal parts, and in the sense are not part of a Jamesian stream of consciousness. As Soteriou develops this idea, the claim is that when we individuate a mental entity in terms of its content, under that description it has merely semantic or logical parts rather than temporal ones. This is a claim about the contribution of mental entities, thus individuated, to phenomenology: their contribution is non-temporal. But I suggest that this is what we need in order to motivate the basic idea that if the vehicles of a cognitive process are purely syntactic they are not essentially processive. The syntax instantiates contents that are not temporal. The question then arises, of course: What else can we say, positively, about the nature of such non-syntactic vehicles? I return to this in a moment, but let me first say a few words about the phenomenological claim.

O'Shaughnessy's claim that perceptual experiences are essentially processive is phenomenologically based. Soterious's appeal to the sense in which contents are non-temporal can also help makes sense of the intuition in the quotation above to the effect that if this is true it means we cannot capture everything there is to say about an experience by characterizing it in terms of representational content. But here too the question arises: If this is true about the phenomenology, in virtue of what is it true? What is it about visual occurrences that makes it the case that there is something essentially processive about their phenomenological nature, in a sense that stands contrasted with characterizing their contribution to phenomenology in terms of their representational content? At this point the idea that naturally suggests itself is that this is true because (at least some of) the vehicles of conscious experience are essentially non-syntactic.

For this to work, though, we need to hit upon a level of description of the mechanism of vision that can engage both with empirical processes we discover and with a priori intuitions about the essential phenomenology of what it is like to see. Now, the strong sensorimotor approach appeals to the role of self-induced movements in collecting information about the environment to explain the sense in which the process of vision is non-syntactic. I return later to the question of whether this particular claim can be right. Before that I want to examine the generalized version of this claim, implicit in the sensorimotor approach here, which is the claim that getting right the sense in which vision is essentially processive turns on getting right the sense in which it is essentially active.

VII

Is the Process of Vision Active or Passive? The right answer is that it is both, of course; the problem is how to get right the mixture of activity and passivity distinctive of it. Very roughly, it is possible to distinguish among three kinds of answer to the sense in which perception is active. The first emphasizes the role of physical action in delivering information and/or in determining its basic content. Much of this kind of work takes its inspiration from J. J. Gibson, who, in rejecting the idea that perception is the passive absorption of the impact on the world on us, proposed a picture on which perception is an activity of picking up information, by looking, smelling, touching, and so on (Gibson 1968, pp. 47–58).

The second two emphasize the role of mental activity, One of these, familiar from John McDowell's development of the Kantian slogan that 'intuitions without concepts are blind', locates the active component in perception in the rational exercise of concepts, treating this exercise as integral to perceptual experience (McDowell 1994, Lecture I). On the second of these, the active component is to be found in attention. This is to be found in many psychological treatments of attention, where the origin of this is said to be William James's characterization of attention as essentially subject to the will. (For more on this and other ways of linking activity and attention, see Eilan 1998).

Now there is some loose sense in which we might want to say that all these kinds of activity are or can be 'involved in' vision. This is not least because we may appeal to activity to answer a whole variety of different questions about the nature of the perceptual process. Which is right depends on what we are trying to explain.

Our particular question here is: Is there a sense in which the process of vision is essentially active that we can appeal to in doing justice to the sense in which it is essentially processive, essentially temporally extended? If we ask the question in this way, it automatically rules out appeal to the capacity for rational thought. For thinking, to the extent that it is a process, is essentially a syntactic process. Moreover, if we take McDowell's attempt to do justice simultaneously to the sense in which experiences are passive, we lose even this sense of process. For, as he puts it, what is distinctive about the way reason and concepts characterize perceptual experience is that in experience we find ourselves 'saddled with content', where the experience is conceived of specifically as a state with content, and where this is contrasted with the activity of judging (McDowell 1994, pp. 9–10).

So direct and exhaustive appeal to the sense in which thought is active will not do here. This leaves us with physical action and attention. Actually, as Clark makes clear, physical action can come in two ways, either by appealing to relatively automatic self-induced movements used in the pick-up of information (for instance, saccades) or by appealing to full-blown intentional action. Let us begin with the first.

Recall: an essential constraint here is that we are looking for a kind of mechanism in perception which can link up directly with relatively a priori claims we make about the sense in which experience is essentially processive. One way of reading versions of the sensorimotor approach of the kind argued for by Susan Hurley and Alva Noë is that they are claiming that the phenomenological claims about the processive nature of experience are true in virtue of the truth of dynamical claims about the mechanisms involved in perception. How could this be so? After all, these minute adjustments of eye movements and so forth do not show up, on the face of it, in consciousness. One ingredient in their answer is to say that that these movements are not the objects of consciousness but rather, its silent, non-syntactic vehicles. It is because the process of vision is mediated by such movements that the phenomenology of conscious perception is essentially temporally extended.

One problem for this, raised by Clark, is that these kinds of processes seem to occur in cases where there is no consciousness at all—so they are certainly not sufficient. But if I have understood him, there is also a deeper reason for rejecting the appeal to such self-induced movements. Loosely put, the objection is that this is simply the wrong place at which to locate the connection between phenomenology and activity: we need to locate it at a level at which it can be said that the subject is doing something, where this is contrasted with movements that are to large extent outside her control. That is, if claims about process are to connect with phenomenological claims about activity, they are to be located at a place at which subjects can identify themselves as doing something when seeing.

One way of reading his positive proposal in 'Visual Awareness and Visuomotor Action', given this objection, is the following. Physical action engages with consciousness on the level of intentional action, action done for a reason. It engages with consciousness because on this level we need to appeal to consciousness of the environment in order to explain the way in which the targets and aims of intentional actions are set. The suggestion then is that the role of such intentions is to activate attention. Attention, in turn, is where we should look to for the sense in which the mechanism of consciousness is non-representational; it involves, rather, the setting into motion of processes of information selection, rather than the actual representation of information.

I end with the question of whether this can be quite right—I mean whether it is right to place the connection between activity and phenomenology at the door of intentional action, with attention brought in only indirectly. One problem is in the account of attention. If we think of it solely as selection of information for the purposes of action, as for example the psychologist Allen Allport suggests we should (Allport 1998, p. 648), then there is no obvious link with consciousness. Presumably in case of blindsight there is also selection of information for the direction of action. So we need so to appeal to a kind of attention that is not activated in blindsight. The natural thought here is to turn to the kind of attention appealed to by Campbell, the kind that yields direct presence of intrinsic or categorical properties. But then the question is whether the most direct way of linking such attention with the sense of which the process of vision is active is to be found in the way attention is put to the service of intentional action. For surely there is a more direct way—the sense captured in the psychologists Daniel Kahneman and Avishai Henik's claim that '... the enduring fascination with the problem of attention can perhaps be traced to the nature of selective attention as a pure act of will (James 1890) which controls experience' (Kahneman and Henik 1981, p. 201). Of course, to say this is just to open up a question of what exactly this means. But if we do pursue this line of thought, appeal to physical action drops out once again. If this is the line we pursue, then one challenge for those who think that appeal to action, intentional or not, is critical to an explanation of the sense in which perception is an active process is to find some other way of bringing it in. My own sense is that direct focus on attention, independently of appeal to the nature of physical action, is the right way to go in explaining the link between temporal extension and activity in visual consciousness. If this is right, then attention really can be the bridging concept we need for beginning to link up claims about content and about mechanisms in accounting for the phenomenology of visual experience.

References

Allport, A. 1989: 'Visual Attention'. In M. I. Posner (ed.), *Foundations of Cognitive Science*. Cambridge, MA: MIT Press, pp. 631–82.

Campbell, J. 2002: *Reference and Consciousness*. Oxford: Oxford University Press.

Clark, A. 1998a: 'Time and Mind'. *Journal Of Philosophy*, 95:7, pp. 354–76.

——— 1998b: 'Embodiment and the Philosophy of Mind'. In A. O'Hear (ed.), *Contemporary Issues in The Philosophy Of Mind: Royal Institute Of Philosophy Supplement 43*. Cambridge: Cambridge University Press, pp. 35–52.

——— 1999: 'Visual Awareness and Visuomotor Action'. *Journal Of Consciousness Studies*, 6:11–12, pp. 1–18.

Demopoulos, W. and M. Friedman 1985: 'Critical Notice: Bertrand Russell's *The Analysis of Matter*: Its Historical Context and Contemporary Interest'. *Philosophy of Science*, 52, pp. 621–39.

Eilan, N. 1998: 'Perceptual Intentionality, Attention and Consciousness'. In A. O'Hear (ed.), *Contemporary Issues in the Philosophy of Mind: Royal Institute of Philosophy Supplement 43*. Cambridge: Cambridge University Press.

Gibson, J. J. 1968: 'The Perceptual Systems'. In *The Senses Considered as Perceptual Systems*. London: George Allen and Unwin, pp. 47–58.

Hurley, S. 1998: *Consciousness in Action*. Cambridge, MA: Harvard University Press.

James, W. 1890: *The Principles of Psychology*. New York: Holt.

Kahneman, D. and A. Henik 1981: 'Perceptual Organisation and Attention'. In M. Kobovy and J. Pomerantz (eds), *Perceptual Organisation*. Hillsdale, NJ: Lawrence Erlbaum Associates.

Marr, D. 1982: *Vision: A Computational Investigation into the Human Representation and Processing of Visual Information*. Cambridge, MA: MIT Press.

McDowell, J. 1994: *Mind and World*. Cambridge, MA: Harvard University Press

Milner, A. and M. Goodale 1995: *The Visual Brain in Action*. Oxford: Oxford University Press.

Newman, M. H. A. 1928: 'Mr Russell's "Causal Theory of Perception"'. *Mind*, 37, pp. 137–48.

O'Regan, J. K. and A. Noë 2001: 'A Sensorimotor Approach to Vision and Visual Consciousness'. *Behavioural and Brain Sciences*, 24:5, pp. 939–73.

O'Shaughnessy, B. 2000: *Consciousness and the World*. Oxford: Oxford University Press.

Rothschild, D. 2002: 'Structure, Knowledge and Ostension'. Unpublished.

Russell, B. [1927] 1992: *The Analysis of Matter*. London: George Allen and Unwin.

Soteriou, M. 2005: 'Content and the Stream of Consciousness'. Unpublished.

Tye, M. 1995: *Ten Problems of Consciousness*. Cambridge, MA: MIT Press.

Van Gelder, T. and R. Port 1995: 'It's About Time: An Overview of the Dynamical Approach to Cognition'. In R. Port and T. van Gelder (eds), *Mind as Motion: Explorations in the Dynamics of Cognition*. Cambridge, MA: MIT Press, pp. 1–44.

PHILOSOPHICAL ANALYSIS AND SOCIAL KINDS

by Sally Haslanger and Jennifer Saul

I—Sally Haslanger

WHAT GOOD ARE OUR INTUITIONS?

ABSTRACT In debates over the existence and nature of social kinds such as 'race' and 'gender', philosophers often rely heavily on our intuitions about the nature of the kind. Following this strategy, philosophers often reject social constructionist analyses, suggesting that they change rather than capture the meaning of the kind terms. However, given that social constructionists are often trying to debunk our ordinary (and ideology-ridden?) understandings of social kinds, it is not surprising that their analyses are counterintuitive. This article argues that externalist insights from the critique of the analytic/synthetic distinction can be extended to justify social constructionist analyses.

I

Introduction. Across the humanities and social sciences it has become commonplace for scholars to argue that categories once assumed to be 'natural' are in fact 'social' or, in the familiar lingo, 'socially constructed'. Two common examples of such categories are *race* and *gender*, but there are many others. One interpretation of this claim is that although it is typically thought that what unifies the instances of such categories is some set of *natural* or *physical* properties, instead their unity rests on *social* features of the items in question. Social constructionists pursuing this strategy—and it is these social constructionists I will be focusing on in this paper—aim to 'debunk' the ordinary assumption that the categories are natural, by revealing the more accurate social basis of the classification.[1] To avoid confusion, and to resist some of the associations with the term 'social construction', I will sometimes use the term 'socially

1. In Haslanger 2003 I contrast this sort of interpretation with one that is more common in the context of 'the science wars' which is discussed at length in, for example, Hacking 1999.

founded' for the categories that this sort of constructionist reveals as social rather than natural.[2]

Let me emphasize: the idea in saying that a category is socially founded is not to say that social factors are responsible for our attending to the category in question (which may be true of wholly natural categories); nor is it to say that the things in the category are less than fully real (material things may be unified by social features and there is no reason to deny that social properties and relations are fully real). The point, roughly, is to shift our understanding of a category so we recognize the real basis for the unity of its members. As we shall see, there are importantly different sorts of cases. But because the difference between a natural and a social category has significance both for what's possible and for what we're responsible, the constructionist's general project, when successful, has important normative implications.

Amongst those who aim to analyse our ordinary racial classifications, social constructionists are often at odds with *error theorists* (sometimes called *eliminativists*) and *naturalists*. Error theorists maintain, in agreement with social constructionists, that the items taken to fall within the category in question do not meet the supposed natural or physical conditions for membership; the error theorist often goes farther to claim that the conditions are vacuous: nothing satisfies them (sometimes even that nothing *could* satisfy them). They conclude, then, that such things are illusory and that talk purporting to refer to such categories is false or misguided. So, for example, an error theorist about race (Appiah 1996; Zack 1997) claims that there are no races, given what we mean by 'race'. Of course it is then open to the error theorist to propose terminology for new categories—perhaps social categories with an extension close to what we thought was the extension of our original categories, such as 'racial identities' (Appiah 1996)—whose conditions for membership are satisfied.

2. I'll continue, however, to speak of those whose project it is to argue that a category is socially founded as 'social constructionists', both because 'social foundationalists' would be a serious misnomer, and also because it is reasonable to cluster those who make a variety of different social arguments together, even if their views are not always compatible. It may be down the road that this acceptance of the 'social constructionist' label is more trouble than it is worth.

Present-day race *naturalists* agree with the eliminativists and constructivists that races are not what they were once thought to be—they are not, for example, groups with a common racial essence that explains a broad range of psychological and moral features of the group's members—but they disagree with both other views in maintaining that the human species can be divided on the basis of natural (biological, genetic, physical) features into a small set of groups that correspond *roughly* to the ordinary racial divisions (Rosenberg et al. 2002; Mountain and Risch 2004). This in itself would not be particularly interesting, however, if the natural basis for the grouping was biologically 'real' but of no real significance for explanation or prediction. Full-blooded race naturalists, however, maintain that there is a biologically significant classification that somehow captures our current racial divisions. Moreover, they argue, recognizing this fact is socially and politically important for the purposes of achieving racial justice, for example, by enabling us to address racially divergent medical needs (Risch et al. 2002; cf. Lee et al. 2001).[3]

In this essay I shall focus on the debate between the constructionist and error theorist; I take up the disagreement between the constructionist and naturalist elsewhere (Haslanger 2006). One way of capturing the difference between the social constructionist and the error theorist is to see them as disagreeing about the content of the relevant concepts. According to the error theorist, there is reason to take our ordinary belief that the category has a natural basis to set a constraint on what could count as an adequate analysis of the concept: a successful analysis must be in terms of natural properties and relations (or involve them at least in the way required for the concept to count as expressing a natural property). In contrast, according to the social constructionist, we may employ the concept successfully even though we have a false belief about what sort of property it expresses or sort of set it determines. For example, a social constructionist about race (such as myself) will claim that there are races and that races are social categories, that is, that race is socially founded, even though it is commonly assumed that

3. The interdisciplinary debate over race naturalism and the relevance of 'race' for medicine is substantial and complex. I have listed only a few of the most controversial articles as examples.

races are natural categories. It is an important part of the social constructionist picture that, to put it simply, our meanings are not transparent to us: often ideology interferes with an understanding of the true workings of our conceptual framework and our language. More specifically, ideology (among other things) interferes with our understanding of our classificatory practices, suggesting to us that we are finding in nature divisions that we have played an important role in creating.

The Concept of Race. To gain a vivid sense of the controversy, it may be helpful to consider briefly two different analyses of *race*, one constructionist, the other defended by the error theorist. These are just two examples of many that are discussed in the literature.

Anthony Appiah is perhaps the most well-known error theorist about race. On his view the concept of race is the core notion in the folk theory of racialism:

> [T]here are heritable characteristics, possessed by members of our species, that allow us to divide them into a small set of races, in such a way that all the members of these races share certain traits and tendencies with each other that they do not share with members of any other race. These traits and tendencies characteristic of a race constitute, on the racialist view, a sort of racial essence; and it is part of the content of racialism that the essential heritable characteristics ... account for more than the visible morphological characteristics—skin colour, hair type, facial features—on the basis of which we make our informal classifications. (Appiah 1993, p. 5)

Races, then, are groups with a common inherited racial essence. The implications of this for our purposes are straightforward: there are no such racial essences, so there are no races. Appiah argues, however, that there is a neighbouring notion—that of *racial identity*—that does not presuppose racial essences and can be accurately attributed to people. Having a racial identity is a matter of identifying with a label (such as 'White' or 'Black')[4] that has been historically associated with a racial essence (Appiah 1996, pp. 81–2).

4. I will use upper-case terms such as 'White' and 'Black' for races, lower-case terms such as 'white' and 'black' for the 'colour' markings associated with the races.

In contrast, I have argued for a constructionist account of race that parallels an account of gender (Haslanger 2000). On my view (to simplify quite a bit) races are racialized groups, and:

> A group is *racialized* (in a context) if and only if its members are socially positioned as subordinate or privileged along some dimension—economic, political, legal, social, etc.—(in that context), and the group is 'marked' as a target for this treatment by observed or imagined bodily features presumed to be evidence of ancestral links to a certain geographical region.

On this view, being White (in a context) is a matter of being seen as conforming to a meaningful bodily schema associated with European ancestry—such schemata I call 'colour'—and being treated (in that context) as positioned in a social hierarchy appropriate for persons of that 'colour'. In the contemporary United States, being marked as 'white' brings with it a broad range of social privileges, at least for the most part. However, because racial hierarchies interact with other social hierarchies—gender, class, sexuality, culture, religion, nationality—the concrete impact of being White varies depending on other aspects of one's social position. For example, a straight young White man and an elderly White lesbian will both reap privileges by virtue of their Whiteness, but the kinds of privileges they enjoy may differ considerably.

Three questions naturally arise at this point. First, it is clear that the analysis of race I offer does not capture what people consciously *have in mind* when they use the term 'race'. The account is surprising, and for many, highly counterintuitive. (Although I myself doubt that Appiah's account captures better what people consciously *have in mind* when they talk of races, it is at least familiar, and has some intuitive plausibility if we are looking for how people generally have thought of races.) Note that this counterintuitiveness will always be a feature of social constructionist analyses because (debunking) social constructionists aim to reveal that the concepts we employ are not exactly what we think they are. But if the adequacy of a philosophical analysis is a matter of the degree to which it captures and organizes our intuitions, and if constructionist analyses are always counterintuitive, then it would seem that philosophers would never have reason to consider social constructionist projects acceptable. However, this seems too fast. Surely philosophers cannot simply rule out constructionist analyses from the start.

Second, does the social constructionist approach make sense? Are there considerations developed in the context of philosophy of language (or related areas) that would prevent one from pursuing a constructionist *analysis* of race or gender and force us to adopt an error theory? I will argue that, in fact, there are considerations in contemporary philosophy of language that not only permit, but in some respects *favour* a constructionist account.

Third, what difference does it make? Does it really matter whether we say, for example, that there are no races but there are racial identities, rather than that there are races but they are social rather than natural? Are there cases where an error theory would be mistaken but a social constructionist account would be warranted? By what criteria do we decide, and is it worth worrying about?

The arguments that follow focus mainly on the first two questions; however, drawing on this discussion I will return to the question of why it might matter whether we adopt a constructionist or error strategy towards the end of the essay. The issues are complex. My own view is that which approach is better will depend on the case at issue, and the betterness will depend on semantic, pragmatic and political considerations. Moreover, pragmatic and political factors will vary with context. Before we proceed, however, it is worth pointing out that one potential advantage of a constructionist account is that it does not simply deny the existence of the allegedly natural category and substitute another (possibly social category) in its place, but it also—at least in the best cases—provides a diagnosis of our role in bringing about the effects that appear to us (mistakenly) as natural, together with an explanation of the illusion. In such cases, the self-deception involved when we mean something, and yet mask that meaning to ourselves, is laid bare. Such unmasking can be an important step in motivating social change.

II

Kinds of Analysis. The project of 'conceptual analysis' in philosophy takes many forms, partly depending on the particular concept in question, and partly depending on what methodological assumptions the philosopher brings to the issue. There are at least three common ways to answer 'What is *X*?' questions: conceptual, descriptive, and ameliorative.[5]

For example, consider the question 'What is knowledge?' Following a *conceptual approach*, or what we might more revealingly call an *internalist approach*, one is asking 'What is *our* concept of knowledge?', and looking to a priori methods such as introspection for an answer.[6] Taking into account intuitions about cases and principles, one hopes eventually to reach a reflective equilibrium. On a *descriptive* approach, one is concerned with what objective types (if any) our epistemic vocabulary tracks.[7] The task is to develop potentially more accurate concepts through careful consideration of the phenomena, usually relying on empirical or quasi-empirical methods. Scientific essentialists and naturalizers, more generally, start by identifying paradigm cases—these usually function to fix the referent of the term—and then draw on empirical (or quasi-empirical) research to explicate the relevant kind or type to which the paradigms belong. Do paradigms project an objective type, and if so, what type? Familiar descriptive approaches in philosophy of mind and epistemology draw on cognitive science.

Ameliorative projects, in contrast, begin by asking: What is the point of having the concept in question; for example, why do we have a concept of knowledge or a concept of belief? What concept (if any) would do the work best? In the limit case a theoretical

5. Quine distinguishes different forms of definition, the third being what he calls (drawing on Carnap) 'explicative'. In giving explicative definitions, 'an activity to which philosophers are given, and scientists also in their more philosophical moments ... the purpose is not merely to paraphrase the definiendum into an outright synonym, but actually to improve upon the definiendum by refining or supplementing its meaning' (Quine 1953, pp. 24–5). 'Ameliorative' captures better than 'explicative' the sort of project Quine is characterizing as especially philosophical; it is this sort of project that I've also called 'analytical' (Haslanger 2000). Because 'analytical' is commonly used to characterize Anglo-American philosophy in general, and because I'm attempting here to introduce a more fine-grained framework, using 'ameliorative' rather than 'analytical' will sometimes avoid ambiguity. It should be understood, however, that on my view, whether or not an analysis is an improvement on existing meanings will depend on the purposes of the inquiry.

6. In previous work I've dubbed this the 'conceptualist' approach. However, I've been convinced by others, and by confusions in discussion, that it may be better described as an 'internalist' approach in order to highlight the contrast with the underlying externalism assumed by the descriptive approach (described next in the text). The change is useful; however, there are different degrees and kinds of internalism and externalism and I am only using the terms suggestively and not precisely here.

7. On objective types see Armstrong 1989.

concept is introduced by stipulating the meaning of a new term, and its content is determined entirely by the role it plays in the theory. If we allow that our everyday vocabularies serve both cognitive and practical purposes that might be well served by our theorizing, then those pursuing an ameliorative approach might reasonably represent themselves as providing an account of our concept—or perhaps the concept we are reaching for—by enhancing our conceptual resources to serve our (critically examined) purposes (see Anderson 1995). Conceptual, descriptive and ameliorative projects cannot, of course, be kept entirely distinct, but they have different subject matters and different goals.

Given the different projects of analysis and different subject matters for 'analysis', it is not surprising that philosophers who may appear to be asking the same question are in fact talking past each other. For example, where one philosopher might assume that an adequate analysis must capture our ordinary intuitions, another may take for granted that a priori reflection is likely to be systematically misleading when we are trying to understand the social domain. In fact, recent work on race provides an excellent example of the diversity of approaches. Some authors are engaged in a conceptual project, attempting to explicate our ordinary understanding of race (Appiah 1996, Zack 1997, Hardimon 2003, Mallon 2004); others are attempting to determine what, if any, natural kind we are referring to by our racial terms (Appiah 1996, Kitcher 1999, Andreason 2000, Zack 2002, Glasgow 2003); others have pursued genealogy (Omi and Winant 1994); still others are invested in what I call ameliorative projects, raising normative questions about how we should understand race, not only how we currently do (Gooding-Williams 1998, Alcoff 2000).

What should we make of these different projects? Should we simply allow that different inquirers are interested in different questions, and nothing can be said to resolve the question what race *really is* or what we mean by 'race'? Although I would not argue that there is one thing that race *really is* or one thing that 'we' mean by 'race', we might hope that through reflection and discussion we could come to the point where (a) the concept we take ourselves to be employing, (b) the concept that best captures the type we are concerned with, and (c) the type we ought to be concerned with coincide. In such cases the conceptual, descriptive and ameliorative projects yield the same concept. It is a mistake, then, for those engaged in conceptual analysis to dismiss other forms of analysis, with the thought that only the conceptual project can discover 'our' concept (See Mallon 2004, Hardimon 2003). For example, if we discover that we are tracking something that it is worthwhile to track in using our racial vocabulary, then even if this is not what we originally 'had in mind', it still may be what we have been and should continue to be talking about.[8] But how should we proceed?

III

Manifest and Operative Concepts. One of the functions of concepts is to enable us to draw distinctions between things. Sometimes the activity of distinguishing things—separating them into groups—comes first, and we develop a concept of what we've distinguished later; sometimes the concept comes first, and we divide things according to it. For example, I might find myself asking my daughter to turn down her music on a regular basis without thinking that there is any pattern in my requests, only to find through conversation with her that I always ask her to turn it down when she is listening to a particular artist; or I might come to judge that a particular artist's lyrics are typically offensive and ask her to turn down the music once I discern that that artist is playing. Moreover, in practice, our activity of grouping things, even when we have a concept in mind, does not involve explicitly applying the concept to each case, that is, making sure that each object meets the conditions for applying the concept. We typically rely on empirical assumptions linking easily accessible criteria with the conditions for membership. In the grocery, I pick up what look and feel like potatoes, without testing them genetically. Once I learn that the store sells genetically modified potatoes, I may want some further assurance of the genetic make-up of the ones I purchase; but even then, I will rely on a sticker or label rather than applying the genetic criteria myself.

Everyday life requires a steady activity of drawing distinctions, an activity which combines both the use of concepts as guides

8. It might be useful to see this by analogy with other terminological developments in science. Although our understanding of, and even our definition of, 'atom' has changed over time, it is plausible that there is something worthwhile we have been and continue to be talking about.

and a rough-and-ready responsivencss to things. In reflecting back on our activity, there are a number of options for describing this sort of give and take. Consider again my requests to Zina (my daughter) that she lower the volume of her music. Suppose I don't want to listen to music with misogynistic lyrics. I have a concept of misogynistic lyrics and I also have a rough-and-ready responsiveness to what she is listening to. When Zina complains about my interventions into her listening, I may come to find that my responses are not tracking misogynistic lyrics after all, even though that's the concept I was attempting to use to guide my interventions. Let's call the concept I thought I was guided by and saw myself as attempting to apply, the *manifest concept*. I find, in other words, that my manifest concept is not in accord with my practice of determining when she has to lower the volume of her music.

There are several ways to resolve the awkward position of having my self-representation, or my intentions, out of line with my practice.

(i) I can be more careful about my interventions so that I only make my request when the lyrics really are misogynist. This would be to change the occasions of my intervention to bring my responsiveness into accord with my manifest concept.

(ii) I might instead find that a different concept conforms to my pattern of interventions. I could find that my responses are prompted by, say, sexually explicit lyrics, not misogynistic ones. Let's call the concept that best captures the distinction that I in practice draw the *operative concept*. In such a case, I allow the operative concept to have priority over the (original) manifest concept in guiding my behaviour; in doing so the operative concept becomes manifest (and, hopefully, is now consistent with my practice).

(iii) Rather than replacing the original manifest concept with a new operative concept, I modify my understanding of the manifest concept in light of the new cases that have emerged in the practice. So rather than being newly guided by the concept of sexually explicit lyrics, I change what I understand misogynistic lyrics to be.

> Let's call the *target concept* the concept that, all things considered (my purposes, the facts, etc.), I should be employing. In the ideal case, I adjust my practice and my self-understanding to conform to the target concept.

So far I've distinguished the manifest, the operative, and the target concept. The manifest concept is the concept I take myself to be applying or attempting to apply in the cases in question. The operative concept is the concept that best captures the distinction as I draw it in practice.[9] And the target concept is the concept I should, ideally, be employing. As illustrated above, the operative concept may not correspond with my understanding of what distinction I'm tracking. This is not to say, however, that the manifest and operative concepts always, or even typically, come apart. Typically, my practice will track the objective type that my manifest concept determines; in other words, my manifest concept and my operative concept coincide.[10] In the best cases, all three (my manifest, operative, and target concepts) will coincide.

The example of my responses to Zina's music locates the issue in the realm of individual consistency: how can I bring my practice in line with my intentions? To see that the phenomenon has broader scope, it may be helpful to consider an example that draws on more collective meanings. Consider the term 'parent'. It is common, at least in the United States, to address primary school memos to 'Parents', to hold a 'Parent Night' or 'Parent Breakfast' at certain points during the school year, to have 'Parent–Teacher Conferences' to discuss student progress, and so on. However, in practice the term 'parent' in these contexts is meant to include the primary caregivers of the student, whether they be biological parents, step-parents, legal guardians, grand-parents, aunts, uncles, older siblings, informal substitute parents,

9. I don't mean to suggest here that there is only one manifest concept and only one operative concept. The manifest and operative concepts may vary from context to context.

10. However, we often make mistakes in applying our manifest concepts. When we make a simple mistake, must we postulate an operative concept distinct from the manifest one? I'm not sure much hinges on this, but it seems to me that if we have a sparse theory of objective types a better approach would be to understand the practice as tracking a nearby (or the nearest?) objective type; if the nearby type is the type also determined by the manifest concept, we have coincidence. The operative concept will be, then, the concept that determines that type in terms that make the most sense in analysing the practice.

etc. However, it is also clear to everyone that those on the list just given are not the student's parents. So, for example, Tara's grandmother Denise (with whom she lives) counts as Tara's parent in all relevant school contexts, but is also known to be her grandmother and not her mother, and so not her parent. Given the distinction between manifest and operative concepts, it would seem that there are two different concepts of 'parent' here: parent as *immediate progenitor*, and parent as *primary caregiver*. Tara's grandmother satisfies the operative concept of *parent* but not the manifest one.

One might resist the idea that the manifest concept of *parent* is of biological mother or father; however, my own experience as an adoptive mother has convinced me that at least in many contexts the dominant understanding of 'parent' frames it as a biological notion. For example, if I were Zina's biological parent, I don't think I would ever be asked (by people who know us), 'Do you know Zina's parents?' If one is uncomfortable with the assumption that the manifest concept of *parent* is biological, then we need only take the case to be describing a possible world in which the manifest concept of *parent* is more narrowly biological, possibly a world much like the US in an earlier era before adoption was common or legally institutionalized.

As in the earlier example of misogynist lyrics, there are three different responses to the gap between idea and practice in our use of the term 'parent':

(i) Bring our practice in line with the manifest concept: insist that one must be an immediate progenitor of a student to participate in Parent Nights, Parent–Teacher Conferences, etc. (This option seems clearly misguided—not necessarily as a semantic matter, but as a social/political matter.)

(ii) Find a new manifest concept that better captures our practice: correct the memos so they are addressed to 'Primary Caregivers'.

(iii) Modify our understanding of the manifest concept, in this case, 'parent', to accord with our practice. This would involve a transition in our understanding from parent as a biological category to parent as a social category.

This example is intended to show that the distinction between manifest and operative concepts is one that concerns public meanings as much as individual beliefs and intentions (see also Haslanger 2005). If we ask, 'What is the concept of "parent"?' we have at least two places to look for an answer: the concept that speakers generally associate with the term, and the concept that captures how the term works in practice. Although so far I've focused on the relatively transparent example of 'parent', of course there are many philosophically rich and more surprising examples available. Feminist and race theorists have been urging for some time that the proper target of analysis is not (or not simply) what we have in mind, but the social matrix where our concepts do their work. For example, Catharine MacKinnon says, '[The verb "to be" in feminist theory] is a very empirical "is". Men define women as sexual beings; feminism comprehends that femininity "is" sexual. Men see rape as intercourse; feminists say much intercourse "is" rape' (MacKinnon 1987, p. 59). Charles Mills argues that the Enlightenment social contract is a Racial Contract (Mills 1997), and that an adequate analysis of personhood reveals that 'all persons are equal, but only white males are persons' (Mills 1998, p. 70). Such analyses purport to show that our manifest understandings of crucial political notions are masking how the concepts in question actually operate (see also Mills 1998, pp. 139–66).

IV

Concepts, Conceptions and the Like. Can we understand the manifest/operative distinction in terms of a more familiar distinction between concept and conception? It is not an unusual circumstance in philosophy to find that 'the concept' we take ourselves to be analysing is not 'the concept' that the students seem to employ in their day-to-day practice. Undergraduates are competent users of terms such as 'knowledge', 'justice' and 'object', and yet are surprised and resistant when they learn philosophical theories of knowledge, justice and objects. One might argue that the philosophical theories are all false and the students are correct to reject them. But this is often not plausible. More plausible is that ordinary usage of a term doesn't require that one has thought carefully enough about the issues to develop consistent accounts of central concepts in one's repertoire. Cases such as these (and in general, accounts of language acquisition) support the idea that we need to distinguish various ways that individuals might be related to the concept, say, of knowledge or justice. For example, James Higginbotham (1998, pp. 149–50) distinguishes:

i) possession
   - merely possessing a word, and so being able to use it with its meaning;
   - merely possessing a concept, so being able to deploy it, without having an accurate or full conception of it.

ii) tacit conception
   - knowing the meaning of the word;
   - having a full conception of a concept.

iii) explicit understanding
   - having an adequate conscious view of the word's meaning;
   - having a adequate conscious view of the nature of the concept.

There may be additional relevant distinctions, but these go some way to making room for competent use without full explicit understanding. Over the course of repeated use of a notion we develop conceptions of what we're talking about, but we might be misguided in various ways. Philosophical inquiry helps us develop more detailed, explicit and adequate conceptions of our concepts.

But this doesn't seem to capture what's at issue in the cases we've been considering. How would we map the distinction between manifest and operative concepts on some pair of the distinctions between possession, tacit conception, explicit understanding? For example, consider Brenda, Tara's teacher. She has a fully conscious and explicit understanding of the concept *parent*; she also enacts a practice that is in some ways at odds with it. And she probably doesn't have a full or explicit conception of the rule that she employs in practice. But the distinction between manifest and operative concepts is not simply a distinction along the continuum of implicit–explicit, or uninterpreted–adequately interpreted. As we saw before, the manifest and operative concepts are at odds; they are, in a sense, competing with each other within the space of practical reason. For example, given the confidentiality laws in place, Brenda may find herself uncertain how or what to communicate with someone she knows to be a primary caregiver of a student, but who is not legally recognized as such. For all intents and purposes the adult in question is the child's parent and no other parent is available, but legally speaking the adult is not the child's parent. In effect, fully developing and making explicit the operative concept does not necessarily yield the manifest concept. And as we saw above, this does not mean that we should reject the operative concept as a 'misguided conception' in favour of the manifest.

V

Is Parent *Socially Founded?* Let us return to consider further the gap between the manifest concept of *parent* and the operative concept. A social constructionist in this case will plausibly claim that the category of *parent* is 'socially founded'. This means both that our manifest concept of *parent* (understood in biological terms) does not accord with our practices involving the notion of *parent* (which extends beyond the biological), and also that we would do well to modify our understanding of 'parent' to include a social dimension.

It appears that the constructionist could pursue more than one strategy for making the modification. One would be to simply replace the manifest concept of *parent* with the operative (e.g., *primary caregiver*), and appropriate the terminology of 'parent'. This would be to adjust, in a brute way, our understandings to conform to our practice. I'll call this the descriptivist strategy.[11] A second strategy would be to reflect on content of the manifest concept and the practice to come up with a concept of *parent* that best suits our needs and legitimate purposes. Let's call this the ameliorative strategy. A third strategy might be to argue for an ambiguity in the term, with one meaning tracking a social kind; the question then is whether a new term should be introduced, or whether there are other ways of resolving the ambiguity.

Those favouring a conceptualist (or internalist) analysis, as I've described it, typically argue that neither of these constructivist approaches—the descriptivist or the ameliorative—is acceptable because both amount to changing the subject. *Our* notion of parent (or *our* notion of race) is of a biological category, and any

11. Given what I say in Haslanger 2005, we could also consider it a genealogical strategy.

modification that disrupts that assumption replaces *our* concept with a different one. In other words, 'parent' just means *immediate progenitor*, and if we start using it to mean *primary caregiver* (or some more philosophically refined notion) then we have changed the meaning.[12] So social constructionists are wrong to say that *parent* is socially founded; what they are really saying is that a different concept, such as *primary caregiver*, is socially founded, which is obvious and not worth pointing out.[13] Moreover, the social founding of *primary caregiver* poses no challenge to our assumptions concerning the concept of *parent*. Similarly, a conceptualist concerned with race maintains that *our* concept of *race* is of a biological category, and nothing satisfies the biological conditions the concept requires. So the best we can do to capture the phenomena is to deny that there are races and invent (or appropriate) a new concept—such as *racial identity*—for the type tracked by our practices.[14]

I am willing to grant that each of these strategies could be reasonable in some context and we cannot decide on the basis of the simplified descriptions I've offered which is the best overall. However, the conceptualist sometimes maintains that

12. Of course, in the case of *parent*, it is not plausible to adopt a thoroughgoing error theory, since there are some people who do satisfy the conditions of being an immediate progenitor. But the internalist strategy would have us adopt a qualified error theory: all of our uses of the term 'parent' aside from the core biological cases are strictly in error because they pick out people who aren't really parents. In response to the charge that this would be inadequate in, for example, a school context, the conceptualist could also maintain that such an approach to the semantics does not entail that we retain the concept or terminology of *parent* in our school practices: perhaps we would do well to address our school memos using 'primary caregivers' or another term.

13. Although Ian Hacking is a constructionist, he concludes that constructionists cannot simply be making the debunking point that the category in question is socially unified rather than naturally unified because the claim would be 'redundant'. I think the distinction between the manifest and operative concept helps show why it need not be redundant and may be important (see Hacking 1999, p. 39).

14. Interestingly, Appiah (1996) does consider a kind of descriptivist approach, and still concludes that there are no races. He does so, however, because he takes it as a constraint on the type that can be projected from the paradigms that it be a natural type, since this is part of the concept, given his explorations of the history of the concept. So he does not consider the possibility that the objective type we designate with the term 'race' is a social type. This seems to be a 'mixed' approach that places, to my mind, too much weight on the history of the concept and does not adequately recognize objectivity of social kinds. My argument against error theories will only address those who defend their view using a conceptualist strategy. Those pursuing an ameliorative strategy who come, ultimately, to the conclusion that an error theory is the best option, I do not address here.

his approach is the *only* reasonable approach and that the descriptive and ameliorative approaches cannot capture the meaning of our terms; the best they can do is propose new meanings.[15] Is there reason to think that a descriptivist or ameliorative approach is simply misguided and that social constructionists aren't really doing philosophical analysis of the terms in question at all?

In the case of *parent*, at least, I think it is fairly clear that the concept has evolved and continues to evolve in response to the changing circumstances of family life; significantly for our purposes, it has changed from functioning as a natural category to functioning—at least in some settings—as a social category. (In some contexts the manifest concept of *parent* seems to allow that step-parents and adoptive parents are fully included; and increasingly there are contexts where it is no longer surprising if a child has two parents of the same sex.) How do we take this evolution into account in doing philosophical analysis? What does this 'evolution' involve? By granting that the concept has evolved, are we conceding to the error theorist that we are analysing a new concept, not the concept of *parent*? If we adjust the manifest concept so that a biological relation to the child is no longer necessary, isn't this 'changing the subject' in the very sense the conceptualist is worried about?

There are at least two ways of thinking of what might be involved when a concept evolves in response to social context: on one hand it may be that the term 'parent' expresses a different concept than it once did. The change is a change in our language. On the other hand it may be that the concept of *parent* remains the same, but what we take to be the shape and content of that concept changes. Perhaps we once took it to be an essential feature of parents that their children were biologically related to them, but we have come to regard this as just an empirical generalization based on a limited survey of cases that does not hold necessarily. This is a change in our conceptual knowledge. In the next two sections I

15. I myself am not opposed to proposing new meanings and, more generally, undertaking revisionary metaphysics. Given the history of our language and our conceptual framework, it would be a miracle if we had landed upon the best framework to describe the world. I only care about what we do mean as a step in an inquiry into what we should mean. Nonetheless, I think the conceptualist is misguided, and it is worth pointing out why, since many are not so happy with radical revisions as I am.

will consider each of these interpretations of 'conceptual change'. I will argue, first, that the constructionist is not changing the subject, or changing our language; rather, the constructionist is revealing that our linguistic practices have changed in ways that we may not have noticed. Second, I will argue that although the constructionist suggests that we come to a new understanding of our concepts, this does not require replacing our old concept with a new one, but understanding our original concept better. I do not commit myself to one or another account of conceptual change here; I also want to leave it open that concepts change like other ordinary things, that is, by altering.

VI

Semantic Externalism. According to the first explanation of conceptual change, the change is in what concepts our terms (such as 'race' or 'parent') express. This is plausibly understood as a semantic shift. It is not within the scope of this paper to take a stand in debates over meaning, for example, whether the *meaning* of the term is a concept to whose content we have privileged access, or the term's extension, or a function from worlds to sets of objects, etc. The point I want to make is quite simple and should be familiar: whatever it is that determines the extension of our social kind terms, it isn't something to which we have privileged access through introspection. If the extension of the term changes over time, it is legitimate to postulate a change in what determines the extension. Those who are familiar with an externalist approach to language and mind will find little new in this section beyond the claim that externalist insights should be applied to our thought and language about the social as well as the natural (so take yourself to be given permission to skip ahead). However, the implications of externalism are much less commonly recognized in social and political philosophy, so I'll provide a quick summary here.

I've suggested that the error theorist typically invests in a conceptualist approach to analysis that emphasizes a priori reflection and ideas that are relatively accessible to introspection. I've also suggested that it is plausible to see this as an investigation of the manifest concept. In undertaking conceptual analysis of, say, *F-ness*, it is typically assumed that it is enough to ask competent users of English under what conditions someone *is F*, without making any special effort to consult those whose daily lives are affected by the concept or who use the concept in practice. After all, if competent speakers know the meaning of their terms, then all that's needed is linguistic competence to analyse a term. A sophisticated internalist might want to allow that if one is sensitive to the possibility that in any actual circumstance there are competing meanings (often quite explicit) that structure alternative practices, then one could and should consider a broad range of speakers that are differently situated with respect to the phenomenon.[16]

However, this approach to understanding race, gender and other social kinds is not plausible if one takes into account arguments in philosophy of language over the past thirty years that call into question the assumption that competent users of a term have full knowledge of what the term means, that is, that what's 'in our heads' determines a term's referent. This assumption was already questioned once we considered the distinction between concept and conception (see Section IV), but is further challenged by the tradition of semantic externalism. Externalists maintain that the content of what we think and mean is determined not simply by intrinsic facts about us but at least in part by facts about our environment. Remember: Sally and Twinsally both use the term 'water', but Sally means H_2O and Twinsally means XYZ (Putnam 1975b). Sally thinks she has arthritis in her thigh, and is wrong because 'arthritis' in her community is an ailment of the joints; Twinsally thinks she has arthritis in her thigh and is right because 'arthritis' in her community is an ailment that is not confined to the joints (Burge 1979).

Most commonly, descriptive analyses—and the externalist picture guiding them—have been employed to provide *naturalistic* accounts of knowledge, mind, etc.; these seek to discover the *natural* (as contrasted with *social*) kind within which the selected paradigms fall. But it is possible to pursue a descriptive approach within a social domain as long as one allows that there are social

16. Although I'm not endorsing the methods of ordinary language philosophy, the complexity of our use of words in different contexts is something ordinary language philosophers were well attuned to, and some of their methods and ideas are tremendously valuable for this project.

kinds or types.[17] In fact I've chosen to speak of 'descriptive' approaches rather than 'naturalistic' approaches for just this reason. Descriptive analyses of social terms such as 'democracy' and 'genocide', or ethical terms such as 'responsibility' and 'autonomy' are methodologically parallel to more familiar naturalizing projects in epistemology and philosophy of mind.

Of course, an externalist analysis of social terms cannot be done in a mechanical way, and may require sophisticated social theory both to select the paradigms and to analyse their commonality; in short, the investigation of social kinds will need to draw on empirical social/historical inquiry, not just natural science. Moreover, it is easily possible that the resulting analysis of the type is highly surprising. For example, it was not intuitively obvious that water is H_2O or that gold is an element with atomic number 79. It took sophisticated natural science to determine what the terms 'water' and 'gold' mean. Likewise it may take sophisticated social theory to determine what 'parent' or 'Black' means. In a descriptive project, intuitions about the conditions for applying the concept should be considered secondary to what the cases in fact have in common: as we learn more about the paradigms, we learn more about our concepts.

17. Because the terminology of 'natural kind' is used in several different ways, it will be helpful to make a few distinctions. The term 'kind' is sometimes used to classify substances, in the ordinary case, (physical) objects. Substances can be classified according to their essence; kinds consist of groups of objects with a common essence. For example, tigers constitute a kind of thing because each tiger has essentially a certain cluster of properties that define the kind. On other occasions, the term 'kind' is used to refer to what are sometimes called *types*. A type is a group of things, sometimes substances, but possibly non-substances, that has a certain unity. This unity need not be a matter of sharing essential properties: red things constitute a type (their unity consists in their all being red), even though redness is seldom an essential property of the things that have it. Unity seems to come in different degrees. The things on my desk might be thought to constitute a weak sort of type (they have in common the fact that they are on my desk), and at the limit there are highly gerrymandered sets of things that don't have any unity at all and so don't constitute a type.

One way to think about the unity of types is in terms of similarity between the members. We can distinguish different sorts of types by distinguishing axes of similarity. Exactly six-foot-tall human beings are a natural type because the commonality between the members is natural (species and height); high school graduates are a social type because the commonality between the members is social. Both of these types are (metaphysically) objective, however. How to draw the line between social and natural types is difficult (as is the distinction between objective and subjective!) and not one I will address here. I'll have to rely on background understandings and familiar cases. However, it is important to keep in mind that as I am using the terms the distinction between objective and non-objective kinds/types is importantly different from the distinction between natural and social kinds/types.

Externalism initially appeared in two forms, supported by the sorts of examples ('water', 'arthritis') just recited:

1. *Natural kind externalism* (Putnam 1973; Putnam 1975b; Kripke 1980): Natural kind terms/concepts pick out a natural kind, whether or not we can state the essence of the kind, by virtue of the fact that their meaning is determined by ostension of a paradigm (or other means of reference-fixing) together with an implicit extension to 'things of the same kind' as the paradigm.
2. *Social externalism* (Putnam 1975b; Burge 1979; Burge 1986): The meaning of a term/content of a concept used by a speaker is determined at least in part by the standard linguistic usage in his or her community.

It then became clear that externalist phenomena are not confined to natural kind terms (properly speaking), but occur quite broadly. For example, in the history of logic and mathematics, inquiry can seem to converge on an idea or concept that we seemed to have in mind all along, even though no one, even the best minds, could have explicated it. (Leibniz's early efforts to define the limit of a series is an example.) In such cases it is plausible to maintain that certain experts were 'grasping a definite sense, whilst also failing to grasp it "sharply"' (Peacocke 1998, p. 50).

Recognizing the possibility of reaching for a concept that is not quite within grasp provides us with a way to think about the ameliorative approach to analysis sketched above. In such cases we have perhaps a partial or vague understanding of the manifest concept, and the operative concept picks out a relatively heterogeneous set, but nonetheless we can say that there is something we mean, an objective type we are approaching. As before, I will use the term 'target concept' for the concept that is plausibly what we are getting at, even if we poorly understand it; the target concept is the object of ameliorative analysis. Although Fregeans are apt to capture this by invoking objective senses that the inquirers 'grasp', an ontology of sparse objective properties will also do the work.

The upshot of this is that the basic strategy of natural kind externalism need not be confined to natural kinds (where it is assumed that things of the same natural kind share an essence). Externalism is an option whenever there are relatively objective types. The notion of objective type needed is not too mysterious:

a set of objects is more an objective type by virtue of the degree of unity amongst its members beyond a random or gerrymandered set. Objectivity is not only to be found in the natural world. There are objective types in every realm: social, psychological, political, mathematical, artistic, etc. We might account for unity in various ways (Lewis 1983), but a familiar way I'll assume for current purposes is in terms of degrees of similarity; the similarity in question need not be a matter of intrinsic similarity; that is, things can be similar by virtue of the relations (perhaps to us) they stand in. Roughly,

> *Objective type externalism*: Terms/concepts pick out an objective type, whether or not we can state conditions for membership in the type, by virtue of the fact that their meaning is determined by ostension of paradigms (or other means of reference-fixing) together with an implicit extension to things of the same type as the paradigms.

Sets of paradigms will typically fall within more than one type. To handle this, one may further specify the kind of type (type of liquid, type of artwork), or may (in the default?) count the common type with the highest degree of objectivity. For the purposes of capturing the operative concept, it is promising (as suggested before) to take the relevant type to be the one that we rely on in our best theory of the social/linguistic practice.

Descriptive projects adopt an externalist approach to content, that is, they set out to determine the (an?) objective type, if any, into which the paradigms of a particular concept fall. Social constructionists can rely on externalist accounts of meaning to argue that their disclosure of an operative or a target concept is not *changing the subject*, but better reveals what we mean. By reflecting broadly on how we use the term 'parent', we find that the cases, either as they stand or adjusted through ameliorative analysis, project onto an objective social, not natural, type. So although we tend to assume we are expressing the concept of *immediate progenitor* by the term 'parent' in fact we are expressing the concept of *primary caregiver* (or some such); the constructionist shows us that our assumptions about what we mean are false, given our practice. This is not to propose a new meaning, but to reveal an existing one.

If one assumes with the conceptualist that the task of philosophical inquiry is simply to explicate through introspection what we think we mean in using a term, then almost any externalist inquiry will seem 'revisionary'. But the conceptualist approach to analysis is wedded to assumptions about mind and language that are certainly contested, if not outmoded. We should also ask ourselves why, given the systematic use of terms such as 'parent' to track a social category, do we persist in thinking that the term picks out a natural category? Might ideology be playing a role in masking how we organize our social lives? In any case, there is no reason to reject out of hand the constructivist's claim that a term whose manifest concept is of a natural kind may be better understood in terms of the operative social concept. The proposed analysis may be surprising; and it may even be that the term has come, through practice, to express a different concept than it used to; that is, the manifest may not have caught up with the operative. But the constructionist is not causing this, or even promoting such a change, but is rather revealing it.

VII

Meaning Holism. We considered before two ways that we might interpret the idea that a concept 'evolves' with social practices. On one interpretation, the point is that a term such as 'parent' expresses, say, the concept of *immediate progenitor* at one time, but, given changes in how the community organizes family life, comes to express a different concept, such as *primary caregiver*, at a later time. I've argued that the constructionist describes this shift by saying that the term 'parent' is socially founded. This is not to invoke or propose a new meaning, but rather, drawing on externalist insights, to reveal an existing meaning that might well be obscured.

However, the other interpretation we considered was that the concept in question 'evolves', not in the sense that the term changes what concept it expresses, but rather, there is a change in our understanding of the concept. For example, empirical investigation might reveal that a generalization we took to be analytically entailed by the concept is in fact only contingent, or even false. The suggestion here is not that the concept itself changes (though it might be useful to spell it out that way), but rather that our understanding of it does.

Nothing I'm saying here is news; the claim that there is, at best, a blurry line between what's true by virtue of fact and what's true by virtue of meaning is one theme in the arguments against the analytic/synthetic distinction. As in the case of externalism, however, the focus of discussion has typically been on cases in natural science and the development of natural kind concepts. For example, in his essay, 'The Analytic and the Synthetic', Putnam contrasts examples in mathematics and science which, he argues, are not happily classified as either analytic or synthetic, with the standard example of 'A bachelor is an unmarried man', which is one of the few claims that he thinks should count as analytic. He says:

> In the case of a law cluster term such as 'energy', any one law, even a law that was felt to be definitional or stipulative in character, can be abandoned, and we feel that the identity of the concept has, in a certain respect, remained. Thus, the conclusions of the present section still stand: A principle involving the term 'energy', a principle which was regarded as definitional, or as analytic, if you please, has been abandoned. And its abandonment cannot be explained always as mere 'redefinition' or as change in the meaning of 'kinetic energy' .... (Putnam 1975a, p. 53)

He continues:

> But 'All bachelors are unmarried' cannot be rejected unless we change the meaning of the word 'bachelor' and not even then unless we change it so radically as to change the *extension* of the term 'bachelor'. What makes the resemblance [to the 'energy' case] superficial is that if we were asked what the meaning of the term 'bachelor' is, we can *only* say that 'bachelor' means 'unmarried man', whereas if we are asked for the meaning of the term 'energy', we can do much more than give a definition. We can in fact show the way in which the use of the term 'energy' facilitates an enormous number of scientific explanations, and how it enters into an enormous bundle of laws. (Ibid.)[18]

But let's consider the example of 'bachelor' more closely. It is still commonly assumed and asserted in philosophy that: it is analytically true by virtue of the meaning of 'bachelor' that:

x is a *bachelor* iff_{df} x is an unmarried adult male (UAM).

But this claim only seems plausible if one assumes that heterosexuality is universal, or that there is no way other than marriage

18. Putnam's paper is famous for going on to argue that there are scenarios in which we would consider evidence that 'All bachelors are unmarried' is false; but such scenarios are ones in which 'bachelor' comes to function as a natural kind term for those with a certain neurosis. So again, on Putnam's account the phenomenon of conceptual evolution occurs in the context of developing natural science.

for one to enter into a formalized lifelong commitment. It seems plausible to say that an unmarried gay man who has made a lifelong commitment to another—perhaps even formalized it as a 'civil union'—is not a bachelor. (So not: if UAM, then bachelor) To press further: is it analytic that marriage is between a man and a woman, or is it only 'deeply embedded collateral information' (Putnam 1975a, p. 41)? Whose intuitions about 'marriage' should settle this?

One might suggest that a weaker claim is analytic by virtue of the meaning of 'bachelor':

> If x is a *bachelor*, then x is unmarried.

But the truth of this claim depends on what sorts of institutions might qualify as 'marriage', and this is an issue that is highly contested and historically complex. For example, marriage as we know it has traditionally combined an economic institution with a quasi-religious institution setting constraints on sexual behaviour. This is, of course, not an accident, since sex tends to produce offspring and offspring are, at least potentially, both an economic drain and an economic resource. However, it is possible to imagine a case in which the economic institution of marriage and the sexual institution of marriage are separated to form two kinds of marriage, a sexual marriage and an economic marriage. (Consider, perhaps, a variation on Margaret Atwood's *The Handmaid's Tale*.) Further, suppose that one can be sexually married to A and economically married to B. I'm inclined to think that bachelorhood is really about sexual availability, so the fact that a man is economically married to A does not compromise his bachelor status, since he is still available to be sexually married to someone else.

In any case, the reliance on a background social framework is apparent in the case of:

> x is a *parent* iff_{df} x is an immediate progenitor.

In some social/historical contexts this may seem analytically true by virtue of what 'parent' means. But laws and customs change so that one can become the legal parent of a child who is not biologically related, and with time, such parents are recognized as 'real parents'.

In the case of *parents* and of *marriage* there are competing models of social life, of what's essential and what's accidental to our existing social structures. But just as what is essential or accidental to being an atom or being energy will depend on the background physical theory in which the term 'atom' is used, so what is essential or accidental to being a parent, or being married, or being a bachelor, will depend on the background model of social life (see also Burge 1986). Putnam suggests that we should contrast cases such as 'Bachelors are unmarried men' with scientific principles, because the former is as close to pure stipulation as we can get and the latter have 'systematic import'. Because of the systematic import of scientific principles, we can give up one or another of them without changing the meaning of the terms used to express them. (Putnam 1975a, p. 40) What Putnam (and others) seem to miss is that 'Bachelors are unmarried men' also has systematic import; that is, the concepts, in particular, of *marriage*, *adult*, and *male*, although familiar from common parlance, can also be the subject of social and political theory and of social contestation. Although the scientific essentialists were apt to claim that the analytic/synthetic distinction stood in the way of scientific progress, they were not as apt to see that it may also stand in the way of social progress.

What these cases reveal is that often what we take to be analytic principles actually encode certain social arrangements, and the relationship between terms encode certain power structures. For example, the term 'parent' brings with it a certain normative weight, entitlement, etc., that the term 'primary caregiver' doesn't. Putnam suggests that it would be difficult to imagine a physical theory that did not employ some notion of *the past*, or of *energy*. These are framework concepts. Similarly it is difficult to imagine a social theory that did not employ some notions of *male*, *female*, *parent*, even something like *marriage*. So there is a reason why social constructionists want to rethink the term 'parent' rather than substituting the term 'primary caregiver'. And it is not surprising that in the United States we are fighting over *what the term 'marriage' means* as part of the struggle for gay rights. The term 'marriage' is a framework concept that links the institution to a broad range of other social phenomena, and does so in a way that 'civil union' cannot approximate.

The constructionist about 'parent' maintains that in cases where the manifest concept of *parent* is of an immediate progenitor, it may nonetheless be appropriate to understand the concept of *parent* as of *primary caregiver* (or some such notion). Is the constructionist simply changing the meaning of the term? If the concept of *parent* is a (social) framework concept, which seems plausible, and if the work we need the term 'parent' to do is no longer best served by assuming that parents are immediate progenitors, then it is reasonable to consider this claim, not as giving the meaning of the term, but as stating a useful, though not universal, generalization.

This, then, suggests a reason to prefer the constructionist to the error-theoretic strategy in analysing at least some social kinds. The conceptualist's insistence that the concept in question, say *parent*, should be analysed only in terms of what is manifest to us, can have the effect of fossilizing our social structure: if we are not allowed to adjust the contents of our framework concepts in light of developments in social theory and social life, then social change will require a wholesale adoption of a new conceptual scheme. Given that this is unlikely, change will be difficult. Moreover, because framework concepts are embedded with normative principles, rejecting the concepts may leave us with old practices and no new principles to guide us. If we combine the conceptualist strategy with the retention of purportedly natural categories, we further entrench the existing framework by suggesting that its analytic structure is just tracking nature's joints, not ours. So, in effect, the constructionist is making two moves that potentially destabilize our social arrangements: revealing that a purportedly analytic statement is in fact a contingent generalization, and revealing that a natural category is in fact social.

VIII

Conclusion. I started this essay by asking whether social constructionist analyses of familiar terms or concepts can ever be philosophically acceptable if such analyses aim to *debunk* our ordinary understandings and so inevitably violate our intuitions. Further, if social constructionist analyses can be counterintuitive, are there any limits on how counterintuitive they can be and still be acceptable; more generally, what makes for goodness in a constructionist analysis, if intuitions don't matter? And finally, are there any reasons why constructionist analyses should be preferred over error-theoretic accounts that remain committed to the manifest naturalizing concept as 'what we mean' and offer a new social concept to capture how the term operates in our practice?

I have argued that constructionist analyses cannot be faulted *in general* for changing the subject, or for being counterintuitive. Semantic externalism allows us to claim that what we are talking about is, in fact, a social category, even if we think it isn't. And in the case of framework concepts, social theory and social life may lead us to reject principles that seemed definitional, while we still retain the concept. So the constructionist can claim to provide an acceptable analysis of a concept, even if it is not intuitive.

A successful constructionist debunking will be one in which the best account of what we are doing (or should be doing) in drawing the distinctions in question—taking into account what legitimate purposes are being served and what objective types there are—has us tracking a social type.[19] Such an account will not be purely a priori and will draw on social theory. I have not, in this essay, argued that a social constructionist account of race is preferable to an error-theoretic or naturalistic account (though I have maintained that it is: see Haslanger 2000); such an argument would have to delve into empirical matters that I haven't touched on here.

It would be a mistake to conclude from what I've argued that constructionist analyses are always preferable to error-theoretic analyses when there is a gap betweeen manifest and operative concepts. Cases have to be examined individually. In particular, the arguments I've offered in this essay only address error theorists who rely on a conceptualist picture, that is, those whose analysis of the controversial concept rests entirely on balancing intuitions. There may be some who adopt an error theory as the result of a broad analysis of our practices and purposes. My arguments do not weigh against such an account. Rather, I have urged that if our manifest concepts are misleading about our practices and mask what we are really doing with our concepts, we should consider whether there is a story to be told about how and why. If there is such a story, our accounts should reflect it.

Grounding philosophical analysis in linguistic competence or a priori intuition concerning our manifest concepts risks

19. On the issue of what counts as a 'legitimate purpose' and how our theoretic purposes should be evaluated, I follow Anderson 1995 and trends in feminist empiricism more broadly.

perpetuating social self-deception. Although we cannot proceed without intuition, neither can we proceed without critical social theory. My hope is that the example of gender and race will encourage philosophers to pay greater attention to the rather ubiquitous gap between manifest and operative concepts, leading to less focus on our intuitions and more on the role of concepts in structuring our social lives. Philosophical analysis has a potential for unmasking ideology, not simply articulating it.[20]

References

Alcoff, Linda 2000: 'Is Latino/a Identity a Racial Identity?' In Jorge J. E. Gracia and Pablo De Grieff (eds), *Hispanics and Latinos in the United States: Ethnicity, Race, and Rights*. New York: Routledge, pp. 23–44.

Anderson, Elizabeth 1995: 'Knowledge, Human Interests, and Objectivity in Feminist Epistemology'. *Philosophical Topics*, 23(2), pp. 27–58.

Andreason, Robin 2000: 'Race: Biological Reality or Social Construct?' *Philosophy of Science*, 67, Supplementary Volume, pp. S653–66.

Appiah, K. Anthony 1996: 'Race, Culture, Identity: Misunderstood Connections'. In K. A. Appiah and A. Gutmann, *Color Conscious: The Political Morality of Race*. Princeton: Princeton University Press, pp. 30–105.

——— 1993: *In My Father's House*. New York: Oxford University Press.

Armstrong, David 1989: *Universals: An Opinionated Introduction*. Boulder, CO: Westview Press.

Burge, Tyler 1979: 'Individualism and the Mental'. *Midwest Studies in Philosophy*, 4, pp. 73–121.

——— 1986: 'Intellectual Norms and Foundations of Mind'. *Journal of Philosophy*, 83(12), pp. 697–720.

Glasgow, Joshua 2003: 'On the New Biology of Race'. *Journal of Philosophy*, 100, pp. 456–74.

Gooding-Williams, Robert 1998: 'Race, Multiculturalism and Democracy'. *Constellations*, 5(1), pp. 18–41.

Hacking, Ian 1999: *The Social Construction of What?* Cambridge, MA: Harvard University Press.

Hardimon, Michael O. 2003: 'The Ordinary Concept of Race'. *Journal of Philosophy*, 100(9), pp. 437–55.

Haslanger, Sally 1995: 'Ontology and Social Construction'. *Philosophical Topics*, 23(2), pp. 95–125.

——— 2000: 'Gender and Race: (What) Are They? (What) Do We Want Them To Be?' *Noûs*, 34(1), pp. 31–55.

20. Thanks to Louise Antony, Lawrence Blum, Alex Byrne, Jorge Garcia, Richard Holton, Erin Kelly, Ishani Maitra, Mary Kate McGowan, Lionel McPherson, Laura Schroeter, Marion Smiley, Sarah Song, Ronald Sundstrom, Ásta Sveinsdóttir, Gregory Velazco y Trianosky, and Steve Yablo for discussing with me the issues raised in this paper. Earlier versions of this paper were given at the Society for Analytic Feminism, the Australian National University, The California Roundtable on Philosophy and Race (2005), the University of Colorado, Boulder, and Tufts University. I am grateful to the participants in the discussions for helpful feedback.

——— 2003: 'Social Construction: The "Debunking" Project'. In Frederick F. Schmitt (ed.), *Socializing Metaphysics: The Nature of Social Reality*. Lanham, MD: Rowman and Littlefield, pp. 301–25.

——— 2005: 'What are we Talking About? The Semantics and Politics of Social Kinds'. *Hypatia*, 20(4), pp. 10–26.

——— 2006: 'Race and Natural Kinds'. Conference presentation, January 9. *Revisiting Race in a Genomic Age*, Stanford Humanities Centre.

Higginbotham, J. 1998. 'Conceptual Competence'. *Philosophical Issues*, 9, pp. 149–62.

Kitcher, Philip 1999: 'Race, Ethnicity, Biology, Culture'. In L. Harris (ed.), *Racism*. New York, Humanity Books, pp. 87–117.

Kripke, Saul 1980: *Naming and Necessity*. Cambridge, MA: Harvard University Press.

Lee, Sandra Soo-Jin, Johanna Mountain and Barbara Koenig 2001: 'The Meanings of "Race" in the New Genomics: Implications for Health Disparities Research'. *Yale Journal of Health Policy, Law and Ethics*, 1, pp. 33–75.

MacKinnon, Catharine 1987: *Feminism Unmodified*. Cambridge, MA: Harvard University Press.

Mallon, Ron 2004: 'Passing, Traveling and Reality: Social Construction and the Metaphysics of Race'. *Noûs*, 38(4), pp. 644–73.

Mills, Charles 1998: *Blackness Visible: Essays on Philosophy and Race*. Ithaca, NY: Cornell University Press.

——— 1997: *The Racial Contract*. Ithaca, NY: Cornell University Press.

Mountain, Joanna L. and Neil Risch 2004: 'Assessing Genetic Contributions to Phenotypic Differences Among "Racial" and "Ethnic" Groups'. *Nature Genetics*, 36 (11 Supp.), pp. S48–53.

Omi, Michael and Howard Winant 1994: 'Racial Formation'. In M. Omi and H. Winant, *Racial Formation in the United States*, New York: Routledge, pp. 53–76.

Peacocke, Christopher 1998: 'Implicit Conceptions, Understanding, and Rationality'. *Philosophical Issues*, 9, pp. 43–88.

Putnam, Hilary 1973: 'Meaning and Reference'. *Journal of Philosophy*, 70, pp. 699–711.

——— 1975a: 'The Analytic and the Synthetic'. In *Mind, Language and Reality: Philosophical Papers, Volume 2*. Cambridge: Cambridge University Press, pp. 33–69.

——— 1975b: 'The Meaning of "Meaning"'. In *Mind, Language and Reality: Philosophical Papers, Volume 2*. Cambridge: Cambridge University Press, pp. 215–71.

Quine, W. V. O. 1953: 'Two Dogmas of Empiricism'. In *From a Logical Point of View*. Cambridge, MA: Harvard University Press.

Risch, Neil, Esteban Burchard, Elad Ziv and Hua Tang 2002: 'Categorization of Humans in Biomedical Research: Genes, Race and Disease'. *Genome Biology*, 3(7), comment 2007.1–2007.12.

Rosenberg, Noah A., Jonathan K. Pritchard, James L. Weber, Howard M. Cann, Kenneth K. Kidd, Lev A. Zhivotovsky and Marcus W. Feldman 2002: 'Genetic Structure of Human Populations'. *Science*, 298, pp. 2381–5.

Zack, Naomi 2002: *Philosophy of Science and Race*. New York: Routledge, pp. 29–43.

——— 1997. 'Race and Philosophic Meaning'. In *RACE/SEX: Their Sameness, Difference, and Interplay*. New York: Routledge, pp. 29–43.

PHILOSOPHICAL ANALYSIS AND SOCIAL KINDS

by Sally Haslanger and Jennifer Saul

II—Jennifer Saul

GENDER AND RACE

ABSTRACT Sally Haslanger's 'What Good Are Our Intuitions? Philosophical Analysis and Social Kinds' is, among other things, a part of the theoretical underpinning for analyses of race and gender concepts that she discusses far more fully elsewhere. My reply focuses on these analyses of race and gender concepts, exploring the ways in which the theoretical work done in this paper and others can or cannot be used to defend these analyses against certain objections. I argue that the problems faced by Haslanger's analyses are in some ways less serious, and in some ways more serious, than they may at first appear. Along the way, I suggest that ordinary speakers may not in fact have race and gender concepts and I explore the ramifications of this claim.

In a series of recent papers, Sally Haslanger has argued for some rather striking analyses of race and gender concepts (Haslanger 2000, 2003, 2004, 2005). One of the most striking features of these analyses is that they are hierarchical in nature—for example, a necessary condition for being a woman is that one be systematically subordinated. Haslanger is well aware that this will strike most of us as counterintuitive, but she offers two quite distinct reasons for thinking that this counterintuitiveness should not count against her analyses. Both reasons involve arguing that counterintuitiveness is not nearly as relevant as we might think to the question of whether her analyses are acceptable. Very roughly: First, Haslanger notes that her analyses need not be taken to be analyses of the concepts that we *actually* use in order to be worthwhile. Instead, she presents them as analyses of the concepts we *should* use—those that would best serve our legitimate purposes. If this is Haslanger's project, then counterintuitiveness need not be an objection to her analyses (Haslanger 2000). Call this reply 'The Revisionary Reply'. In more recent papers (Haslanger 2005, 2006), however, she has begun to argue that counterintuitiveness is not necessarily relevant even to the question of what concepts we are actually using: an analysis may be deeply counterintuitive and yet still be an analysis of *our* concepts.[1] Her analyses, then, may—despite appearances—still lay claim to being non-revisionary analyses of our race and gender concepts. Call this 'The Non-Revisionary Reply'.

Haslanger explores these sorts of defences very carefully, but she does not actually apply them in detail to her analyses of race and gender concepts. In this paper, I discuss the prospects for doing so. I begin with the Non-Revisionary Reply. Here I start by suggesting that Haslanger has indeed shown that an analysis may be counterintuitive and yet not revisionary; but I argue that the prospects for showing her analyses to be of this sort are not good. However, the problems that would render such a demonstration difficult also offer a new reason for doubting the significance of intuitions about race and gender concepts. In fact, I suggest, it may well be that ordinary speakers do not *have* race and gender concepts at all. If this is right, then it makes no sense to worry about whether an analysis of our race and gender concepts is revisionary. Nonetheless, we can still worry about suggested changes to our language—to the meanings of words like 'woman' and 'Black' (whether or not these are gender and race terms). And a version of the Revisionary Reply is highly relevant to this issue. I argue that this reply also faces problems. How serious these problems are, however, is largely a matter for empirical study rather than philosophy.

I

Haslanger's Analysis of Gender and Race Concepts. Haslanger adopts the traditional feminist distinction between sex and gender. Very roughly, gender is a social notion while sex is a biological one: sex is determined by features such as chromosomes or genitalia, and gender is determined by social features. Drawing this distinction helped feminists to argue that biology was not destiny—that women's social roles were quite a separate matter

1. The 'our' here is Haslanger's term, and there are many concerns that can be raised about it. One important issue is that of who 'our' refers to: all English speakers, all English speakers from a particular country or region, all members of a particular cultural subgroup, etc.?

from their biology, and that it is possible to change social roles without changing biology.[2] Haslanger also follows the practice of using 'woman' and 'man' as gender terms and 'female' and 'male' as sex terms. Although people who are biologically female will usually be gendered as women, this need not (and does not) always happen: someone who is male may live out the life of a woman. Women are not always female, and men are not always male. Both sex and gender pose serious theoretical difficulties: the two-fold, clear-cut sex distinction that ordinary speakers generally take to exist does not;[3] and gender has proved extremely difficult for feminist theorists to analyse.[4]

Parallel distinctions can be drawn, Haslanger suggests, for race. She takes race to be a social notion, using the term 'colour' for its biological counterpart. Again, both terms are extremely problematic. For Haslanger, however, 'race is the social meaning of "colour"' (2003, p. 5). Race is analogous to gender, while colour is analogous to sex: 'colour' is a term for something (not a natural kind) that is determined by the superficial clusters of physical traits that are taken to be markers of race (facial features, skin colour, etc.).

1.1 Gender Concepts. Haslanger's understanding of gender is very different from many in the feminist literature. It focuses not on self-conceptions, or patterns of behaviour, but instead on position occupied in a hierarchical society. Here are her definitions of 'woman' and 'man':[5]

> *Woman*: S is a woman iff S is systematically subordinated along some dimension (economic, political, legal, social, etc.) and S is 'marked' as a target for this treatment by observed or imagined bodily features presumed to be evidence of a female's biological role in reproduction.
> *Man*: S is a man iff S is systematically privileged along some dimension (economic, political, legal, social, etc.) and S is 'marked' as a target for this treatment by observed or imagined bodily features presumed to be evidence of a male's biological role in reproduction. (Haslanger 2003, pp. 6–7)

2. I think good questions can be raised about whether the sex/gender distinction was needed in order to make these arguments, but this is not the place for such questions.
3. See, for example, Fausto-Sterling 1992, 2000.
4. See, for example, Butler 1990, Spelman 1988.
5. Haslanger has given slightly different definitions in other papers.

It is built into Haslanger's definitions, then, that women are systematically subordinated to men; a female who escapes systematic subordination is not, for Haslanger, a woman.

1.2 Race Concepts. Haslanger's analysis of race concepts begins with a definition of what it is for a group to be racialized:

> A group is *racialized* (in context *C*) iff its members are socially positioned as subordinate or privileged along some dimension (economic, political, legal, social, etc.) (in *C*) and the group is 'marked' as a target for this treatment by observed or imagined bodily features presumed to be evidence of ancestral links to a certain geographical region. (Ibid., p. 7)

Of course, this does not yet tell us what it is for an individual to be of a particular race. Haslanger is less explicit on this point. She writes, '*S* is of the White (Black, Asian . . .) race (in *C*) iff Whites (Blacks, Asians) are a racialized group (in *C*) and *S* is a member' (ibid., p. 7). In a footnote, she tells us a bit more about what is required for such membership: 'I recommend that we view membership in a racial/ethnic group in terms of how one is viewed and treated regularly and for the most part in the context in question' (ibid. p. 26, n. 8).

Since this is a little more complicated than Haslanger's 'gender' definition, it's worth going through an example. Suppose that in context *C* people taken to have a certain cluster of bodily features (which are taken to be evidence of geographical origin in Africa) are marked for subordination. Such people will then constitute a racialized group, which we'll take to be called 'Black'. Fred will count as being of the race Black if he is a member of this racialized group, and Fred will count as a member if he is generally treated as a member. To be treated as a member of the group called 'Black' is to be treated as subordinate on the basis of certain (real or imagined) physical features taken to be evidence of geographical origin in Africa. Fred, then, is Black just in case he is subordinated for this reason. Just as with gender, then, hierarchy is crucial: Fred is not Black unless he is subordinated in this way.

1.3 The Counterintuitiveness Worry. Haslanger's definitions are, as she concedes, at odds with intuitions. For most of us, Haslanger's definitions are just not the sort of thing we are likely to come up with if asked about the nature of race and gender, and when presented with them we will very likely reject them. Moreover, reflection on certain specific cases can make them seem even odder. To see this, take *woman* as our example:

- A man who decides that he wants to become a woman would not take himself to be deciding that he wants to be subordinated.
- Many females consider themselves women but do not take themselves to be systematically subordinated.
- An unsubordinated woman does not seem, intuitively, to be logically impossible. Indeed, most feminists take themselves to be working for an end to women's subordination, and take this goal to be possible.

II

Haslanger's Defences Against the Counterintuitiveness Worry. Haslanger is well aware that many will find her analyses counterintuitive. Nonetheless, she thinks this counterintuitiveness should not motivate a rejection of these analyses. As noted earlier, she has offered two interestingly distinct arguments for setting aside worries stemming from counterintuitiveness. The Revisionary Reply accepts that her analyses are revisionary, but defends the project of giving revisionary analyses of these concepts; the Non-Revisionary Reply suggests that her analyses may not be as revisionary as they seem, despite their counterintuitiveness. Both of these responses draw on some important distinctions Haslanger draws between kinds of projects and concepts. I will begin with these.

2.1 Kinds of Projects, Concepts. Haslanger distinguishes three kinds of conceptual inquiries one might conduct. I will illustrate these with a different example from those Haslanger uses, one that I think helps us to see how useful these distinctions can be.

2.1.1 Conceptual Inquiry Into Our Manifest Concept. A *conceptual* inquiry proceeds by examining our intuitions about various cases, both actual and hypothetical, and also by examining the definitions that we formulate when asked to reflect upon our concepts. Such an inquiry is very likely to proceed by way of reflective equilibrium. It is concerned with arriving at what

Haslanger calls our *manifest* concept. If we are investigating our manifest concept of democracy, then, we will probably arrive at a standard that requires (at least) elections that are free of voter intimidation, the counting of all ballots, equal access to polling places for all voters, and so on.

2.1.2 Descriptive Inquiry Into Our Operative Concept. A *descriptive* inquiry is not so much concerned with what we *take* our concepts to be when asked about them, or with our intuitions about hypothetical cases. Instead, a descriptive inquiry into *F*-hood might start by examining the things in the world to which we apply the predicate *F*. It would then ask what kind (natural or other), if any, we seem to be tracking with our use of *F*. The concept that we arrive at through this method is our *operative* concept.[6] If we are investigating our operative concept of democracy, then, we may well find that we apply the term far more broadly than our manifest concept would suggest. It may turn out that our operative concept of democracy requires only regular elections and that all adult citizens be formally permitted to vote. This is compatible with substantial voter intimidation, great variation in access to polling places, and ballots going uncounted. We could find out that this is our operative concept by noticing that in fact we apply the term 'democracy' even when we know that voters were intimidated, ballots went uncounted, and so on.

2.1.3 Ameliorative Inquiry Into Our Target Concept. An ameliorative inquiry is very different from either of the above. It attempts to discover what concept we *should* be using. This concept—the *target* concept—will be the one that best serves our legitimate purposes in talking about *F*s. We might have many purposes in using the word 'democracy'. Some of these purposes, such as working toward genuinely representative governments, will be best served by our manifest concept of democracy, with its high standards. Others, such as defending the claim that some current government *G* is democratic, may be best served by our operative concept of democracy. Arguably, however, the first purpose is

6. Importantly, not all uses needed to be accommodated by the operative concept—some may simply be the results of errors. The operative concept will be the concept that picks out the kind that is the *best* fit for our uses of the term in question—it need not be a perfect fit.

more legitimate than the second, as the second seems motivated only by a concern to protect the status quo while the first is motivated by a seemingly far more defensible concern with representative government. (Nothing hangs on this judgement of relative legitimacy of purposes, so don't worry if you disagree.) Perhaps in this case, then, our manifest concept and our target concept are the same. Once we discover this, we can reflect upon what sort of thing we really think the term 'democracy' should apply to, and possibly revise some of our judgements about which governments are democracies, thus opening up new lines of enquiry and rendering our views more coherent. Indeed, Haslanger suggests in the paper preceding this one that—if we do have some target concept that serves a legitimate purpose—we should ultimately work to bring manifest, operative, and target concepts into line with each other.

Exploring the case of *democracy* has helped us to see how important these distinctions are. Before the manifest and operative concepts are distinguished, we may all too easily associate elements of the manifest concept with the things to which we apply the operative concept. For example, our belief that all and only democratic governments are legitimate may be based on our manifest concept of democracy. Employing our operative concept of democracy, we classify some government *G* as democratic. Before noticing that our operative and manifest concepts fail to coincide, we may unthinkingly take *G* to be legitimate. But once we have noticed the disparity, we will (or at least should) hesitate to do this. We now see that even though we have classified *G* as democratic, many questions remain that are relevant to *G*'s legitimacy—questions that we might well have neglected if we had not noticed the disparity.

In the example described above, it may seem just obvious that we have been *wrong* in classifying *G* as a democracy. But this is very likely because it seems clear which concept we *should* be using—the manifest concept. In other cases, however, it may not be so clear which concept we should use, or it may be that the operative concept is the one that we should use.

2.2 The Revisionary Reply. In the example above, it seemed plausible to suppose that our target concept was in fact also our manifest concept, and in other examples it may seem plausible to suppose that it is our operative concept. But our target concept may also be different from either of these. It may well be that the concept we *should* be using—the one that best suits our legitimate purposes—is neither our manifest nor our operative concept. And this offers a way to defend a very revisionary analysis—simply by arguing that it is an analysis of the concept we should be using: our target concept. This was the first defence that Haslanger offered of her hierarchical analyses of race and gender (Haslanger 2000). On this line of defence, whether or not the analyses are revisionary is irrelevant. All that matters is that they are the best for our legitimate purposes. What are these legitimate purposes? Haslanger takes our legitimate purposes (for these concepts) to be the fighting of oppression. More specifically, in the case of gender,

> A primary concern of feminist and antiracist theorizing is to give an account of the social world that will assist us in the struggle for justice. Given this goal, I take the primary motivation for distinguishing sex from gender to arise in the recognition that societies, on the whole, privilege individuals with male bodies. (Haslanger 2003, p. 6)

The (legitimate) point of gender concepts, then, is to help us to fight oppression on the basis of sex. It seems natural to assume that Haslanger takes the (legitimate) point of race concepts to be helping us to fight oppression on the basis of colour. So, the analyses that best serve us in the struggle against oppression on the basis of sex and colour will be the correct analyses of our target concepts. This reply, then, sidesteps the issue of whether Haslanger's analyses fit our manifest or operative concepts.

Haslanger recognizes that the proponent of a revisionary analysis faces an additional issue: when does an analysis cross the boundary from being revisionary to being an analysis of something entirely different? As she puts it, ' [I]n an explicitly revisionary project, it is not at all clear when we are warranted in appropriating existing terminology' (2000, p. 34). She suggests two criteria for deciding this, a semantic and a political one. (Presumably these are meant to be necessary and jointly sufficient.) First, the political condition: 'The politics of such appropriation will depend on the acceptability of the goals being served, the intended and unintended effects of the change, the politics of the speech context, and whether the underlying values are justified' (ibid., p. 35). (This is, as she concedes, not really a condition as it stands. Later we will discuss what it comes to in a bit more detail.) The semantic condition, she suggests, is far more straightforward: '[T]he proposed shift in meaning of the term would seem semantically warranted if central functions of the term remain the same, e.g., if it helps to organize or explain a core set of phenomena that the ordinary terms are used to identify or describe' (ibid., p. 35). Haslanger seems to think that her analyses of race and gender terms will pass these tests, although she does not argue this in detail.

2.3 The Non-Revisionary Reply. Both our manifest and our operative concepts have some claim to be called 'our concepts'. Where the operative and manifest concepts of *F* come apart, however, an analysis of our operative concept of *F* might well turn out to violate some important intuitions of ours about *F*s. After all, it is only the manifest concept that is discovered by consulting our intuitions. We might, for example, find a concept of democracy that does not require freedom from voter intimidation to be deeply counterintuitive. Nonetheless, our operative concept of democracy might well have this feature. Such a concept, then, is arguably not revisionary—it is, in an important sense, *ours* despite its violation of our intuitions.

The mere fact that an analysis is counterintuitive cannot, then, be taken to show that it is revisionary. Demonstrating that Haslanger's analyses of race and gender concepts violate our intuitions, then, does not show these analyses to be revisionary ones. If they are, in fact, non-revisionary—and in addition they are the concepts we *should* be using (our target concepts)—then her analyses are in very good shape, despite their violation of intuitions. This is the basis for Haslanger's second defence against the charge of counterintuitiveness. (It is important to note that Haslanger does not claim to have established that her analyses are in fact non-revisionary, but just to have shown that their counterintuitiveness does not prove them to be revisionary.)

III

Examining the Non-Revisionary Reply. Haslanger's recent suggestion that her analyses may not be so revisionary as they at first appear depends upon the manifest/operative concept distinction. Our intuitions, which her analyses do seem to violate, tell us only about our manifest concepts and not about our operative concepts. Despite their counterintuitiveness, then, her analyses may well have a claim to be analyses of our operative concepts, and therefore to being non-revisionary. This defence is perfectly adequate as a response to an objection that moves directly from counterintuitiveness to rejection of Haslanger's analyses as revisionary. However—as I'm sure she would admit—it is another matter entirely to *argue* that the analyses are non-revisionary. This would require that a case be made for supposing that Haslanger has in fact captured our operative race and gender concepts. Haslanger has not attempted to make this case. Here I examine the prospects for making this case, calling attention to some likely problems. Then I explore further ramifications of these problems.

3.1 The Difficulty of Discovering Operative Race and Gender Concepts. A crucial part of the non-revisionary defence is the idea that some concept may count as *ours* even if it is not our manifest concept. It may be ours by virtue of being our operative concept, and one result of this is that a correct analysis of our concept may nonetheless be a counterintuitive one. This seems to me both right and important. But can a case be made for the claim that Haslanger's analyses of race and gender are correct analyses of our operative concepts of race and gender? This is trickier.

As we have noted, one key aspect of Haslanger's analyses of race and gender concepts is that they are hierarchical. An individual is not, for example, a woman, unless she is systematically subordinated on the basis of (real or imagined) physical markers generally taken to indicate female sex. If we want to learn whether our operative gender and race concepts are those Haslanger describes, clearly one thing we need to know is whether (our knowledge of) the presence or absence of such subordination affects our willingness to call someone 'woman' or 'Black'.

This is more difficult to learn—for both race and gender concepts—than we might at first suppose. I will illustrate the problem by looking at the concept *woman*. A first problem is that it will do us no good to simply ask, 'Suppose that we come across a female who is not subordinated. Could she still be a woman?' This will do us no good because this sort of consultation of intuitions about necessary and sufficient conditions would tell us only about our manifest concept, not our operative one. To learn about the operative concept, what we really need to do is find some females who are not subordinated on the basis of real or perceived sex characteristics and check to see whether people apply the term 'woman' to them. But this is far from straightforward: we will differ on what counts as subordination; we will differ in our views on whether particular individuals are subordinated; and we will differ on our views about what causes the subordination that particular individuals suffer. (And these differences will not be easily resolved: the nature of subordination, for example, is a highly contentious matter even within feminism.) This will cast doubt on any conclusions that we might want to draw from our study of the way that people use the term 'woman'. Suppose we find, for example, that someone we take to be non-subordinated is still classified as a woman by most people. This could be taken to show either that Haslanger has failed to capture most people's operative concept or that most people take this person to be subordinated. We could, however, attempt to resolve this by studying people's willingness to apply the term 'subordinated' to such a person. I am genuinely unsure how successful this would be: one problem is that most people do not use this term in their everyday classification of other people. Explicit questioning could easily start to inform us about not an operative question but a manifest one. Perhaps these problems could be overcome, however. Nonetheless, other, more serious, ones would remain.

3.2 Confusion and Operative Race and Gender Concepts. The most serious problems arise from the fact that ordinary speakers frequently do not draw the same distinctions that Haslanger does (and when they do, they do not do so as clearly as she does). We will first examine this problem in the case of gender. Haslanger draws a clear distinction between sex and gender, and she uses 'woman' exclusively as a gender term (with 'female' as a sex term). But ordinary speakers are not like this. First, ordinary speakers may not have the sex/gender distinction at all. Even if they do, they may not apply it consistently or coherently. Here I offer just two examples:

- The terms 'gender' and 'sex' are used interchangeably in many discussions—both in news articles and in fertility clinics' web sites—that make reference to 'gender selection of embryos'.[7]
- An article in the *Journal of Forensic Sciences* discusses 'gender identification of dried human blood stains'.[8]

These clearly represent instances in which the word 'gender' is used—inaccurately—in place of the word 'sex'. Moreover, these are examples that have passed muster with editors and even scientific referees.

In addition, Haslanger's careful distinction between the meanings of 'woman' and 'female' is not one that is reflected in ordinary usage. Most speakers use 'woman' as both a sex and a gender term. None of the following would strike an ordinary speaker as strange:

- 'Darren is a woman on Friday nights.' (Here 'woman' is used as a gender term.)
- 'I (like everyone else) never realized Ed was a woman until I saw Ed naked.' (Here 'woman' is used as a sex term.)
- 'I am a man, but I want to become a woman.' (It is not so clear here whether 'woman' is being used as a sex or a gender term—this depends on whether the transition is taken to involve change of sex or just gender. But this uncertainty doesn't lead us to any uncertainty about whether the term is correctly used.)
- 'This is the skeleton of a woman.' (Here 'woman' is used as a sex term.)

Given these facts of usage, it becomes difficult to conduct a study of our operative gender concept *woman*. Any data that we

7. See, for example, J. Kahn, 'High Tech Sex Selection', at http://archives.cnn.com/2001/HEALTH/10/01/ethics.matters/; 'Gender Selection overview' at http://www.centerforhumanreprod.com/gender_selection.html; 'Gender Selection: Ask the Expert' at http://news.bbc.co.uk/1/hi/talking_point/3258423.stm.

8. Discussed in Saul and Saul 2004, which also discusses other examples of this confusion in forensic science.

obtain might concern instead the operative sex concept that is (perhaps wrongly) associated with the word 'woman'. If it turned out, then, that speakers readily applied the term 'woman' to unsubordinated females, this might count against Haslanger's definition. On the other hand, it might instead be a product of these speakers using 'woman' as a sex term, not a gender term—or of their using it as both, or as some muddle of the two.

One could instead look just to the usage of those who do carefully and consistently distinguish between sex and gender, and who also use 'woman' only as a gender term. However, these speakers are likely to be theorists who may be quite invested in one theory or another of gender, and such people are extremely unlikely to agree in their usage. In addition, to turn exclusively to theorists' usage suggests that we are treating 'woman' as a technical term. And if that is what we are doing, then the issue of whether Haslanger has captured 'our' concept *woman* is a strange one.

Finally, one might suggest that I have been too focused on use of the term 'woman'. Perhaps speakers' usage of this *term* is muddled, but they nonetheless have a concept, the *woman* concept, that they apply reasonably consistently to all and only those who occupy a particular social role. Although studying linguistic usage may be an easy way to learn about operative concepts, it is not the only one. In order to support this view, we would need to find behavioural evidence that speakers do in fact classify people in this way. It seems to me that such evidence is unlikely to be forthcoming, given both the muddled linguistic usage and its tendency to go unnoticed.

A brief look at the situation with our race concepts will suffice to show that the problems here are, if anything, even more intractable. Haslanger distinguishes two uses we might make of terms like 'Black', 'White', and so on. One use of these words is as colour terms, and the other is as race terms. Race terms refer to social kinds, while colour terms refer to those who share a collection of superficial physical features. This distinction is, if anything, even more absent from everyday usage than that between sex and gender. Moreover, even theorists do not have distinct terms for the race and colour versions of 'Black' and 'White'. (Contrast this with the distinct terms 'woman' and 'female': even if these are not consistently used to draw the distinction Haslanger draws, at least distinct terms exist and they are sometimes used in this way.) How, then, could we ever hope to study our actual usage of race concepts, as opposed to colour concepts? Consider some instance in which the term 'Black' is applied. Can this instance tell us anything about the operative race concept *Black*? In order to do so, it would have to be an instance of this concept in use rather than our operative colour concept *Black*. This would be fairly straightforward to discover when dealing with someone like Haslanger, who draws these distinctions: we could ask questions designed to elicit whether the category is taken to be a social one or not. (Though there would still be a worry that such explicit questioning would be revealing only about the manifest concept, not the operative one.) But it is far less straightforward when dealing with someone who has never thought to distinguish social and physical concepts associated with such terms. It is not even clear that it is right to attribute such a distinction to a person like this. (Once more, it would be possible to draw on non-linguistic data, but it does not seem likely to be available.) It strikes me as unlikely that we would have much evidence enabling us to attribute such a distinction in a non-question-begging manner, collecting together one set of usages of 'Black' as telling us about a race concept and another as telling us about a colour concept.

3.3 Nullifying the Counterintuitiveness Worry? I have been arguing that ordinary speakers do not generally distinguish between race and colour, or between gender and sex, and that even when they appear to distinguish these they do not do so in a consistent manner. If this is right, then ordinary speakers' intuitions are a very poor source of information about race and gender concepts. When people are deeply confused about a subject matter, it is not a good idea to look to them as sources of information. And it seems to me that people are, at the very least, deeply confused about race and gender. This suggests a much quicker reply to the counterintuitiveness worry than those that Haslanger has offered: people are deeply confused on this topic, so their intuitions should not serve as a guide to these concepts.

We can take this response yet further. It seems to me that there is no good reason to even attribute gender or race concepts to ordinary speakers. Ordinary speakers do, of course, have concepts associated with the terms 'woman' and 'Black', but there is no reason to take these to be gender and race concepts—that is, to take them to be social correlates of sex and colour concepts. Moreover, it does not seem as though ordinary speakers have a tendency to organize the world (linguistically or otherwise) according to categories that really look like gender and race categories—rather than sex and colour categories, or some muddled amalgams. Why should we, then, attribute race and gender concepts to ordinary speakers? I'd like to tentatively suggest that we should not do so, although properly establishing this would require more argument than I am in a position to make here. If this is right, then it makes no sense to even ask whether Haslanger's analyses of race and gender concepts are revisionary with respect to ordinary ones: *there are no ordinary race and gender concepts*. If this is right, then Haslanger can surely help herself to whatever race and gender concepts she finds most useful. These are theoretical notions, and Haslanger should be guided by her theoretical needs.

3.4 A New Counterintuitiveness Worry. Despite all this, it seems to me that there is still a counterintuitiveness worry. This worry concerns not our concepts, but our words. Ordinary speakers do undeniably have the words 'woman' and 'Black', and Haslanger is proposing definitions for these words that seem counterintuitive. Call this 'the linguistic counterintuitiveness worry'. Since we are not, it seems to me, expressing gender and race concepts with our ordinary use of these words, it is hard to see how to apply the Non-Revisionary Reply to the linguistic counterintuitiveness worry. In the next section, we explore the prospects for applying some version of the Revisionary Reply.

IV

The Revisionary Reply and Linguistic Counterintuitiveness. The Revisionary Reply to the counterintuitiveness worry with which we began argues that Haslanger's analyses are to be viewed as analyses of our target concepts. These are the concepts we *should* be using—the concepts that best serve our legitimate purposes in using race and gender concepts. If I am right that we do not really use race and gender concepts, then this reply as it stands does not make sense. But then neither does the worry that motivated it.

Can some version of this reply, however, be applied to the linguistic counterintuitiveness worry? It seems to me that it can. This reply would argue that the analyses Haslanger has offered best serve our legitimate purposes in using terms like 'woman' and 'Black' (whether these express gender and race concepts is irrelevant). My goal here is to assess the prospects for this reply. In considering this reply, Haslanger's semantic and political conditions for terminological appropriation are clearly of great importance. We will consider these in turn. I will argue that the semantic condition as it stands is in need of work, and that a case can certainly be made that the political condition will not be satisfied.

4.1 The Semantic Condition.

> [T]he proposed shift in meaning of the term would seem semantically warranted if central functions of the term remain the same, e.g., if it helps to organize or explain a core set of phenomena that the ordinary terms are used to identify or describe. (Haslanger 2000, p. 35)

It seems to me that more work needs to be done to make the above condition really do what it needs to do. To see this, suppose that I were to propose an explicitly revisionary definition for 'woman' that was just like Haslanger's analysis of *man*:

> *S* is a woman iff *S* is systematically privileged along some dimension (economic, political, legal, social, etc.) and *S* is 'marked' as a target for this treatment by observed or imagined bodily features presumed to be evidence of a male's biological role in reproduction.

I could defend this revisionary definition by arguing, 'The phenomenon that I am concerned to describe is that of inequalities between males and females. A term "woman", meaning what I suggest above, will be very useful to me in organizing and explaining this phenomenon.' Haslanger cannot deny that a term with this meaning would be useful for explaining the phenomenon at issue—after all, this is how she defines 'man'. This shift in meaning, then, would seem to meet Haslanger's semantic criterion.

Most likely, the way to respond to this worry is to insist that that the phenomenon specified above is not the right one.[9] But it is far from obvious how the phenomenon in question should be specified. One could try an extensional specification: the new meaning for the term should result in the same extension as the old one. But this clearly won't do. Recall that the main way Haslanger's definition is counterintuitive is in its inclusion of a hierarchical requirement: according to Haslanger, one is not a woman unless one is subordinated. This is counterintuitive to those who think that it is possible to be a woman and not be subordinated. Let's assume that the existing meaning for 'woman' allows for this possibility. Haslanger's clearly does not. The two concepts, then, have different extensions (at least in some possible world, and arguably in the actual one as well). If preservation of extension is required for 'same phenomenon', then, Haslanger's proposed revisionary understanding fails the test. This is not, of course, the only option for further specifying Haslanger's requirement. It may be possible to refine it in a way that answers my worry. My point is simply that further work is needed on Haslanger's semantic condition.

4.2 The Political Condition.

> The politics of such appropriation will depend on the acceptability of the goals being served, the intended and unintended effects of the change, the politics of the speech context, and whether the underlying values are justified. (Haslanger 2000, p. 35)

The political condition, as Haslanger acknowledges, is not really a condition as it stands. But it seems fair to assume that a definition yielding the concept that best serves our legitimate purposes in using a term (the target concept) should meet Haslanger's intended condition. Our question, then, is whether Haslanger's definitions pass this test.

9. Alternatively, one could use the pragmatic criterion to rule out my proposed change—it really wouldn't be a very good idea, practically speaking, after all. But it seems as though the change really *should* be ruled out semantically as well.

4.3 Haslanger's Suggested Purposes. Haslanger argues that her definitions are the best suited to the purposes she describes as 'our legitimate purposes' in using race and gender concepts. Here we will examine the idea that these definitions are the ones best suited to our legitimate purposes in using words like 'woman' or 'Black'. Our legitimate purposes, she maintains, are the fighting of oppression on the basis of sex and colour. In order to determine what definitions will serve us well in this fight, it seems to me, we need to look a little more closely at what is involved in it. Haslanger mentions two key elements: identifying and explaining inequalities, and provoking a re-evaluation of our identities.

4.3.1 Identifying and Explaining Inequalities. According to Haslanger, we 'need to identify and explain persistent inequalities between females and males, and between people of different "colours"; this includes the concern to identify how social forces, often under the guise of biological forces, work to perpetuate such inequalities' (2000, p. 36.) Our question now is whether terms like 'woman' and 'Black', as defined by Haslanger, are useful for this project.

These terms, as understood by Haslanger, can indeed be used to do the work described above. To take one example, using 'women' and 'men': very roughly, the explanation of persistent inequalities between females and males would begin from the fact that females tend overwhelmingly to be women, and that women are systematically subordinated to men. The next step would be to analyse this systematic subordination and how it is perpetuated.

It does not seem to me, however, that the terms 'women' and 'men', as understood by Haslanger, are essential to this explanation. We could easily rewrite the explanation in a way that does not make use of these terms: 'The explanation of persistent inequalities between females and males would begin from the fact that females tend to be systematically subordinated to males. The next step would be to analyse this systematic subordination and how it is perpetuated.' A term needn't, of course, be essential in order to be useful, but it is unclear to me why utilizing Haslanger's terminology should be seen as adding something to this explanation. This does not mean, however, that it does *not* add anything. It may be that the final step of the explanation—analysing the details of the systemic subordination and its perpetuation—will benefit from employing these terms. But it seems to me far from obvious that discussions of social forces such as stereotyping, discrimination, and so on, will benefit from using hierarchical gender terms. We can, after all, discuss power differentials between two groups even if these are not built into the meanings of our terms for these groups (take, for example, cats and mice, or the Labour Party and the Tory Party). It is far from clear, then, that Haslanger's definitions offer us the best ways of using 'women' and 'men' for the purpose of identifying and explaining inequalities.

One might even suppose that identifying and explaining inequalities could become *more* difficult if we utilize Haslanger's hierarchical terminology than if we make use of non-hierarchical understandings. One thing we might (pre-theoretically) want to do is to investigate whether, for example, there are women who are not subordinated—and to learn what factors bring this about. On Haslanger's understanding, however, *all* women are subordinated to men, so investigating the case of women who escape subordination is not possible. This is not to say, however, that Haslanger cannot examine such cases: she can, but she cannot do so in the very natural terminology just used. This is, then, one use for the term 'woman' that might seem important to the identification and explanation of inequalities—and it isn't available to Haslanger.

4.3.2 Challenging Self-conceptions. For Haslanger, one key advantage of using the definitions she suggests for 'woman', 'Black', and so on, is the following:

> By appropriating the everyday terminology of race and gender, the analyses I've offered invite us to acknowledge the force of oppressive systems in framing our personal and political identities. Each of us has some investment in our race and gender: I am a White woman. On my accounts, this claim locates me within social systems that in some respects privilege and in some respects subordinate me. Because gender and racial inequality are not simply a matter of public policy but implicate each of us at the heart of our self-understandings, the terminological shift calls us to reconsider who we think we are. (2000, p. 47)

There is no question, it seems to me, that Haslanger's suggestion could have the sort of effect suggested above. It is a shocking shift she suggests, and it is a shift that—if adopted—would very likely alter the way we feel about claiming identities in terms like 'woman', 'man', 'Black' or 'White'. But there are many uncertain empirical matters. One uncertainty is what sort of effect such a shift would have. Haslanger takes it that the shift would be a positive one, causing us to question our identities in a productive manner that furthers the cause of social justice. But would this happen? Those in subordinated positions might instead become trapped in a feeling of powerless to change their own fates. It could be quite disempowering, for example, for a woman to come to believe that women are by definition subordinated. And those in powerful positions might feel even more secure and deserving of their power if they come to see it as built into being (for example) a man. Certainly such sentiments are not at all unheard-of amongst the subordinated and the subordinators. Whether these responses or those Haslanger suggests would occur is a matter of human psychology. Gambling on the positive responses Haslanger expects is risky.

We might also reflect on which people are likely to adopt Haslanger's terminology and be affected by it in the way that Haslanger hopes. It seems to me likely that such people will already be committed to the cause of fighting racism and sexism. Others, it seems to me, are unlikely to be won over to the cause by Haslanger's suggestions (more on this below). There is nothing wrong, of course, with provoking those already committed to feminism or anti-racism to think harder about the inequalities they are trying to fight and their role in perpetuating them. But I worry that this may be less important than the need to win new converts, and I argue below that Hasanger's definitions may be counterproductive as far as this goal goes.

4.3.3 Other Ways of Fighting Injustice. There are many things that one might want to do in fighting 'sex- and colour-based' oppression. Some of these, at least, seem as though they would be rendered *more* difficult by the use of Haslanger's hierarchical terminology.

4.3.3.1 Convincing Others That There Is an Injustice. One important step in correcting injustices is convincing others that there are injustices to be corrected. Haslanger's terminology might at first seem ideally suited to this purposes. After all, if we use her vocabulary it is very clear that 'All women are subordinated to men' is true—and this seems undeniably an enormous injustice. However, this claim is likely to be misunderstood as a claim about all females, and many (perhaps most) people—including many females—do not think that all females are subordinated to men. We can then explain to them how the word 'woman' is being used, and show them that 'All women are subordinated to men' must be true. After all, it is true by definition. But upon learning that this is simply a definitional truth the injustice is no longer so clear: it would remain true even if we succeeded in eradicating subordination (and thereby created a world without women). So Haslanger's terms are not necessarily the best ones for alerting people to injustice.

4.3.3.2 Avoiding Misunderstanding. If we accept that Haslanger's definitions *are* revisionary (as we have done), then any use of them will clearly require us to spend time making our new use of familiar terminology clear. This may not be the best use of our time, and if people forget or do not listen to our explanations we will be misunderstood.

4.3.3.3 Stating Goals. It is useful if a political movement states its goals in a clear and appealing manner, in order to rally people to the cause. As Haslanger notes, her understandings of race and gender commit her to political movements whose goals are the elimination of women and Blacks. These goals are extremely likely to be misunderstood and the statement of these goals may well alienate many of those who would be most likely to support anti-oppression movements.

None of the worries raised in this section of the paper are decisive. It may well be that Haslanger's terminology is so useful that this usefulness outweighs the ways in which I have worried that they might be counterproductive. But we need to know more in order to be able to evaluate this. It would be very useful to have more detail and more examples regarding the ways in which Haslanger's concepts are useful, and more empirical information.

Without this, it is far from clear that the political criterion for terminological appropriation is met.

V

Contextualism. At times, it is not entirely clear how contextualist Haslanger's proposals are. She suggests in the paper preceding this one that we should be working toward an ideal in which our manifest, operative and target concepts are the same. This does not sound contextualist at all: it sounds as though she thinks that we should agree on our concepts once and for all. However, at other points she sounds very contextualist:

> [W]hether the terminological shift I'm suggesting is politically useful will depend on the contexts in which it is employed and the individuals employing it. The point is not to legislate what terms to use in all contexts, but to offer resources that should be used judiciously. (2000, p. 48)

On this contextualist understanding, all that Haslanger is proposing is *one* way to understand the terms 'woman', 'man', 'Black', and so on. Her proposals are not proposals about what these terms should always mean, but instead about what these terms should *sometimes* mean. Understood this way, one might think, Haslanger's proposals are hard to argue with. If her understandings are useful for some purposes (such as provoking a re-thinking of our identities), why not simply use them for those purposes? If they are counterproductive for other purposes, as I have suggested above, we need not use them for these purposes. On this line, it might seem, everyone gets what they want at very little cost. All of the practical objections raised above would seem to fade away.

It seems to me, however, that the cost of this proposal is greater than it at first appears. To see this, recall the realities of the societies we live in. Haslanger and I agree that we are, most of us, living in societies that have a long way to go in combating and even acknowledging racism and sexism. (If we have already won these battles, then this also gives a good reason to resist her proposals—fighting racism and sexism isn't necessary if the battles have been won.) We are also living in a world that does not often draw distinctions between race and colour, or gender and sex. The contextualist proposal would be that we should sometimes use words like 'woman' or 'Black' as gender and race terms, understood along Haslanger's lines. But we should also try to use these terms in a more ordinary manner at other times. We must, then, be careful to code-shift at the appropriate times, and to make sure that things written or said in one context are not misunderstood in another. It seems to me that communication is difficult enough as it is, and that we should instead try to use ordinary terms in as ordinary a way as possible. We may well have a need for technical terms that work as Haslanger's do, but it seems to me a mistake to risk confusion by using ordinary vocabulary to do this work.

Other worries about this proposal may seem more like technical ones, but I think they point to something important. Let's look at some, far too briefly. Imagine that Amanda takes a feminist philosophy class and is convinced by Haslanger's views. She decides to use the terms 'woman' and 'man' in the way that Haslanger suggests in order to explain to her friend Beau what she has learned. Amanda utters (1):

(1) All women are subordinated by men.

Beau does not use 'woman' and 'man' in the way that Amanda uses these terms. He uses them, let's say, as sex terms. A first question is what Amanda has said. Since the speaker and audience have different meanings in mind for the contextually-shifting terms, it is genuinely unclear what the right answer is. Possibly, the right answer is that Amanda has failed to say anything. This seems strange. Perhaps more plausibly, Amanda has said one thing and Beau has understood her as saying another. But if that's the case, Beau will have trouble even reporting what Amanda has said. It should be, it seems to me, that Beau's utterance of (2) is true.

(2) Amanda said that all women are subordinated by men.

But we're assuming that the content of 'women' in Beau's mouth is different from its content in Amanda's. What Amanda has said is not something that Beau can report (at least not without a lot of work). There are other options, but all face difficulties. These difficulties—regarding what is said in a mixed context, and what we say when we report the speech of those who use the terminology in a different way—point to the seriousness of the confusion that is possible with a contextualist version of Haslanger's view. In so doing, they offer some reason for resisting it.

VI

Conclusion. Haslanger has done a great deal of important theoretical work in order to offer defences of her analyses of race and gender concepts against charges of counterintuitiveness. I have suggested that, to some extent, such defences may have been unnecessary: it seems to me unlikely that we have race and gender concepts—and if we do they are so muddled that our intuitions about them should not be taken very seriously. Nonetheless, I think Haslanger does face some important issues regarding her revisionary definitions of the words 'woman', Black', and so on (whether or not we take these words, in ordinary usage, to be race and gender terms). Most significantly, I think Haslanger's proposals face real political difficulties. Many of my worries, however, turn on empirical matters. So, in the end, it seems to me that what really needs to be done is some careful empirical work on the most effective vocabulary for combating racism and sexism. And this takes us outside the purview of philosophy.[10]

References

Butler, J. 1990: *Gender Trouble*. New York: Routledge.

Fausto-Sterling, A. 1992: *Myths of Gender: Biological Theories about Women and Men*. New York: Basic Books.

—— 2000: *Sexing the Body: Gender Politics and the Construction of Sexuality*. New York: Basic Books.

Haslanger, S. 2000: 'Gender and Race: (What) Are They? (What) Do We Want Them To Be?' *Noûs*, 34(1), pp. 31–55.

—— 2003: 'Future Genders? Future Races?' *Philosophic Exchange*, 34, pp. 5–27.

10. I am very grateful to Michelle Garvey, Chris Hookway, Jules Holroyd, Mari Mikkola and Lina Papadaki for reading and discussing drafts of this paper (especially Chris and Mari, who read multiple drafts!), and to Ray Drainville, Rosanna Keefe, Steve Laurence and Frank and Julie Saul for discussing the issues in this paper with me. I learned a great deal from these discussions, and the paper was much improved by many suggestions that I received.

—— 2004: 'You Mixed? Racial Identity Without Racial Biology'. In S. Haslanger and C. Witt, *Adoption Matters*. Ithaca, NY: Cornell University Press.

—— 2005: 'What Are We Talking About? The Semantics and Politics of Social Kinds'. *Hypatia*, 20(4), pp. 10–26.

—— 2006. 'Philosophical Analysis and Social Kinds: What Good are Our Intuitions?' *Proceedings of the Aristotelian Society, Supplementary Volume 80*, pp. 89–118.

Saul, F. P. and J. M. Saul 2004: 'Sex vs Gender: Does It Really Matter?' Poster, *Proceedings of the American Academy of Forensic Sciences*, 10, pp. 271–2, Dallas, TX.

Spelman, E. 1988. *The Inessential Woman: Problems of Exclusion in Feminist Thought*. Boston: Beacon Press.

DISJUNCTIVISM

by John Hawthorne & Karson Kovakovich
and Scott Sturgeon

I—John Hawthorne & Karson Kovakovich

DISJUNCTIVISM

ABSTRACT We examine some well-known disjunctivist projects in the philosophy of perception, mainly in a critical vein. Our discussion is divided into four parts. Following some introductory remarks, we examine in part two the link between object-dependent contents and disjunctivism. In part three, we explore the disjunctivist's use of discriminability facts as a basis for understanding experience. In part four, we examine an interesting argument for disjunctivism that has been offered by Michael Martin.

I

When we report upon perceptual experience, certain descriptions encode perceptual success. Other descriptions are neutral with respect to success. Yet others encode failure. We can, in the abstract, imagine various analytic projects whereby one or more varieties of perceptual state types are taken as more basic and the remaining state types are analysed in terms of them. In this connection, one might take certain neutral states as basic,[1] factorizing both the success and failure states into a combination of the neutral states and certain further ingredients. One might instead take both the success and failure states as basic, analysing the neutral state in terms of them. Finally, one might take just the success states as basic, analysing the neutral and failure states in those terms.[2] Certain versions of the latter project are often classified as 'disjunctivist' within the philosophy

1. Those disjunctivists who are used to saying 'There are no such things as neutral states' should not think that we have prejudged the cogency of their view. Here and elsewhere we deploy a very lightweight conception of 'state'. For lightweight purposes, there is a state of being either a fork or a rock that is shared by rocks and forks. The ideology of naturalness that we are about to introduce allows for the articulation of a more heavyweight conception, one that will allow us to articulate various disjunctivist proposals in ways that are not apt to produce confusion.
2. We trust that no one will want to take the failure states as basic and then analyse the neutral and success states in terms of them.

of perception.[3] As we shall see, their details depend, *inter alia*, on which concept of success is at work.

The so-called 'disjunctivist' obviously won't analyse some given neutral state by conjoining a set of conditions that include a success state plus some further ingredients. This is out of the question, since the neutral state is insufficient for the success state. But a natural form of analysis remains, namely that of analysing the neutral state as a state that is either the success state or else a state that bears a certain relation to the success state.[4] And, indeed, standard disjunctivisms conform to something like this recipe—hence the name.[5] We shall be investigating some well-known disjunctivist projects in some detail, mainly in a critical vein. Before looking at those projects, however, some preliminary ground-clearing is in order.

First, let us remember that there are various positions that the disjunctivist might take concerning the sense in which success states are more basic.

One might hold that they are conceptually more basic, and that the proposed analysis somehow mirrors the conceptual order—the order of understanding, so to speak. On this construal, the relevant analyses might plausibly be presented as something like conceptual or semantic analyses that represent the structure of the relevant ordinary concepts.

But the analyses need not be so construed. One might instead put a more metaphysical spin on the project. Many of us recognize a distinction between properties that mark joints in nature—highly *natural* properties, as David Lewis puts it—and

3. Early examples include Michael Hinton 1967, 1973 and Paul Snowdon 1980/81, 1990. John McDowell 1982, 1986 is a little harder to classify, since it is not clear whether and how he wishes to analyse the failure state of 'mere appearing' in terms of the success state of 'taking in a fact'. Other influential discussions, some friendly, some hostile include Child 1994, Dancy 1995, Robinson 1994, Martin 1997, and Williamson 1995. Austin 1962 is undoubtedly an inspiration for British disjunctivists, but here is not the place to explore points of similarity and difference. Martin 2006 tentatively suggests in a footnote that the label 'disjunctivism' is due to Howard Robinson 1985. Our concern in this paper is to evaluate a certain family of ideas, not to speculate as to what exactly is meant by that term of art in the mouths of our contemporaries.

4. The failure state is then naturally analysed as requiring the presence of the neutral state and the absence of the success state.

5. In this respect the philosophers that we discuss here are not the 'Disjunctive Quietists' described by Sturgeon who offer 'no positive story about hallucination at all' (1998, p. 184).

properties that are more gerrymandered, or 'gruesome' (recalling Goodman).[6] One gloss on the thesis that success states are more basic is that success-encoding properties are far more natural, more joint-like, than the properties that encode neutral or failure states. From such a perspective, it may be tempting to offer a metaphysical account of the more gerrymandered properties in terms of more natural ones, and the relevant 'disjunctivist' analysis might be offered in this spirit. Of course, if the order of concepts mirrors the order of being, then some such analysis might satisfy both the conceptual and metaphysical construals of the project.

In what follows we shall assume a metaphysical construal, according to which the central goal is to carve perception at its joints. These natural contours may in turn be underappreciated or in some cases overlooked by our ordinary conceptual scheme. Certainly, many of the writers that we are interested in pay lip service on occasion to the metaphysical construal. Better not to pin them with a priori or conceptual commitments when their project does not require them. For the most part, though, our choice of construal is not particularly important, since the worries that we raise here for the metaphysical project apply with at least equal force to the conceptual one. (The main effect of our choice is that we do not pursue certain criticisms that have the conceptual project as their distinctive target.)

Second, let us emphasize that even if the project of analysing neutral and failure states in terms of success states runs aground, certain of the ideas that motivate disjunctivism may yet be defensible and important. Let us briefly mention three such themes.

(a) Disjunctivists might be right in thinking it mistaken to try to factorize success states into neutral states plus some further ingredients. Just as it may be a mistake to try to factorize knowledge into belief and some further ingredients, it may similarly be misguided to try to, say, analyse *visually perceiving that P* into *looking that P* plus further ingredients, and also misguided to try to analyse *seeing an object* into its *(visually) appearing*

6. See Lewis 1983, Goodman 1954.

that there is an object plus some further ingredients. Even if an analysis of neutral states in terms of success states fails, that hardly means that some analysis in the opposite direction will work.

(b) Disjunctivists might be right that certain success states play a role in explaining action that cannot be happily taken over by neutral states. Even if neutral states are natural, joint-like states in their own right, that hardly entails that they will leave success states with no explanatory work to do.

(c) Disjunctivists might be right that certain success states play a fundamental *evidential* role in epistemology. Even if neutral states are natural, that hardly entails that pairs of individuals that are duplicates with respect to neutral states are to be reckoned to have the same perceptual evidence. Perhaps differences with regard to success states make for an evidential difference.[7]

We think that there is much that is illuminating and suggestive in disjunctivist discussions of themes (a), (b) and (c) above, and by no means intend the critical remarks in this paper to suggest otherwise.

Third, let us be clear that even if no analysis of the neutral in terms of success is possible, there may yet be some reasonable sense in which success concepts are more fundamental. For one thing, it may well turn out that *developmentally*, success conceptions of our perceptual life are grasped prior to neutral conceptions. For another, the discussion that follows is consistent with a claim that there are deep teleological links between the success and neutral states: one might think that looking that *P* is a state that somehow aims at constituting a case of seeing that *P*. (Just as belief aims at knowledge, so perceptual appearances aim at perceptual success.) We are altogether pessimistic that an analysis of neutral states can be wrought from such reflections, but they may yet point to some kind of dependence (conceptual or

7. For discussion of the explanatory role of veridical perception see Martin 2004. For discussion of the epistemic role of perceptual success, see Brewer 1999 and McDowell 1982, 1986 and 1994. For discussion of themes (a) to (c) in connection with knowledge and belief, see Williamson 2000.

metaphysical) of the neutral upon the successful. At any rate, it is not the purpose of this paper to contest such speculations.

Fourth, our main targets in this paper are certain analyses that have been put forward in the disjunctivist literature. A thoroughly general argument that no analysis of the neutral in terms of the successful is possible would require, *inter alia*, getting more clear than we do here about what is to count as an 'analysis', and about what kinds of properties and relations are fair game to be used along with the success states in providing an analysis of the neutral states.[8]

The remaining discussion will be divided into three parts, designed to highlight some key moves in recent disjunctivist discussions. We shall first examine the link between object-dependent contents and disjunctivist projects. We shall then investigate the prospects for analysing neutral states in terms of their *epistemic relation* to success states, and in particular their indiscriminability from such states. Finally, we shall look at one important line of argument that has been offered by Michael Martin on behalf of a disjunctivist programme.

II

Object-Dependence. According to one influential semantic tradition, the contents of singular thoughts are *object-dependent*. A thought t has an object-dependent content iff there is some object x such that (i) t is about x and (ii) at any world in which a thought with t's content occurs, the existence of x explains the

8. One style of analysis that we shall not evaluate here is modelled on Timothy Williamson's (tentative) account of belief: a case of looking that P is a case that the subject treats as a case of being in a position to see that P, where 'treats' marks similarity of functional role (cf. Williamson 2000, pp. 46–7: 'If believing p is, roughly, treating p as if one knew p, then knowing is in that sense central to believing.' See also p. 48, n. 9). As Williamson is aware, the inchoateness of 'treats', functionally construed, leaves the proponent of this style of account with many loose ends. We note in passing one interesting test case: is it possible that there be a being with looks states that are not treated by the subject as a source of knowledge, and indeed occur in an agent utterly incapable of perceptual knowledge—and the relevant factive perceptual states—through vision? Can we, for example, imagine a creature who uses vision merely as a source of questions and uses touch as a basis for answers? (Thanks to Williamson for helpful discussion here.)

availability of a thought with that content.[9] When I look at the laptop in front of me and think that it is mainly black, then (assuming that this is indeed a genuine singular thought), this thought is made possible by the existence of the laptop. A natural corollary of this way of thinking is that there are cases where one may be under an illusion as to whether one has had a thought at all: owing to the lack of a requisite object, an episode may seem to one as if it is a contentful one when in fact it is contentless.[10] (This may be so, for example, when a hallucination victim attempts to think demonstratively.) When we move to the realm of perceptual experience, this kind of semantic framework has a natural application.[11]

We begin with some ideological scene-setting. When describing perceptual engagement with some particular object (or objects), it has seemed natural to many to distinguish the *contents of the perceptual experience* with the contents one believes, or has some impulse to believe, or has some evidential basis for believing, about the scene. If one looks at an apple, it may in some sense look French, or look like it is from one's parents' backyard, or look like an apple that has been nibbled at by an animal. But arguably these are not all contents presented by the experience itself.[12] Perhaps only a small subset of the contents that might be

9. In the modern era, notable examples are Gareth Evans 1982, David Kaplan 1989, and John McDowell 1984 and 1986. We prefer the formulation in the text to the simpler idea that a singular thought about x is one which is not possible without x, since this modal gloss is vacuously satisfied for certain non-singular thoughts about necessary beings. For discussion of further subtleties in the vicinity, see Martin 2002. One take-home point from that discussion is that if we do not type mental states by their contents, then there is no easy inference from object-dependence to the conclusion that any thought whose content is object-dependent is such that a thought of that type could not exist in the absence of the relevant object.

10. For relevant discussion, see Evans 1982, p. 71. We only say 'natural corollary'. There are in principle ways to block the inference. One might, for example, hold that any case of a singular thought would have been a case of some other kind of thought if no suitable object existed. Such a view would be especially compelling if one were an advocate of free logic.

11. For an overview, see Siegel 2005, Section 3.

12. For fear of incurring the wrath of disjunctivists, we try as much as possible to avoid the verb 'represents'. While we shall not pursue the point here, we find certain of their anti-representationalist slogans confusing. In particular, the claim that experience does not have its content by representing is often driven by a false dichotomy between a representationalist picture and one according to which real-world items are constituents of the experience. Suppose structured propositions are built out of real-world constituents. Then we can say that a person perceptually represents a structured proposition while admitting the there are real-world constituents of the relevant event.

casually described as part of how the apple looks are manifest in the experience *per se*.[13] (We are not concerned here to defend such a distinction, only to note that it has seemed plausible to many.) Let us use 'LOOKS' to mark the contents that are contents of the experience.[14] Here are two theses that will be of interest:

> WEAK SINGULARISM: In non-hallucination cases, *some* of the propositional contents of experience are typically singular contents about external objects, contents that are presented in a way akin to demonstrative thought (call these demonstratively presented singular contents).
> STRONG SINGULARISM: In non-hallucination cases, none of the propositional contents of experience have quantificational structure. *All* such contents are demonstratively presented singular contents about external objects.[15,16]

Suppose one sees a red apple. It is natural enough to suppose that among the ways things LOOK are: there is an x such that it LOOKS to be the case that x is red; there is an x such that it LOOKS to be the case that x is roughly spherical; and so on. The weak singularist view is happy, in addition, to recognize experiential contents that are non-singular, notably ones that can be described quantificationally: it LOOKS to be the case that something is red; it LOOKS to be the case that something is rolling; and so on. She will no doubt also be happy to recognize experiential contents that contain a mixture of singular and quantificational elements: there is some x such that it LOOKS to be that case that x is covered with many small dots. Finally, she may recognize singular components that are not demonstratively presented. Suppose some x is such that it LOOKS to be the case that x is identical to Richard Nixon. Here, Richard Nixon might appear as part of the content

13. For relevant discussion see Siegel 2006.
14. Chisholm 1957 draws attention to the epistemic use of 'appear words'. In the epistemic use, 'appears that *P*' marks the presence of evidence for *P*. Obviously, the advocate of 'LOOKS' talk will not intend her vocabulary to be understood epistemically.
15. A variant: all the contents are singular contents about the subject and a time and various external objects, where the subject is presented *de se*, the time presented *de nunc*, and the external objects are presented demonstratively. We do not propose to agonize over the choice of variant.
16. Some prominent disjunctivists are quite clearly not strong singularists. McDowell, for example, is very liberal about the kinds of facts that can be 'taken in' perceptually.

even if in fact he is not part of the visual scene and thus not available for demonstrative identification.

Let us see what is implied by weak and strong singularism that is of relevance to disjunctivist projects. Compare someone who hallucinates an apple—call this the bad case—with a molecule-for-molecule duplicate who sees an apple—call this the good case. (The latter person may, of course, be under certain illusions.[17] He may see the apple as bigger than it is, as redder than it is, and so on. What matters here is that the person sees the apple.) Suppose further that, as both singularisms would suggest, at least some of the ways things LOOK in the good case are singular. Let us suppose, for example, that the apple is such that it LOOKS to be the case that *it* is red. On this assumption, we will not think that the contents perceptually presented in the good case are just the same as those in the internally matching case where no apple is seen. If the hallucination occurs in a world where the apple doesn't exist, then the relevant content is not available in that world. And even if the apple does exist, the singular content is not plausibly present in the bad case, since demonstrative access to the apple is unavailable.[18]

Now of course, the weak singularist can still hold that there are perceptual contents that are straightforwardly common to the good and bad case. Perhaps in both cases, it LOOKS to be the case that there is a roughly spherical thing. Perhaps in both cases it LOOKS to be the case that a roughly spherical thing has a large brown spot on it. And so on. She might take such descriptions at face value, as being 'non-gruesome' descriptions of part of what is going on perceptually, not to be analysed in other terms. She might thus think that while there are some contents that divide the cases, there are others that make them fundamentally similar.

17. We are following Sturgeon 1998 and Smith 2002 in stipulating cases of illusion to be those where an object is perceived but is in some sense misperceived and cases of hallucination to be ones in which there is no object of perception. Note that in this paper we shall not pursue views according to which hallucination—as opposed to illusion—is scarcely possible. Such a position would be encouraged by a view (entertained in passing by William Alston (1999)) that in *so-called* hallucinations, a region of empty space is the direct object of perception.

18. Recalling the Nixon case, let us suppose that this is not a case where there is also non-demonstrative singular perceptual representation of the apple.

The preceding discussions point to an unclarity in some of Paul Snowdon's recent remarks about the commitments of disjunctivism. He notes that some philosophers—his non-disjunctivist opponents—hold of experiential occurrences (that include both hallucinations and genuine perceptions of the environment) that they

> are, in a fundamental sense, alike. Clearly, there are different and competing accounts of what their similar nature is, but one aspect of this similarity must be that the experiences themselves, in their nature, do not involve or have as constituents, any items in the external environment. This is a consequence of the thesis of a shared nature, together with our conviction that the non-perceptual experiences do not have such items as constituents. (Snowdon 2005, p. 136)

As we have just seen, there is no logical incompatibility in supposing (a) that there is *a* fundamental similarity between certain hallucination cases and certain non-hallucinatory cases while maintaining (b) that the non-hallucination cases involve, in their nature, items in the external environment.

Consider an analogy with action. Imagine a pair of people, one of whom is playing a guitar, one of whom is playing air guitar. It is plausible that a complete list of the natural, joint-like, action-theoretic properties instantiated by the former individual would include properties that encode engagement with an external object. But that hardly shows that there is no fundamental similarity between the two actions.[19]

Things come out rather differently when we turn to strong singularism. Suppose that the only contents that LOOK to be so in the good case are demonstratively presented singular contents about external objects. One now has to concede there is no propositional content that LOOKS to be the case in both the good and bad case. Given strong singularism, one will be forced to find a LOOKS-content for the bad case that is not present at all in the good case, or else claim that in the bad case no proposition LOOKS to be the case. Suppose one subscribes to the further principle:

19. Granted, one might extend disjunctivism to the case of action. But we cannot imagine any plausible version that would deny a natural similarity between this pair of actions.

BAD CASE PRINCIPLE: There are no propositional contents that LOOK to be so in the bad case that do not LOOK to be so in a relevantly similar good case.

Then one will be forced to the second option just mentioned. Now of course, even if nothing LOOKS to be so in a bad case, one will naturally think that there is *some* good sense in which, when one hallucinates a red apple, something perceptually looks to be red. But one does not need to contrive some singular proposition about some inner episode in order to account for this. One merely needs to find some reasonable sense in which, in the bad case, *it is as if* there is an *x* which LOOKS to be red. And there seems to be every prospect of finding some such reasonable sense.

Strong singularism seems to us to be the driving force behind Paul Snowdon's influential 'Perception, Vision and Causation'. Consider his proposal for how to understand ordinary claims of the form 'It looks to *S* as if there is an *F*':[20]

> It looks to *S* as if there is an *F*; (there is something which looks to *S* to be *F*) $\vee$ (it is to *S* as if there is something which looks to him (*S*) to be *F*). (1980/81, p. 185)

Suppose that strong singularism is true. Then this style of truth conditions for ordinary looks claims (where the 'looks' that appears in the analysis means LOOKS) would appear to have some promise. After all, if 'it looks to *S* as if there is an *F*' is treated as requiring that it LOOKS to be the case that there is an *F*, then every such statement will be false.[21] But if it is glossed as above, such reports can be unproblematically true, even in hallucination cases where it might be argued that nothing LOOKS to be the case.

(We note in passing that, assuming that 'There is something which looks to *S* to be *F*' entails 'It is to *S* as if there is something which looks to him (*S*) to be *F*', the left disjunct is superfluous.[22] But that there is no deep need for disjunctions in articulating the

20. He is interested here in perceptual and not doxastic uses of 'looks'. His account is not designed to extend to the mathematician who says, 'It looks as if the continuum hypothesis is unprovable.'

21. Strong singularism tells us that there are no contents with quantificational structure.

22. Where *P* entails *Q*, '*P* or *Q*' will entail and be entailed by '*Q*'.

central ideas of disjunctivism is a point that Snowdon (2005) later explicitly acknowledges.)

Suppose instead that weak singularism is true. Then Snowdon's proposal is altogether unpromising. Suppose that the LOOKS relation can take quantificational contents as objects. Then there would be no special reason to suppose that when it LOOKS to be the case that there is an *F*, then there is, inevitably, a singular content of the form *a* is *F*. Suppose for example, that in vision a chair can look to have a back.[23] We might still have considerable pause at the claim that there is something that looks to be the back of the chair. In any case, subtleties aside, if the contents of the LOOKS relation often has existential structure, then won't it be overwhelmingly natural to treat perceptual reports of the form 'it looks as if something is *F*' as reporting such structure, rather than as reporting the appearance of a singular content? (The shortcomings of a Snowdon-style analysis are even more obvious for other kinds of quantificational phrases. Supposing quantificational structures can LOOK to be so, there seems no reason in principle why it cannot LOOK to be the case that *most Fs are Gs*. One could hardly treat such a state as equivalent to the disjunction: either most *F*s look to be *G*s or it is as if most *F*s looks to be *G*s. If there are, unbeknownst to *S*, three tigers in the world and two of them look sleepy to *S*, then most of the tigers look sleepy to *S*; but it hardly follows that it looks to *S* as if most tigers are sleepy.)

Meanwhile, with strong singularism in place, we can construct a disjunctivist package that builds upon the following three key ideas:

(D1) The natural perceptual features of experience, by involving relations to objects, require a certain kind of perceptual success—perceiving an object—in order to be instantiated.

(D2) There are no natural perceptual commonalities common between the good case and the bad case.

(D3) There are no natural perceptual features at all instantiated in the bad case.

(D1) is underwritten by the idea that the natural perceptual properties always encode singular contents. The move from (D1)

23. We are grateful for discussions with Richard Price here.

to (D2) can be supported by the idea that in the good case, the objects that figure in the natural perceptual properties are external. And the move from (D2) to (D3) is supported by the Bad Case Principle. This kind of picture should be familiar to those acquainted with disjunctivist discussions. With such a picture in place, one would then, as discussed, set out to make sense of 'looks' ascriptions in the bad case by way of various relationships that the bad case has to ones in which certain natural perceptual properties are instantiated. (Note that within the current framework the distinction between one who sees an object and correctly perceives it as red and one who sees an object and incorrectly perceives it as orange is not pertinent. For the purposes of this particular brand of disjunctivism, illusion—as opposed to hallucination—and veridical perception are lumped together as 'success states'. A very different perspective would result if we treated objects and properties analogously, maintaining that, like the case of an object, a property can only figure as part of what is presented by an experience if that property causally impacts on that experience. This idea is no part of Snowdon's view. We shall return to it at various points in due course.)

Let us voice two concerns about the package just outlined. The first is very simple. As we have seen, the package requires not just weak but strong singularism. Establishing that some perceptual contents are object-dependent singular contents that are demonstratively presented is simply not sufficient to vindicate the disjunctivist ideas that we have just been outlining. We thus stand in need of a compelling set of reasons for favouring strong singularism over weak singularism.[24]

The second concern is that even if all the propositional contents of experience are singular, that hardly secures the conclusion that all the natural perceptual features of experience encode singular contents. One way of developing this concern is well trodden: even granting that there is no content-theoretic natural commonality between the good and bad cases, might there not be other

24. Not that we couldn't imagine a framework that made strong singularism attractive. Some might be drawn to Tractarian picture thinking: The facts out of which the world is built include only objects, properties and relations. There are no quantificational states of affairs—quantification arises at the level of linguistic representation of the world. Suppose further that perceptual mechanisms are built to take in states of affairs, and it will be no surprise that quantificational structures are beyond their ken. (Discussions with Elizabeth Camp were helpful here.)

kinds of natural similarities having to do with phenomenal character? (After all, if there are such similarities, it seems to be little more than wordplay to claim that they aren't 'perceptual'.) While by no means unsympathetic to that version of the concern, we shall in what follows develop it in a slightly different direction.

Let us focus on constructions of the form 'It is as if' as they figure in discussions of perceptual experience. One approach to understanding those constructions is familiar from standard disjunctivist discussions. One glosses 'It is as if *S* has perceptual feature *F*' in terms of epistemic facts about discriminability. At a first pass: It is as if *S* has perceptual feature *F* iff *S* cannot discriminate his situation from one in which *S* is *F*. In this way, one can acknowledge a fairly natural *epistemic* commonality between the good case and the bad case while denying a natural *perceptual* commonality. And one will have made good on understanding the neutral case in terms of the success case: the neutral case turns out to amount to one's standing in a certain epistemic relation to the success case. We shall return to this style of analysis (and its shortcomings) in due course. For now, we simply wish to urge that it is far from obligatory, even for one who thinks that there are no propositional contents that are perceptually presented in the bad case. Let us begin with an analogy. Suppose an English speaker utters

(1) That is red

in a situation where his demonstrative fails to refer. Here we might find it natural to say:

(2) It was as if there was something such that the speaker said of it that it was red.

Now, one way to gloss (2) is in terms of discriminability: the speaker was unable to discriminate his situation from one in which there was some *x* such that he said that *x* is red. But there is another natural way to gloss (2). When we consider an English sentence that contains a singular term that fails to refer, we can describe what that sentence expresses relative to an arbitrary assignment to the empty singular term. Relative to the assignment Bush, the relevant utterance of (1) says of Bush that he is red. And so on. Building on this, we can say something about what a sentence expresses relative to every arbitrary assignment to empty singular terms. And in particular, we can say:

(3) Relative to every arbitrary assignment to empty singular terms in (1), there is some *x* such that (1) says of *x* that *x* is red.

We have arrived at a second way of glossing (2), one which exploits the semantic machinery of assignments, familiar from basic model theory, and which bypasses epistemology altogether. In asserting (3) we can still accept that there was no proposition semantically expressed by (1). But we might still insist that there are fairly natural semantic properties that are common to a pair of utterances of 'That is red', where only one of them enjoys referential success. And the natural commonality, we will say, is captured fairly well by (3). (There is nothing mysterious here. Consider by analogy the open sentence '*x* is red'. That does not express a proposition. Yet that fact does not prevent us from giving it a semantic profile in a fairly direct manner. That open sentences do not express whole propositions hardly induces us to think that they do not have fundamental semantic properties. Why then think that in the case of demonstrative failure, the semantic contribution of 'red' in sentences like (1) has to be cashed out in terms of discriminability?)

Now it is certainly arguable that a similar approach—call it the incomplete proposition strategy—can be taken in the perceptual case.[25] In hallucination, it is natural to suppose that an episode occurs with singular demands that go unsatisfied, and on that account no complete proposition is perceptually presented. But that ought not lead us to think that some such property as redness is not perceptually presented. Just as it is a basic semantic fact that redness is semantically manifest in the failed demonstrative 'That is red', so it is natural to think that redness is, in a very basic way, perceptually manifest in a case where one hallucinates a red thing. Moreover, it seems natural enough to apply something like the above model, suitably adapted to that case. In the bad case, we can speak intelligibly about how things LOOK relative to an arbitrary assignment to its unsatisfied singular demands, and, building on this, make claims such as the following:

25. This is examined briefly in Siegel 2005 and 2006.

> When someone hallucinates a red thing, there is an episode such that, relative to every arbitrary assignment to its unsatisfied singular demands, there is some x such that it LOOKS to be that case that x is red.

In embracing this mode of description, we need not be contesting strong singularism. We might still concede that in the bad case there is no proposition that LOOKS to be the case. But this does not stop us recognizing natural perceptual commonalities of a content-theoretic nature, common to the good and bad case, ones that can be captured fairly well by some such strategy as that noted.

The preceding sketch provides one way of combining strong singularism with the admission of natural perceptual commonalities between the good and bad case, one that is not deeply dependent on considerations having to do with phenomenal qualia. Here is another. Consider a particular bad case that consists of a being with intrinsic structure I embedded in environment C. Let us agree that no proposition LOOKS to be the case to that individual. Yet we can perfectly well recognize a function from possible embeddings $C_1, \ldots, C_n$ to LOOKS facts that displays the way that I generates LOOKS facts according to its environmental surround. (Note that the existence of such a function is unproblematic for even the most diehard disjunctivist.) Now one might introduce such a function by way of proposing a semantics for certain ordinary 'looks' claims, maintaining that the function is, at least in some contexts, the semantic value of the that-clause in a 'looks' ascription. We are rather pessimistic about any such semantic ambition. But the function need not earn its keep by constituting the semantic value of 'looks that' ascriptions. Why not instead fall back on the view that it constitutes a rather natural similarity between the good case and the bad case (even given strong singularism), one that does not depend on facts of discriminability or other epistemic relations between the good and bad case? (Call this the possible embeddings strategy.) This poses a challenge to the disjunctivist: why not see such functions as coding natural similarities between hallucinations and successful experiences, similarities that deserve to be called 'perceptual'?

We have noticed an important conceptual gap between the combined forces of strong singularism and the Bad Case Principle on the one hand, and each of (D1), (D2) and (D3) above. How might the disjunctivist shore up his position? It would certainly help the disjunctivist were the ideas associated with object-dependence to be extendable to the case of properties. Suppose that a property can only be present in experience if it is actually instantiated in the environment and actively impacting the sensory organs. In that case, the incomplete proposition strategy would be far less promising. Yet while instantiation-dependence would certainly help motivate the disjunctivist vision, it requires careful defence in its own right.[26] (Note that the semantic tradition concerning singular thought provides little encouragement here: while the real-world existence of an object is plausibly required for that object to serve as the semantic value of a singular term, the real-world instantiation of a property is not plausibly required for that property to serve as the semantic value of a predicate.) And what of the possible embedding strategy? One option is to trenchantly deny that the commonalities revealed by the embedding strategy deserve the name 'perceptual'. Another would be to retreat from (D1) to (D1*):

> (D1*) All the natural perceptual commonalities between the good and bad case involve relations to perceptual success.

(Coordinately, one might allow that there are natural perceptual features present even in the bad case, namely those encoded by the function that figures in the embedding strategy.)

(D1*) is hardly undermined by the embedding strategy, whose whole point is to trade on functions that encode relations to perceptual success. Sure enough, a package that combines (D1*) with the possible embedding strategy is not conducive to the standard disjunctivist idea of using epistemic relations to connect the good and bad cases. But it is thoroughly in accord with the larger goal of understanding perceptual states via their relations to states of perceptual success.

A compelling disjunctivism may yet emerge from some development of object-dependent themes. But much of the hard work remains to be done.

26. We do not mean to imply that nothing has been done by disjunctivists to motivate such a view. But we do believe that more attention to the specific thesis of instantiation-dependence is in order.

III

Discriminability and Experience. We have already touched on the strategy of providing a negative epistemic characterization of non-success cases, where facts of indiscriminability are given a central role. In this section we wish to examine this idea in some detail. We should note that it is not the only conceivable basis for holding that there are no natural perceptual commonalities between good and bad cases. One might, for example, hold that a good case—perceiving that *P*—involves a relation to a fact (where this is construed as something other than a true proposition), and that a bad case—that of a mere appearing that *P*—involves a different, *sui generis* relation to a proposition. One might then hold further that the neutral case is to be analysed as a disjunction of these two relations.[27] Such a view need not maintain that mere appearing can be analysed in terms of a negative epistemic characterization. This view, like more standard disjunctivisms, claims that there is no natural perceptual state that is common between the success and failure cases, but unlike standard disjunctivisms, does not try to provide an account of failure states in terms of success states. The *sui generis* view of mere appearing does not seem very promising. We shall not explore it here. Discriminability-based approaches have more prima facie promise, and are thus more deserving of serious attention. In exploring the discriminability-based idea, our focus will be on some work by Michael Martin, whose papers on the topic offer a rich and systematic defence of disjunctivism. Within disjunctivist literature, his argumentation is the most intriguing, his discussion the most thorough. There is much in those papers that is worthy of extended treatment. Our aim in this section is the limited one of making salient certain obstacles to discriminability-based accounts.

Martin's conception of a success case is veridical perception. His standard gloss on the paradigm is this: one veridically sees an *F* thing as *F*. His preferred way of distinguishing success from failure is thus rather different to Snowdon's: while they both count hallucination as failure, Snowdon, but not Martin, counts illusion as success. Martin tells us that his motivating

27. Arguably, this is McDowell's view.

picture is 'Naïve Realism' according to which, when I veridically perceive a scene, 'I am conscious of the various elements that make it up' in such a way that 'the concrete individuals, their properties, the events these partake in' are 'constituents of the experience' (Martin 2004, p. 39). Presumably Martin thinks that this partaking is what is distinctive of veridical perception. Even allowing that external elements can be constituents of experience, there is more to be worked out here by way of linking his stated version of Naïve Realism to his choice of success state. Suppose you misperceive an individual as running quickly when he is only running slowly. Arguably both the individual and the running event are constituents of your experience. And supposing that your experience ascribes the property of slow running to another individual in the scene, the property of running slowly can also be a constituent of the experience. One general issue lurking in the background here is this: are there *any* objects such that seeing *them* is sufficient for someone's seeing that the individual is running quickly? Seeing me is not enough. And, as noted, it does not seem that seeing the running event is enough. Are there perhaps some more recherché objects such that seeing them is enough? The state of affairs? A certain trope/property instance? Even if such objects exist, one wonders whether, for each candidate, one might see it and yet fail to see that the individual is running quickly (owing to illusions concerning the object seen).[28] The relation between constituency and success requires further investigation.

Martin's gloss on the paradigm case of veridical perception as one in which one sees an *F* thing as *F* is also a little unsatisfactory. Consider veridical illusions: one sees a spinning object as spinning but one sees it as spinning not because it is spinning but because of a quirk in one's brain that compensates for a trick of the light that would make a normal perceiver in that environment see the object as stationary.[29] In this sort of case, while one perceives veridically—one sees the object as how it is—it is not so clear that one sees the event of spinning. Assuming with orthodoxy the link between naked infinitivals and event perception, we can put

28. And as Siegel noted in correspondence, it is not plausible that such recherché objects are parts of the naïve conception of things.
29. The importance of veridical illusion to the theory of perception is stressed by Johnston (2004, 2006).

the point as follows: granted, one perceives the object as spinning when it is in fact spinning. But one does not see it spin. Even having decided to pick on a factive state, considerations such as these invite a choice of fundamental success state other than the one that figures in Martin's explicit statements of disjunctivism.[30] Perhaps *perceiving that an object is F* (or at least: being in a position to perceive that an object is *F*) is a better paradigm for a suitably 'naïve realist' account of perception.[31] Having voiced our reservations, we shall persist with Martin's choice of success state as the starting point for a discriminability-based analysis. Many of the concerns will transfer to other disjunctivist applications of the discriminability approach.

Martin offers the following as a key commitment of disjunctivism:

> The notion of a visual experience of a white picket fence is that of a situation being indiscriminable through reflection from a veridical visual perception of a white picket fence as what it is. (Martin 2006)

Generalizing, we can say that a situation visually presents *P* iff the subject, *S*, is unable to know through reflection that s is not having a veridical visual presentation that *P*. This implements the abstract strategy of analysing neutral states (and failure states) in terms of success states: the fundamental perceptual states are veridical perceptions, while neutral descriptions merely encode epistemic relations to the fundamental states.

Martin adds 'through reflection' to rule out certain sources of information. If I am hallucinating, I may know this by testimony even though I cannot know by 'reflection' that I am not perceiving a white picket fence as white (Martin 2004, p. 76; 2006). It is clear that for the purposes of the analysis Martin wants us to 'bracket' information from testimony. It is not clear what else he wants us to bracket, however. Suppose I am under the visual illusion that something is at rest, but am also touching it and learning thereby that it is spinning. Does this count as knowing 'by reflection' that one is not visually perceiving a stationary object as stationary?

30. We realize, of course, that Martin is well aware of the category of veridical illusion. Our concern is with how he chooses to describe the paradigm case of success.

31. Perhaps instead the relation of 'taking in', as a relation between a subject and a fact is basic (cf. McDowell 1994), where this may not correspond to any ordinary piece of natural language vocabulary—ordinary language may not carve perception at its joints.

If so, we have a problem for the analysis. If not, then we need a more careful gloss on 'by reflection'. Some natural restrictions are also potential trouble spots. Suppose we said 'through reflection on one's visual experience'. Such a gloss risks implying that there is a visual episode with a positive nature that is present to be reflected upon in the bad case—an idea that Martin does not seem comfortable with. The pressure towards a positive gloss will intensify if we wish to rule out knowledge acquired from processes like blindsight as relevant to what can be known by reflection. (And presumably we will, since blindsight is irrelevant to how things look.) The problem may be very serious. We shall now press some other concerns.[32]

Degraded Epistemic Powers. Martin is well aware that some people, not to mention animals, have degraded powers of discrimination. A being that did not have the concept of a veridical visual presentation is always unable to know that he is not having a veridical visual presentation as of a white picket fence. Same for a being who does not have the concept of a white picket fence. And a being that is extremely poor—through drunkenness, carelessness, wishful thinking, or belief-tampering Martians—at discriminating veridical presentations of cream from those of white is unable to tell that he is not having a veridical presentation of a cream picket fence when in fact he is having a veridical presentation of a white one. However, no one wants to be forced into holding that under such circumstances the relevant being is suffering from a visual illusion, wherein the veridical perception of white is accompanied by an illusion of cream. Martin's solution is to idealize:

> [I]t is entirely consistent with this appeal to indiscriminability to grant that two experiences might be indiscriminable through reflection for some particular agent, John, without the two experiences thereby being of the same kind. For John may be unable to know the difference between them due to some specific incapacity on his part—the excess of alcohol or lack of interest in the matter—which would not generalize to other individuals. (Martin 2004, p. 76)

32. For overlapping critical discussion, see Siegel 2004 and her unpublished commentary on Martin 2006. There are also points of overlap with Gendler and Hawthorne 2006.

Consider two particular successive veridical experiences, one of a white picket fence, another of a cream picket fence, that some individual John, who is drunk, or canine, or endemically inattentive, is unable to discriminate. There are two particular experiential episodes, e_1 and e_2, that John is unable to discriminate. Now what could it mean to say that those episodes were nevertheless discriminable? One way of making sense of this would be to deploy a quite extravagant metaphysics of events. One might claim that there is a possible world where *those very experience tokens*, e_1 and e_2 occur in a being that is able to discriminate them. Suppose John is a kind of creature that is unable to pay sufficient attention or is unable to achieve sufficient conceptual sophistication in order to make the relevant discrimination. The extravagant approach would either need to maintain that the subject of an experience *token* is inessential to it, or else that there is a world where the actually mediocre creature has a radically different cognitive architecture. We very much doubt that any, naïve, common-sense view of the mind would seriously entertain this kind of metaphysical radicalism. And in any case, even leaving common sense out of it, the relevant metaphysical commitments seem very dubious.

There are further worries about the extravagant approach. Arguably some features of an event or experience are inessential to it. A killing that is quick might have been a little less quick. An explosion that is very loud might have been a little less loud. But this raises a problem. We need to screen off the following possibility: an experience e_1 might have been discriminable from e_2 on account of the fact that it might have been different in certain ways that are relevant to how things look. Now what one wants to say here is that the look of the experience is, in its entirety, essential to it. But how do we say this if we disallow ourselves any positive characterization of hallucinatory experiences? We wish to say of some hallucinatory experience e that it could have been discriminated from an experience as of a cream picket fence. Intuitively, we think this is because, *holding the character of the experience fixed*, there is a world where one has that very experience and knows one is not veridically perceiving a cream picket fence as cream. But how is this thought to be captured within a framework that allows only a negative epistemic characterization of hallucinatory experiences?

Here is a second, more natural, way of making sense of the contrast between what is discriminable for John and what is discriminable *simpliciter*. Suppose John is unable to discriminate e_1 and e_2. In claiming that the pair is nevertheless discriminable, we can naturally be understood to be claiming that there is some possible being with a *duplicate* pair of experiences e_3 and e_4 (where e_3 duplicates e_1 and e_4 duplicates e_2) such that e_3 is discriminable from e_4. We would then have:

> An experience e is an experience as of a white picket fence if there is no possible experience e_2 such that e_2 duplicates e and such that the subject s of e_2 knows by reflection that s is not having a veridical perception as of a white picket fence.

This is all natural enough, but it is not conducive to Martin's project. For notice that some such predicate as 'duplicate' now appears as an ineliminable feature of the analysis. The ambition of making do with negative epistemic characterizations of hallucinatory experiences can only be made good upon in this setting if the predicate 'duplicate' can itself be given an epistemic gloss. But given that it is now playing a fundamental role in making sense of the facts of discriminability, there seems little prospect of analysing it away using epistemic notions.

In his 2006 paper, Martin is sensitive to concerns of this sort. He pursues a third approach, one that makes the notion of what is discriminable *simpliciter* part of his primitive ideology, not to be analysed in other terms. He introduces the notion of 'impersonal indiscriminability' to mark what is 'impossible *simpliciter*' (and not just impossible for the subject) to tell apart by introspective reflection on that subject's experiences. And having done so, he makes clear that he does not think that there is any counterfactual or modal account of what it means for my experiences to be impersonally discriminable from cases of veridically perceiving a cream object.[33] Where most of us have looks states as the primitive building blocks of non-veridical experience, Martin has irreducible facts of impersonal discriminability. (He would of course be happy to concede a neurological supervenience base for such states.) But crucially they are stand-ins for the primitive perceptual looks states

33. See especially n. 44 in Martin 2006, which responds to worries raised by Siegel that are similar to those voiced in the preceding paragraphs.

of the non-disjunctivist, not epistemic conditions that are to be ultimately explained by states of that sort. A primitive impersonal epistemic condition thus plays the role that others would give to a primitive perceptual condition. Martin sees that such primitivism offers by far the best prospect for a stable version of his position. Readers who hope for negative epistemic characterizations of looks states will have to learn to live with primitivism of this sort.

Of course, some of us will certainly worry about the ground-floor role accorded to primitive states of impersonal indiscriminability, where such facts about me are detached from what I am able to do (since that would bring in my own failings) and what other people are able to do (since that risks bringing in bizarre counterpossibles). Suppose a verificationist in the old days were to shore up his claim that to be true is to be verifiable by remarking, 'By verifiable I mean impersonally verifiable, and so our limitations are irrelevant.' We would be outraged. It is not clear that heavy reliance on an impersonal notion of verifiability is much more satisfying in the restricted domain of experience.

Intransitivity of Indiscriminability. Let us turn to Martin's discussion of problems posed by the intransitivity of indiscriminability. Here is the problem, in its starkest form: indiscriminability, construed as a relation between token experiences, is intransitive. But 'things look the same to the subject of x as to the subject of y' ('same in look', for short) is an equivalence relation on experiences. So indiscriminability with respect to experiences cannot underwrite sameness of look. Consider two *token* veridical perceptions, one of which happened yesterday, the other the day before. Supposing those experiences were discriminable, then we can say with confidence that how things looked yesterday was different to how things looked the day before. Suppose now I have an hallucination that I cannot discriminate from either yesterday's experience or the one that occurred the day before. If we hold that indiscriminability is sufficient for sameness in look, we will be pushed to say that how things look now is both the same as how things looked yesterday and also the same as how things looked the day before. But the transitivity of 'same in look' blocks any such conclusion.

Let us turn to Martin's treatment of the matter. He suggests various strategies.[34] One is to claim that there is no fact of the matter as to what kind of illusion is occurring on a particular occasion: 'All the facts about experiences in general are to be stated just in terms of whether a subject could know the distinctness of these experiences ... This pattern of facts is just not well enough behaved to ground the existence of kinds' (2004, p. 77). Focusing on the identity of how things look colour-wise, the suggestion is, in effect, that one gives up on classifications such as the one provided by 'It looks as if there is something white'.[35] If my hallucination is not known to be other than a veridical perception of white, and not known to be other than a veridical perception of cream, then there is no further question as to whether things now look white to me or cream to me (or whether instead I have a look that presents a determinable of which white and cream are determinates but which does not present either determinate). Note that this is to give up on the analysis presented earlier of 'visual experience as of a white picket fence', since the current suggestion is that such a predicate is defective. This view seems very hard to sustain. For one thing, it is extremely hard to shake off the idea that if I am an intrinsic duplicate of another member of my community that is veridically perceiving cream but not white, then I am someone for whom things look cream—whether or not I have the epistemic wherewithal to take this in. But more generally, we should think twice about dismissing large segments of natural language vocabulary as defective.[36]

We should also not forget that claims of defectiveness can easily spread in uncomfortable ways to other segments of language, via their conceptual links with the vocabulary that has been indicted. One particular worry is that we will now no longer be well placed

34. Apart from those discussed in the body of the text, there is a further strategy available, one that unabashedly relies on the primitive ideology of impersonal indiscriminability. The key move would be this: while personal indiscriminability is intransitive, impersonal indiscriminability is transitive. We are not attracted to an impenetrable fortress built upon the rock of impersonal indiscriminability.

35. After all, the suggestion is that there is no such kind, not merely that it has borderline cases.

36. It has been suggested to us that certain disjunctivists have a general sympathy to the idea that talk of accuracy conditions for perceptual experience is ultimately misconceived. It is far from clear that such a view can be reconciled with our ordinary ways of describing perceptual experience.

to understand questions about whether someone is under an illusion, even in a relatively normal case. Suppose someone perceives a non-cream picket fence. Suppose the colour is a shade that is close to cream but falls just short of cream, so that the person (even when we idealize away from inattention, and so on) is unable to know he is not perceiving a cream picket fence as having a certain shade of cream. So is this person under the illusion that the fence is a certain shade of cream or not? With the kind 'looks cream' discarded as defective, we are deprived of our normal way of understanding the question (which would be in terms of whether the fence looks cream even though it isn't).

Let us examine some less radical approaches to the problem, ones that allow for the classification of illusory and hallucinatory experience into kinds. One idea in the vicinity is to combine idealization with extravagant metaphysics: an ideal perceiver with those very experience tokens could discriminate between them if they do not look the same. We have already indicated our concerns about an approach of this kind. Of more interest is an alternative proposal, sympathetically entertained by Martin, to 'follow Williamson's suggestion that while in a given context a subject may fail to discriminate two samples, this does not show that there is no context in which the samples are discriminable and hence one can hold on to the claim that distinct samples are discriminable in at least some context' (Martin 2004, p. 77).

Now, Williamson's discussion is built around a sharp distinction between *presentations*, the token episodes that present visual experiences, and the looks—or *characters*—that are enjoyed by those experiences. With this in place, he shows that the phenomenon of intransitivity can be reconciled with the principle that for any pair of characters *a* and *b*, *a* and *b* are identical iff they are indiscriminable (call this Subjectivity).[37] The key notion of discriminability, as a relation between characters, is one according to which a pair of characters are discriminable iff there is some possible pair of presentations *x* and *y* of those characters such that one knows that the character of *x* is not the character of *y*. Subjectivity is perfectly compatible with (a) the possibility that

37. Williamson (1990) had some sympathy towards but never outright endorsed this idea.

there be a pair of presentations x and y that have distinct characters but where one does not know that the character of x is not the character of y and (b) the scenario where there are a series of presentations x, y, z such that one does not know whether the character of x is the character of y, and one does not know whether the character of y is the character of z, but one does know that the character of x is not the character of z.

It is altogether unclear to us how Martin thinks that this framework can underwrite the idea that truths about how things look are to be grounded in negative epistemic properties. The equivalence relation *same in look* determines various disjoint sets of experiences. For each set, every pair of members is the same in look, and nothing outside the set is the same in look as a member of it. In this setting, Williamson's framework can be applied by regarding the token experiences as presentations and the sets given by the equivalence class as characters. Suppose that a subject has two successive presentations, p_1 and p_2. When undergoing p_1, things look F to S (where the extension of 'things looks F to x' is the set of people with experiences with the character of p_1). When undergoing p_2, things look G and not F. Suppose now that the subject is not able to tell that the way things look when undergoing p_1 is distinct from the way things look when undergoing p_2 (even though the way things looks when undergoing p_1 is in fact distinct from the way things look when undergoing p_2). Subjectivity (in combination with the simplifying assumption that all the relevant possibilities are actual) tells us that there is some pair of presentations p_3 and p_4 with the characters of p_1 and p_2 such it is known that the character of p_3 is not the character of p_4. But none of this implies that the subject who undergoes p_1 is able to know that the character of p_1 is not the same as the character of x. Nor does it even imply that for some presentation x with the character of p_2, he is able to know that the character of p_1 is not the character of x. We are left with a mismatch between 'things looking F' and 'not being able to know that the character of one's experience is other than looking F'. For all that we learn from Subjectivity, Martin's proposal is still a failure.

We have some difficulty reconstructing Martin's own reasoning about the matter. Here is one bit of reasoning in the vicinity that is tempting but fallacious: 'Given Subjectivity, it is possible for a subject to know that F-ness is not G-ness—via two possible experiential episodes/presentations. If so, can't we imagine the subject bringing such knowledge to bear with the result that he knows by reflection that p_2 is not a presentation of *F*-ness?' To reason in this way would be to miss much of the point of the apparatus that Williamson introduces. To put the relevant point by way of informal analogy: Suppose there are two people, *x* and *y*. There is a possible circumstance in which I know *x* and *y* are different—suppose in scenario *A*, I see that *x* is sitting at one end of the room and *y* at the other. Suppose in another scenario, *B*, *x* is standing behind me and puts his hand on my shoulder, and then shortly afterwards, *y*, who is standing behind me, puts his hand on my shoulder. In that situation I cannot tell that the person presented by the first experience is the same as the person presented by the second experience. And nor would I be able to tell this even were I to have had the benefit of scenario *A* prior to scenario *B*. True enough, it can be argued that thanks to scenario *A* I would have the *de re* knowledge that *A* is not *B*. But I would not be able to bring that knowledge to bear in order to know that the person presented by the second shoulder-touching experience is distinct from the first. The reason is clear enough: it is because I do not know such facts as that the person presented by a certain shoulder-touching experience is the person presented by such-and-such an experience in scenario *A*.

In the 'The Reality of Appearances', Martin writes:

> On either of Goodman's or Williamson's proposals, a subject may be unable to determine whether succeeding experiences have the same phenomenal character. Nevertheless, consistent with this, one can hold that the phenomenal character of the experience is determined by (or at least coincident with) the subject's powers of discrimination. There seems to be an intuitive sense in which Goodman's and Williamson's suggestions do still hold on to the intuitive appeal of assimilating identity of conscious state to subjective indistinguishability. (Martin 1997, p. 99)

But this altogether misunderstands Williamson's discussion of the logics of phenomenal character (including his critique of Goodman),[38] which is driven by the formal result that, even

38. See Williamson 1990, pp. 65–87, which also contains his critique of Goodman 1951.

assuming (a) the obvious fact that sameness in character entails indiscriminability with regard to character and (b) Subjectivity, the global pattern of facts of discriminability, as between presentations, do not fix the facts of sameness in character as between presentations.[39] Thus Martin is mistaken if he thinks that some such principle as the Subjectivity principle is going to save his indiscriminability-based analysis of looks statements. The Subjectivity principle institutes some sort of connection between non-identity of characters and the possibility of *de re* knowledge of non-identity of characters. But it provides no reason whatsoever to suppose that *looks the same*, an equivalence relation on experiences, can be analysed using negative epistemic properties.

Note also that we should not ignore the distinction between maximally determinate characterizations of experience and more determinable ones. Suppose a particular experience e_1 is not a presentation of cream, but is not known not to be (suppose it presents a colour rather similar to cream). There is a certain determinable which experiences as of cream (that may vary in the shade presented and other respects) share. Call that CREAM. Subjectivity tells us that for any experience e^* that does not look the same as e_1, there is a pair of possible experiences x and y that duplicate e_1 and e^* respectively that are known to be different in character. But it says little about our ability to classify experiences under determinable kinds. In particular it does not tell us that there is a possible experience that duplicates e_1 that is known *not to have* the determinable CREAM. Safety-theoretic considerations—of the kind that figure in Williamson's recent (2000) anti-luminosity discussions—can easily be brought against any such proposal. For it may well be that any veridical perception experience that duplicates e_1 could easily be mistaken for a veridical perception of cream. In that case a belief that one was not veridically perceiving cream, made in the presence

39. As Williamson acknowledges, it is possible to give this result a 'no fact of the matter' spin: in so far as the global facts of discriminability between episodes underdetermine sameness of character, there is no fact of the matter as to which relation is denoted by 'same in character'. This spin would take us back to the first of Martin's ideas for handling the intransitivity problem.

of a duplicate of e_1, would not be safe enough to count as knowledge.[40]

De Re Beliefs. As the shoulder-touching analogy would indicate, certain of the problems just posed for indiscriminability-based accounts of looking *F* can be easily adapted to generate problems for indiscriminability-based accounts of what it for it to look as if a particular individual is present. Suppose I see a certain tree as tall. There is an *x* such that I perceive that *x* is tall. Suppose I recently saw a tree *y* that is in fact different to *x*, but I do not know that *y* is different to *x*. Under such circumstances I may not know that I am not veridically perceiving *y* as tall. Similarly for hallucination. Suppose I hallucinate a tall leafy tree falling. I have seen a number of tall leafy trees recently, including *x* and *y*. I may not be able to know by reflection that I am not now veridically perceiving *x* falling. And I may not be able to know by reflection that I am not now veridically perceiving *y* as falling. But it hardly seems that under such circumstances it must look to me that *y* is falling and that *x* is falling. After all, my hallucination may be altogether silent as to which particular tree appears to be present. There is a difference between my hallucinating talking to some particular person *x*, and my hallucinating talking to someone or other who is *F*, *G* and *H*, where in fact *x* is *F*, *G* and *H*. One further example (built upon Williamson 1990, p. 56): Suppose I see a stick *x* pointing out of the left side of a blanket and then see a stick pointing out of the right side of the blanket. Now it is true that I may not be able to know that I am not veridically perceiving *x* as pointing out of the right side. But it hardly follow that it looks to me as if *x* is pointing out of the right side. On the contrary, my experience may be neutral as to whether the stick pointing out of the right side is or isn't the stick pointing out of the left. That two things do not look to be different is not the same as two things looking to be the same. The negative epistemic characterizations, as applied to *de re* beliefs, risk conflating such distinctions among how things look. The structure of the problem is the same

40. Safety considerations may ultimately make trouble for the Subjectivity principle itself. If we are so constituted as to be prone to mistaken judgements of identity and difference as between experiences that are close in character, judgements of difference as between very close characters may never be safe enough to count as knowledge. Here is not the place to pursue this issue further.

in these cases as in the problems induced by the intransitivity of indiscriminability. There are cases where we cannot reliably tell x is absent from our perceptual life (x may be an object or a property) even though x does not look to be present. Scenarios of this shape make trouble for the negative epistemic gloss on looks statements.

IV

Martin's Master Argument.[41] We wish finally to look at a style of argument that Martin (2004, 2006) uses against those who believe that there is more to looks properties than is captured by negative epistemic characterizations. This argument is intended, *inter alia*, to tell against those who hold that there are phenomenal characters that are instantiated by experiences and which cannot be captured by the negative epistemic gloss. And it is intended to tell against those who hold that there are representational properties instantiated by experiences which cannot be captured by the negative epistemic gloss.

If a view embraces 'positive characterizations' of non-veridical experiences, Martin labels it 'immodest'. If a view endorses only negative epistemic characterizations of such experiences, he labels it 'modest'. He argues that proponents of the immodest view are under considerable pressure to concede that the immodest view is extensionally correct in its account of the conditions under which things look a certain way. But such a concession is then reckoned to make real trouble for the immodest view. We shall focus on that portion of the argument that attempts to force a concession of extensional equivalence from proponents of an immodest view.

First he argues that if an experience is, by immodest lights, an experience as of a certain kind of street scene, then it will, by modest lights, also be an experience of that kind of street scene. The immodest view holds that such an experience involves the instantiation of properties $E_1 \ldots E_n$. But:

> After all, by immodest lights the kind of experience one has when seeing such a street scene is of just the same kind as any

41. For further critical discussion of this argument, with a different emphasis, see Siegel 2004.

> non-perceptual event which is not a perception but still an experience as of a street scene, namely an event with the properties $E_1 \dots E_n$. Since nothing can be discriminated from itself, the immodest approach will hold that the modest one should agree that these events are indiscriminable from a veridical perception of a street scene and hence are perceptual experiences as of a street scene. (Martin 2004, p. 48)

The key move 'since nothing can be discriminated from itself' is too quick. Again we should take care to distinguish particular token presentations from more and less determinate characters that are instantiated by those presentations. There are both facts of identity and difference as between presentations and also facts of identity and difference between characters. Granted the character given by $E_1 \dots E_n$ cannot be discriminated from itself. But it does not follow immediately that any token that has $E_1 \dots E_n$ cannot be known to be a token that is not a veridical perception of the relevant kind of street scene. (Certainly, it is numerically distinct from those perceptions, so the facts of identity and difference do not settle the matter.)

There are two assumptions driving Martin's discussion, both of which one might question. First, he seems to assume on behalf of the immodest view that if an experience is to be known not to be *F* (where *F* is the property of veridically perceiving that *P*, for some *P*), then one's ability to know this will be explained merely by invoking the properties that the immodest view cites as constituting the looks properties. It is not clear that this should be conceded. Consider an analogy. Some might think that if I know that I am not dreaming, this will be because my experience has certain distinct phenomenal properties. But it is far from clear that this is so—a reliable belief-forming mechanism might proceed via causal paths that do not rely on the phenomenal character of the experience. Similarly in the case of illusion. Suppose a person was able to contort his face to produce certain visual appearances. When he did this he might know that he was not veridically perceiving a scene even though the character of the experience was just the same as if he were experiencing that scene. Similarly, we might be wired to believe as false certain illusory experiences that make the world look certain ways. In such a case the belief might be very safe and thus the subject knows himself not to be having a veridical perception that *P*; but it would still look to the subject that *P*. Is there a way to tweak 'reflection' so that none of these cases count as knowing *by reflection* that onc is not veridically perceiving thus and so? It is not clear how this is to be done. It thus seems that there is here a class of cases where the immodest and modest approaches potentially come apart.

Turning to the second assumption, Martin assumes that the only properties exemplified by any visual presentation of that kind of street scene will be E_1 to E_n. But this in general is not a fair assumption to make. He is in the business of comparing modest and immodest accounts of looks properties. Some of those looks properties will be rather determinable-like: certainly, few, if any, will correspond to maximally specific characters. Thus presentations as of the relevant kind of street scene may have immodest properties in *addition* to E_1 to E_n. But this raises the possibility that one may exploit one or more of those other properties to know by reflection that one is not veridically perceiving the relevant kind of street scene. (Notice that the remark that 'nothing can be discriminated from itself' has absolutely no force in this connection.) We might imagine a being for whom a certain immodest property *F* was the hallmark of fatigue-induced hallucination, and who was wired to believe that experiences with *F* were not veridical. Such a person might know that a certain experience (with *F*) was not a veridical perception as of a certain kind of street scene. (Suppose for example that the street scene appeared to be taking place directly above one's head, or that an experience had immodest properties distinctive of perception of a street scene but also additional immodest properties that gave it a dreamlike quality.) Such an experience might certainly possess E_1 to E_n and thus, by immodest lights, count as a visual presentation of that kind of street scene.

Step one of the argument was intended to show that if something is an immodest perception of a street scene, then it is a modest one. Step two is designed to induce proponents of an immodest view to accept the conclusion that if something is a modest perception as of a street scene, then it is an immodest one. According to this line of argument, the immodest view would be embarrassed were it to claim that the modest view is 'too catholic in its conception of what can be an experience as of a street scene' (Martin 2004,

p. 49). The key idea is that in a case of veridical perception of a kind of street scene, all that we ordinarily notice is the presentation of certain bits of external reality: 'Even if the experience does also possess the characteristics $E_1 \ldots E_n$ it need not manifest to the perceiver that these are present as opposed to Naïve realist aspects of experience' (ibid., p. 49). Given that this is all that we know about in the good case, it then seems plausible, argues Martin, to think that the link between the good case and the bad case (illusion or hallucination) is 'the seeming presence of Naïve phenomenal properties', where Naïve phenomenal properties are ones that encode the presence of certain bits of external reality. Thus Martin argues that common sense will count any case in which the relevant bits of external reality seem to be present as cases of looking a certain way. If the immodest view is not to collide with good common sense, it will have to claim that $E_1 \ldots E_n$ is present whenever common sense says that a street scene of the relevant kind seems to be present. This is then to concede that if something is a modest perception of a street scene then it is also an immodest one. This conclusion, in combination with the previous argument, is supposed to push the immodest view into the position of conceding that the modest account is at least extensionally adequate.

The relevant line of argument does not strike us as convincing. Let us begin by granting that all that we ordinarily know about in the good case are Naïve phenomenal properties that are constituted by relations to objects and properties out there in the world. Is Martin right that 'the seeming presence of Naïve phenomenal properties' would be the natural way to link the good and bad cases? Let us distinguish 'seeming that *P*', construed as 'not knowing that *P* is not the case', with 'seeming *P*', construed as 'having some strong inclination to believe that *P* is the case'. Now the former does not seem like any reasonable gloss on 'seeming' as it is used in English. The latter is in the vicinity of the familiar 'doxastic' use. We would have thought that it is some such doxastic use that provides the natural link in the set-up that Martin envisages (at a first pass: what makes something a bad case is that we have some inclination to believe that we are veridically perceiving certain things), especially when we emphasize that a strong inclination to believe may not yield belief when competing forces stand in the way. But in that case, it is not plausible to set out to capture ordinary looks statements by a negative epistemic gloss.

The contrast between the doxastic and the negative epistemic links becomes particularly evident in cases where one's ability to know is compromised. Suppose you sometimes disguise yourself as *S*'s brother. Someone hallucinates *S*'s brother as being in the room. That person does not know that she is not veridically perceiving you in the room. For you could easily have been in the room. By the negative epistemic test it looks to be the case that you are in the room. By the doxastic test it does not. Clearly the doxastic test is the more natural one here.

It also bears emphasis that common sense may maintain other kinds of links between the good case and the bad case (even on the assumption that it is only aware of Naïve phenomenal properties in the good case.) Let us suppose that redness is a real-world property. Supposing that naïve common sense reckons *being red* to be a constituent of the experience in the good case when one veridically perceives a red tie, isn't it arguable that naïve common sense reckons it also a constituent of experience when one hallucinates a red tie? Let us be naïve for a moment. If someone had never actually seen a real red thing but had hallucinated a red tie, then doesn't it seem right to say that the person had *encountered redness* in experience?[42] Prior to the hallucination the person may not have had a grip on what redness was like. But doesn't naïve common sense tell us that the person got a good long look at redness during the hallucination—such a good look that he now knows what it is like for something to be red? It thus seems like Martin's own proposal fails to square with a naïve conception of hallucination. It is also worth adding in this connection that Martin's favoured approach will, by naïve lights, be short on explanatory material. Let us focus on a case where someone hallucinates a white picket fence and cannot know by reflection that she is not veridically perceiving a white picket fence as a white picket fence. Let us ask the natural question

42. Some such common sense reflections lie behind Price's remark that even in a case of hallucination, there is no doubting the fact that a 'field of colour is directly present to my consciousness' (1932, p. 3). The naïve conception of hallucination is one of the driving forces of Mark Johnston's approach to perceptual experience, though we do not wish to imply that his reasons for holding the view are merely naive (see Johnston 2004, 2006).

'Why is the person unable to know (by reflection) that she is not veridically perceiving a white picket fence as a white picket fence?' A natural answer suggests itself to common sense: because it looks to that person as if there is a white picket fence there. But suppose that the property of being someone for whom it looks that there is a white picket fence *is* the property of being someone who cannot tell by reflection that she is not veridically perceiving a white picket fence. Then the explanation that common sense offers takes on a quite different shape. It has the feel of 'Because he is an unmarried male' as an answer to 'Why is he a bachelor?' But it is quite clear, intuitively that the original explanation was offered as a causal explanation, not a definitional one. Thus Martin's approach appears to deprive common sense of an explanation that it finds altogether compelling.

Let us turn briefly to Martin's idea that naïve reflection on our veridical experience construes it as constituted by presentation of real-world properties. As he sees it, naïve common sense populates the world with a rich array of properties. When something looks amusing, naïve common sense tell us that there is a property—being amusing—that it looks to have. A slightly trickier case is one where a circular object has an oval look. In such a case it does not seem that one needs to be under any kind of visual illusion. Naïve common sense, as Martin construes it, will in this sort of case populate the world not merely with shape properties such as being circular, but also with looks: whether or not anyone is there to see it, there is that oval look that the plate has.

We do not wish here to get too caught up in quibbles about whether naïve common sense reckons that it is only real-world properties that are known about in veridical perception. Some will say that common sense does not suppose that the mood of an experience or the blurriness of an experience is constituted by the presentation of 'naïve phenomenal properties'. Others will try to finesse such examples (though their methods for doing so seem far from naïve). And some will have sympathy with Thomas Reid who, having declared his 'resolve ... always to pay a great regard to the dictates of common sense' (Reid 1764, p. 113), distinguishes the smell of the rose construed as a quality of the object from the sensation that the smell produces in the mind, noting that 'The smell in the rose, and the sensation which it causes, are not conceived, even by the vulgar, to be things of the same kind,' and that when our sensations 'are so quick and lively as to give us a great deal either of pleasure or of uneasiness . . . we are compelled to attend to thc sensation itself and to make it an object of thought or discourse' (ibid., p. 114). And some will have general worries about attributing broad philosophical judgements on quite delicate matters to ordinary people. (What exactly is the basis for our supposing that the folk think that only naïve phenomenal properties are manifest in, say, veridical auditory experience? We need some methodology for sorting out some putative common-sense view if we are not simply to end up fusing strands of our own philosophical tradition with off-hand conjectures about our family and friends.) For now, though, let us concede that vulgar common sense conceives of veridical visual and olfactory experiences and so on in such a way that they are wholly constituted by relations to external qualities and objects.

Still, it is worth wondering why vulgarity is to be celebrated. Martin himself does not appear to have much patience with vulgar conceptions of hallucination. Why then be so enamoured with vulgar conceptions of perceptual success? Suppose naïve common sense tells us that when people have varying colour perceptions of a single thing owning to slight variations in lighting or contrast conditions or biological constitution, then at most one of the perceptions is veridical. And perhaps naïve common sense tells us that there is a single real-world colour, pure green, that is the test for veridicality of the visual experiences of any creature that looks at certain samples and a set of real-world timbres whose presence or absence determines the veridicality of the auditory experience of one who is in fact exposed to the Doppler effect. But we can't see much point in pursuing the philosophy of perception in a setting where it is assumed that such commitments will survive philosophical and scientific reflection. After all, we shouldn't think that vulgar common sense has seen in advance how to handle various challenges to its commitments. When confronted with the fact that under normal lighting conditions there is wild divergence among normal observers concerning which shades are pure green, naïve common sense gets confused and throws up its hands. And when it learns that perceived pitch timbre and loudness is largely determined by a little membrane inside the ear that performs a kind of Fourier analysis on the incoming perturbations, naïve common sense expects to receive new and potentially confounding insights about which real-world properties he is sensitive to in audition, and about where they are instantiated.[43] Granted, some clever philosophers have found ways to cling on to something like the naïve commitments in the face of such challenges and discoveries. But the ways that they do it are not naïve—nor is it even clear that naïve common sense would find the resultant package at all natural or appealing.

Martin is well aware, of course, that there are philosophical pressures on us to say that naïve common sense mistakes properties that concern our inner life for properties that are detected in the world. Clearly he is unmoved. But it bears emphasis that those of us who have succumbed to those pressures will find nothing persuasive in the above line of argument for the modest view. For in that case, we will think that, whatever vulgar common sense has to say about the matter, the nature of veridical experience is not wholly constituted by Naïve phenomenal properties.[44]

References

Alston, W. 1999: 'Back to the Theory of Appearing'. *Philosophical Perspectives*, 13, pp. 181–203.

Austin, J. L. 1962: *Sense and Sensibilia*. Oxford: Clarendon Press.

Brewer, B. 1999: *Perception and Reason*. Oxford: Oxford University Press.

Broad, C. D. 1925: *The Mind and Its Place in Nature*. London: Kegan Paul.

Child, W. 1992: 'Vision and Experience: The Causal Theory and the Disjunctive Conception'. *Philosophical Quarterly*, 42, pp. 297–316.

—— 1994, *Causality, Interpretation and the Mind*, Oxford: Oxford University Press.

Chisholm, R. 1957: *Perceiving*. Ithaca, NY: Cornell University Press.

Crane, Tim. 1992: 'The Nonconceptual Content of Experience'. In T. Crane (ed.), *The Contents of Experience*. Cambridge: Cambridge University Press.

Dancy, J. 1995: 'Arguments from Illusion'. *Philosophical Quarterly*, 45, pp. 421–38.

43. And imagine how we might have been forced to reconfigure common sense were we to have discovered that Descartes was right that perceptual imagery is determined by 'ideas ... which are traced ... on the surface of gland H [which are] the forms or images which the rational soul united to this machine will consider directly when it imagines some object or perceives it by the senses' (1664, p. 106). On such a discovery it seems that we would be encouraged to think that perceptual experience—typed at its joints—is constituted by relations to animal spirits on the surface of the pineal gland and not, after all, by relations to objects that lie outside the confines of our bodies.

44. We are grateful to audiences at Brown University and Oxford University for helpful discussion, and to Elizabeth Camp, Richard Heck, Richard Price, Susanna Siegel, Scott Sturgeon, Dmitri Tymoczko and Timothy Williamson for helpful comments and discussion.

Descartes, R. 1664: *Treatise on Man*. In J. Cottingham, R. Stoothoff and D. Murdoch (eds), *The Philosophical Writings of Descartes*. Cambridge, Cambridge University Press, 1985, pp. 99–108.

Evans, G. 1982: *The Varieties of Reference*. Ed. J. McDowell. Oxford: Clarendon Press.

Gendler, T. S. and J. Hawthorne 2006: *Perceptual Experience*. New York: Oxford University Press.

Goodman, N. 1951: *The Structure of Appearance*. Cambridge, MA: Harvard University Press.

—— 1954: *Fact, Fiction and Forecast*. Cambridge, MA: Harvard University Press.

Hinton, J. M. 1967: 'Visual Experiences'. *Mind*, 76, pp. 217–27.

—— 1973: *Experiences*. Oxford: Clarendon Press.

Jackson, F. 1977: *Perception*. Cambridge: Cambridge University Press.

Johnston, M. 2004: 'The Obscure Object of Hallucination'. *Philosophical Studies*, 103, pp. 113–83.

—— 2006: 'The Function of Sensory Awareness'. In Gendler and Hawthorne 2006.

Kaplan, D. 1989: 'Demonstratives'. In J. Almog, J. Perry and H. Wettstein (eds), *Themes from Kaplan*. Oxford: Oxford University Press.

Lewis, D. 1983: 'New Work for a Theory of Universals'. *Australasian Journal of Philosophy*, 61, pp. 343–77.

Martin, M. G. F. 1997: 'The Reality of Appearances'. In M. Sainsbury (ed.), *Thought and Ontology*. Milan: FrancoAngeli.

—— 2001: 'Beyond Dispute'. In T. Crane and S. Patterson (eds), *The History of the Mind–Body Problem*. London: Routledge.

—— 2002: 'Particular Thoughts and Singular Thought'. In A. O'Hear (ed.), *Logic, Thought, and Language*. Cambridge: Cambridge University Press.

—— 2004: 'The Limits of Self-Awareness'. *Philosophical Studies*, 120, pp. 37–89.

—— 2006: 'On Being Alienated'. In Szabo and Hawthorne 2006.

McDowell, J. 1982: 'Criteria, Defeasibility and Knowledge'. *Proceedings of the British Academy*. Reprinted in McDowell 1998.

—— 1984: '*De Re Senses*'. *Philosophical Quarterly*, 34, pp. 283–94. Reprinted in McDowell 1998.

—— 1986: 'Singular Thought and the Extent of Inner Space'. In P. Pettit and J. McDowell (eds), *Subject, Thought, and Context*. Oxford: Clarendon Press.

—— 1994: *Mind and World*. Cambridge, MA: Harvard University Press.

—— 1998: *Meaning, Knowledge, and Reality*. Cambridge, MA: Harvard University Press.

Price, H. H. 1932: *Perception*. London, Methuen.

Prichard, H. A. 1950: *Knowledge and Perception*. Oxford: Clarendon Press.

Reid, Thomas 1764: *An Inquiry Into the Human Mind, or Principles of Common Sense*. In *The Works of Thomas Reid*. Edinburgh: Maclachlan, Stewart and Co., 1849.

Robinson, H. 1985: 'The General Form of the Argument for Berkeleian Idealism'. In J. Foster and H. Robinson (eds), *Essays on Berkeley: A Tercentennial Celebration*. Oxford: Clarendon Press.

—— 1994: *Perception*. London, Routledge.

Smith, A. D. 2002: *The Problem of Perception*. Cambridge, MA: Harvard University Press.

Snowdon, P. F. 1980/81: 'Perception, Vision and Causation'. *Proceedings of the Aristotelian Society*, 81, pp. 175–92.

—— 1990: 'The Objects of Perceptual Experience'. *Proceedings of the Aristotelian Society Supplementary Volume*, 64, pp. 121–50.

—— 2005: 'The Formulation Of Disjunctivism: A Response To Fish'. *Proceedings of the Aristotelian Society*, 105, pp. 129–41.

Siegel, S. 2004: 'Indiscriminability and the Phenomenal'. *Philosophical Studies*, 120, pp. 90–112.

—— 2005: 'The Contents of Perception'. In Edward N. Zalta (ed.), *The Stanford Encyclopedia of Philosophy (Summer 2005 Edition)*. Available at: http://plato.stanford.edu/archives/sum2005/entries/perception-contents/.
—— 2006: 'Which Properties are Represented in Perception?' In Gendler and Hawthorne 2006.
—— unpublished: Comments on Martin 2006.
Sturgeon, S. 1998: 'Visual Experience'. *Proceedings of the Aristotelian Society*, 98, pp. 179–200.
—— 2000: *Matters of Mind*. London: Routledge.
Valberg, J. J. 1992: *The Puzzle of Experience*. Oxford: Clarendon Press.
Williamson, T. 1990: *Identity and Discrimination*. Oxford: Basil Blackwell.
—— 1995: 'Is Knowing a State of Mind?' *Mind*, 104, pp. 533–65.
—— 2000: *Knowledge and Its Limits*. New York: Oxford University Press.

DISJUNCTIVISM

by John Hawthorne & Karson Kovakovich
and Scott Sturgeon

II—Scott Sturgeon

REFLECTIVE DISJUNCTIVISM

ABSTRACT The paper aims to do five things: sketch the backbone of disjunctivism about visual experience, explore the view of our title, defend a version of that view from two objections, press two more objections of my own, and sketch a more radical variety of disjunctivism which avoids much of the bother.

I

Working to a Disjunction. There are three types of visual experience: veridical perception, illusion and hallucination. The first two involve perceptual contact with the world but the third does not. All three involve conscious portrayal of the world as being some way. Veridical perception, illusion and hallucination have two key sides: a perceptual side and a conscious portrayal side.

There is widespread disagreement about what they come to. There is no serious consensus about how experience portrays the world as being; and there is none about how it makes for perceptual contact. Most agree visual experience has portrayal and perceptual sides, but no one agrees on the details. Except for this: everyone thinks the two sides are deeply connected. Whether an event counts as a veridical perception, illusion or hallucination turns on the way its conscious portrayal of the world is grounded in its perceptual contact with it.

An event is a veridical perception, for instance, if its portrayal of the world is fully grounded in its perceptual contact with it. Veridical perception is a more demanding category of consciousness than is often supposed, more than just accurate perceptual contact with the world. Veridical perception is accurate perceptual contact the accuracy of which comes through, but only through, perceptual contact as such. Veridical perception is the best kind of visual experience, occurring when the portrayal side of an experience springs fully from its perceptual side.

Or again: an event is an illusion if its conscious portrayal of the world springs partly from its perceptual contact with it. Illusion is a less demanding category of consciousness than is often supposed, less than just inaccurate perceptual contact with the world. Illusion is perceptual contact the accuracy or otherwise of which comes through, but not only through, perceptual contact as such. Illusion is the second-best kind of visual experience, occurring when an experience's portrayal side comes some but not fully through perceptual contact. There are veridical as well as delusive illusions. Old chestnuts involve inaccurate perceptual contact with the world—say when a partially submerged stick looks bent despite being straight—but new chestnuts involve accurate perceptual contact too—say when a red herring looks red not because it is so but because of the ambient light. What makes for illusion—what old and new chestnuts have in common—is conscious portrayal of the world yoked to, but not drawn wholly from, perceptual contact with it.

Or again: an event is an hallucination if its conscious portrayal of the world is not grounded in perceptual contact with that world. Hallucination too is a less demanding category of consciousness than is often supposed, more than just inaccurate non-perceptual portrayal of the world. Hallucination is the worst kind of visual experience, occurring when an experience manifests fully non-perceptual portrayal of the world. There are veridical as well as delusive hallucinations. Old chestnuts involve delusive portrayal of the world—say when Macbeth hallucinates his dagger—but new chestnuts involve accurate portrayal too—say when a red herring is hallucinated to be where a red herring chances to be. What makes for hallucination—what old and new chestnuts have in common—is conscious portrayal of the world unyoked to perceptual contact with it.

There are three types of visual experience: veridical perception, illusion and hallucination. They have portrayal and perceptual sides; and the former can be grounded in the latter to various degrees. We shall remain neutral about how all this works, taking no stand on how exactly visual experience portrays the world, no stand on how it perceptually connects to the world, and none on how the former might be grounded in the latter.

We shall simply speak—to simplify things—of Good and Bad experiences, Good and Bad episodes, Good and Bad cases. And we shall assume without argument that every experience is either Good or Bad but not both.[1]

This leads to a thought prominent in work on disjunctivism:

$$(1)\quad VE^{\Phi}(x) \leftrightarrow [G^{\Phi}(x) \vee B^{\Phi}(x)].$$

Put in English: an episode is a visual experience as of Φ exactly when it's either a Good Φ-case or a Bad one. This comes to the idea that an episode is a visual experience as of Φ exactly when one of two things occurs: either the episode is a conscious portrayal of the world as of Φ aptly grounded in its perceptual contact with the Φ-side of the world, or the episode is a conscious portrayal of the world as of Φ not so grounded.

II

The Backbone of Disjunctivism. Disjunctivism is not so much a theory of visual experience as a rough approach to the topic. Its defenders include Michael Hinton, Mike Martin, John McDowell and Paul Snowdon. These philosophers believe all manner of things about visual experience. Often those things conflict with one another. One must tread carefully, then, when shooting for the backbone of the approach. One stands no chance of hitting it unless one aims at a high level of abstraction. That will be my strategy.

I suggest two views are jointly the backbone of disjunctivism (or at least should be). One concerns the conscious character of Good cases—what it's consciously like to enjoy Good visual experience. The other concerns the conscious character of Bad cases—what it's consciously like to enjoy Bad visual experience. The backbone claim about Good character is this:

(Good) Good character derives from bits of the physical world standing in an explanatorily basic relation to percipients.

1. Sturgeon forthcoming shows how to preserve our discussion yet relax this assumption. I take no stand here (or there) on the Good–Bad status of illusion. Sturgeon forthcoming discusses this further.

The idea here, roughly, is that what it's like to enjoy Good experience is fixed by the explanatorily fundamental perceptual contact one has with the world. That loose idea can be understood in various ways. McDowell says that Good cases involve real-world facts manifesting themselves to percipients; and he treats the manifestation relation as explanatorily basic. Martin says that Good cases involve objects, events and features being taken in by percipients; and he treats the taking-in relation as explanatorily basic. Other disjunctivists spell out (Good) in their own way. But all claim—or at least should claim—that Good character comes from explanatorily basic conscious perceptual contact with the world. This idea is the soul of disjunctivism's take on Good character. It is said to be drawn directly from perceptual contact with the world, contact that cannot be explained in more basic mental idioms. This is the most important half of disjunctivism's backbone.

The other half concerns Bad character:

(Bad) Bad character does *not* derive from bits of the physical world standing in an explanatorily basic relation to percipients.

The idea here, roughly, is that what it's like to enjoy Bad experience is not fixed by explanatorily basic perceptual contact with the world. This thought can be spelled out in multiple ways too; and that yields a range of disjunctive positions. In turn they can be ordered by the degree of difference seen between Good and Bad cases.[2] Our target today—Reflective Disjunctivism—sees a very great difference indeed.

Like all versions of disjunctivism, the Reflective version claims that Good character derives from bits of the physical world standing in an explanatorily basic relation to percipients. Like all versions of disjunctivism, the Reflective version claims that Bad character does not derive in that way. But Reflective Disjunctivism distinguishes itself from other versions of disjunctivism—and thereby earns its name—by claiming that Bad character derives from *negative epistemics*: in particular, it says that Bad character derives from Bad cases being reflectively indiscriminable from Good ones. As we'll see in a moment, the key idea is that

2. Sturgeon forthcoming lays out the range in detail.

visual experience as such is nothing but a state of reflective indiscriminability from Goodness.

There are many ways to fill out the picture. They all result in a view which claims that Good cases involve people standing on the catching-end of an explanatorily basic relation to bits of physical reality, while Bad ones involve nothing like that at all. Reflective Disjunctivism insists that Bad cases are just situations which cannot be reflectively discriminated from Good ones; and Bad character is spelled out by appeal to negative epistemics: when Macbeth hallucinates his dagger, for instance, what it's like for him is said to derive *solely* from his inability to discriminate his case by reflection from one of seeing a dagger properly. Reflective Disjunctivism denies that Good and Bad cases share a deep metaphysical structure. It sees Good ones as relational and Bad ones as epistemic. It is a radical form of disjunctivism. Our next task is to explore its details, merits and demerits.

III

Sketching the Approach. Recall that a Bad case involves conscious portrayal of the world as being a way to which the portraying case is not aptly grounded. Reflective Disjunctivism spells out such cases by appeal to reflective indiscriminability from Goodness—by appeal, that is to say, to indiscriminability from Goodness by introspective reflection.[3] An episode is said to be a Bad Φ-case only if it is so indiscriminable from Good Φ-cases:

(2) $B^{\Phi}(x) \rightarrow x\mathbf{IND}g^{\Phi}$.[4]

3. As Siegel 2006 notes, however, it seems possible that visual experience portrays the world as being a way it could not be—Escher-wise, so to say. If that is right, such experience will almost certainly be reflectively discriminable from veridical perception. Martin's way with the issue—sketched at the end of his 2004—is to apply his reflective construction in the first instance to elements of experience rather than whole experiences. He does not say enough for me to know what to think of his proposal, so I ignore the whole issue in this paper. Chapter 5 of Sturgeon 2001 reinforces the worry.

4. Here and in much of what follows I am vague in my symbolization. This is done for a reason: I want to use English idioms quite common to the literature on visual experience—some of which I wrote myself—along with natural-but-multiply-interpretable symbolizations of them. This should raise pointed questions of interpretation as we go. The hope is that all of those questions will be resolved into recognizably clear symbols by the end.

On the broad conception of indiscriminability used by Reflective Disjunctivism, moreover, Good Φ-cases turn out to be automatically indiscriminable from themselves. We'll see why that's so in a moment; for now we note merely that facts of this form turn out to be conceptual truths:

(3) $G^{\Phi}(x) \rightarrow x\mathbf{IND}g^{\Phi}$.

Put in English: an episode is a Good Φ-case only if it is indiscriminable from Good Φ-cases.

Now recall that (1) is the claim that an episode is a visual experience as of Φ exactly when it's either a Good Φ-case or a Bad one. This, (2) and (3) jointly entail the following claim about visual experience:

(4) $VE^{\Phi}(x) \rightarrow x\mathbf{IND}g^{\Phi}$.

Put in English: an episode is a visual experience as of Φ only if it is indiscriminable from Φ-Good cases. A striking feature of Reflective Disjunctivism—to be vetted in due course—is that it accepts the converse idea:

(5) $x\mathbf{IND}g^{\Phi} \rightarrow VE^{\Phi}(x)$.

Put in English: an episode is indiscriminable from Φ-Good cases only if it is a visual experience as of Φ.[5] Reflective Disjunctivism is thus led, via (4) and (5), to its *über*-commitment about the extension of visual experience:

(6) $VE^{\Phi}(x) \leftrightarrow x\mathbf{IND}g^{\Phi}$.

Put in English: an episode is a visual experience as of Φ exactly when it is indiscriminable from Good Φ-cases.

If that is right—and we'll consider whether it is in a moment—the most natural explanation would be the identity of visual experience and indiscriminability. (6)'s truth would be most cleanly explained by Reflective Disjunctivism's *über*-commitment

5. Reflective Disjunctivism must find a non-question-begging way to delineate the episodes available to introspective reflection. In a sense, after all, episodes unavailable to it are automatically indiscriminable from anything else by its means. I shall take this as read in what follows, always assuming that episodes under discussion are introspectable. For relevant discussion, see Siegel 2006's distinction between strong and weak indiscriminability properties and the last note of this paper.

about the nature of visual experience:

$$(7)\quad \lambda x \mathrm{VE}^{\Phi}(x) = \lambda x(x\mathbf{IND}g^{\Phi}).$$

Put in English: being a visual experience as of Φ is identical to being a state indiscriminable from Good Φ-cases; in other words, being a Φ-experience is the same thing as being an episode that cannot be reflectively discriminated from such cases. This is the view's core conception of visual experience. It sees it as nothing but reflective indiscriminability from Goodness.[6]

To understand the view properly we need a better grip on its notion of reflective indiscriminability. There are several versions of this notion at work in the philosophical literature. In principle, each could be used to build a version of Reflective Disjunctivism. Exhaustive treatment of the approach thus requires inspecting every (7)-like claim got by appeal to a working notion of indiscriminability; it might even require inspecting every such claim got by appeal to a coherent notion of indiscriminability. We have no time for that here—thank goodness—so we focus instead on the prominent type of indiscriminability notion found in philosophical discussion of perception. That notion turns on the idea of *knowledge*.

To see how, note that indiscriminability is inability to discriminate. On a knowledge-based understanding of indiscriminability,

6. After putting forth its own version of (Good), Martin 2006 defends restricted versions of

> (N=) The notion of a visual experience as of Φ is that of an episode being indiscriminable from a Good Φ-case;

and

> (C=) The conscious character of Φ-experience as such is nothing but indiscriminability from a Good Φ-case.

The first claim identifies the notion of being a visual experience as of Φ and the notion of being indiscriminable from a Good Φ-case. If that identification is right, (6) is true as well; for the identification claims that notions mentioned in (N=) are co-extensive, and their identity would guarantee that co-extension. Moreover, (C=) says that visual character as such is nothing but indiscriminability from Goodness. If this identification is right, (7)—and thus (6)—must be true as well; for (7) claims that the state of being a visual experience is identical to that of being indiscriminable from Goodness; and that must be so if conscious character is nothing but indiscriminability from Goodness. In defending restricted versions of (N=) and (C=), Martin 2006 defends such a version of Reflective Disjunctivism. The view is also defended in Martin 2004, and Martin suggests it can be found in Hinton 1967 and 1973.

moreover, discrimination is itself the activation of knowledge; in particular, it is the activation of knowledge that things are not a certain way. This means that a knowledge-based take on indiscriminability sees it as the inability to activate knowledge that things are not a certain way. When the root idea is applied to (6) the result is

$$(8)\quad \mathrm{VE}^{\Phi}(x) \leftrightarrow \neg\Diamond\mathbf{K}[\neg(x \approx g^{\Phi})];$$

and when it is applied to (7) the result is

$$(9)\quad \lambda x \mathrm{VE}^{\Phi}(x) = \lambda x \neg\Diamond\mathbf{K}[\neg(x \approx g^{\Phi})].$$

Put in English: the first claim is that an episode is a visual experience as of Φ exactly when it cannot be known not to be a Good Φ-case; and the second claim is that an episode's being a Φ-experience is identical to its being not possibly known not to be a Good Φ-case.

Pulling all this together, then, Reflective Disjunctivism plumps for (Good), (Bad), (9), and so (8). The view claims that Good character derives from bits of the physical world standing in an explanatorily basic relation to percipients. It continues that Bad character does not derive in that way. And it accounts for the source of Bad character by appeal to the purely experiential nature of Bad cases. This is then fleshed out via negative epistemics. The picture is one on which visual consciousness as such is a state of reflective indiscriminability from Goodness—a state of such indiscriminability from bits of the physical world standing in an explanatorily basic relation to percipients.

IV

Working Through Some Details. Our take on Reflective Disjunctivism should depend on how principles (8) and (9) are fleshed out. That can be well understood by seeing how proponents of them might deal with challenges put to their view. Working through several such challenges turns out to be a useful way to see how Reflective Disjunctivism must be interpreted if it's to be credible. To that end, note the right-hand sides of (8) and (9) each lean on three non-trivial items: modality, knowledge, and the claim that x is not a Good Φ-case. The rest of this section presents challenges to these principles. Responses to them help fix a take on the modality, knowledge and claims used by Reflective Disjunctivism.

What About Everyday Knowledge of Badness? It is a datum of everyday life that we can know—in certain contexts at least—that we suffer visual illusion; and it is a datum of everyday life that we can know—in certain contexts at least—that we suffer visual hallucination. It is part of everyday life, therefore, that we can know—in certain contexts at least—that our visual experience is not Good. That seems to conflict with (8) and with (9); for if we know that a given visual episode is not Good, it must *be* not Good by the factiveness of knowledge. It follows that we *can* know of a Bad one that it is not Good; and that looks to mean that visual experience pulls apart from inability to know by reflection that one's experience is not Good. In turn, that looks to conflict with the extensional claim at (8) and the identity claim at (9). Everyday knowledge of Badness puts pressure on Reflective Disjunctivism from the start.

That pressure must be alleviated by restricting the source of knowledge used in the approach. Specifically, Reflective Disjunctivism must say that its knowledge can only come by introspective reflection. For short: it can only come *by reflection*. The thought must be that when one knows in everyday circumstances that one's visual episode is not Good, that knowledge is got other than by such reflection. It could be got by appeal to testimony, as Martin notes in his 2004; so Reflective Disjunctivism must stipulate that knowledge got in that way is not reflective in the experience-making sense. This is how everyday knowledge of Badness will be marked as compatible with the intended readings of (8) and (9). That knowledge will be said not to refute Reflective Disjunctivism from the start; for the view will be said not to cover every kind of knowledge in its founding principles. It will be said to cover only knowledge got by reflection.

Later we'll see whether a restriction like this can be made to work. Here we take it for granted and mark it in our notation:

$$(8)_{kr} \quad \mathrm{VE}^{\Phi}(x) \leftrightarrow \neg\Diamond\mathbf{KR}[\neg(x \approx g^{\Phi})];$$

$$(9)_{kr} \quad \lambda x \mathrm{VE}^{\Phi}(x) = \lambda x \neg\Diamond\mathbf{KR}[\neg(x \approx g^{\Phi})].$$

Put in English: the first claim is that an episode is a visual experience as of Φ exactly when it cannot be known by introspective reflection not to be a Good Φ-case; and the second claim is that an episode's being a Φ-experience is identical to its being not possibly known by such reflection not to be a Good Φ-case.

What Claim is Involved Here? Reflective Disjunctivism is grounded in a knowledge-based understanding of reflective indiscriminability. Before we can understand it properly we must know what kind of claim is used in the (negative) knowledge facts said to make for such indiscriminability. The symbolization of this at (8) and (9)—along with its expression in English—was left purposefully vague on this issue. Now we must fix the detail in line with Martin's take on the topic.[7]

In his 2004 and 2006, Martin appeals to a knowledge-based notion of reflective indiscriminability; and he understands his notion in terms of claims about the Goodness or otherwise of episodes. Discrimination from Goodness turns on knowledge of non-Goodness; so discriminability turns on the possibility of such knowledge, and indiscriminability turns on its impossibility. On his approach,

$$(\mathbf{ind})_{\mathbf{m}} \quad x\mathbf{INDG}^{\Phi} \leftrightarrow \neg\Diamond\mathbf{KR}\neg G^{\Phi}(x).$$

Put in English: an episode is indiscriminable from Good Φ-cases exactly when it is not possible to know by reflection that it does not have the feature of Φ-Goodness—exactly when it is not possible to know by reflection, that is to say, that the episode in question fails to have the nature which makes for Φ-Goodness.

When this take on indiscriminability is applied to (9), the result is a Martinized version of Reflective Disjunctivism's main claim about the extension of visual experience:

$$(8)_{\mathbf{kr\text{-}m}} \quad VE^{\Phi}(x) \leftrightarrow \neg\Diamond\mathbf{KR}\neg G^{\Phi}(x).$$

Put in English: an episode is a visual experience as of Φ exactly when it is not possible to know by reflection that it fails to have the feature of being a Good Φ-experience. Indiscriminability here is understood via knowledge got by reflection; and that

7. Other takes are discussed in Farkas 2006, Siegel 2006 and Sturgeon forthcoming. Each generates its own version of Reflective Disjunctivism.

knowledge is understood to concern a claim about the episode failing to have Φ-Goodness. When one cannot know by reflection that a given episode is distinct from Φ-Good cases, on this view, *what* cannot be known is the claim that the episode does not have the feature of being a Φ-Good case.

When Martin's take on indiscriminability is applied to (9), the result is a Martinized version of Reflective Disjunctivism's main claim about the nature of visual experience:

$$(9)_{\textbf{kr-m}} \quad \lambda x \mathrm{VE}^{\Phi}(x) = \lambda x \neg \Diamond \mathbf{KR} \neg \mathrm{G}^{\Phi}(x).$$

Put in English: an episode's being a Φ-experience is identical to its being not possibly known by reflection to lack the feature of Φ-Goodness. Here indiscriminability is understood via knowledge got by reflection; and that knowledge is understood to concern a claim about the lack of a certain feature.

What About Kids, Puppies and the Like? It is a fact of everyday life that some visual experiencers *lack* the capacity for reflective knowledge seemingly presupposed by (8) and (9). Small children cannot reflect introspectively yet they enjoy visual experience; and the same is true of puppies and other creatures of diminished epistemic capacity. There are visual experiencers who cannot reflect introspectively and thus cannot know anything by doing so. This puts pressure on (8) and on (9).[8]

That pressure must be relieved, in my view, by de-coupling the possibility of knowledge used in the approach from capacities enjoyed by visual experiencers. The idea would be to read (8) and (9) so that manifestation of visual experience does not oblige personal epistemic capacity. Rather, visual experience would be said to require *impersonal* epistemic impossibility of some kind. The key question would then be: What kind of possibility is that?

This is a good question; but I do not think it is an unanswerable one. Nor do I think such impersonal modality is a creature of darkness to be avoided if possible. The challenge to Reflective Disjunctivism posed by kids, puppies and the like does not

8. Hawthorne and Kovakovich 2006, Siegel 2006 and her unpublished object to Reflective Disjunctivism on these grounds. The response in Martin 2006 is critiqued at the end of the sub-section. Note 9 explains why I think Hawthorne and Kovakovich misconstrue that response.

amount to refutation of the view. There is a straightforward response to the challenge. Here's how it goes.

A common thought in epistemology is that its subject matter includes impersonal norms or idealizations. When degrees of belief are said to be rational only if measured by probability functions, for instance, the idea need not be that rational agents must actually possess the personal capacity to make their degrees of belief conform to the probability calculus if they are to be subject to probabilistic norms. The idea could be that such norms are impersonal, that they limn the contours of rationality divorced from epistemic capacity. Or when belief sets are said to be rational only if logically consistent, for instance, the idea need not be that rational agents must actually possess the personal capacity to make their entire set of beliefs conform to logic if they are to be subject to norms of logic. The idea could be that logic-based norms are impersonal, that they limn the contours of rationality divorced from epistemic capacity.

Impersonal idealizations are the meat and potatoes of epistemic theory. There is no reason Reflective Disjunctivism should be disallowed from using them. They provide a good resource for dealing with challenges to the approach based on diminished epistemic capacity. On my view defenders of that approach should use them to do so. They should deal with kids, puppies and the like by appeal to idealization implicit in their theory. The idea would be to read modality on the right-hand sides of (8) and (9) as impersonal idealized epistemic possibility. Just as norms of consistency can be seen to involve impersonal epistemic modality—namely, an impersonal epistemic impossibility of contradiction lurking within rational belief—so (8) and (9) could be seen to involve impersonal epistemic modality—namely, an impersonal epistemic impossibility of reflective knowledge that one's case is not Good. On this interpretation of (8) and (9), their modal operator is an idealized epistemic operator abstracting from real-world capacity to know by reflection.

Norms of logic are often thought to make for an impersonal space of possibility concerning justified belief. The idea is that they fix what is impersonally possible for such belief. Similarly, norms of probability theory are often thought to make for an impersonal space of possibility concerning rational degrees of belief. The idea is that they fix what is impersonally possible for such credence. My view is that (8) and (9) should be thought of as resting on similar norms, only this time the norms should be said to apply to reflective judgement rather than belief or credence. Reflective norms—as we might call them—make for an impersonal space of possibility concerning reflective judgement. They fix what is impersonally possible for knowledge grounded in such judgement.

On this approach, reflective norms—together with logic, conceptual links and other a priori tools, of course—make for a space of impersonal possibility. Modal operators in (8) and (9) reflect the contours of that space. Martinized Reflective Disjunctivism makes use of impersonal idealization; and the resulting view is one on which (Good) and (Bad) are true along with these principles:

$$(8)_{\mathbf{m}} \quad \mathrm{VE}^{\Phi}(x) \leftrightarrow \neg\Diamond_{\mathbf{imp}}\mathbf{KR}\neg\mathrm{G}^{\Phi}(x).$$

$$(9)_{\mathbf{m}} \quad \lambda x\mathrm{VE}^{\Phi}(x) = \lambda x\neg\Diamond_{\mathbf{imp}}\mathbf{KR}\neg\mathrm{G}^{\Phi}(x).$$

Put in English: the first claim is that an episode is a visual experience as of Φ exactly when it is not impersonally possible to know by reflection that it fails to have the feature of Φ-Goodness; and the second claim is that an episode's being a Φ-experience is identical to its being not impersonally possible to know by reflection that it lacks that feature.

Epistemic idealization is an impersonal matter. Reflective Disjunctivism tries to pin down the nature of visual experience in epistemic terms. When those terms are said to involve epistemic idealization, the resulting view entails that the nature of visual experience is an impersonal matter, one unfixed by capacities of those who visually experience. The resulting view de-couples the nature of visual experience from capacities of those who enjoy it; and for this reason, the resulting view is not threatened by visual experiencers of diminished capacity. Proponents of Reflective Disjunctivism are well advised, then, to see their resources to involve idealization. That is the lesson of kids, puppies and the like.

Here I depart from Martin's response (2006) to the worry of this sub-section. He argues that that worry itself presupposes that reflective knowledge is the upshot of non-trivial faculties or mechanisms of introspection. He then claims that Reflective

Disjunctivism is implicitly committed to the denial of that presupposition; and he spells out that denial by appeal to the rejection of non-trivial necessary conditions for reflective judgement.

My view is that the worry of this sub-section has nothing to do with faculties or mechanisms, nothing to do with non-trivial necessary conditions on introspective judgement. After all: there are sufficient conditions for such judgement—as Martin concedes (2006, p. 392)—so let C be the condition which holds exactly when an agent satisfies one of them—exactly when, that is to say, she satisfies one of the nomically possible sufficient conditions for reflective judgement. Do children or puppies ever satisfy C? As they are incapable of introspective judgement, it does not seem that they do—nor does it seem that they *can*—so the worry of this sub-section can be raised while rejecting faculties and mechanisms in Martin's sense. It does not presuppose that there are such things.

Defenders of Reflective Disjunctivism should sidestep the worry of this sub-section by appeal to epistemic idealization. They should see visual experiencers of diminished capacity as enjoying sufficiently robust background states—beliefs, veridical perceptions, and so forth—to fall under impersonal norms of reflective judgement. They should then make use of the impersonal nature of such norms to clarify how agents of diminished capacity can be visual experiencers despite their diminished capacity.[9]

What about the Non-transitivity of Indiscriminability? There is a worry for Reflective Disjunctivism that turns on the non-transitivity of indiscriminability. It can be roughly sketched as follows: there might be episodes *u*, *v* and *w* so that *u* is indiscriminable from *v*, *v* is indiscriminable from *w*, while *u* is discriminable from *w*. Were this to happen, one could not tell

9. Hawthorne and Kovakovich misconstrue Martin's response to the worry of this sub-section. They see his 2006 as resolving it by appeal to impersonal indiscriminability. Section VI of that paper explicitly rejects such an approach to the problem: '[I]t really is not clear,' Martin says on p. 383, 'how establishing the possibility of impersonal claims of indiscriminability will help with our initial problem in respect of the dog.' He goes on to argue that the key to resolving the problem turns on whether introspective judgement rests on non-trivial faculties or mechanisms. Hawthorne and Kovakovich do not speak to this. They argue instead that the approach defended above is no good, unsuccessfully in my view.

that u was not the same as v, one could not tell that v was not the same as w, but one could tell that u was not the same as w. For reasons to be spelled out in a moment, that possibility puts pressure on the idea that a feature of episodes is pinned down by indiscriminability facts concerning them; and that, in turn, puts pressure on Reflective Disjunctivism's claim that experiential features as such are pinned down by indiscriminability.

This all takes some explaining. Our game plan will be to spend a paragraph setting out a general fact about relations and properties; then we'll examine whether that general fact makes trouble for Reflective Disjunctivism. Here are the steps in order:

General Fact. No non-transitive relation **R** and feature **F** can be so that for variable x and y:

$$(^*)\quad [\mathbf{F}(x)\ \&\ \mathbf{F}(y)] \leftrightarrow x\mathbf{R}y.$$

To see this, suppose a non-transitive relation **R** and feature **F** do make $(^*)$ true for variable x and y. Then by **R**'s non-transitivity there can be a, b, and c so that a stands in **R** to b, b stands in **R** to c, but a does not stand in **R** to c. Since a stands in **R** to b, the right-to-left direction of $(^*)$ entails that a and b each have feature **F**. Since b stands in **R** to c, that direction of $(^*)$ entails that b and c each have feature **F**. This means a and c both have feature **F**. The left-to-right direction of $(^*)$ then entails that a stands in relation **R** to c. This contradicts our assumptions about **R** and **F**, so those assumptions must be wrong. No non-transitive relation **R** and feature **F** can make $(^*)$ true for variables x and y.

The Rub. Reflective Disjunctivism uses indiscriminability to build a conception of visual experience. The general fact constrains how this might be done. To see how, recall the view's basic take on the extension of visual experience:

$$(6)\quad \mathrm{VE}^{\Phi}(x) \leftrightarrow x\mathbf{IND}g^{\Phi}.$$

Put in English: an episode is a visual experience as of Φ exactly when it is indiscriminable from Good Φ-cases. This claim looks a lot like $(^*)$ in our general fact; in particular, it looks to have this form:

$$\mathbf{F}(x) \leftrightarrow x\mathbf{R}y.$$

That isn't quite the general fact's (*); but we can get to it with no difficulty.

After all, Reflective Disjunctivism sees the claim that x is indiscriminable from Good Φ-cases as meaning *something* to the effect that x cannot be known not to be a Good Φ-case. The factive nature of knowledge ensures that Good Φ-cases cannot be known not to be Good Φ-cases (however the item of knowledge is understood). For this reason—as mentioned before—the view sees claims of this form as conceptual truths:

(3) $\mathrm{G}^{\Phi}(x) \rightarrow x\mathbf{IND}g^{\Phi}$.

The right-to-left direction of (6) then ensures that Good Φ-cases conceptually count as visual experiences as of Φ. But that fact joins with (6) to entail

(10) $[\mathrm{VE}^{\Phi}(x)\ \&\ \mathrm{VE}^{\Phi}(g^{\Phi})] \leftrightarrow x\mathbf{IND}g^{\Phi}$.

And this claim looks very much like our general fact's (*). Indeed: when **F** is set equal to the feature of being a visual experience as of Φ, **R** is set equal to a binary relation of indiscriminability, and '$x\mathbf{IND}g^{\Phi}$' is read to involve that relation, (10) is revealed as a claim of this form:

(*) $[\mathbf{F}(x)\ \&\ \mathbf{F}(y)] \leftrightarrow x\mathbf{R}y$.

The general fact then has bite; for when (10) is so read, it ensures that (10)'s relation of indiscriminability is transitive. Yet the indiscriminability of episodes can look clearly non-transitive.

For instance, suppose you see a given white picket fence on Monday, Wednesday and Friday. Each time you see it from the same point of view; and each time the fence and its surroundings are exactly the same, save for this: the fence changes colour each day, shifting subtly from one shade of white to another. Suppose there are five shades of white involved. The fence has the first one on Monday, the second one on Tuesday, and so forth. It looks possible that your veridical perception on Monday is indiscriminable from your veridical perception on Wednesday, your veridical perception on Wednesday is indiscriminable from your veridical perception on Friday, yet your veridical perception on Monday is discriminable from your veridical perception on Friday. After all, the shades of white may render Monday–Wednesday differences and Wednesday–Friday differences vanishing, while making for just noticeable Monday–Friday differences in colour. If the shades themselves are indiscriminable in this way, it's plausible your Good cases of them are too. Thus we have

(11) $g^{m}\mathbf{IND}g^{w}$ & $g^{w}\mathbf{IND}g^{f}$ & $\neg(g^{m}\mathbf{IND}g^{f})$.

This contradicts our current reading of (6).

After all, (11) ensures that its relation of indiscriminability is non-transitive. The general fact then entails that there can be no feature **F** which joins with that relation to make something of (*)'s form variably true. That is just what (10) asserts under its present reading. Since that reading is entailed by a certain reading of (6), the latter must be wrong. Reflective Disjunctivism cannot employ a non-transitive notion of indiscriminability. It is essential to the view that it uses indiscriminability of some kind to pin down the nature of visual experience; so the general fact ensures that it must employ a notion of indiscriminability which is not that of a non-transitive relation.

Notionally, at least, defenders of the approach have two options. They can work with a transitive notion of indiscriminability; or they can work with a non-binary notion. With the first option, proponents of the view insist that their notion of indiscriminability is transitive after all; and if that is right, their view uses a different notion of indiscriminability from the one used in the picket fence example. The present option involves proponents of Reflective Disjunctivism using a notion of indiscriminability distinct from any non-transitive ordinary one we may have. The burdens of the approach thus involve clarifying the motivations for its notion of indiscriminability, setting out details of that notion, and showing how they add up to a transitive relation on episodes.[10]

With the second option, proponents of Reflective Disjunctivism insist their notion of indiscriminability is non-binary. Note that only binary relations are in the business of being transitive or non-transitive. Only they are preserved, or fail to be so, by iteration across pairs of things; for only they show up across

10. Sturgeon forthcoming argues that a version of Reflective Disjunctivism faintly inspired by Williamson 1990 can plausibly take this option when dealing with the putative non-transitivity of indiscriminability.

pairs of things. If proponents of Reflective Disjunctivism use a non-binary notion of indiscriminability, therefore, they use a notion other than that of a non-transitive relation. For this reason, they use a notion distinct from the one found in our picket fence example. This means the present option also involves use of its own notion of indiscriminability; so it too must clarify motivations for its notion, set out its details, and show how they add up to a non-binary phenomenon.

On either option no difficulty will spring from the general fact plus the use of indiscriminability to pin down the nature of visual experience. The first option will avoid bother by using a transitive notion of indiscriminability. The second option will do so by using a non-binary notion of discriminability. Either way the general fact will have no bite. To think otherwise would be to confuse the notion of indiscriminability used in the pre-theoretic run up to the picket fence example with the one used by proponents of Reflective Disjunctivism. But that would be a mistake. Once either option is taken, the non-transitivity of the notion of indiscriminability used in the challenge to Reflective Disjunctivism is simply irrelevant to that view's take on visual experience. Therefore: proponents of the view have a principled response to the picket fence worry if either option can be motivated. Once that is done, they have a principled reason to reject the idea that a pre-theoretically non-transitivity notion of indiscriminability can be used to show that visual experience is unfixed by indiscriminability of some kind.

We must ask, then, whether either option is *apt* for use by Martinized Reflective Disjunctivism. Set aside that each of them opens a notional route around an objection to his view. Ask yourself this: is there any other reason for that view to use a transitive notion of indiscriminability? Is there any other reason for it to use a non-binary notion of indiscriminability?

Well, recall the view builds a notion of indiscriminability from reflective knowledge. To understand its notion of indiscriminability properly, therefore, we must understand such knowledge. But that has not yet been fully spelled out; for we have not yet been told what one must reflect *upon* if one is to achieve knowledge by reflection. Getting a bit clearer on that reveals the radical nature of Martin's view and a principled response to the picket fence worry.

To see this, note the most natural thought here can be shelved right away. Reflective Disjunctivism in general—and the Martinized version of it in particular—cannot say that reflective knowledge is got solely by reflection on the *visual character* of episodes. After all, the view is in the business of spelling out a theory of such character by appeal to indiscriminability. Since Reflective Disjunctivism builds a view of visual character from facts about indiscriminability, and builds a view of indiscriminability from facts about reflective knowledge, Reflective Disjunctivism cannot spell out such knowledge by appeal to reflection on visual character. That would put things back to front, yielding no theory at all about episodes with only visual character (i.e. hallucinations). For this reason, Reflective Disjunctivism must see reflective knowledge in a broad way, as something like knowledge got by reflection on one's epistemic context.

As we'll see in a moment, it is unclear this idea can be spelled out properly. What matters here, though, is simply that Reflective Disjunctivism is built on the idea that visual experience is itself made from the modal limits of knowledge got by reflection on one's epistemic context. Martinized Reflective Disjunctivism sees its notion of indiscriminability this way:

$$(\mathbf{ind_c})_\mathbf{m} \quad x\mathbf{IND_c}\mathrm{G}^\Phi \leftrightarrow \neg\Diamond_{\mathbf{imp}}\mathbf{KR_c}\neg\mathrm{G}^\Phi(x).$$

Put in English: an episode is indiscriminable in context **c** from Φ-Goodness exactly when it is not impersonally possible to know by reflection on **c** that it does not have the nature which makes for such Goodness.

This is the full-dress notion of indiscriminability used by Martinized Reflective Disjunctivism. It does not concern a binary relation. It concerns a contextually indexed reflective phenomenon. Martinized claims of the syntactic form '$x\mathbf{IND_c}g^\Phi$'—for instance, the claim that one's current episode is indiscriminable from Good Φ-cases—do not have the logical form $x\mathbf{R}y$; nor do they have the logical form $x\mathbf{R_c}y$; nor are they generalizations or schematizations of such binary phenomena. Deep down they are predicative claims relativized to context. Deep down they have the logical form $\mathbf{F_c}(x)$. This means Martinized Reflective Disjunctivism faces no difficulty from our general fact. The view's construction of visual experience—from facts about indiscriminability—is simply not pressed by the non-transitivity of any pre-theoretic take on the indiscriminability of episodes we may have; for the view does not use a binary notion of indiscriminability in that construction. It uses a different notion instead.[11]

V

A Pair of Worries and a Modest Proposal. Martinized Reflective Disjunctivism sees visual experience as the impersonal limit of reflective knowledge. I want to close my discussion by probing that conception a bit. First I'll present a well-known worry for the view and say why Martin's way with it is problematic. Then I'll present a new worry for the view. And then I'll sketch how defenders of Reflective Disjunctivism like Martin should react to the cumulative force of what's gone before.

(a) *The Zombie Problem.* Here is Martinized Reflective Disjunctivism's take on the nature of visual experience:

$$\text{(Nat)}\quad \lambda x\mathrm{VE}^{\Phi}_{\mathbf{c}}(x) = \lambda x\neg\Diamond_{\mathbf{imp}}\mathbf{KR}_{\mathbf{c}}\neg\mathrm{G}^{\Phi}(x).$$

Put in English: an episode in **c**'s being a visual experience as of Φ is identical to its being not impersonally possible to know by

11. Martin's view does face a worry similar to the one of this sub-section; and it too can be set up by reference to our picket fence example. To see this, recall your veridical perceptions on Monday, Wednesday and Friday in that example. They have characters $\mathrm{Good}_{\mathrm{mon}}$, $\mathrm{Good}_{\mathrm{wed}}$ and $\mathrm{Good}_{\mathrm{fri}}$ by hypothesis. Those characters are just like one another save for indexing to tiny shifts in colour. This prompts a tough question for Martin: can you know on Wednesday, by reflection on context alone, that your visual episode then fails to have $\mathrm{Good}_{\mathrm{mon}}$ or $\mathrm{Good}_{\mathrm{fri}}$? If not, Martin's view looks to entail that your Wednesday episode has more visual character than it should. It looks subject to an overcrowding-of-character objection. (Hawthorne and Kovakovich speak to this too, in connection not only with the non-transitivity of indiscriminability but also with reference to visual experiencers of diminished epistemic capacity, and also *de re* belief. See the section devoted to the last topic in Hawthorne and Kovakovich 2006.) On the other hand, if Martin says that you can know on Wednesday, by reflection alone, that your episode then fails to have $\mathrm{Good}_{\mathrm{mon}}$ or $\mathrm{Good}_{\mathrm{fri}}$, his view looks to entail—or at least to rely upon—some kind of 'self-intimation' thesis concerning phenomenology. This would be a view on which one is always well placed to know the character of one's phenomenal states. Martin considers such a view sympathetically. He does accept an approach to knowledge that would yield, in conjunction with a self-intimation thesis, a Yes answer to our tough question above—see pp. 390 ff. of Martin 2006. But I have not been able to satisfy myself that Martin is committed to an answer to that tough question. The overcrowding worry is taken up again in the next section, when I critique Martin's response to a zombie-like challenge to his view.

reflection on **c** that it lacks the feature of Φ-Goodness. But what about physical-functional duplicates of us who lack consciousness? What about *zombie twins*, as they say? Don't they make trouble for the idea? After all, their episodes look to satisfy (Nat)'s right-hand side while failing to satisfy its left-hand side. The possibility of zombies thus shows that no cognitive condition can capture visual experience as such; for none can capture what it's like.

This is the zombie objection. Martin reacts to something much like it by sketching a view of the relation between phenomenal consciousness and self-awareness. As Siegel (unpublished) notes, however, his reaction is a two-step affair. The first step involves a link from Martinized indiscriminability to a certain kind of cognitive awareness:

(i) $\neg\Diamond_{\mathbf{imp}}\mathbf{KR}_{\mathbf{c}}\neg G^{\Phi}(x) \rightarrow$[it seems to one in **c** that x is a Good Φ-case];

and the second step involves a link from that kind of cognitive awareness to visual consciousness:

(ii) [it seems to one in **c** that x is a Good Φ-case] $\rightarrow \mathrm{VE}_{\mathbf{c}}^{\Phi}(x)$.

In this way, Martin gets *from* something cognitive-cum-epistemological—Martinized indiscriminability from Goodness—*to* something evidently phenomenological—visual experience as of Φ.

We needn't work through the details of Martin's take on the relation between phenomenal consciousness and self-awareness. He uses them primarily to support the second step in his line, to push for the claim that possession of a certain kind of self-awareness is sufficient for phenomenal consciousness. But I worry about the first step in his line. After all, (i)'s general form is this:

$$\neg\Diamond_{\mathbf{imp}}\mathbf{KR}_{\mathbf{c}}\neg\Psi \rightarrow \text{[it seems to one in } \mathbf{c} \text{ that } \Psi\text{]}.$$

The item of knowledge in the antecedent of this conditional is the logical opposite of the embedded claim in its consequent. Shifting negations yields another expression of the idea:

$$\neg\Diamond_{\mathbf{imp}}\mathbf{KR}_{\mathbf{c}}\Psi \rightarrow \text{[it seems to one in } \mathbf{c} \text{ that } \neg\Psi\text{]}.$$

Put in English: the first claim is that if it cannot impersonally be known that ¬Ψ—by reflection on context **c**, of course—then in **c** it seems intellectually that Ψ; and the second claim is that if it cannot impersonally be known that Ψ—again by reflection on **c**—then in **c** it seems intellectually that ¬Ψ. These claims amount to a single idea: when something cannot be ruled *out* by reflection on context it thereby seems intellectually to be ruled *in*.

Here I don't follow. For one thing, *mute* epistemic contexts make trouble for (i). They are devoid of information about whether one sees, for instance, a white picket fence. Idealized impersonal reflection on them will not rule out that one sees such a fence; but nor will it rule out that one does not see in that way. Whenever one occupies a mute epistemic context—of this sort anyway—Martinized Reflective Disjunctivism entails that it seems to one that one sees a white picket fence; but the view also entails that it seems to one that it's not the case that one sees such a fence. Whenever one occupies a mute epistemic context—of this sort anyway—Martinized Reflective Disjunctivism entails that one's perspective on things is explicitly contradictory. But this seems wrong. No contradictory perspective follows from being in an epistemic context which does not decide—because it does not speak—to whether or not one sees a white picket fence. Being in such a context does not cripple perspective on things. It only limits reflective knowledge. This suggests that perspective is not fixed by such knowledge.

For another thing, *mixed* epistemic contexts make trouble for (i). They contain mixed information about whether one sees, for instance, a white picket fence. Idealized impersonal reflection on them will not rule out that one sees such a fence; but nor will it rule out that one does not see in that way. Whenever one occupies a mixed epistemic context—of this sort anyway—Martinized Reflective Disjunctivism entails that it seems to one that one sees a white picket fence; but the view also entails that it seems to one that it's not the case that one sees such a fence. Whenever one occupies a mute epistemic context—of this sort anyway—Martinized Reflective Disjunctivism entails that one's perspective on things is explicitly contradictory. But this too seems wrong. No contradictory perspective follows from being in an epistemic context which does not decide—because it speaks with a mixed voice—to whether or not one sees a white picket fence. Being in such a context does not cripple perspective on things. It only limits reflective knowledge. This too suggests that perspective is not fixed by such knowledge.

And finally, *corrupt* epistemic contexts make trouble for (i). These are contexts containing unreliable belief-forming mechanisms, ill-designed belief-forming mechanisms, causally deviant chains, evidence just out of sight, and all manner of external-to-perspective knowledge precluders.[12] That fact and (i) jointly entail that when one occupies a corrupt epistemic context, it seems from one's perspective as if one sees all kinds of things to be so, that one's take on things is once again explicitly contradictory. But this seems wrong as well. No contradictory perspective follows from being in an epistemic context which does not decide—because of corruption—to whether or not one sees a white picket fence. Being in such a context does not cripple perspective on things. It only limits reflective knowledge. This is yet another reason to think that perspective is not fixed by such knowledge.[13]

12. Arguably: like the veridical perception two days hence of a subtly different version of what one sees now, as in the picket fence example of the last section (see note 10).

13. Martin 2004 defends the idea that in a certain range of cases, at least, whenever something cannot be ruled *out* by reflection on context it thereby seems intellectually to be ruled *in*. The key passage is this:

> [W]e can determine which consequences of experiences will be co-present in cases of perception and matching hallucination [by appeal to indiscriminability]. For example, if veridical perception gives rise to rational judgement about the environment, then an hallucinating subject will be equally inclined to judgement as a perceiving one. A propensity to make a judgement is one, one can normally detect through reflection on the situation. If an agent had no propensity to judge that a lavender bush is present when having the hallucination of one, then the absence of inclination here would be a detectable difference from the case of veridical perception and hence a ground for discriminating the two situations. In this way, we can say in the basic case it is not merely that an agent does not know that they are not perceiving when hallucinating, where this indicates something consistent with agnosticism on the matter. If an agent in the case of veridical perception can judge that there is a bush there, or that they are seeing a bush, then in a case of perfect hallucination they cannot be left with no inclination one way or the other to judge the presence of bushes or the sighting of bushes. Rather they must equally be inclined to judge that there is a bush there and that they see one. In this case then, positively it must seem to them as if a bush is there and the sighting of a bush is occurring. (p. 67)

It's unclear how the argument of this passage proceeds exactly. Martin seems to presuppose something like standard or canonical dispositions to judgement associated with a given type of veridical perception—and he also relies on the claim, of course, that such dispositions are available to reflection on context. I am unsure what he is talking about here—whether said dispositions are meant to be background-belief-independent, for instance; or whether they can vary from

(b) *The Alignment Problem.* It does not seem that reflection on context can yield knowledge in line with the demands of Martinized Reflective Disjunctivism.[14] To see why, note the view's main take on the extension of visual experience:

$$\text{(Ext)}\quad \mathrm{VE}^{\Phi}_{\mathbf{c}}(x) \leftrightarrow x\mathbf{IND}_{\mathbf{c}}\mathrm{G}^{\Phi} =_{\text{df.}} \neg\Diamond_{\mathbf{imp}}\mathbf{KR}_{\mathbf{c}}\neg\mathrm{G}^{\Phi}(x).$$

Put in English: an episode in **c** is a visual experience as of Φ exactly when it's indiscriminable in **c** from Φ-Good cases—exactly when, that is to say, it's not impersonally possible to know by reflection on **c** that the episode lacks the feature of Φ-Goodness. Negating each bit of (Ext)—and dropping a double negation—yields an equivalent idea:

$$\text{(Ext}^{*}\text{)}\quad \neg\mathrm{VE}^{\Phi}_{\mathbf{c}}(x) \leftrightarrow \neg x\mathbf{IND}_{\mathbf{c}}\mathrm{G}^{\Phi} =_{\text{df.}} \Diamond_{\mathbf{imp}}\mathbf{KR}_{\mathbf{c}}\neg\mathrm{G}^{\Phi}(x).$$

Put in English: an episode in **c** is *not* a visual experience as of Φ exactly when it's *not* indiscriminable in **c** from Φ-Good cases—exactly when, that is to say, it *is* impersonally possible to know by reflection on **c** that the episode lacks the feature of Φ-Goodness.

But it's a datum of everyday life, recall, that we can know—in certain contexts at least—that we suffer visual illusion as of Φ; and it is a datum of everyday life that we can know—in certain contexts at least—that we suffer visual hallucination as of Φ. It follows that we can know—in certain contexts at least—that our visual episode does not have a Φ-Good nature. As we have seen, proponents of Reflective Disjunctivism must say that knowledge like this does not make for visual experience—it is not reflective, in their terms. But they must tell us what *does* make for such knowledge. In particular, Reflective Disjunctivists

doxastic context to context. There is no agreement about this kind of thing in the epistemic literature, to be sure, even concerning a non-normative claim about disposition to judgement. One way to see my critique in this bit of the paper, then, is simply as a call to clarification. It would be good to know more about how the argument of this passage works, exactly, more about the background psychological assumptions driving it; and how those assumptions undermine worries I've sketched for something like (i).

14. The problem generalizes to other forms of Reflective Disjunctivism, as I argue in Sturgeon forthcoming, and the text here is meant to make clear.

must tell us exactly what goes into reflection on context—in Martin's phrase, they must tell us exactly 'what is available to you in reflecting on your circumstances' (Martin 2006, p. 365).

It does not seem any specification of detail will work out. To see why, recall Martin's point that testimonial information will have to be barred from reflection on context. He is certainly right to make it: one can learn by reflection on information got by testimony that one suffers a Bad Φ-case. Martin does not say what else must be ruled out of reflection on context if everyday knowledge of Badness is not to refute Reflective Disjunctivism. But it is clear that non-testimonial routes to everyday knowledge of Badness exist too. Here is a case drawn from last summer:

> My wife and I used a big fan in the living room. We then stopped monitoring our toddler's sleep for the first time in twenty months. The result was a distinctive pattern of auditory hallucination: every night I would 'hear' Sascha, our daughter, crying. After several trips down the hall—over several nights—the hallucinatory nature of the set-up became known. Then I had everyday knowledge of Badness.

Reflection on information like this applies to visual episodes as well as auditory ones. It can yield everyday knowledge of visual Badness too. For this reason, Reflective Disjunctivism must rule out a lot more than testimonial information from the base upon which reflective knowledge is built. It must bar any information which could be involved in a normal route to knowledge by reflection. But there are all manner of such routes available—situations well within the sphere of quotidian possibility which permit the visually deceived to work out, by simple reflection on circumstance, that they are so deceived. As a result, Reflective Disjunctivism must say this:

(iii) Background beliefs do not generally make for reflective knowledge.

The information involved in background beliefs cannot be generally available to reflection on circumstance. Otherwise the possibility of everyday knowledge of Badness will slip through the net, count as knowledge obtainable by reflection, and falsify the left-to-right direction of (Ext).

But now let *h* be an hallucination as of Ψ—say as of a white picket fence. Then for a huge number of Φ,[15] *h* is *not* a visual experience as of Φ. When Φ concerns portrayal of a green field, for instance, *h* is not a visual experience as of Φ; for *h* is not a conscious portrayal as of a green field. When Φ concerns portrayal of a blue sky, for instance, *h* is not a visual experience as of Φ; for *h* is not a conscious portrayal as of a blue sky. And so on. For a huge number of Φ, *h* is not a visual experience as of Φ since it's not a conscious portrayal as of Φ. The left-to-right direction of (Ext)* entails that for each of the Φs one *can* know, by reflection alone, that *h* is not a Good Φ-case.

That is a huge amount of knowledge to be got solely by reflection. In layman's terms, one can know by reflection alone that one is not seeing a green field, that one is not seeing a blue sky, that one is not seeing all kinds of other things. For each of the Φs here, Reflective Disjunctivism entails that one can know by reflection alone—and *not* by reflection on the visual character of *h*, recall—that one is not seeing Φ. The only way that could be true, I submit, is if background beliefs were generally available to reflection on context. Otherwise one could not know all these things by reflection. Reflective Disjunctivism must also say this:

(iv) Background beliefs generally make for reflective knowledge.

The problem is that (iii) and (iv) jointly entail that there is no such thing as reflection on context. They entail that no source of knowledge can do what Reflective Disjunctivism obliges reflective knowledge to do: namely, square with the datum that ordinary background information can make for everyday knowledge of Badness yet secure the extensional adequacy of (Ext). There is a sharp misalignment between the datum and Reflective Disjunctivism's take on the extension of visual experience.

(c) *A Modest Proposal.* Reflective Disjunctivism accounts for Bad character with an epistemic resource: reflective knowledge.

15. Perhaps all Φ not equal to Ψ; perhaps only Φs not entailed by Ψ; perhaps something else again. We won't bother with this here, as it turns on the exact way that visual experience portrays the world. We abstract from that issue in this paper.

Other disjunctivisms do so with other resources—mere appearance, sensory items, and so forth.[16] Reflective Disjunctivism's ideology is pleasing when compared to that of its cousins, then, for reflective knowledge is there for everyone to use. It is a non-partisan resource. Moreover, Reflective Disjunctivism has internal resources to deal with worries based on diminished epistemic capacity and the putative non-transitivity of indiscriminability. Reflective Disjunctivism is a surprisingly resilient view.

Having said that, it faces considerable theoretical pressure. Most importantly, its details need to be spelled out more clearly than they have been so far. No matter how that is done, however, it is hard to see how indiscriminability alone can make for an epistemic perspective sufficient for visual experience; and it is hard to see how everyday knowledge of Badness can be reconciled with the approach's take on the extension of visual episodes. These pressures call into question the viability of the view. They raise serious doubt as to whether it can be made to work. But what is the choice point at this stage of discussion? What should a proponent of Reflective Disjunctivism begin to contemplate if struck by the force of what's gone before? I close with a modest proposal about that.

Initially, the choice point seems to be this: one should either drop disjunctivism about visual experience or go in for a version which uses murky resources to deal with Bad character. But I do not think that correctly diagnoses the situation; for there is a version of disjunctivism which avoids murky resources along with theoretical pressures faced by Reflective Disjunctivism. It does this by hearing the second backbone claim of disjunctivism in a surprising way. Recall that claim:

> (Bad) Bad character does *not* derive from bits of the physical world standing in an explanatorily basic relation to percipients.

To this point we've heard (Bad) to involve narrow-scope negation. We've assumed—with common sense, of course—that there is such a thing as Bad character; and we've heard (Bad) to state of it that it does not derive like Good character. But the main

16. Sturgeon forthcoming lays out a range of disjunctive positions by way of illustration.

motive for Reflective Disjunctivism—at least that of its prime defender, Mike Martin—also suggests a reading of (Bad) on which its negation takes wide scope.[17]

In a nutshell, the motivation is simple enough: introspection of visual experience leads always and only to naïve realism. In our terminology, it leads always and only to endorsing the presence of Good character. It never seems to us introspectively as if we enjoy Bad character. Introspection says visual experience is Good; and it says nothing else at all.

Suppose that is so. Then a pure form of disjunctivism comes into focus, one which avoids both the murky resources used by non-reflective disjunctivisms and the theoretical pressures faced by their reflective cousin. The view I have in mind—Pure Disjunctivism—accepts (Good) and (Bad), of course; but it accepts (Bad) for a startling reason. It says there is no such thing as Bad character. The view rejects the very idea of delusive phenomenology.

This rejection entails that when one suffers an hallucination as of a green field, for instance, there is nothing it is like to enjoy the episode. In this it disagrees with Reflective Disjunctivism and common sense. But all three positions agree that it *seems* to one introspectively as if there is something it is like to enjoy such a case. After all, all three agree—we're assuming here—that it always introspectively seems to one as if one enjoys a Good case. For this reason, Pure and Reflective Disjunctivism will both say that it seems to one as if the episode in question is phenomenally just like a Good one of a green field. And more generally, they will agree that introspection insists on Good character and only Good character for Bad cases.

Further, both views entail that introspection is *flat wrong* about what Bad cases are like; for they both say that such cases do not involve Good character despite seeming solely to do so on the basis of introspection. Although introspection prompts the idea that Bad cases are a Good thing, both views insist, introspection is flat wrong about what those cases are like. Pure and Reflective

17. For Martin on this motivation see especially his 2002, but also his 2004 and 2006. Sturgeon forthcoming argues that none of the standard motivations for disjunctivism—neither epistemic, phenomenological nor semantic motivations—brings with them a commitment to Bad character. The only serious motive for that commitment, so far as I know, is the one to be emphasized now.

Disjunctivism disagree about why introspection goes wrong in this way. The former says it does so because Bad cases have no character at all, because there is nothing it is like to be in them. Reflective Disjunctivism says that introspection gets the character of Bad cases flat wrong because introspection says it is Good when it is really something else, when it is really reflection-based character. Reflective Disjunctivism agrees with common sense that there is something it is like to be in a Bad case; but it claims what it's like isn't at all what we think it's like introspectively. Pure Disjunctivism steps off the boat upstream.

Like its Reflective cousin, Pure Disjunctivism insists that introspection is our best initial guide to what experience is like; and like its Reflective cousin, Pure Disjunctivism insists that introspection generates no knowledge of what Bad experience is like. Unlike its Reflective cousin, however, Pure Disjunctivism takes the view that *if* our source for thinking that Bad cases *have* character in the first place is flat wrong about that character—completely and totally wrong—then we should give up the consequences of what that source leads us to accept about that character. Pure and Reflective Disjunctivism agree that introspection of Bad cases leads to the view, and only the view, that such cases are Good. And from this it follows that they *have* character of some kind. But both views say that introspection is flat wrong about the character it attributes to Bad experience. As a result, Pure Disjunctivism drops commitment to the view that there is such a thing as Bad character in the first place, plumping instead for the simpler view that Bad cases are characterless. There is nothing it is like to be in them. Pure Disjunctivism takes the view that Good character is character enough, and that Bad character is a theoretical dangler foisted upon us by hamstrung introspection.

This view can accept, of course, that there are visually delusive episodes. Pure Disjunctivism need only deny that their delusive nature is like anything. For this reason: the view contains no commitment about the nature of Bad character; nor need it contain any about the extension or nature of visual experience as such. Pure Disjunctivism need only involve a take on what visual experience is like. It need only commit to a pure reading of (Good) and (Bad). That is why it can avoid murky resources to deal with Bad character. That is why it can avoid theoretical pressures generated by Reflective Disjunctivism's take on the nature of visual experience.

There are several ways to spell out the approach. At bottom they all defend a disjunctivism about visual episodes, splitting them into two groups: on one side of the divide are episodes with visual character; on the other side are episodes with no visual character. Moreover, some versions of the approach will see visual experience as such as possessing a nature specifiable in other terms. It is compatible with Pure Disjunctivism as sketched to this point, for instance, that an episode is a visual experience as of Φ exactly when it plays a certain functional role. But it is also compatible with the picture as sketched that visual experience as such has no underlying nature at all, that visual experience makes for a hodgepodge class of event tied together by nothing of theoretical note. To the extent that disjunctivists like to think there is no such thing as a visual experience, then, their sentiment is compatible with Pure Disjunctivism.

One bitter aspect of the view—by my lights, anyway—is that it is committed to visual episodes within the purview of introspection but outside that of phenomenology. Pure Disjunctivism is committed to the possibility of episodes unlike anything being introspect-able nonetheless. One might reasonably query the coherence of that. Matt Soteriou did in discussion, and I feel his pain. I've worried about this too while reading Martin 2006, having been prompted to do so by a point repeatedly stressed in that paper. As Martin puts it on p. 390, 'the impossibility of one's experience merely seeming a certain way without being so is not established solely by supposing that phenomenal states have the distinctive property of being self-intimating, by which I mean: being such that a subject who is in such a state is thereby in a position to know that she is in it.' I do not aim to question the truth of Martin's claim. Its use of the word 'solely' may well shield it from serious critique (depending, of course, on how serious the restriction on supposition is meant to be). But I do want to note that Martin's claim requires for its truth the bitter possibility mentioned above, *if* we are allowed to make an obvious assumption about phenomenal knowledge.

To see this, let Self-Intimacy be the claim that any phenomenal way an episode could be is a way its owner will be well placed to know about by introspection if the episode turns out to be that way; and let Infallibility be the claim that perforce an episode introspectively seems to be a given way only if it is that way. Martin claims that Infallibility is not established solely by supposing Self-Intimacy. That may or may not be so; but if a plausible claim about phenomenal knowledge is also supposed, Martin's claim will hold only if bitter possibilities are lent credence.

Here's the argument. Suppose Self-Intimacy is true. Suppose also that no source of knowledge about an episode's phenomenology can be shaky about its subject matter: none can suggest relevant falsehoods about that as well as relevant truths. Let *e* be an arbitrarily chosen phenomenal episode. There is a phenomenal way *W* such that *e* is *W*.[18] By Self-Intimacy, *e*'s owner is well placed to know by introspection that *e* is *W*. That will be so only if *e* seems to be *W* by introspection. Suppose there is a W^* so that *e* seems introspectively to be W^* when it is not. Then introspection turns out to be shaky about *e*'s phenomenology. It suggests relevant falsehoods about that as well as relevant truths. This means introspection cannot be a source of knowledge about what *e* is like. But that contradicts Self-Intimacy; so there cannot be such a W^* after all. If our first two suppositions are true, therefore, Infallibility is also true when restricted to phenomenal episodes. The only way Infallibility could turn out false, under present assumptions—the only way it could fail to be established under those assumptions—is if credence were lent to the possibility that a *non*-phenomenal episode cut against the principle. But that would be to lend credence to a bitter possibility, to leave open the possibility—if only a tad—that an episode unlike anything introspectively seemed to be like something. When combined with a plausible claim about phenomenal knowledge, therefore, Martin's claim entails the coherence of bitter possibilities. Without lending them some credence, after all, one can establish Infallibility by supposing Self-Intimacy alone. That is why Martin 2006 prompts me to worry about the coherence of bitter possibilities,

18. For present purposes it does not matter if *W* is maximally specific. The argument could be altered in an obvious way were that assumption to be made. It would then rely on a different claim about knowledge than the shaky-theoretic one mentioned above; but it would then rely on a claim about knowledge actually used by Martin on p. 390. Readers are thus invited to augment the reasoning here as suggested if they see fit.

why Martin's intriguing defence of Reflective Disjunctivism leads to the thought of them.[19]

References

Farkas, K. 2006: 'Indiscriminability and the Sameness of Appearance'. *Proceedings of the Aristotelian Society*, 106, pp. 205–25.

Hawthorne, J. and K. Kovakovich 2006: 'Disjunctivism'. *Proceedings of the Aristotelian Society Supplementary Volume 80*, pp. 145–83.

Hinton, J. M. 1967: 'Visual Experiences'. *Mind*.

——— 1973: *Experiences*. Oxford: Oxford University Press.

Martin, M. G. F. 2002: 'The Transparency of Experience'. *Mind & Language*.

——— 2004. 'The Limits of Self-Awareness'. *Philosophical Studies*.

——— 2006. 'On Being Alienated'. In T. Szabo Gendler and J. Hawthorne (eds), *Perceptual Experience*. Oxford: Oxford University Press.

Siegel, S. 2006. 'Indiscriminability and the Phenomenal'. *Philosophical Studies*.

——— Unpublished: Comments on Martin 2006. Available at: http://www.people.fas.harvard. edu/~ssiegel/papers/dogandzombie.htm.

Sturgeon, S. 2001: *Matters of Mind*. London: Routledge.

——— forthcoming: 'Disjunctivism about Visual Experience'. In Fiona Macpherson and Adrian Haddock (eds), *Disjunctivism: Perception, Action, Knowledge*. Oxford: Oxford University Press.

Williamson, T. 1990: *Identity and Discrimination*. Oxford: Basil Blackwell.

19. The following deserve special thanks for help with the paper: Alex Byrne, David Chalmers, Tim Crane, Kati Farkas, John Hawthorne, Eli Kalderon, Mike Martin, Susanna Schellenberg, Susanna Siegel, Paul Snowdon, Matt Soteriou and the Birmingham Philosophy Department. Each suffered through a very rough draft of this material. Worse still: Maja Spener had to deal with all my crazy thoughts on the topic. I am extremely grateful for the help.

GAMES AND THE GOOD

by Thomas Hurka and John Tasioulas

I—Thomas Hurka

ABSTRACT Using Bernard Suits's brilliant analysis (*contra* Wittgenstein) of playing a game, this paper examines the intrinsic value of game-playing. It argues that two elements in Suits's analysis make success in games difficult, which is one ground of value, while a third involves choosing a good activity for the property that makes it good, which is a further ground. The paper concludes by arguing that game-playing is the paradigm modern (Marx, Nietzsche) as against classical (Aristotle) value: since its goal is intrinsically trivial, its value is entirely one of process rather than product, journey rather than destination.

Our societies attach considerable value to excellence in sports. In Canada hockey players are named to the highest level of the Order of Canada; in Britain footballers and cricketers are made MBE and even knighted. And this attitude extends more widely. Sports are a subclass of the wider category of games, and we similarly admire those who excel in non-athletic games such as chess, bridge, and even Scrabble.

I take this admiration to rest on the judgement that excellence in games is good in itself, apart from any pleasure it may give the player or other people, but just for the properties that make it excellent. The admiration, in other words, rests on the perfectionist judgement that skill in games is worth pursuing for its own sake and can add value to one's life. This skill is not the only thing we value in this way; we give similar honours to achievements in the arts, science and business. But one thing we admire, and to a significant degree, is excellence in athletic and non-athletic games.

Unless we dismiss this view, one task for philosophy is to explain why such excellence is good. But few philosophers have attempted this, for a well-known reason. A unified explanation of why excellence in games is good requires a unified account of what games are, and many doubt that this is possible. After all, Wittgenstein famously gave the concept of a game as his primary example of one for which necessary and sufficient conditions cannot be given but whose instances are linked only by looser 'family resemblances'.[1] If Wittgenstein was right about this, there can be no single explanation of why skill in games is good, just a series of distinct explanations of the value of skill in hockey, skill in chess, and so on.

But Wittgenstein was not right, as is shown in a little-known book that is nonetheless a classic of twentieth-century philosophy, Bernard Suits's *The Grasshopper: Games, Life and Utopia.* Suits gives a perfectly persuasive analysis of playing a game as, to quote his summary statement, 'the voluntary attempt to overcome unnecessary obstacles'.[2] And in this paper I will use his analysis to explain the value of playing games. More specifically, I will argue that the different elements of Suits's analysis give game-playing two distinct but related grounds of value, so it instantiates two related intrinsic goods. I will also argue that game-playing is an important intrinsic good, which gives the clearest possible expression of what can be called a modern as against a classical, or more specifically, Aristotelian, view of value.

But first Suits's analysis. It says that a game has three main elements, which he calls the prelusory goal, the constitutive rules, and the lusory attitude. To begin with the first, in playing a game one always aims at a goal that can be described independently of the game. In golf, this is that a ball enter a hole in the ground; in mountain climbing, that one stand on top of a mountain; in Olympic sprinting, that one cross a line on the track before one's competitors. Suits calls this goal 'prelusory' because it can be understood and achieved apart from the game, and he argues that every game has such a goal. Of course, in playing a game one also aims at a goal internal to it, such as winning the race, climbing the mountain, or breaking par on the golf course. But on Suits's view this 'lusory' goal is derivative, since achieving it involves achieving the prior prelusory goal in a specified way.

1. Ludwig Wittgenstein, *Philosophical Investigations*, 3rd edn, trans. G. E. M. Anscombe, Oxford: Blackwell, 1972, Sect. 66.
2. Bernard Suits, *The Grasshopper: Games, Life and Utopia*, Toronto: University of Toronto Press, 1978; repr. Peterborough, ON: Broadview Press, 2005, p. 41/55 (page references are first to the University of Toronto Press edition, then to the Broadview Press edition).

This way is identified by the second element, the game's constitutive rules. According to Suits, the function of these rules is to forbid the most efficient means to the prelusory goal. Thus, in golf one may not carry the ball down the fairway and drop it in the hole by hand; one must advance it using clubs, play it where it lies, and so on. In mountain climbing one may not ride a gondola to the top of the mountain or charter a helicopter; in 200-metre sprinting, one may not cut across the infield. Once these rules are in place, success in the game typically requires achieving the prelusory goal as efficiently as they allow, such as getting the ball into the hole in the fewest possible strokes or choosing the best way up the mountain. But this is efficiency within the rules, whose larger function is to forbid the easiest means to the game's initial goal.

These first two elements involve pursuing a goal by less than the most efficient means, but they are not sufficient for playing a game. This is because someone can be forced to use these means by circumstances he regrets and wishes were different. If this is the case—if, for example, a farmer harvests his field by hand because he cannot afford the mechanical harvester he would much rather use—he is not playing a game. Hence the need for the third element in Suits's analysis, the lusory attitude, which involves a person's willingly accepting the constitutive rules, or accepting them because they make the game possible. Thus, a golfer accepts that he may not carry the ball by hand or improve his lie because he wants to play golf, and obeying those rules is necessary for him to do so; the mountaineer accepts that he may not take a helicopter to the summit because he wants to climb. The restrictions the rules impose are adhered to not reluctantly but willingly, because they are essential to the game. Adding this third element gives Suits's full definition: 'To play a game is to attempt to achieve a specific state of affairs [prelusory goal], using only means permitted by the rules ... where the rules prohibit the use of more efficient in favour of less efficient means [constitutive rules], and where the rules are accepted just because they make possible such activity [lusory attitude].' Or, in the summary statement quoted above, 'playing a game is the voluntary attempt to overcome unnecessary obstacles.'[3]

3. Ibid., p. 41/54–5.

This analysis will doubtless meet with objections, in the form of attempted counterexamples. But Suits considers a whole series of these in his book, showing repeatedly that his analysis handles them correctly, and not by some ad hoc addition but once its elements are properly understood. Nor would it matter terribly if there were a few counterexamples. Some minor lack of fit between his analysis and the English use of 'game' would not be important if the analysis picks out a phenomenon that is unified, close to what is meant by 'game', and philosophically interesting. But the analysis is interesting if, as I will now argue, it allows a persuasive explanation of the value of excellence in games.

Suits himself addresses this issue of value. In fact, a central aim of his book is to give a defence of the grasshopper in Aesop's fable, who played all summer, against the ant, who worked. But in doing so he argues for the strong thesis that playing games is not just an intrinsic good but the supreme such good, since in the ideal conditions of utopia, where all instrumental goods are provided, it would be everyone's primary pursuit. The grasshopper's game-playing, therefore, while it had the unfortunate effect of leaving him without food for the winter, involved him in the intrinsically finest activity. Now, I do not accept Suits's strong thesis that game-playing is the supreme good—I think many other states and activities have comparable value—and I do not find his arguments for it persuasive. But I will connect the weaker thesis that playing games is one intrinsic good to the details of his analysis more explicitly than he ever does.

Consider the first two elements of the analysis, the prelusory goal and constitutive rules. By forbidding the most efficient means to that goal, the constitutive rules usually make for an activity that is reasonably difficult. They do not always do so. Rock, paper, scissors is a game whose prelusory goal is to throw rock to one's opponent's scissors, scissors to his paper, or paper to his rock, and the rules forbid the easiest means to this goal by forbidding one to make one's throw after he has made his. But though the rules make achieving this goal more difficult than it might be, they do not make it by absolute standards difficult; rock, paper, scissors is not a challenging activity. But then rock, paper, scissors is not a very good game, and certainly not one the playing of which has much intrinsic value. It is characteristic of good games to be not only more difficult than they might be but also in absolute terms reasonably difficult. They cannot be so difficult that no one can succeed at them, but also cannot lack all challenge; they must strike a balance between too much and too little difficulty. In what follows I will defend the value only of playing good games, because they realize what seems an internal goal of the design of games. If the constitutive rules of a game make achieving its prelusory goal more difficult than it might be, this is surely because they aim at making it simply difficult.

If the prelusory goal and rules of a good game make succeeding at it reasonably difficult, they will also give it one ground of value if difficult activities are as such intrinsically good. And I believe that difficult activities are as such good. Though not often explicitly affirmed by philosophers, this view can be defended in at least two ways.

Many contemporary philosophers include among their intrinsic goods achievement, by which they mean not just moral but also non-moral achievement, for example, in business or the arts.[4] But what exactly is achievement? It clearly involves realizing a goal, but not every such realization counts as an achievement; for example, tying one's shoelace does not unless one has some disability. And among achievements some are more valuable than others; thus, starting a new business and making it successful is a greater achievement than making a single sale. If we ask what explains these differences—between achievements and non-achievements, and between greater and lesser achievements—the answer is surely in large part their difficulty: how complex or physically challenging they are, or how much skill and ingenuity they require. It is when a goal is hard to bring about that doing so is an achievement. So reflection on our intuitive understanding of the value of achievement suggests a first reason for holding that difficult activities are as such good.

A second reason, which is complementary but more abstract, is suggested by Robert Nozick's fantasy of an 'experience machine'.[5] This machine, which can electrically stimulate the

4. See, for example, James Griffin, *Well-Being: Its Meaning, Measurement and Moral Importance*, Oxford: Clarendon Press, 1986, p. 67.
5. Robert Nozick, *Anarchy, State, and Utopia*, New York: Basic Books, 1974, pp. 42–5.

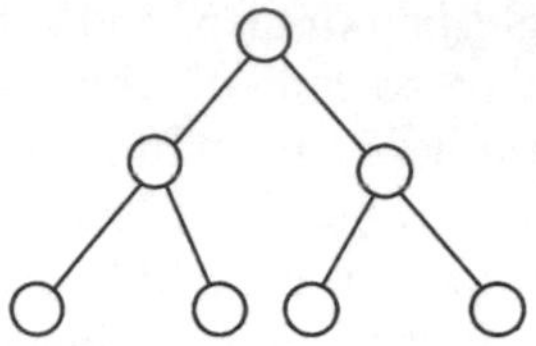

Figure 1

brain to give one the pleasure of any activity one wants, is intended as a counterexample to the hedonistic view that only pleasure is good, but it also makes a positive point. If life on the machine is less than ideal, this is largely because people on it are disconnected from reality. They have only false beliefs about their environment and never actually realize any goals: they may think they are discovering a cure for cancer or climbing Everest, but in fact they are not. This suggests that an important good is what we can call 'rational connection to reality', where this has two aspects, one theoretical and one practical.[6]

The theoretical aspect is knowledge, or having beliefs about the world that are both true and justified. The beliefs' truth means there is a match between one's mind and reality; their being justified means the match is not a matter of luck but something one's evidence made likely. But a full account of this good must explain which kinds of knowledge are most worth having. Classical philosophers like Aristotle thought the best knowledge is of the intrinsically best objects, such as the divine substances, but the more plausible view is that the best knowledge has the most of certain formal properties that are independent of its subject matter. More specifically, the best knowledge is explanatorily integrated, with general principles that explain middle-level principles that in turn explain particular facts. This integration results in an explanatory hierarchy like that represented in figure 1, where items of knowledge higher up in the hierarchy explain those below them. And this hierarchy embodies more intrinsic value than if one knew only isolated unexplanatory facts, like the number of grains of sand on seven beaches (figure 2). We can give an artificial but illustrative

6. I give a fuller account of this value in my *Perfectionism*, New York: Oxford University Press, 1993, Chs 8–10.

○ ○ ○ ○ ○ ○ ○

Figure 2

model for measuring this value if we imagine that each item of knowledge initially has one unit of value in itself, but gains an extra unit for every other item of knowledge subordinate to it in a hierarchy. Then the seven isolated items in figure 2 have just one unit of value each, for a total of seven units. But in figure 1 the middle items have three units, since they each explain two further facts, and the top item has seven units, for a total of seventeen units in the hierarchy as a whole. The explanatory relations between them give an integrated set of beliefs more value than ones that are unconnected.

This model can be enriched. We may think it especially valuable to give unifying explanations of diverse facts, or to make surprising connections between what seemed unrelated phenomena. If so, we can count not just the number of individual items a given item of knowledge has subordinate to it, but the number of items of different kinds, so there is more value in explaining more types of fact. We may also value precision of knowledge, such as knowing that the constant of gravitational acceleration is not just somewhere between 5 and $15\,m/s^2$ but exactly $9.8\,m/s^2$. And we can capture this view both by giving more value to precise knowledge in itself and by giving it more additional value for explaining further precise truths.

Finally, we may think that knowing truths concerning many objects is better than knowing highly particular ones, even apart from the former's explanatory role; thus, knowing a scientific law is better than knowing the number of grains of sand on some beach even if one has not used the former to explain anything else.

The practical parallel to knowledge, and the other value missing on the experience machine, is achievement, or realizing a goal in the world given a justified belief that one would do so. Here again there is a match between one's mind and reality, though now reality has been made to fit one's mind, and a justified belief that makes the match not just lucky. Again we must specify which achievements are best. A classical view might say they are of the goals that are independently best, but we can maintain the parallel with knowledge, and give a better account of achievement as achievement, if we say they are of the goals with the most of certain formal properties that again centre on hierarchical integration. This time, however, the integrating relation is not explanatory but means–end. Thus, in figure 1 we achieve the goal at the top of the hierarchy by achieving the two middle-level goals as means to it, and each of those by achieving the two below them. And if each non-luckily achieved goal has one unit of value in itself plus an additional unit for every other goal achieved as a means to it, the achievements in this hierarchy again have seventeen units of value as against the seven in seven unrelated achievements. Just as more complex explanatory relations make for more value in knowledge, so more complex means–end relations make for more value in achievement.

Again this model can be enriched. We may think achievements are especially valuable if they require subsidiary achievements of varied kinds, and can capture this view by counting the number of goals of different types a given one has subordinate to it. More strongly, we may deny significant value to achievements that involve only subordinate goals of the same repetitive type. We may also value precision in achievement—hitting a particular target rather than just some vague area—and can give achievements additional value for that. And we can think that, apart from means–end relations, achieving goals whose content extends more widely, through time or in the number of objects they involve, is likewise more valuable.

This model deepens the value of achievement by showing it to be parallel to knowledge and, with it, one aspect of a more abstract good of rational connection to reality. It also makes many difficult activities good for the very properties that make them difficult. First, the more complex the means–end hierarchy an activity involves, the more places there are where one can fail at something crucial and the harder success in the activity becomes. Second, the more complex the hierarchy, the more deliberative skill it requires, since one has to monitor one's progress through a more elaborate sequence of tasks. There is a further increment of difficulty if the hierarchy involves a greater variety of subordinate goals, since then it requires a greater variety of skills, and likewise if the activity demands more precision. And it is more difficult to achieve goals with more extended contents, both because holding them in one's mind is more difficult and because achieving them requires changing more of the world.[7]

Moreover, these are precisely the aspects of difficulty found in good games. These games usually require one to go through a complex sequence of tasks rather than do one simple thing such as throw rock, paper or scissors. The tasks in question often demand varied skills: thus, golf requires one not only to drive the ball a long distance but to drive it accurately, play from bunkers, putt, and make strategic decisions. Good golfers are also precise, hitting their approach shots to a particular part of the green rather than just somewhere near it. And many games, such as chess, hockey and basketball, require players to grasp an extended content, including all the pieces on the board or all the players on the ice or court, in a single act of consciousness. That again is difficult, and requires years of practice to master.

Not all the difficulty in games involves this complex ratiocination. Weightlifters have to go through a precisely ordered sequence of moves in order to lift their weights, but also need brute strength: if one of two lifters has less perfect technique but is stronger and therefore lifts more, he wins the competition. Boxing, too, depends in part on raw power. These purely physical forms of difficulty do not instantiate the value of rational connection, and their role in making game-playing good is unclear. Why do we value the physical aspects of weightlifting and boxing but not those found in, say, pie-eating contests? Does this reflect just the historical accident that weightlifting and boxing began long enough ago that we can value them now for their traditions? Or do we value physical difficulty only when it accompanies more rational forms of challenge but not on its own? I will not pursue this issue, taking the rational connection model to capture what makes purely cerebral games such as chess difficult, and also much of what makes sports such as golf and hockey difficult.

I have argued that the prelusory goal and constitutive rules make playing a good game difficult, and have given two reasons

7. Some may deny that difficulty is as such good, on the ground that an activity aimed at evil, such as genocide, is not in any way made good by its difficulty. The issue here is complex (see my *Virtue, Vice, and Value*, New York: Oxford University Press, 2001, pp. 144–52), but those moved by this objection can retreat to the weaker claim that only activities with good or neutral aims gain value by being difficult. This weaker claim is sufficient to ground the value of games.

to believe that difficulty is as such good. But I have not yet used the third element in Suits's analysis, the lusory attitude. Let us examine it more closely.

In his 1907 book *The Theory of Good and Evil* Hastings Rashdall remarked that '[s]port has been well defined as the overcoming of difficulties simply for the sake of overcoming them'.[8] This definition is close to Suits's, but differs on one point. It in effect takes the lusory attitude to be one of accepting the rules because they make the game difficult, whereas Suits takes it to be one of accepting the rules because they make the game possible. For Rashdall, the golfer accepts the rule against improving one's lie because it makes golf harder; for Suits, it is because it makes golf golf. Which view is correct?

Suits's view is preferable if we are analysing the generic concept of playing a game. Consider what we can call a pure professional golfer, who plays golf only as a means to making money and with no interest in the game for itself. He does not cheat as a means to making money; he knows that to make money he must play golf, which means obeying all its rules. But his only reason for accepting the rules is to make money. If we used Rashdall's view to define the generic concept, we would have to say the pure professional is not playing golf, which is absurd. But on Suits's view he is playing golf: though he accepts the rules only as a means to money, he does accept them in order to play golf and so has the lusory attitude.

But though Suits defines the generic concept of game-playing, this is not what he defends as the supreme intrinsic good. His argument, recall, is that in utopia, where all instrumental goods are provided, game-playing would be everyone's primary activity. But this description of utopia implies that it would contain no professional players; since no one would need to play a game as a means to anything, all players would be amateurs who chose the game for itself. But then they would have Rashdall's lusory attitude of accepting the rules because they make the game difficult, and Suits explicitly agrees. He describes how one utopian character decides to build houses by carpentry rather than order them up telepathically because carpentry requires more skill. And

8. *The Theory of Good and Evil*, 2 vols, London: Oxford University Press, 1907, vol. 2, p. 105.

he starts his discussion of utopia by saying he will defend the value of game-playing as a specific form of play, where he has earlier denied that playing a game necessarily involves playing: to play is to engage in an activity for its own sake, and a pure professional does not do that.[9] So the activity Suits defends as supremely good is game-playing that is also play, or what I will call 'playing in a game'. And that activity involves accepting the rules not just because they make the game possible, but also because they make it difficult.

I will follow Suits here and narrow my thesis further: not only will I explain the value only of playing good games, I will explain the value only of playing *in* these games, or of playing them with an at least partly amateur attitude. But this is not in practice much of a restriction, since most people do play games at least partly for their own sakes. Consider Pete Rose, an extremely hard-nosed baseball player who was disliked for how much he would do to win. Taking the field near the end of the famous sixth game of the 1975 World Series, and excited by the superb plays that game had involved, he told the opposing team's third base coach, 'Win or lose, Popeye, we're in the fuckin' greatest game ever played'; after the game, which his team lost, he made a similar comment about it to his manager. Intensely as he wanted to win, Pete Rose also loved baseball for itself.[10]

So the game-playing whose value I will explain involves accepting the rules of the game because they make it difficult. But then the elements that define this type of game-playing are internally related: the prelusory goal and constitutive rules together give it a feature, namely difficulty, and the lusory attitude chooses it because of this feature. More specifically, if difficulty is as such good, the prelusory goal and rules give it a good-making feature and the lusory attitude chooses it because of that good-making feature. This connects the lusory attitude to an attractive view that has been held by many philosophers, namely that if something is intrinsically good, the positive attitude of loving it for the property that makes it good, that is, desiring, pursuing

9. Suits, *The Grasshopper*, pp. 166/149, 144/130.

10. Tom Adelman, *The Long Ball: The Summer of '75—Spaceman, Catfish, Charlie Hustle, and the Greatest World Series Ever Played*, New York: Back Bay Books, 2003, p. 313.

and taking pleasure in it for that property, is also, and separately, intrinsically good. Thus, if another person's happiness is good, desiring, pursuing and being pleased by her happiness as happiness is a further good, namely that of benevolence; likewise, if knowledge is good, desiring, pursuing and being pleased by knowledge is good. Aristotle expressed this view when he said that if an activity is good, pleasure in it is good, whereas if an activity is bad, pleasure in it is bad,[11] and it was accepted around the turn of the twentieth century by many philosophers, including Rashdall, Franz Brentano, G. E. Moore, and W. D. Ross. And it applies directly to playing in games, which combines the good of difficulty with the further good of loving difficulty for itself. The prelusory goal and constitutive rules together give playing in games one ground of value, namely difficulty; the lusory attitude in its amateur form adds a related but distinct ground of value, namely loving something good for the property that makes it so. The second ground depends on the first; loving difficulty would not be good unless difficulty were good. But it adds a further, complementary intrinsic good. When you play a game for its own sake you do something good and do it from a motive that fixes on its good-making property.

This two-part explanation deepens Suits's claim that playing in games is an intrinsic good, by connecting it to more general principles of value with application beyond the case of games. At the same time, however, it makes playing in games a derivative rather than a fundamental intrinsic good. It would not appear on a list of basic goods, since it combines two other, more fundamental, goods in a particular way.

But a good that is not fundamental can nonetheless be paradigmatic because it gives the clearest possible expression of a certain type of value. If difficult activities are as such good, they must aim at a goal: it is achieving that which is challenging. But their value does not derive from properties of that goal considered in itself, depending instead on features of the process of achieving it. Yet this can be obscured if the goal is independently good, since then the activity, if successful, will be instrumentally

11. Aristotle, *Nicomachean Ethics*, trans. W. D. Ross and J. O. Urmson, Oxford: Oxford University Press, 1980, 1175b24–30. I discuss this view at length in *Virtue, Vice, and Value*.

good, and this can seem the most important thing about it. If the farmer who works by hand successfully harvests a crop, his work contributes to the vital good of feeding his family, and this can distract us from the value it has in itself. But there is no such danger if the goal is intrinsically valueless, as it most clearly is in games. Since a game's prelusory goal—getting a ball into a hole in the ground or standing atop a mountain—is intrinsically trivial, the value of playing the game can depend only on facts about the process of achieving that goal. And this point is further emphasized by the lusory attitude, which chooses that process just as a process, since it willingly accepts rules that make achieving the goal harder. Game-playing must have some external goal one aims at, but the specific features of this goal are irrelevant to the activity's value, which is entirely one of process rather than product, journey rather than destination. This is why playing in games gives the clearest expression of a modern as against an Aristotelian view of value: because modern values are precisely ones of process or journey rather than of the end-state they lead to.

The contrary Aristotelian view, which denigrates these values, was expressed most clearly in Aristotle's division of all activities into the two categories of *kinēsis* and *energeia*, and his subsequent judgements about them.[12] An Aristotelian *kinēsis*—often translated as 'movement'—is an activity aimed at a goal external to it, as driving to Toronto is aimed at being in Toronto. It is therefore brought to an end by the achievement of that goal, which means that a *kinēsis* can be identified by a grammatical test: if the fact that one has *X*-ed implies that one is no longer *X*-ing, as the fact that one has driven to Toronto implies that one is no longer driving there, then *X*-ing is a *kinēsis*. But the main point is that a *kinēsis* aims at an end-state separate from it. By contrast, an *energeia*—translated variously as 'actuality', 'activity', or 'action'—is not directed at an external goal but has its end internal to it. Contemplation is an *energeia*, because it does not aim to produce anything beyond itself, as is the state of feeling pleased. And *energeiai* do not pass the above grammatical test, and therefore, unlike *kinēseis*, can be carried on indefinitely: that one has contemplated does not imply that one is not

12. *Nicomachean Ethics*, 1094a1–7, 1174a13–b8, 1176b1–8, 1177b2–4.

contemplating now or will not continue to do so. Contemplation, like driving to Toronto, is an activity, but it does not aim to produce anything apart from itself.

Now, Aristotle held that *energeiai* are more valuable than *kinēseis*, so the best human activities must be ones that can be carried on continuously, such as contemplation. This is because he assumed that the value of a *kinēsis* must derive from that of its goal, so its value is subordinate, and even just instrumental, to that of the goal. As he said at the start of the *Nicomachean Ethics*, 'Where there are ends apart from the actions, it is the nature of the products to be better than the activities.'[13] But it is characteristic of what I am calling modern values to deny this assumption, and to hold that there are activities that necessarily aim at an external goal but whose value is internal to them in the sense that it depends entirely on features of the process of achieving that goal. Suits cites expressions of this modern view by Kierkegaard, Kant, Schiller, and Georg Simmel,[14] but for an especially clear one consider Marx's view that a central human good is transforming nature through productive labour. This activity necessarily has an external goal—one cannot produce without producing some thing—and in conditions of scarcity this goal will be something vital for humans' survival or comfort. But Marx held that when scarcity is overcome and humans enter the 'realm of freedom' they will still have work as their 'prime want', so they will engage in the process of production for its own sake without any interest in its goal as such. Or consider Nietzsche's account of human greatness. In an early work he said the one thing 'needful' is to 'give style to one's character', so its elements are unified by 'a single taste', and that it matters less whether this taste is good or bad than whether it is a single taste.[15] Later he said the will to power involves not the 'multitude and disgregation' of one's impulses but their coordination under a single predominant impulse.[16] In both discussions he deemed activities good if they involve organizing one's aims around a

13. Ibid., 109414–5.
14. Suits, *The Grasshopper*, pp. 93–94/92.
15. Friedrich Nietzsche, *The Gay Science*, trans. Walter Kaufmann, New York: Vintage, 1974, Sect. 290.
16. Nietzsche, *The Will to Power*, trans. Walter Kaufmann and R. J. Hollingdale, New York: Vintage, 1968, Sect. 46.

single goal whatever that goal is. So for both Marx and Nietzsche a central human good was activity that on the one side is necessarily directed to a goal but on the other derives its value entirely from aspects of the process of achieving it. This is why the type of value they affirm is paradigmatically illustrated by playing in games; when one's goal is trivial, the only value can be that of process. Marx and Nietzsche would never put it this way, but what each valued is in effect playing in games, in Marx's case the game of material production when there is no longer any instrumental need for it, in Nietzsche's the game of exercising power just for the sake of doing so.

Playing in games also clearly straddles Aristotle's division between *kinēseis* and *energeiai*. It has the logical structure of a *kinēsis*, since it aims at a goal external to itself, and passes the relevant grammatical test: if one has parred a golf hole or climbed a mountain, one is no longer doing so. But it also has value in itself, as an *energeia* does, based on properties internal to it as an activity. We can show this more precisely using our formal model of the value of achievement, on which the value of any goal depends in part on the number of other goals achieved as means to it. In figure 1 the lower-level goals are pursued as means to higher-level ones, and contribute to those goals' value only if they are both successfully achieved and contribute causally to them. And the higher-level goals must themselves also be successfully achieved. Since the hierarchy is precisely one of *achievements*, a highest-level goal that is not achieved does not qualify for inclusion in the hierarchy, and so does not gain any value from having other goals achieved as attempted means to it. This means that if two people go through the same complex process as a means to a given goal, and the first achieves the goal while the second through bad luck does not, the first's activity has more intrinsic value: his hierarchy contains his highest-level goal, which has his greatest value, but the second's does not. (If Pete Rose's opponents played as well as he did but Rose's team won the World Series, his play was intrinsically better.) So the activities valued by our formal model are directed at an external goal, as *kinēseis* are, and have their full value only if that goal is achieved. But their value does not depend on properties of the goal considered by itself; if the same goal were achieved without complex means, it might have just one unit of value. Instead, their value depends on means–end relations between their components, and so depends on internal features of the activity as does that of an *energeia*.

If playing in games is the paradigm expression of modern values, it helps us see similar value in other activities not normally associated with games. One, emphasized by Nietzsche, is a life organized around a single goal; it embodies through a longer stretch of time the same hierarchical structure present in individual difficult activities. The relevant activities also include ones in business and the arts. Business activity sometimes aims at an independent good such as relieving others' suffering or increasing their comfort. But often its goal is just to win market share and profits for one company, which is morally trivial; there is no intrinsic value in people's drinking Coke rather than Pepsi or using Microsoft rather than Apple. Aristotle should therefore deny this activity value, and he did, arguing that if money has no intrinsic value, the activity of money-making must likewise have no value.[17] But if winning market share is difficult, requiring a complex series of finely balanced decisions, a modern view can grant it significant worth. And its pursuit can also involve something like the lusory attitude, since business people who aim partly for profits can also value the exercise of business skill just as skill, or for its own sake. Artistic creation too, to cite a different activity, has an independently good product if it aims, say, at communicating truths that cannot be communicated by non-artistic means. But a distinctively modern view (which is not to say the only view held nowadays) says that art aims only at beauty, where that consists in organic unity, or having the different elements of a painting, novel or piece of music form a coherent, dynamic whole. This view makes the value of artistic production rest on its intentionally creating all the complex relations that define its product's beauty, that is, on its itself being complex. And its value will be greater if it has

17. *Nicomachean Ethics*, 1096a5–10. An obvious suggestion is that an activity like money-making can be a *kinēsis* when described in one way and an *energeia* when described in another. But, plausible though it is, this does not seem to have been Aristotle's view. He seems to have treated the distinction as a metaphysical one, between types of activities as they are in themselves. Nor could he have accepted the suggestion and continued to give his arguments about the inferiority of money-making and the superiority of contemplation, however described, based on their properties as *kinēsis* or *energeia*.

more of the supplementary qualities mentioned above: if it unifies more varied elements, if it requires more precise brushstrokes, notes or words, and if it involves grasping more extended contents in a single act of consciousness, as Henry Moore could see his sculptures from all sides at once.[18] And of course artistic creation can involve a lusory attitude, if the artist enjoys and values the skill his work involves for its own sake.

But playing in games is also in one respect a lesser good, and I want to close by explaining why. Imagine two activities that are equally complex and difficult, one of which produces an intrinsically good result while the other does not. Perhaps one is political activity that liberates an entire nation from oppression while the other involves winning a high-level chess tournament. The first activity will, of course, be instrumentally better, because it produces a separate intrinsic good. But it will also arguably be on that basis intrinsically better. Consider Derek Parfit's example of a person who spends his life working for the preservation of Venice. Parfit claims, plausibly, that if after this person's death Venice is preserved, and in a way that depends crucially on his efforts, that will make his life and activities intrinsically better than if Venice had been destroyed.[19] This conclusion already follows from our formal model of achievement, since any realization of a topmost goal adds value to a hierarchy. But I think there is an extra ground for its truth if, as Parfit clearly intends, the preservation of Venice is independently good. Whatever additional value there is in achieving a goal just as a goal, there is further value in achieving one that is good. When an activity aimed at a valuable end successfully achieves that end and therefore is instrumentally good, its being instrumentally good is an extra source of intrinsic goodness.[20]

Now, because game-playing has a trivial end result, it cannot have the additional intrinsic value that derives from instrumental value. This implies that excellence in games, though admirable, is less so than success in equally challenging activities that produce a

18. Howard Gardner, *Frames of Mind: The Theory of Multiple Intelligences*, New York: Basic Books, 1983, p. 188.

19. Derek Parfit, *Reasons and Persons*, Oxford: Clarendon Press, 1984, p. 151.

20. On this see Shelly Kagan, 'Rethinking Intrinsic Value', *Journal of Ethics*, 2, 1998, pp. 277–97; and my 'Two Kinds of Organic Unity', *Journal of Ethics*, 2, 1998, pp. 299–320.

great good or prevent a great evil. This seems intuitively right: the honour due athletic achievements for themselves is less than that due the achievements of great political reformers or medical researchers. Whatever admiration we should feel for Tiger Woods or Gary Kasparov is less than we should feel for Nelson Mandela. It also implies that, whatever their other merits, Suits's utopia and Marx's realm of freedom would lack an important intrinsic good. Their inhabitants could play the game of, say, farming or medicine by going through the same complex procedures as farmers and doctors today. But if food could be produced and diseases cured by pushing a button, as they can in Suits's vision, their activity would not have the additional intrinsic value that comes from actually feeding or curing people and that is found in present-day farming and medicine.[21] The very perfection of Suits's and Marx's utopias prevents them from containing the distinctive good of producing intrinsic goods that would not otherwise exist.

The point that an ideal world may exclude certain intrinsic goods should not be unfamiliar: G. E. Moore noted that the best possible world could not contain compassion for real pain, which he plausibly held was a greater good than compassion for merely imaginary pain.[22] And Suits's and Marx's utopias can still contain, alongside such goods as pleasure and knowledge, the distinctively modern good of achieving a difficult goal regardless of its value. Moreover, their doing so can help make them better on balance than any world in which successful instrumental activity is possible. Many philosophers have assumed, with Aristotle, that the value of a process aimed at producing some end-state must derive entirely from the end-state's value, so if the latter is negligible so is the former. But there is no reason to believe this. Even if some of the process's intrinsic value depends on its instrumental value, in the way just described, there can also be intrinsic value in its properties just as a process and apart from any value in its product. To return again to figure 1, this value will depend not on any qualities of

21. This claim is defended, with specific reference to Suits, in Shelly Kagan, 'The Grasshopper, Aristotle, Bob Adams, and Me' (unpublished ms.).
22. G. E. Moore, *Principia Ethica*, Cambridge: Cambridge University Press, 1903, pp. 219–21.

the topmost goal considered in itself, but only on the means–ends relations between the various goals whose sequential achievement constitutes the process. I have argued that this distinctively modern value is illustrated most clearly by playing in games, especially when that is analysed as in Bernard Suits's wonderful book *The Grasshopper*.[23]

REFERENCES

Adelman, Tom 2003: *The Long Ball: The Summer of '75—Spaceman, Catfish, Charlie Hustle, and the Greatest World Series Ever Played*. New York: Back Bay Books.

Aristotle 1980: *Nicomachean Ethics*. Trans. W. D. Ross and J. O. Urmson. Oxford: Oxford University Press.

Gardner, Howard 1983: *Frames of Mind: The Theory of Multiple Intelligences*. New York: Basic Books.

Griffin, James 1986: *Well-Being: Its Meaning, Measurement and Moral Importance*. Oxford: Clarendon Press.

Hurka, Thomas 1993: *Perfectionism*. New York: Oxford University Press.

——— 1998: 'Two Kinds of Organic Unity'. *Journal of Ethics*, 2, 1998, pp. 299–320.

——— 2001: *Virtue, Vice, and Value*. New York: Oxford University Press.

Kagan, Shelly 1998: 'Rethinking Intrinsic Value'. *Journal of Ethics*, 2, 1998, pp. 277–97.

——— unpublished: 'The Grasshopper, Aristotle, Bob Adams, and Me'.

Moore, G. E. 1903: *Principia Ethica*. Cambridge: Cambridge University Press.

Nietzsche, Friedrich 1968: *The Will to Power*. Trans. Walter Kaufmann and R. J. Hollingdale. New York: Vintage

——— 1974. *The Gay Science*. Trans. Walter Kaufmann. New York: Vintage.

Nozick, Robert 1974: *Anarchy, State, and Utopia*. New York: Basic Books.

Parfit, Derek 1984: *Reasons and Persons*. Oxford: Clarendon Press.

Rashdall, Hastings 1907: *The Theory of Good and Evil*, 2 vols. London: Oxford University Press.

Suits, Bernard 1978/2005: *The Grasshopper: Games, Life and Utopia*. Toronto: University of Toronto Press. Repr. Peterborough, ON: Broadview Press, 2005.

Wittgenstein, Ludwig 1972: *Philosophical Investigations*, 3rd edn. Trans. G. E. M. Anscombe. Oxford: Blackwell.

23. I am grateful for helpful conversations to my former student Gwendolyn Bradford, whose essay 'Kudos for Ludus' first linked the value of games and the details of Suits's definition of a game.

GAMES AND THE GOOD

by Thomas Hurka and John Tasioulas

II—John Tasioulas

ABSTRACT This paper contends that play, not achievement, is the primary intrinsic good internal to game-playing, and supports a relational, as opposed to formal, conception of achievement.

Thomas Hurka endorses three arresting claims in his contribution to this symposium: (a) that game-playing can be defined as 'the voluntary attempt to overcome unnecessary obstacles',[1] where the obstacles are created by constitutive rules with respect to a goal that can be specified and achieved independently of those rules; (b) that this definition enables us to identify the two intrinsic or non-instrumental goods internal to game-playing: they consist, primarily, in the good of engaging successfully in difficult activity (achievement), and, derivatively, in loving (that is, desiring, enjoying, and so on) such activity for its own sake; and (c) that the primary good realized through game-playing—success in achieving a difficult goal regardless of its value—is a distinctively modern, as opposed to classical, type of authentic good. In this paper, I take issue with all three claims. In the course of doing so, I put forward the rival hypothesis that the primary intrinsic good internal to game-playing—a good worth pursuing for its own sake and so capable of making one's life go better in so far as one participates in it—is that of play itself.

I

Games and their Value. Hurka's thesis (a) invokes Bernard Suits's definition of game-playing, according to which

> To play a game is to attempt to achieve a specific state of affairs [prelusory goal], using only means permitted by the rules ... where the rules prohibit the use of more efficient in favour of less efficient means [constitutive rules], and where the rules are

1. B. Suits, *The Grasshopper: Games, Life and Utopia*, Boston, Godine, 1990, p. 41.

> accepted just because they make possible such activity [lusory attitude].[2]

Yet this definition seems wildly over-inclusive. Neither the justified infliction of punishment nor the waging of a lawful war is the playing of a game. But consider a Hartian understanding of the former. Here the 'prelusory' goal is to prevent criminal behaviour and the rules that make its attainment more difficult include those that forbid punishing the innocent or punishing the guilty disproportionately. Moreover, officials of the criminal justice system may adopt a 'lusory attitude' towards its rules, voluntarily accepting them just so that they can engage in the activity thereby made possible, i.e. the justified punishment of offenders. Whatever the defects of Hart's theory of punishment, that it turns punishment into a game is not plausibly among them. A similar verdict holds in the case of a war, aimed at repelling an attack by another state, which is conducted in accordance with humanitarian law, since the latter prohibits such potentially efficient means as the torture of enemy soldiers and the terror bombing of civilians.[3]

Perhaps these intended counterexamples misfire because they do not involve 'intrinsically trivial' goals (p. 285), unlike the prelusory goals of golf (putting a ball in a hole) or chess (bringing about a certain arrangement of chessmen). But it is not obvious what the requirement of 'triviality' amounts to, nor that all the activities Hurka considers to be games meet it. Are the prelusory goals of poker (increasing one's money) or boxing (incapacitating or outpunching one's opponent) also trivial? The answer is unclear, partly because the goals admit of a variety of descriptions that seem to differ in point of triviality. In any case, other activities with more obviously trivial goals may serve as counterexamples. Consider a goal-involving ritual, such as a pilgrimage. Here, a

2. Ibid. pp. 54–5, quoted in T. Hurka, 'Games and the Good', p. 275. All otherwise unspecified page references are to Hurka's article.

3. Suits would presumably seek to exclude these putative counterexamples on the grounds that those who engage in the practices of punishment and legal warfare accept the rules for general and independent *moral* reasons (op. cit., pp. 31–2). But players often accept the rules of paradigmatic games for moral reasons, for example, rules disallowing dangerous tackles in football. More importantly, from the fact that there are independent moral reasons for accepting the rules of a practice, it does not follow that those who engage in it accept them for those reasons. Some may simply wish to be judges or soldiers and therefore accept the rules that apply to these roles.

trivial goal (being present in location *X* at time *t*) is to be achieved only by complying with certain rules (such as travelling on foot via a circuitous route) that make the accomplishment of the goal more difficult. Moreover, the rules may be complied with for the sake of the activity they make possible, e.g. a pilgrimage.

Not only is Suits's definition over-inclusive in so far as it appears to be satisfied by activities that Hurka himself would not count as games, it is also over-inclusive by virtue of embracing activities that he implausibly considers to be games. The problem here is with the unqualified contention that sports are 'a subclass of the wider category of games' (p. 273). Some of the sports Hurka mentions, such as golf, baseball and hockey, are unquestionably games, whereas others, such as sprinting, weightlifting and mountaineering, would not ordinarily be so described. Naturally, this observation is hostage to the vagaries of linguistic usage, but an underlying rationale can be adduced in its favour.[4] Sports are activities the successful pursuit of which characteristically invites the display of some kind of physical prowess; indeed, having the opportunity to display such prowess is part of the point of engaging in sporting activities. This is why many jib at awarding unathletic indoor games such as tiddlywinks, darts or billiards the honorific description 'sport'. And just as not all games are sports, so too not all sports are games. Sports that are not games tend to be institutionalized—or rule-governed—versions of some form of activity that involves the display of physical prowess, and in which one might intelligibly engage, or take an interest, pre-institutionally. Thus, boxing is a rule-governed fist fight, the 100 metres sprint a rule-governed foot race, weightlifting a rule-governed trial of strength of a certain kind, and so on. The goings-on in a cricket match, by contrast, notoriously cannot be understood without pervasive reference to a system of 'arbitrary' rules, that is, rules that do not essentially structure and facilitate the realization of some fairly specific pre-institutional activity. Of course, this leaves the distinction between sports that are games

4. There is a Wittgensteinian irritant here, but not the thesis that 'game' is indefinable that irritates Hurka. Instead, it is the mistranslation of 'Kampfspiele' as 'Olympic games' in the English-language edition of the *Philosophical Investigations* (see L. Wittgenstein, *Philosophical Investigations*, 3rd edn, trans. G. E. M. Anscombe, Oxford: Blackwell, 1972, §66). Greeks continue to call them '*agones*', which is best rendered 'contests'. On the view I am advancing, 'games' in the expression 'Olympic games' operates as a metonym.

and those that are not occasionally indeterminate, but that is as it should be.

The reply might now be that even if true, everything I have said so far is innocuous to the success of Hurka's project. And this because the concept of 'game-playing' he deploys is a term of art, one that captures what is importantly common to participating in both games and sports. Perhaps so; but this reply skates over the dialectical significance of treating all sports as games and concentrating heavily, as Hurka does, on sports in elucidating the value of game-playing. The overall effect is to confer far greater plausibility on thesis (b) than would have been the case had a different set of examples been employed, since most people are inclined to believe that sporting success is a genuine form of achievement. This tendency to skew the dialectic in (b)'s favour is compounded by three other features of Hurka's discussion.

The first is his brisk dismissal of many games, for instance, rock-paper-scissors, as not 'good games' because they are not 'challenging' or 'reasonably difficult' (p. 276). Yet, like snakes-and-ladders, this is a perfectly good game when played by or with a child, and its goodness has little to do with any form of achievement as opposed to the fun of playing it. And there are, of course, adult analogues: games that involve no significant room for skill in meeting difficult challenges. The most conspicuous category, which is entirely absent from Hurka's discussion, is games of chance such as bingo or roulette.[5] Of course, even these can be played in a way that eliminates or curtails the influence of chance on the outcome (for example, one might buy up all the tickets in a lottery). But to play them in this spirit is to miss their distinctive appeal. Moreover, many games combine skill with luck, and one of the determinants of the extent to which the latter figures may be the players' comparative levels of competence.[6] Still, the presence of luck seems to be a

5. For the observation that, notwithstanding the dominance of the rhetoric of skill and achievement over that of fortune or fate among the professional classes, the amount of money spent annually on games of chance in the United States ($400 billion) exceeds that spent on all others combined, as well as the defence budget, see B. Sutton-Smith, *The Ambiguity of Play*, Cambridge, MA: Harvard University Press, 1997, p. 66.

6. Mae West: Is poker a game of chance?
W. C. Fields: Not the way I play it.—*My Little Chickadee*

valuable feature of many games despite having nothing to do with striving and achievement, and everything to do with the thrill of surrendering to fate and delighting in good fortune.

Relatedly, Hurka focuses on 'excellence' manifested in skilful game-playing and the 'admiration' it merits. Yet there are innumerable instances of game-playing in ordinary life that we judge worthwhile even though they do not, and often cannot in virtue of the nature of the relevant game, realize the excellence/admiration pairing. Here, the perspective of those who participate in games, and not merely that of potential spectators, needs to be taken into account. Consider, for example, young children playing blind man's bluff, factory workers engaged in an impromptu football match during their lunch break, or an Old Age Pensioner enjoying a weekly game of bingo. One would be hard-pressed to deny that these activities have value for those engaged in them, and so are properly desired by the latter. But the realization of this value is typically no cause for admiration on the part of onlookers. Instead, what seems to be at stake is an interest, like our interest in autonomy or freedom from pain, the meeting of which makes a person's life go better. In so far as this interest is fulfilled, some attitude of approval other than admiration is usually in order; conversely, its non-fulfilment may rightly provoke frustration and indignation.[7] It is primarily under this decidedly non-elite aspect that our interest in play is protected by various human rights instruments, such as Article 31(1) of the United Nations Convention on the Rights of the Child and Article 24 of the Universal Declaration of Human Rights. But it is a dimension of the value of game-playing that is screened from view by Hurka's analysis.

7. For an attempt to understand human well-being itself in terms of the enjoyment of excellence, see R. M. Adams, *Finite and Infinite Goods: A Framework for Ethics*, Oxford: Oxford University Press, 1999, Ch. 3. This thesis faces the difficulty that 'excellence', if it is not simply identical with goodness, is either a high level of (attainable) goodness or else a type of goodness, for example, that which merits admiration. Either way, it is radically incomplete as an account of well-being, since engagement with good (but not excellent) things can enhance one's life. Moreover, Adams makes strained judgements—both about the source of an activity's value and the presence of excellence—that only confirm this incompleteness, for example, that physical pleasure is 'normally an enjoyment of healthy life, which ... is an excellence', or that 'bad' art can enhance our lives only because the latter 'typically has excellences, in some degree' (op. cit., pp. 100–1).

Finally, not everyone accepts the claim that engaging in games and sports can manifest a form of excellence that merits admiration. Indeed, some take a dim view of the widespread adulation of leading sporting figures in contemporary society—a phenomenon Hurka invokes in order to lend credence to this claim—attributing it to some such cause (or complex of causes) as the distorting influence of nationalist sentiment, the commodification of sport under capitalism or the cultural 'levelling-down' wrought by democratization. George Orwell, for example, diagnosed the modern preoccupation with sporting success as 'merely another effect of the causes that have produced nationalism', and he went on to ridicule those spectators and nations 'who work themselves into furies over these absurd contests, and seriously believe—at any rate for short periods—that running, jumping and kicking a ball are tests of national virtue'.[8] Such scepticism is not obviously perverse, especially when recast as the less uncompromising claim that modern culture grossly overvalues sporting success. But an approach that simply deems it a platitude that the primary good internal to sport is a form of excellence that merits admiration is scarcely well-placed to counter it.

II

Play as a Basic Good. The provisional upshot of our discussion is that, in so far as there is a good 'internal' to game-playing, that is, one in terms of which the nature and point of that activity is primarily to be elucidated, it is not best thought of as a kind of 'excellence' that rightly evokes 'admiration'. So, *contra* (b), it is not achievement which is presumably a good of that sort. Someone might respond that this conclusion is vitiated by a failure to distinguish between intrinsic and instrumental value: Hurka aimed to elucidate the intrinsic value of game-playing—the good accruing to game-playing as such, independently of its consequences—whereas the supposed counterexamples identify aspects of its instrumental value. Of course, claims about the instrumental value of game-playing are well-rehearsed.

8. George Orwell, 'The Sporting Spirit', in *George Orwell: Essays*, London: Penguin, 2000, pp. 322, 324.

According to Herodotus, the Lydians purported to have invented all games common to them and the Greeks as a way of mitigating the effects of a famine. And evolutionary psychologists in our day attribute adaptive value to play as preparation for coping with future challenges, both expected and unexpected.[9] So, it might be said in connection with our illustrative cases, that the bingo player's weekly game is a means to enjoyment and friendship; that the factory workers' football match affords a period of recreation and diversion that helps them go back to work with renewed vigour; and so on.

Without disputing that game-playing can be instrumentally valuable in myriad ways, in this section I contend that the primary intrinsic value internal to game-playing is play itself. Moreover, one can affirm this without first having defined game-playing, so to that extent Hurka's thesis that a unified account of the value of game-playing must be erected on the back of a definition of that activity is mistaken. Achievement in game-playing is also a good, and when instantiated it typically constitutes a form of excellence that merits admiration; but in the next section I argue that it is a relational good. In other words, although achievement is an intrinsic value that can be realized through game-playing, when it is so realized it is typically dependent on the value of play itself.

The thesis that play is a basic good opposes the contention that playing in games is 'a derivative rather than a fundamental intrinsic good', combining the two goods of difficult activity and the love of such activity (p. 284). Still, it is a claim with a notable pedigree, even if its proponents have not usually accorded it the benefit of a sustained defence.[10] Of course, it faces the immediate objection that there seems to be a world of difference between, say, chess and football; so much so, it will be said,

9. Herodotus, *The Histories* I.94; Sutton-Smith, op. cit., Ch. 2.

10. For some examples from English-language philosophy in recent years, see J. Finnis, *Natural Law and Natural Rights*, Oxford: Oxford University Press, 1980, p. 87 (listing play as a basic form of human good); G. Grisez and R. Shaw, *Beyond the New Morality: The Responsibilities of Freedom*, 3rd edn, Notre Dame, IN: University of Notre Dame Press, 1988, Ch. 7; M. Nussbaum, *Women and Human Development: The Capabilities Approach*, Oxford: Oxford University Press, 2000, p. 80 (listing play as a 'central human functional capability'); and M. Oakeshott, 'Work and Play', in *What is History? and Other Essays*, Exeter: Imprint Academic, 2004.

that it is highly artificial to suppose that the same good is instantiated by both activities. The first line of response must be that the value of play is a determinable, one that assumes different determinate shapes in the context of the various activities instantiating it. After all, subscribers to an objective list of goods will have to make some such claim about other items on it. Notice, too, that play need not be any more definable than other putative goods, such as enjoyment, friendship and knowledge. But we can be satisfied with this response only if an informative characterization of the value of play can be given at a fairly high level of generality, one that confirms its status as a distinct and irreducible value.

The most promising way to formulate such an account is by adopting a bottom-up approach that identifies characteristic features of instantiations of the value of play. Such an approach contrasts sharply with Hurka's subsumption of game-playing under a pre-established theory of value, according to which pleasure, achievement and knowledge are basic goods. An important source for this enterprise is Johan Huizinga's classic study *Homo Ludens*, in which play is characterized as follows:

> [A] free activity standing quite consciously outside 'ordinary' life as being 'not serious', but at the same time absorbing the player intensely and utterly. It is an activity connected to no material interest, and no profit can be gained by it. It proceeds within its own proper boundaries of time and space according to fixed rules and in an orderly manner. It promotes the formation of social groupings which tend to surround themselves with secrecy and to stress their difference from the common world by disguise or other means ... The play-mood is one of rapture and enthusiasm, and is sacred or festive in accordance with the occasion. A feeling of exaltation and tension accompanies the action, mirth and relaxation follow.[11]

It is worth elaborating some of the elements, whether explicit or implicit, in this formulation.

(1) *Free Activity*. At its best play is a free activity, voluntarily entered upon (and exited) and without any sense of material or moral compulsion. Of course, sometimes play is not engaged in

11. J. Huizinga, *Homo Ludens: A Study of the Play Element in Culture*, Boston: Beacon Press, 1955, pp. 13, 132. I have also benefited from R. Caillois, *Man, Play and Games*, Urbana, IL: University of Illinois Press, 2001.

freely, or not straightforwardly so—for instance, compulsory sport at school—but, to the extent that this is so, it lacks an important dimension of the good of play. Leaving aside any instrumental concern with health, discipline or the prevention of delinquency, a key justification for dragooning schoolchildren into sports and other worthwhile forms of play is that they may eventually acquire a liking for them and engage in them freely in their own time.

(2) *Separation from Ordinary Life*. Play takes place outside the routine of 'ordinary' life, especially those aspects concerned with reproducing the material and moral conditions of our existence. It typically unfolds during one's leisure or 'free' time, often within spatial boundaries marked out in advance (court, stage, field, etc.) and sometimes with participants wearing distinctive attire. Its separation from ordinary life lends it a quality of being 'not serious' or 'only pretend', which is related to the fact that what takes place in play is not supposed to have significant (especially, significantly *negative*) repercussions for the rest of life. The inconsequential nature of play explains our disinclination to classify duelling or any other activity that involves the deliberate infliction of serious harm, or even a very high risk of severe injury, as a form of play.[12] It also explains the familiar denunciations of the commercialization of sport as a corruption of play. Ordinary life, in these cases, oversteps the boundaries that separate it from play. Hence also the tendency of play to lose its value when it becomes an obsession, so all-pervading that the player loses touch with ordinary life, or when participation in games of chance fosters a superstitious or fatalistic attitude to life as a whole, or when players of mimetic games come to identify with their fictional persona. Play in these cases is corrupted by invading ordinary life. None of this, of course, prevents play from interposing itself benignly into even the most serious activities, from the administration of justice to philosophical disputation, as Huizinga's work famously showed.

(3) *Significant Order*. Play tends to be ordered by rules, roles or expectations that confer a point on the activity for those engaged

12. By contrast, on Suits's definition, a fight to the death (provided it is governed by at least one constitutive rule, e.g. one that sets a start time, that is accepted by the fighters in order to engage in the activity made possible) is just as much a game as chess (op. cit., Ch. 6).

in it. This is certainly true of sports, with their formally defined rules, but it applies equally to chess, dancing, the telling of jokes, etc. Two dimensions of the order exhibited by play are worth stressing. The first is the aesthetic character of play, which is evident in the vocabulary often used to describe it: tension, balance, variation, harmony, grace, rhythm, resolution, and so on. The second is the important role that uncertainty, and the tension it creates, assumes within this order. Resigning one's will to an uncertain outcome, beyond one's control, belongs to the essence of games of chance. But uncertainty is also a significant factor in competitive games that call for intellectual or physical skill. Here, the rules set difficult challenges for the participants, which they might fail to meet. Indeed, were they assured of meeting them without too much effort, the game would lose much of its appeal.

(4) *Valued for Its Own Sake*. Play is activity (capable of being) valued and engaged in exclusively for its own sake, as opposed to any instrumental benefit, such as the meeting of needs or desires of the player or of others in society. This marks a basic contrast with activity that counts as 'work', which is typically directed at the creation of a product or outcome that has intrinsic or instrumental value, where this value in turn provides at least a partial basis for the intrinsic value of engaging in work. Yet despite not being 'serious' in the sense discussed under (2), play is capable of being taken seriously in virtue of its perceived intrinsic value, and in its most worthwhile manifestations it absorbs the player 'intensely and utterly'.

(5) *Enjoyment*. The enjoyment of playful performances for their own sake is an important source of their intrinsic value. There is a temptation to think that in the absence of being enjoyed, such performances lack intrinsic value. But this claim is too strong. Many instances of play, especially of the sporting variety, are imbued with a kind of tension, concentration or physical exertion that renders enjoying them whilst one is whole-heartedly engaged in them very difficult, if not impossible.[13] But this does not mean that they have no value when engaged in without enjoyment. Where enjoyment is not incompatible with being whole-heartedly

13. 'There are no pleasures in a fight but some of my fights have been a pleasure to win' (Muhammad Ali).

engaged in play, the absence of enjoyment can diminish the value of a particular instance of game-playing. Still, we should not discount the possibility that, as John Finnis has suggested, 'participation in basic goods which is emotionally dry, subjectively unsatisfying, nevertheless is good and meaningful as far as it goes.'[14] The obvious caveat is that in the case of play it might not go very far at all, since with many kinds of play it is virtually unintelligible why anyone should choose to engage in them if they do not enjoy them (leaving aside any instrumental benefit, such as exercise or sociability). This seems especially true of games that are in no sense challenging. At this point one might be attracted to a disjunctive account of the intrinsic value internal to games and sports, with achievement and enjoyment as the two disjuncts (but, unlike Hurka's theory, the latter not being dependent on the former). Although not without its merits, this account fails to capture the strong sense that play often involves participation—whether enjoyed or not—in an independently valuable activity, where the independent value is not plausibly characterized as achievement. Thus, someone might think that a low-grade game of football was intrinsically worthwhile, even though they did not enjoy it because they were upset at missing a 'sitter' early on or were anxious throughout about the outcome of the match. This, however, is not to exclude the possibility that some forms of play need to be enjoyed if they are to have value, or at least if they are to contribute to the well-being of those participating in them.

(6) *Social Dimension.* A component of the value of many forms of play is their being socially acknowledged, at least potentially so, as valuable. In the passage quoted above, Huizinga characterizes the social dimension of play in terms of the propensity of devotees of various forms of play to establish clubs and associations. Equally, we have noted that play often depends on rules, roles and expectations, and these are typically socially generated. But the deeper point is that it can belong to what makes a form of play worthwhile that there are spectators or competitors who can or do 'play along', engaging in or valuing the activity as worthwhile in itself. The goodness of games can consist, in part, in the fact that their goodness is—and is generally known

14. Finnis, op. cit., pp. 96–7.

to be—acknowledged by others who engage in or with the playing of it as fellow participants or as spectators. This is especially so with games of skill, which have a natural tendency to become competitive and seek out an audience, but it also applies to games of chance, which explains why many prefer gambling at a casino or racetrack to the solitary activity of placing their bets by telephone or through the Internet. The phenomenon of fads for certain games, puzzles and toys, which suddenly flare up and just as quickly peter out only to be replaced by the latest craze, is partly to be understood by reference to the social dimension of play.

The recognition of play as the basic good internal to games yields a number of advantages over Hurka's account. First, it remedies one way in which Suits's definition is over-inclusive. If the primary intrinsic value internal to games is play—that is, if games are activities that are characteristically worth engaging in for the sake of play—this suffices to distinguish them from activities that involve the pursuit of goals subject to voluntarily accepted constitutive rules, such as punishment, lawful warfare and pilgrimages, which are engaged in for the sake of goods other than play. This way of distinguishing game-playing seems preferable to Hurka's suggestion that games can be engaged in with a 'pure' lusory attitude, one whereby the rules in question are accepted because they make the resultant activity difficult, and not just possible. One reason is that this attitude is inapplicable to games that do not pose a reasonably difficult challenge; another is that the attitude seems to be present in difficult rule-bound and goal-directed activities that are not the playing of a game: for example, an adult who teaches himself Russian in his spare time might decide to sit the A level examination in the subject as a test of his competence, but no game is being played as a result.

Second, it corrects Hurka's tendency to focus on games in which there is scope for the realization of excellence, or instances of game-playing in which excellence is realized, thereby depriving an implausibly large number of everyday instances of game-playing of any significant intrinsic value. Instead, acknowledging play as a basic good brings to light the intrinsic good internal to the four broad, and overlapping, categories of games: competitive games (e.g. chess), games of chance (e.g. roulette), games of simulation (e.g. charades), and those of vertigo (e.g. drinking games).[15] Moreover, we are equipped to identify the key feature that unites game-playing with activities that do not count as games because they are not governed by (arbitrary) rules. We can thus keep hold of the common-sense idea that when a child, in the course of an afternoon, moves from playing in his sandpit, to playing with his toy animals, to bouncing a ball, to playing hide-and-seek, and so on, he is, throughout, ultimately engaged in the same kind of activity, one that broadly realizes the same intrinsic value.

Third, specifying the nature of games by reference to the value of play preserves the valid insight buried in the misleading claim that sports are a sub-class of games. This is the idea that play is the primary good internal to both games and sports. Indeed, one might understand (I do not say define) the concept of a game, in its focal sense, as an activity that is characteristically engaged in for the sake of play, the rules of which tend to be pervasively 'arbitrary', that is, not primarily facilitative of some pre-institutionally meaningful form of activity. The 'arbitrariness' of the rules is perfectly compatible with their being purposely adapted to facilitate enjoyable, imaginative, intellectually or physically challenging, etc., instantiations of the good of play. Sports are activities in which this good is realized indirectly, in a way intended to manifest the participants' physical prowess. This potentially unstable combination of play and physical prowess is reflected in the uneasiness many feel about classifying as sports activities in which the relevant form of prowess essentially involves the deliberate infliction of severe pain or the assumption of a significant risk of injury, since these features threaten to crowd out anything obviously recognizable as play. Some observations in Joyce Carol Oates's *On Boxing*, although perhaps going too far in denying that boxing is a form of play and insufficiently attentive to the distinction between sports and games, help bring out the tension:

15. Here I invoke Roger Caillois's fourfold classification of games according to the characteristic attitude that animates them: 'the desire to win by one's merit in regulated competition (*agôn*), the submission of one's will in favor of anxious and passive anticipation of where the wheel will stop (*alea*), the desire to assume a strange personality (*mimicry*), and, finally, the pursuit of vertigo (*ilinx*)' (op. cit., p. 44; see also pp. 14–26).

> I have no difficulty justifying boxing as a sport because I have never thought of it as a sport . . . There is nothing fundamentally playful about it; nothing that seems to belong to daylight, to pleasure. At its moments of greatest intensity it seems to contain so complete and so powerful an image of life—life's beauty, vulnerability, despair, incalculable and often self-destructive courage—that boxing *is* life, and hardly a mere game. During a superior boxing match (Ali–Frazier I, for instance) we are deeply moved by the body's communion with itself by way of another's intransigent flesh. The body's dialogue with its shadow-self—or Death. Baseball, football, basketball—these quintessentially American pastimes are recognizably sports because they involve play: they are games. One *plays* football, one doesn't *play* boxing.[16]

The point is not simply about the negation of enjoyment by pain, fear and despair, but also the blurring of the boundary between 'ordinary' life and 'non-serious' play. It is worth observing that Hurka also registers the problematic status of boxing as an exemplification of the good internal to sport. But he ascribes it to the influence of 'raw power' (and also, presumably, speed, endurance, etc.) in determining the outcome of a bout, since this sits uncomfortably with his emphasis on a 'rational connection to reality' in specifying the value of achievement. In other words, whereas I have suggested boxing's problematic character *qua* sport stems from its being all too consequential for 'real life', Hurka attributes it to a lack of 'complex ratiocination' (p. 281). But not only is this a curiously intellectualized account of the good internal to sport, one that implausibly ranks golf (or sailing, lawn bowls, etc.) above boxing (or swimming, sprinting, etc.) despite the limited role of physical prowess in the former. It is also a questionable explanation of the problematic status of boxing as an exemplification of the good internal to sport, since the importance of raw power and other non-rational capacities is also a feature of swimming, weightlifting, javelin-throwing, sprinting, and other sports that are quite properly found unproblematic on this score.

Fourth, the good of play provides a general, albeit not exhaustive, account of the intrinsic good internal to games and sports that neatly sidesteps—or, at least, postpones—a

16. J. C. Oates, *On Boxing*, New York: Harper Collins, 2002, pp. 18–19.

confrontation with Orwellian scepticism regarding the presence of admiration-meriting excellence in such activities. However things may stand with respect to achievement in sports and games, engagement in both can have intrinsic value in so far as it instantiates the value of play itself. Even Orwell did not deny that sports can be played in a way that is (intrinsically?) valuable for their participants: 'On the village green, where you pick up sides and no feeling of local patriotism is involved, it is possible to play simply for the fun and exercise.'[17]

Finally, we can respect an intuitive distinction between play and work activities, one that survives the complication that for some, such as professional sportspeople, their work consists in a form of play. For Hurka, presumably, achievement is the key intrinsic value internal to both games and sports, on the one hand, and work, on the other, even though it is only in the latter case that the activity's value derives in significant measure from its product or outcome. But whereas lack of personal achievement, or of any prospect of it, is always a good *pro tanto* reason for dissatisfaction with one's work, the same is not true of one's play. From this perspective, Hurka's argument for (b) is a sophisticated manifestation of a problematic trend in modern life, one that has been aptly described as 'the invasion of play by the rhetoric of achievement'.[18] As such, it is a defence of games in the spirit of the work ethic, and so yet another expression of the imperialist tendencies of the latter in our culture.[19]

III

Achievement and Difficulty. There are two reasons why we still need to examine Hurka's account of achievement. I have disputed (b) in part by relying on a common-sense grasp of the nature of achievement, one according to which it is instantiated

17. Orwell, op. cit., p. 322.
18. C. Lasch, *The Culture of Narcissism: American Life in an Age of Diminishing Expectations*, New York: Norton, 1978, p. 65.
19. 'Instead of regarding "work" and "play" as two great and diverse experiences of the world, each offering us what the other lacks, we are often encouraged to regard all that I have called "play", either as a holiday designed to make us "work" better when it is over, or merely as "work" of another sort' (Oakeshott, op. cit., p. 313).

by activities characterized by certain kinds of excellence that merit admiration. But Hurka's account of achievement might be compelling, and so provide a basis for affirming (b), even though it deviates from this ordinary notion. Second, even if play is the primary value internal to games and sports, it is plausible to suppose that achievement is also an important intrinsic good that can be realized through playing them. So it is worth considering whether Hurka offers a compelling account of achievement independently of its use to support (b).

On Hurka's construal, achievement involves 'realizing a goal in the world given a justified belief that one would do so' by means of a process that is 'reasonably difficult' in absolute terms (pp. 223, 220), for example, one that involves complexity, physical prowess, skill and ingenuity. In contrast to a supposed 'classical' or Aristotelian view, which would assess the value of goal-directed pursuits exclusively by reference to the independent value of the goal they realize, Hurka claims that the intrinsic value of such activities *qua* achievements is fundamentally dependent on certain 'formal properties' that make them difficult. On this view, the intrinsic value of difficult activity is increased to the extent that its goals, and the hierarchical means–end relations that obtain among them, exhibit properties such as *complexity* (which relates not just to the number of goals to be achieved, but also their diversity and the complexity of their interrelations), the level of *precision* required in achieving the goals, and the *breadth of content* of the goals, for example, across time or in the number of objects they involve. The important point is that these intensifiers of the good of achievement are among the very properties that make an activity—including every kind of 'good game'—difficult (p. 224–5): achievement is successful engagement in difficult activity as such.

Now, Hurka's 'formal model' contrasts with two other plausible accounts of achievement, which I shall label the 'deep' and the 'wide'. According to the former conception, achievement is one prudential value among others, so that its instantiation in a person's life can enhance their well-being by conferring weight or point on it.[20] A person's life can contain deep achievements, and

20. It is in this vein that James Griffin defends the value of 'accomplishment', which he describes as 'roughly the sort of value that gives life weight or point'—see J. Griffin, *Value Judgement: Improving our Ethical Beliefs*, Oxford: Oxford University Press, 1996, p. 24.

to that extent be admirable, despite not going well for them overall—for example, they might have fought heroically in a just cause, but died tragically young—and also despite not being admirable overall. The other, 'wide' conception of achievement is instantiated when a person's life as a whole *does* go well for them. On an objectivist construal of well-being, one according to which a good life is not ultimately or predominantly a life in which certain mental states obtain, this is a life in which the person living it is active, and to a significant degree successful, in pursuing worthwhile goals, both shorter-term and longer-term in character, that make up an overarching network of goals. A good life will involve self-direction, choice, discipline, etc., on the part of the person whose life it is, and so can be thought of as an achievement of theirs, something actively secured through their efforts, rather than a condition that might have come into being primarily through the benevolent actions of others, the workings of a Nozickian 'experience machine', etc.[21] On a wide, as opposed to a deep, conception of achievement, its presence in someone's life does not necessarily merit admiration.

Success in difficult activity as such is not achievement in either of these senses. One must go beyond the bare fact of an activity's difficulty, and its possession of the formal qualities mentioned earlier, to see it as instantiating either deep or wide achievement; some other value, or combination of values, must be appropriately related to difficult activity if engaging in it is to be an achievement. Since the dependence of 'wide' achievement on other values is fairly obvious, let me concentrate on 'deep' achievement. Regarding the latter, James Griffin denies that even very difficult activities, such as flagpole-sitting of 'Guiness-Book-of-Records duration', constitute accomplishments: 'bare, even rare, achievement' does not suffice.[22] I think this denial is best understood as reflecting the following thesis: whether an activity is a deep achievement depends on its being appropriately related to evaluative qualities that make it worth overcoming the difficulties it involves, and so capable of conferring weight or

21. This understanding of happiness or well-being as achievement is explicitly presented in J. Annas, 'Happiness as Achievement', *Daedalus*, Spring 2004, pp. 44–51. However, it can also be found (without explicit reference to achievement) in J. Raz, *Ethics and the Public Domain*, Oxford: Oxford University Press, 1994, Ch. 1.
22. Griffin, op. cit., p. 20.

point on one's life. In this connection, Griffin mentions Darwin as someone who accomplished great things; yet his accomplishment consisted not just in the bare fact that he surmounted difficulties, but that in doing so he made a momentous scientific breakthrough. Here the value of understanding needs to be registered for the very fact of Darwin's achievement, not just its magnitude, to come into view. Similarly, a poor immigrant's achievement may consist in the great sacrifices he made to secure the welfare of his children, but again only because both his relationship with them and their welfare are independently valuable.

This last example brings out the limitations of specifying difficulty in terms of formal properties and achievement as the display of skill in overcoming them. For we can elaborate it in such a way that the difficulties in question essentially consist in the *substantive* costs that the father willingly bore—for example, many years of mind-numbingly repetitive and physically draining factory work that seriously impaired his own self-development, to the extent perhaps that his own life did not go well overall—rather than the complexity, precision, etc., of the means–end reasoning required to attain his goal. Some of the finest achievements combine skill or ingenuity with a willingness to incur considerable substantive costs in realizing an objective. For instance, the magistrate protagonist in the Costa-Gavras film *Z* displays both investigative prowess and moral courage in bringing to justice the high-ranking officials complicit in the murder of a left-wing politician. Nor does this exhaust the kinds of difficulty the overcoming of which can make for achievement without any skill being displayed. To give one more example: it is an achievement for a victim of serious crime to overcome powerful feelings of anger and resentment, and the incomprehension and suspicion of their community, in coming to forgive their attacker. The difficulty here consists in retaining or coming to an appreciation of the value of forgiveness in such circumstances, and having the compassion and courage needed to forgive despite countervailing pressures, both internal and external. In the last three cases I have described, the overcoming of difficulty manifests not (or not merely) the agent's skill, but their possession of a moral virtue. Moral virtues contrast with skills in always being directed towards the realization of a good end. One consequence of this is that an agent's voluntary error within a domain of decision-making governed by a virtue would undermine the ascription to him of that virtue; by contrast, an agent's possession of a skill is fully compatible with his making voluntary errors within its domain: for example, a master-builder might deliberately use the wrong technique for a job in order to test an apprentice's understanding of the craft.[23]

The phenomenon of dependence exhibited in these cases involves an intentional relation: the agent engages in difficult activity in order to realize one or more values. The mode of realization is not confined to situations in which difficult activity acquires intrinsic value through bringing about, in an instrumental manner, an independently valuable outcome, for instance in the way that a physician's activities cause his patients' improved health. It is also possible for the relationship to be constitutive, such that engagement in an independently valuable activity (e.g. being a good friend) inherently involves overcoming certain difficulties. Notice, further, that the relevant value to which difficult activity is related need not itself be a manifestly 'prudential value', that is, one that constitutes some aspect of human flourishing. On the contrary, the relevant value may be moral (e.g. justice), and so only indirectly related to individual flourishing, or even non-anthropocentric—someone's achievement might consist in helping preserve a rainforest from destruction, but the value of the latter's existence is not exhausted by its instrumental or constitutive bearing on human interests.

Both deep and wide achievement, I contend, have a relational character, in that some other value must appropriately characterize a difficult activity before it can be an achievement. Activity that amounts to an achievement is always a difficulty-overcoming mode of participation by an agent in some value, such as deep personal relations, knowledge, justice, beauty, and so on, one that rightly commands our admiration. Although a necessary element, overcoming difficulty by itself does not suffice to constitute achievement. Let us call the relevant other value(s) the 'framing value(s)'.[24] By contrast, goods such as play or understanding

23. Cf. Aristotle, *Nicomachean Ethics*, 1140b.
24. The relational view is thus anticipated by Aquinas: 'When something is more difficult, it is not for that reason necessarily more worthwhile, but it must be more difficult in such a way, as also to be at a higher level of goodness' (*Summa Theologiae* II-II, Q.27, a.8, ad 3um).

seem to be relatively self-standing, in that they can be instantiated independently of any instrumental or constitutive relationship to another good. Against this view, Hurka grounds achievement in difficult activity as such, independently of its connection to any other intrinsic value, although of course he also allows that such a connection can *enhance* the value of the activity (but presumably not *qua* bare achievement). How might the bare account of achievement be defended against the relational view?

Two lines of defence emerge in Hurka's article. The first is to countenance, at least *arguendo*, a negative version of the relational thesis: in order for an activity to be valuable by virtue of its difficulty it must not (exclusively?) aim at producing a (very) bad or evil outcome.[25] This blocks the inference that, on a bare account of achievement, the complex planning and execution of a terrorist atrocity has intrinsic value (even if it is bad overall, and so appropriately condemned, in light of its evil goal). This is a welcome result, since it is reasonable to suppose that the terrorists' success in overcoming difficulties, instead of possessing any intrinsic value (let alone the sort of intrinsic value that merits admiration), only serves to aggravate both the heinousness of their crime and the blight it casts on their lives. This is partly because an agent who deliberately surmounts difficulties in order to realize an evil end is typically more volitionally identified with that end, and hence more morally culpable, than someone who does not. Presumably something similar must be said about the adoption of evil yet difficult means to the attainment of a neutral or good objective.

But Hurka's second line of defence resists the apparently plausible flip side of the negative thesis, that is, the positive claim that for achievement to be instantiated the overcoming of

25. Hurka's concession here is grudging (see p. 225, n. 7): 'Some may deny that difficulty is as such good, on the ground that an activity aimed at evil, such as genocide, is not in any way made good by its difficulty. The issue here is complex, ... but those moved by this objection can retreat to the weaker claim that only activities with good or neutral aims gain value by being difficult.' In the end, he would not allow the concession to stand, because achievement figures as a 'base-level value' in his recursive theory of virtue, and it is essential to its having that status that it can be specified independently of both (a) other base-level values, and (b) any reference to morally good or evil attitudes. See, T. Hurka, *Virtue, Vice, and Value*, New York: Oxford University Press, 2001, pp. 144–52. One way of reading my argument in this section is as denying that achievement is a 'base-level value' in this sense.

difficulty must exhibit an appropriate connection to some framing value. Instead, he believes that defenders of the relational view of deep achievement are mistaken, and that their error is best exposed through reflection on game-playing, since a game's prelusory goal lacks value. Game-playing shows us, on this view, that the essence of achievement is success in difficult activity as such. Now, a defender of the relational view should readily agree that the prelusory goal of valuable instances of game-playing, even those that manifest achievement, is usually neutral considered by itself. But it does not follow that game-playing does not instantiate framing values that are capable of entering into the right kind of relation with difficult activity to ground deep achievement. Drawing on the discussion in Section II, he should say that these values include the good of play itself. After all, my aim in playing golf is not simply to put the ball in the hole; on the contrary, I have that aim precisely because I want to participate in the good of play (specifically, the determinate version of that good instantiated by playing the game of golf). Overcoming the difficulties imposed by the rules of golf is a constitutive means of pursuing the framing good of play, in the specific version of that good represented by the playing of golf.

To adjudicate between the bare and the relational accounts of achievement, consider an exemplar of perversity familiar from recent value theory: let us call him Joe, a man whose dominant pursuit in life is counting blades of grass in various well-delineated lawns. We can describe his activity in such a way that it involves considerable difficulty and, moreover, constitutes a Suitsian game. The prelusory goal is to count the exact number of blades of grass in as many lawns of a certain size as possible within a given calendar year, remembering at the end of the year how many blades each area contained and also accurately describing its general condition. The constitutive rules that make the attainment of this goal more difficult include that the counting must be done manually and without assistance, that it must continue uninterrupted for twelve hours per day, that on every other day the player must entirely abstain from food, that no resort may be had to aide-mémoires, etc. Moreover, Joe accepts these rules because of the very difficulties they create, so he manifests a 'pure' lusory attitude. Let it also be the case that the grass-counting game is his own creation, that it affords him a sense of fulfilment but little pleasure, and that no one else engages in or sees the point of this activity; on the contrary, others in his society treat Joe as an object of ridicule, pity or bewilderment.

Let us suppose that Joe becomes highly proficient at the grass-counting game, able to count and accurately recall the details of ten times as many lawns of a given size annually as the average hypothetical amateur. Does this amount to an achievement on his part? It seems Hurka must say so. Joe's game demands great physical stamina and mental concentration, it also requires some fairly impressive feats of memory. Over the years, he attains rare levels of manual dexterity and perfects a very effective counting technique. His activity exhibits a significant degree of complexity, precision and breadth of content—certainly as compared with sports such as weight-lifting or sprinting. And yet, we should rightly judge it an appalling waste of time, hence as utterly devoid of achievement. Perhaps it will be countered that *some* intrinsic value is realized in Joe's life as a result of this activity, since even a life of grass-counting is preferable to a supremely indolent existence. This suggestion may be correct, but then it seems we are according value to activity informed by practical and theoretical reasoning *per se*, rather than to anything recognizable as an achievement. For surely there is nothing to be admired in what Joe does.

How might achievement come to grace this dismal scene? Well, although I said Joe's activity was a game on Suits's definition, it is hardly a clear-cut instantiation of the good of play as understood in Section II. But imagine now grass-counting transformed into play: not only freely engaged in, but enjoyed by Joe for its own sake, yet regarded by him as not serious, so that it takes place in his free time, filling no more than seven days in a year and imposing no health-endangering burdens. Imagine also that others take part in it competitively, for instance, that it is an all-day event during an annual community festival. Now the elements of play are more obviously present, and as a result playing the game seems to acquire real value—the value of play itself. And this value, in characterizing the point of the activity, provides a framework within which some performances might conceivably be judged genuine achievements, that is, admirable displays of skill, physical dexterity, speed, endurance, memory, and so on. It need not be (exclusively) the good of play that performs this framing role; it might have been some other good, such as friendship, religion or deep personal relations. Even flagpole-sitting, or some comparable feat of endurance, might qualify as an achievement if appropriately framed by other values. St Simeon Stylites, who spent thirty-six years on a column as an expression of religious devotion, is venerated for his spiritual achievement, whereas a present-day imitator who did the same thing simply because it is difficult would rightly be judged perverse.

Of course, not any connection between difficult activity and a framing value grounds achievement. Whether the overcoming of specific kinds of difficulty is an achievement depends on the nature of the framing value in question. The point is especially compelling regarding difficulties that impose what I called substantive costs. Thus, it is an achievement for a mother to sacrifice her life in order to save her child's life; but someone who is prepared to lay down their life purely in order to secure victory in a football match has a distorted grasp of the value of playing games, and therefore also a distorted grasp of what counts as achievement in playing them. Notice, in this connection, that scope for achievement was created in the grass-counting game precisely through the activity being made in certain respects *less* difficult—in particular, less consequential in its potentially negative impact on players' interests—since this was necessary for it to be seen as a genuine instantiation of the value of play.

Consider, finally, how the two opposing views of achievement bear on the proposal that the use of performance-enhancing drugs be permitted in athletic competitions. Abstracting from moral or public policy considerations, this proposal might be advanced as a way of making athletics more challenging; for example, athletes might be required to determine and administer their own dosage, thus necessitating some chemical and medical expertise on their part. On the bare view of achievement, this seems to be a way of increasing the difficulty, hence also the potential level of achievement, in sports such as sprinting or weight-lifting, adding an element of ratiocination to pursuits that Hurka believes to be overly dominated by 'raw power'. On the relational view, by contrast, the proposal works to diminish the scope for achievement. This is because sports realize the good of play through displays of physical prowess, and the introduction of performance-enhancing drugs strikes against both framing values: the health risks of drug-taking contravene the inconsequentiality that characterizes the good of play, and the artificial enhancement of performance is inimical to the kind of physical prowess that sport is traditionally concerned to elicit. The relational view thus provides a means of justifying the plausible and widely held view that legalizing drug use would be corrosive of sporting achievement.

To sum up: the bare account denatures achievement by reducing it to the counterfeit intrinsic good of success in difficult activity as such, thereby ignoring its relational character. Since this account collapses, it cannot be used to prop up thesis (b).

IV

A Comment on 'Modernity'. If modern goods are a subset of authentic goods, then achieving a difficult goal regardless of its value cannot be a modern good, since it is not an authentic good.[26] Thesis (c), therefore, is false. Is the value of play, as I have described it, a modern good, at least when realized by the playing of games? If we follow Hurka in using Aristotle's notoriously slippery distinction between *energeia* and *kinēsis* as a touchstone for the classical/modern divide—so that distinctively modern goods are realized by activities that have an external goal and satisfy the Aristotelian grammatical test for *kinēseis*, but which resemble *energeiai* in deriving intrinsic value from properties internal to the activity itself (pp. 229ff.)—then the good of play may well be no less modern than the putative good of bare achievement.

Assuming we retain the structure of prelusory goal, constitutive rules and lusory attitude in characterizing game-playing, we can still describe instances of it as *kinēseis* that possesses intrinsic value not derived from the value of their prelusory goal, since in the case of games the latter is typically valueless. Instead, the intrinsic value of game-playing derives from the fact that the process of achieving the prelusory goal is a way of participating in the good of play. But it also seems that game-playing can be

26. It is not the good of achievement; and I leave aside the possibility mentioned in Section III, that overcoming of difficulty may have some intrinsic value *qua* expression of practical and theoretical reasoning.

re-described as a form of *energeia* if the adoption of the prelusory goal, and the activity aimed at achieving it, are treated as constitutive means to the good of play itself. Now, the goal of the activity is no longer external to it, in so far (for example) as it is not possible to specify the goal of playing golf (a determinate form of the determinable good of play) without reference to activities such as teeing off, putting, etc. Moreover, the grammatical test for an *energeia* is also satisfied: from the fact that I have played golf (that is, realized this particular form of the good of play) at *t*, it does not follow that I am not still playing golf at *t*. More generally, a particular phase or instance of play will always come to an end, but an agent's potential engagement with the basic value of play itself is inexhaustible.[27] But presumably something similar may be said about the putative good of overcoming difficulty: from the fact that I have already overcome difficulties at *t*, it does not follow that I am not still doing so at *t*. This is an instance of the well-known problem that whether an activity counts as an instance of *energeia* or *kinēsis* seems worryingly sensitive to apparently insignificant variations in its description.

Given among other things its malleability, it is doubtful that the hybrid Aristotelian criterion tracks a historically resonant distinction between classical and modern conceptions of value. And yet the bare account of achievement *is* unmistakably 'modern' in a way that both the basic good of play and the relational account of achievement are not, since it displays the hallmarks of large-scale cultural tendencies associated with modernity. These include the exaltation of considerations of efficacy, form and procedure in evaluating an agent's adoption, ordering and realization of their goals, whatever their content—hence the significance that instrumental reasoning, consistency, integrity, skill, power, and so on assume in modern thought—and a corresponding down grading of substantive concerns about the worth of those goals. But we are now in the shadow of one of modern ethical thought's dark sides, a fact to which

27. Cf. '[W]e must recall the distinction between, on the one hand, values in which we participate but which we do not exhaust and, on the other hand, the particular projects we undertake and objectives we pursue (normally, if we are reasonable, as ways of participating in values) and which can at a given point of time be said to have been fully attained, or not, as the case may be' (Finnis, op. cit., p. 155).

Hurka's invocation of Nietzsche's conception of human greatness as a distinctively modern good should alert us (p. 286). The idea that there is value, let alone supreme value, in subordinating one's impulses to an overarching master-impulse irrespective of the latter's content,[28] amounts to a *reductio ad absurdum* of the modernist tendencies just described. Indeed, Charles Taylor's critique of the prevailing modernist, essentially Nietzschean, conception of authenticity on the grounds that it fatally detaches creativity, originality, opposition to convention, and so on from 'horizons of significance' nicely parallels my argument that the bare account of achievement ignores its inherently relational character by severing the overcoming of difficulty from framing values.[29]

Lest it be thought that I have simply adopted a neo-Aristotelian party line, one that is hopelessly nostalgic in its antipathy to certain features of modernity and disquietingly illiberal in its focus on the value of ends, let me conclude by quoting a philosopher whose modernist and liberal credentials are unassailable:

> [I]n times of social doubt and loss of faith in long established values, there is a tendency to fall back on the virtues of integrity: truthfulness and sincerity, lucidity and commitment, or, as some say, authenticity ... Now of course the virtues of integrity are virtues, and among the excellences of free persons. Yet while necessary, they are not sufficient; for their definition allows for most any content: a tyrant might display these attributes to a high degree, and by doing so exhibit a certain charm, not deceiving himself by political pretenses and excuses of fortune. It is impossible to construct a moral view from these virtues alone; being virtues of form they are in a sense

28. F. Nietzsche, *The Will to Power*, trans. W. Kaufmann and R. J. Hollingdale, New York: Vintage, 1968, Sect. 46.

29. '[W]e can say that authenticity (A) involves (i) creation and construction as well as discovery, (ii) originality, and frequently (iii) opposition to the rules of society and even potentially to what we recognize as morality. But it is also true ... that it (B) requires (i) openness to horizons of significance (for otherwise the creation loses the background that can save it from insignificance) ... That these demands may be in tension has to be allowed. But what must be wrong is a simple privileging of one over the other ... This is what the trendy doctrines of "deconstruction" involve today. They stress (A.i), the constitutive, creative nature of our expressive languages, while altogether forgetting (B.i)...' (C. Taylor, *The Ethics of Authenticity*, Cambridge, MA: Harvard University Press, 1991, pp. 66–7).

> secondary. But joined to the appropriate conception of justice ... they come into their own.[30]

What Rawls says about the virtues of integrity applies *mutatis mutandis* to personal achievement. Achievement only comes into its own—in other words, admirable activity that confers weight or point on a person's life only exists—when the overcoming of difficulty is appropriately joined to some framing value or other. It is a characteristically modern illusion, not an insight, to suppose otherwise.[31]

References

Adams, R. M. 1999: *Finite and Infinite Goods: A Framework for Ethics*. Oxford: Oxford University Press.

Annas, J. 2004: 'Happiness as Achievement', *Daedalus*, Spring 2004.

Aquinas: *Summa Theologiae*.

Aristotle: *Nicomachean Ethics*.

Caillois, R. 2001: *Man, Play and Games*. Urbana, IL and Chicago: University of Illinois Press.

Finnis, J. 1980: *Natural Law and Natural Rights*. Oxford: Oxford University Press.

Griffin, J. 1996: *Value Judgement: Improving our Ethical Beliefs*. Oxford: Oxford University Press.

Grisez, G. and R. Shaw 1988: *Beyond the New Morality: The Responsibilities of Freedom*, 3rd edn. Notre Dame, IN: University of Notre Dame Press.

Herodotus, *The Histories*.

Huizinga, J. 1955: *Homo Ludens: A Study of the Play Element in Culture*. Boston: Beacon Press.

Hurka, T. 2001: *Virtue, Vice, and Value*. New York: Oxford University Press.

——— 2006: 'Games and the Good'. *Proceedings of the Aristotelian Society, Supplementary Volume 80*, pp. 273–91.

Lasch, C. 1978: *The Culture of Narcissism: American Life in an Age of Diminishing Expectations*. New York: Norton.

Nietzsche, F. 1968: *The Will to Power*. Trans. W. Kaufmann and R. J. Hollingdale. New York: Vintage.

Nussbaum, M. 2000: *Women and Human Development: The Capabilities Approach*. Oxford: Oxford University Press.

Oakeshott, M. 2004: 'Work and Play'. In *What is History? and Other Essays*. Exeter: Imprint Academic.

Oates, J. C. 2002: *On Boxing*. New York: HarperCollins.

Orwell, G. 2000: 'The Sporting Spirit'. In *George Orwell: Essays*. London: Penguin.

Rawls, J. 1999: *A Theory of Justice*, rev. edn. Oxford: Oxford University Press.

Raz, J. 1994: *Ethics and the Public Domain*. Oxford: Oxford University Press.

30. J. Rawls, *A Theory of Justice*, revised edn, Oxford: Oxford University Press, 1999, pp. 455–6.

31. I wish to thank Roger Crisp, James Griffin, John Ma, Joseph Raz, Helen Steward, Christopher Taylor, David Wiggins and Susan Wolf for helpful comments and discussion. I am also grateful to Constantine Tasioulas for the valuable insights into this topic that he has afforded me.

Suits, B. 1990: *The Grasshopper: Games, Life and Utopia*. Boston: David R. Godine.

Sutton-Smith, B. 1997: *The Ambiguity of Play*. Cambridge, MA: Harvard University Press.

Taylor, C. 1991: *The Ethics of Authenticity*. Cambridge, MA: Harvard University Press.

Wittgenstein, L. 1972: *Philosophical Investigations*, 3rd edn. Trans. G. E. M. Anscombe. Oxford: Blackwell.

SUFFICIENCY AND EXCESS

by Lloyd Humberstone and Herman Cappelen

I—Lloyd Humberstone

ABSTRACT This paper assembles examples and considerations bearing on such questions as the following. Are statements to the effect that someone is too young (for instance) or that someone is old enough always to be understood in terms of someone's being too young or too old for such-and-such—for example, for them to join a particular organization? And when a 'such-and-such' has been specified, is it always at least tacitly modal in force—in the case just given, too young or old enough *to be able* to join the organization? These questions are explored by means of a critical examination of the (affirmative) answers given to them by Eric Nelson in a 1980 paper on the subject, with part of the intention being to rescue Nelson's thoughtful discussion from the oblivion into which it appears to have fallen, judging by more recent contributions on the subject by semanticists.

I

Introduction. Our subject is the semantics of the extent modifiers *too* and *enough*, which combine with gradable adjectives and adverbs (and perhaps further material) to form phrases themselves behaving like adjectives and adverbs, respectively. The treatment will be informal and taken up more with raising than with settling questions. We concentrate mainly on adjectives (ADJ) for illustrative purposes, so that, simplifying away some further possibilities here, the constructions of special interest are of the forms we may provisionally represent as (1) and (2):

(1) NP_1 is too ADJ (for NP_2) (to VP)
(2) NP_1 is ADJ enough (for NP_2) (to VP)

in which either or both of the parenthesized constituents may be absent in each case, NP_i ($i = 1, 2$) is a noun phrase and VP is a (finite) verb phrase, perhaps with a transitive verb and a gap for an object noun phrase, understood as NP_1, though with NP_1 taken as the subject in case the verb is intransitive, together with any further adjuncts or arguments licensed by the verb. (These parenthetically indicated parts of (1) and (2) are what was meant by 'further material' in our opening sentence.) Note that in the oversimplified description provided by (1) and (2), we have not made explicit provision for *too/enough* with a prenominal adjective—cf. (13) below—let alone for the case in which it is an adverb that is modified by *too* or *enough* (though some of the latter cases will find their way in examples).

A detailed description of how the missing constituents are understood and of exactly what the syntactic possibilities are—especially with regard to pronominalization and null anaphora (gaps or 'traces')—may be found in Nelson 1980; we merely remind the reader that in the oft-noted (Quirk et al. 1985, p. 1142) case of threefold ambiguity,

(3) It is too hot to eat.

the 'it' can be taken as a candidate subject of *eat* ('The pig is too hot for it to eat [anything]'), or as the object ('The pork is too hot [for us] to eat [it]'), or as a weather *it* ('It is too hot [for us] to eat [anything]'), the third of which cases suggests that the general form of the construction is better given by (4) than by (1):

(4) NP_1 is too ADJ for–to S.

where, given S of the form NP_2+ VP 'for–to S' (a representation we prefer from now on) is to be understood as 'for NP_2 to VP', and again not all of this material need be explicit (as indicated by the parentheses in (1)). The role of the discontinuous sentence complementizer *for . . . to___* in these constructions is emphasized in Nelson 1980, from p. 101 of which comes the following further example, indicating that it is not just in the case of the rather specialized 'dummy *it*' cases that we have the initial NP not corresponding to any pronoun or gap in the sentence complement:

(5) The lecture was too exciting for anyone to fall asleep.

(The relevant contrast here, for our purposes, is with the variant of (5) with '. . . fall asleep in', where 'in' is understood as followed by a gap for 'the lecture'.[1]) Similar points hold in the case of

1. In some cases there may be no such immediately available version with a gap, such as 'Life is too short to worry about things like that', 'The music was too loud for me to follow what he was saying', and (3) above, with a weather *it*.

enough.[2] Note that this account rules as grammatical some sentences which might give us pause on semantic grounds, such as 'Harry was too fast for John to outrun Sam'. Whereas it is easy—for the case of (5)—to imagine its being because of how exciting the lecture was that people didn't fall asleep, it is not easy to imagine circumstances in which it is because of how fast one person was that a second person didn't outrun a third. (The 'because' here is not specifically a causal 'because'. For instance, a geometrical figure with eleven sides has *too many sides* to be a decagon.)

The interconnected questions with which we shall be concerned can be grouped under the headings (i) relationships, (ii) the 'complete thought' issue, and (iii) the question of evaluativity. The intended coverage of (i)—the main topic for Sections II–V below—is the semantic relationships between the two constructions, and of the availability of illuminating paraphrase relationships between either of them and constructions couched in other terms. We include under this heading not only relations of paraphrase or equivalence but also inferential relations in general. For example, we should consider whether arguments of the form (6) are valid:

(6) NP_1 is too ADJ for–to S
NP_0 is ADJ-er than NP_1
———————————
∴ NP_0 is too ADJ for–to S.

Here 'ADJ-er' just represents the appropriate comparative form of ADJ. An argument of this form would take us from premisses

2. There are some quite subtle grammaticality distinctions in this area raised by Nelson (1980), who notes (p. 105) the contrast between 'He was too quick to catch' and *'He ran too quickly to catch' (though both 'He was too quick for me to catch him' and 'He ran too quickly for me to catch him' are fine); Nelson offers a syntactic account which explains such differences. On the other hand, Quirk et al. (1985, p. 1140) disagree, giving the following without an asterisk anywhere in sight: 'It moves too quickly for most people to see (it)'. Rothstein, in various publications, has a more refined account, agreeing with the grammaticality judgements just cited from Nelson 1980, but at p. 110 of Rothstein 2001, for example, noting the grammaticality of 'He knocked too gently for us to hear', with transitive *hear* having as object the event of knocking—to put it somewhat loosely—rather than its agent (the subject of *knocked*). (This particular example Rothstein credits to Anita Mittwoch. It raises a question about whether the understood object of 'see' in the Quirk et al. example without the 'it' is the object said to be moving or rather the movement itself. The claim that the example paralleled the 'catch' sentence assumed the former.)

'This fence is too high for me to climb' and 'That fence is higher than this fence', to the conclusion 'That fence is too high for me to climb'. Is such an argument valid in virtue of its having the form (6)? There is a similar question for *enough*, and the form of argument:

(6′) NP_0 is ADJ enough for–to S
NP_1 is ADJ-er than NP_0

∴ NP_1 is ADJ enough for–to S.

An argument of this form would take us from premisses 'Chris is tall enough to join the police force' and 'Alf is taller than Chris' to the conclusion 'Alf is tall enough to join the police force'. Again we can ask whether this argument is valid in virtue of having the form (6′).

Under (ii)—the 'complete thought' issue—we have in mind the question of whether sentences of the forms collected under the schemata (1) and (2) are, on the one hand, in some way incomplete or (loosely speaking) elliptical, or, on the other, whether such a sentence should be seen as expressing a complete thought in its own right. In particular we have the question: when the material instantiating the parenthesized portions of (1) and (2) is absent, is the sentence in question an incomplete version of one in which those portions are supplied?[3] The issue under (iii), which along with (ii) will be addressed in Section VI, can be introduced with the observation that there seems to be something evaluative (or perhaps even normative) about constructions (1) and (2). More specifically, they seem at first sight, and when no special considerations are available to cancel this impression, to be respectively unfavourably and favourably evaluative. Calling a cup of coffee *too hot* seems to be passing an adverse judgement on it, while calling it *hot enough* seems to be recording a point in its favour. What are we to make of this?

By way of introduction, let us consider a preliminary proposal falling under heading (i), as to how the meanings of *too* and *enough* are related to each other. We shall call this the *Simple-Minded Account*. The suggestion—readily elicited in casual

3. There may even remain some indeterminacy after this material is specified. See the closing paragraph of Section VI below.

conversation with 'semantically naïve' subjects, and, as we shall see in the following section, surfacing occasionally in print—would have it that (1), rewritten as (4), may be paraphrased as (7), in which:

(7) NP_1 is more than ADJ enough (for–to S).

The Simple-Minded Account can be dismissed on the grounds that it wrongly predicts that (8) means what (9) means:

(8) Tom is too old to join the police force.
(9) Tom is more than old enough to join the police force.

If the minimum and maximum entry ages, for entry into the police force in question, are 18 and 35, respectively, and Tom is 20, (9) is true though (8) is false. The general point is that for the simple case of 'one-dimensional' adjectives[4] and a given choice of NP_2 (where appropriate) and VP in (1) and (2), we have the following situation, in which the orientation indicates ADJ-ness to a greater and greater extent, and 'min' and 'max' indicate points below and above which, respectively, NP_1 is not ADJ enough and is too ADJ (for NP_2 to VP):[5]

(10) ————o————————o————→
min max

Some special settings may give misleading encouragement to the Simple-Minded Account. More than enough of something may come to count as too much of it in those cases in which some independent consideration favours minimizing the something in question. An Australian retailer of beers, wines and spirits, advertises itself (in 2005) with the line 'If you're not buying your liquor at Dan Murphy's, you're paying too much.' The message is that a given product in the range costs less at Dan Murphy's than elsewhere, so if you are buying elsewhere, you are parting with more than enough money to buy the product:

4. Kamp 1975, p. 141.
5. There may or may not be 'absolute' end-points for the scale depicted in (10), depending on the choice of ADJ, in the sense of degrees below and above which it is not possible for ADJ to apply. (According to Unger 1975, Chapter 2, for instance, adjectives like *flat* and *full* are absolute in the sense that there is an absolute maximum, and the extent constructions such as comparatives and *too* and *enough* phrases require a reinterpretation of the adjective so that the extents are the degrees to which this maximum is approached.)

this gets to count as parting with too much money on the principle that, *ceteris paribus*, one should minimize one's expenditure.[6] But without such a tacit further premiss, there is no legitimate inference from *more than enough* to *too much*, as the police age entry example shows: there is no special reason for wanting police recruits to be as young as possible, while there is a general presumption in favour of not spending more money than necessary (on a given product).

The 'more than ADJ' construction in (7) is, we note in passing, somewhat special, and in particular is not what was indicated under 'ADJ-er' in (6). The latter was the usual comparative form of ADJ, which may be 'more ADJ' and may be, especially (and we simplify here) for short adjectives in English, literally formed by adding the '-er' suffix. It is in general a delicate question as to how to draw the line between semantically significant and semantically insignificant syntactic facts. In the case of *too* and *enough* the fact that the former does and the latter does not create contexts licensing negative polarity items (already illustrated by (5)),[7]

(11) They were too tired to carry any more cases.
(12) *They were strong enough to carry any more cases.[8]

lie on the former—semantically suggestive—side of any such line, while the word order anomalies belong on the latter—purely syntactic—side:

(13) He was too weak a child to defend himself in the playground.
(14) *He was a too weak child to defend himself in the playground.

6. Thus the circumstances can be such as to make the min and max points in (10) coincide. Sometimes they may even appear to cross sides, but this is due to varying the complement sentence mid-example: enough sleeping tablets (to get to sleep) may already be too many (to have a clear head in the morning).
7. Krifka 1995 provides a useful survey discussion for the benefit of readers not familiar with the theme of negative polarity. The contrast between *too* and *enough* in this respect was noted at p. 774 of Quirk et al. 1972.
8. What about 'After years of training, this fighter was strong enough to defeat any challenger'? Well, the *any* here is not a negative polarity *any*. For this reason, it is actually better to choose examples with (e.g.) *ever*, which stands in for 'at any time' with the genuine polarity 'any' but not for the other (sometimes called *free choice*) 'any' (as in 'Come at any time').

(15) Mary was perceptive enough to realize that something was amiss.
(16) *Mary was enough perceptive to realize that something was amiss.

In the case of (11) and (12), the presence of negative polarity items in the complements of *too* seems semantically suggestive because it seems linked, as Nelson 1980 proposes, to the fact that being too tired to do something is a matter of being so tired that one *cannot* do that thing (or cannot do it well). Once this modal element of inability or impossibility is made explicit, one naturally sees it as responsible triggering the relevant polarity items (*any*, in the case of (11)). We will return to Nelson's suggestions several times, and to do justice to his pioneering discussion—which appears to have been completely overlooked in the more recent linguistic literature[9]—include two sections devoted to some of them (IV and V).

As for the other cases, one reason for thinking of the grammaticality distributions illustrated by (13)–(14) as superficial from a semantic point of view is that the ungrammatical entries become grammatical when *too* and *enough* are replaced by *excessively* and *sufficiently*, respectively (even though (14), in which, of course, this change will force 'a' to become 'an', is somewhat strained stylistically).[10] This point would be more compelling if the longer modifiers did not differ in meaning from *too* and *enough*, but it must be conceded that this is not the case for *too*, where the substitute *excessively* does not sit well with *for–to* complements in general and could certainly not

9. Under this heading I have in mind Heim 2001, Section 3.2 of which is relevant, and—devoted to our topic—Meier 2003 and Hacquard 2005*a*; Hacquard 2005*b* touches on many of the same topics. The present paper was written in ignorance of this literature, whose existence was drawn to my attention by Hacquard, and most references to it accordingly appear in notes or parentheses. (Meier's paper also contains references to work on our topic in the 1980s by M. Bierwisch and by A. von Stechow.)

10. A second reason may come from familiarity with other languages in which the words usually translating *too* and *enough* do not display the word order anomalies. But this consideration should not be overstressed, since most other languages lack a range of specifically negative polarity items and so do not present the contrast between (8) and (9). The latter contrast is well known, being mentioned for example on p. 1140 of Quirk et al. 1985, an invaluable source which in particular has the merit over what might otherwise be regarded as superseding it—Huddleston and Pullum 2002—of discussing *too* and *enough* in the same breath, especially in Section 15.72, headed 'Comparisons of sufficiency and excess'.

replace the *too* in, for example, (8).[11] We will return to this point in Section VI. It is worth noting that one possible source encouraging the Simple-Minded Account dismissed above is the phrase 'in excess of' which simply means 'more than' and does not imply *too many* (or *too much*). Sometimes it is not clear which kind of case we are dealing with. The 'over' in *overact, overdo, overreact* and *overeat* indicates doing something to excess, but what about claims that this or that ethnic minority is *over-represented* in the prison population? Such claims may be intended as purely statistical in content, but when so expressed they tend in public discussion to be interpreted in a 'too much' kind of way, with the attendant negatively evaluative tone we have noted is associated with *too*—perhaps in this case in respect of the fairness of the judicial system.

II

Relations of Paraphrase and Entailment: The Received Account. The obvious successor to the Simple-Minded Account's equation of (1), alias (4), with (7) of the previous section is one based on the notion of antonymy, which postulates instead what we call a Scale Reversal Equivalence. Although the notion of antonymy is philosophically problematic, we shall simply take it for granted here, trusting that the plausibility of the Scale Reversal Equivalence—or more accurately, equivalences—will be not be undermined by any such problems. This replacement for the Simple-Minded Account forms part of what we shall call the *Received Account*, in view of the authoritative statement it

11. *Pace* Quirk et al. 1985, p. 1140, where we read that 'Sufficient(ly) and excessive(ly) are more formal synonyms of *enough* and *too*.' Bolinger 1972, p. 22, says that *excessively* is a 'close synonym' of *too*. Similarly, Huddleston and Pullum 2002, wanting to distinguish the special 'too' which after 'not' means something like *very* ('You don't look too good this morning') and which they write as too_{n}, say 'Too_{n} means "very", as opposed to ordinary *too* meaning "excessively".' (Naturally we are ignoring this use of *too* here, as well as various idiomatic uses of 'ordinary' *too* as in 'Too bad' meaning something in the vicinity of 'Bad luck' or 'So much the worse', 'Too right I will' (emphatic agreement), to which list we might also add an *enough* example, 'True enough' (concession): Bolinger 1972, p. 49, lists more 'stereotyped phrases' in this vein. Also not covered here, this time purely for reasons of space, are double *too* constructions, as in 'She had spent too long in water that was too cold.'

receives in Quirk et al. 1985.[12] The Received Account combines with Scale Reversal Equivalences with a pair of further proposals relating *too* and *enough* constructions to constructions with *so* or *such*; we shall get to them presently. The first part of this package is explained by the authors in the following words:

> Paraphrase pairs may be constructed with antonymous items, in which one sentence is positive and the other negative; one sentence has *enough* or one of its synonyms, and the other *too* or one of its synonyms. (Quirk et al. 1985, p. 1140)

They illustrate with (17) and (18)—numbering added here—in which the *a* and *b* sentences are paraphrases of each other:[13]

(17*a*) They're rich enough to own a car.
(17*b*) They're not too poor to own a car.

(18*a*) The book is sufficiently simple to understand.
(18*b*) The book is not excessively difficult to understand.

To illustrate the claim of the quoted passage inset above, one should perhaps supplement these examples by some in which it is the *too* claim that is un-negated and the *enough* claim that is negated, as in:

(19*a*) They're too poor to own a car.
(19*b*) They're not rich enough to own a car.

Indeed, the latter pair are what one would expect Quirk et al. to emphasize in view of their citing the negative polarity differences (our (11)–(12) from the preceding section) between *enough* and *too* on the same page: emphasizing the mutuality of the relationship as in the above inset quotation detracts from seeing the negative paraphrase as in any way explanatory of why it is the *too* constructions rather than the *enough* constructions that trigger negative polarity items. At any rate, let us offer a schematic description of how excess and sufficiency are related according to

12. Also Quirk et al. 1972, §§11.62–63 or the abridged version of this discussion in Quirk and Greenbaum 1973, §§11.43–44. This account is, as we shall see below, essentially defended also in Nelson 1980.
13. This claim of paraphrase requires us to understood the adjectives involved in a 'neutralized' sense; as it stands, (17*a*) arguably implies that the people under discussion qualify as rich *tout court*, which (17*b*) does not. See Nelson 1980, esp. Appendix II, Lehrer and Lehrer 1982, Lehrer 1985, and Cruse 1992, for further information, as well as Horn 1989, at the pages indexed under 'Antonymy'.

the received view; here Un-ADJ and ADJ are scalar antonyms, and the content of this view is that for any single filling of their positions (marked by NP_1, ADJ and S) (20*a*) and (20*b*) are paraphrases, as with (21*a*, *b*):[14]

THE SCALE REVERSAL EQUIVALENCES:

(20*a*) NP_1 is too ADJ (for–to S)
(20*b*) NP_1 is not Un-ADJ enough (for–to S)

(21*a*) NP_1 is ADJ enough (for–to S)
(21*b*) NP_1 is not too Un-ADJ (for–to S)

Since for many adjectives there is no appropriately antonymous form, this schematic description cannot be instantiated in their case. It claims only to offer equivalences for the case in which there are antonymous pairs, and amounts to saying that for such pairs, the un-ADJ scale, as in (10), is obtained by inverting the ADJ scale. One must of course be careful to get the relative scope of the *too* and the *un-* right: a news report on children in hospital, broadcast on Australian television a few years ago ran as follows: 'About 140 children were unwell enough to be sent home for Christmas Day.' What the reporter of course meant to say was that they were not well enough to be sent home, or—by the above equivalences—too unwell to be sent home for Christmas Day.[15] (The most famous case of how we get confused with *too* and *enough* is perhaps the sentence 'No head injury is too trivial to be ignored', or '... to ignore', either of which we naturally hear as a sensible remark, without realizing that what should have been said is that no head injury is too trivial to *pay attention to*.[16] The phenomenon—with this example and others—was studied in detail in Wason and Reich 1979.[17])

14. Amongst such examples, Nelson 1980, p. 108, lists *angry*, *sleepy*, *embarrassed*.
15. Channel 9 (Melbourne) news bulletin of December 25, 2002. (I have also heard 'We lacked enough bread', to mean 'We didn't have enough bread', which seems similarly misformulated, though it has its defenders.)
16. Alternatively: No head injury is trivial enough to ignore. These mistakes are very common, and a few days after the preceding words were written (October 12, 2005), a scientist interviewed on television was asked what would be needed to convince sceptics that *Homo Floresiensis* constituted a genuine species in its own right and he replied: 'More fossils. You can never have too few fossils ...' The interview transcript is available (at the moment, at least) at http://www.abc.net.au/lateline/content/2005/s1480975.htm.
17. Some cross-linguistic results on the phenomenon are reported in Natsopoulos 1985.

One obvious but important case subsumed under the Received Account—the claim that the (*a*, *b*)-pairs under (17) and (18) are paraphrases—with some indirectness is the truism that 'not enough' (e.g., water) amounts to 'too little' (water). Here we take *little* as ADJ in (17*a*)—recalling that adjectives are not all of them either predicates or predicate modifiers (supposing the latter to be a plausible rendering of semantically attributive adjectives)—with the antonymous *much* as UN-ADJ, noting that the **much enough* is rendered as *enough* (by contrast[18] with the case of *too much*). When in the place of water in the preceding example we have the name of a quality capable of coming in degrees, the Scale Reversal Equivalences amount to saying that having too little of the quality (e.g., height, bravery) is the same as not having enough of it, so that a deficiency is the same as an insufficiency: a platitude that sums up what these equivalences amount to. The leftmost of the three segments into which the line in (10) is divided represents the range of deficiency of the corresponding quality and the rightmost segment, that of excess. The example of bravery here is intended to recall the relevance of this tripartite division to Aristotle's doctrine of the mean—in the present instance courage being the virtuous mean and cowardice and foolhardiness the flanking vices (see Urmson 1973). If one plays up the negative evaluativity of *too*, one obtains the view that this doctrine is vacuous (Puccetti 1964), since too much or too little of a quality is 'by definition' unacceptably much or unacceptably little of it.

Now the Scale Reversal Equivalences clearly represent an advance over the Simple-Minded Account, and it is interesting to see that in spite of making this advance, Quirk et al. 1985 retains an echo of that superseded account in the following passage from another part of the book—perhaps illustrating the effect of multiple authoring—namely in a passage[19] which reads:

> *Too* in the sense of 'more than enough' might also be mentioned here:
>
> - It's *too long*. ['longer than it should be']
> - He speaks *too quickly*. ['more quickly than he should speak']

18. Nelson 1980, p. 123.
19. 'Bullets' have been added in the following quotation; the passage appears on p. 467 of Quirk et al. 1985.

The relation of the parenthetical glosses offered here to the point supposedly being illustrated is not clear, though they bear clearly on the question of the evaluativity of *too*-statements. For them to serve here the glosses should presumably have been 'more than long enough' and 'more than quickly enough', respectively, and it is plain that these by no means successfully paraphrase the examples for the reasons already given apropos of (10). Indeed the passage just quoted is strikingly reminiscent of the following remarks from Jespersen 1924:

> Further we have a latent comparative in *too* ... which means 'more than enough,' or 'more than decent, or proper, or good'. (p. 248)

in which the first disjunct corresponds to the first sentiment quoted above from Quirk et al., and the second to the parenthetical glosses there offered—so as we cross the disjunction we lurch from the erroneous Simple-Minded Account to a rather hastily assumed negatively evaluative interpretation.[20] These glosses do raise a question of interest in its own right, however, and that is of how they themselves manage to mean what they do. In particular, it would be good to have an account—none will be proposed here—as to why (22) and (23) are respectively associated with the claim that Simon eats too much and with the claim that Simon eats more than enough:

(22) Simon eats more than he should/ought to.
(23) Simon eats more than he needs to/has to.

For the moment let us set to one side all questions about the precise modal 'filling' and also ignore the above vestige of the Simple-Minded Account, taking Quirk et al. (1985) to have

20. A trace of the Simple-Minded Account might even to be discerned in Heim 2001, at p. 236 of which it is argued that 'John needs (to have) too much money' is ambiguous, with a reading on which it says 'that John's financial needs are too high', and another on which, Heim writes, 'it means that what John needs is to have too much money. Imagine he is the type of person who only feels secure when he has more money than he can spend. Unless he has too much money (for him to spend), his (emotional) needs are not satisfied.' The case is complicated by the importance of the parenthetical 'for him to spend', in whose absence we have a negatively evaluative remark (according to a proposal sympathetically aired in Section VI below) which is odd given the close proximity of a reference to John's evaluative perspective.

committed themselves firmly to what we are calling the Received Account of the relation between *too* and *enough*.

That is not all they do. In the course of setting out this account, our authors go further and offer what we might call a 'reduction' of *too* and *enough* constructions alike to clauses with *so* and *that* (or with *such* and *that* in the case of a prenominal adjective) as illustrated (Quirk et al. 1985, p. 1142) by their:

(24*a*) It's too good a movie to miss.
(24*b*) It's such a good movie that we mustn't miss it.

(25*a*) It flies fast enough to beat the speed record.
(25*b*) It flies so fast that it can beat the speed record.

Abstracting from these cases, we have the schematic form of the proposal we shall dub the 'so/such' reductions, stated here openly with the paraphrases using *so*, and with the aid of some logical notation: $\neg$ for 'it is not the case that' and $\Diamond$ for 'it is possible that/possible for–to'. In the latter case we use the usual symbol from the study of normal modal logics, dual to the necessity-style operator $\Box$ (equivalent to $\neg\Diamond\neg$). We recall that the normal modal logics include those, such as the basic deontic logic **KD** in which $\Box p$ does not provably imply p, but only $\Diamond p$ (to say nothing of the minimal normal logic **K** from which even the latter implication is missing). For the case of (24) we have a deontic reading, while for (25) an (approximately) alethic reading of the relevant operators (which the reader may be more used to seeing as 'O' and 'P' rather than '$\Box$' and '$\Diamond$' in the deontic case).

THE SO/SUCH REDUCTIONS:

(26*a*) NP_1 is too ADJ for–to S
(26*b*) NP_1 is so ADJ that $\neg\Diamond$S

(27*a*) NP_1 is ADJ enough for–to S
(27*b*) NP_1 is so ADJ that $\Diamond$S

The *so* (or *such*, for the instantiation to constructions where this precedes an indefinite noun phrase) figuring in these reductions is the familiar *so* involved in resultative (or 'consecutive') clauses—as in 'The play was so dull we left at interval'—which is why these equivalences capture the *because* aspect of our constructions noted in the opening remarks (after (5)).[21] In the case of the example just given, the claim is that it was because of how dull the play was that we left at interval. For (26), it is because of how ADJ NP_1 is that it is not possible that S.

There is one respect in which Quirk et al. acknowledge that the so/such equivalences do not hold, and that is when the 'so' (or 'such') forces a non-neutral reading onto an adjective which in the *so*-free construction is interpreted as neutral ('unmarked', as it is sometimes put). They illustrate this (1985, p. 1143) with the examples (28), in which the *b* form does not imply that the lion was tame *tout court* while the *a* form does:

(28*a*) The lion was tame enough for the lionkeeper to enter its cage.
(28*b*) The lion was so tame that the lionkeeper was able to enter its cage.

In the same vein, the authors discussion on p. 1140 of the example

(29) She's old enough to do some work.

pairs it not with a paraphrase in the style of the So/Such Reduction above, but instead with (30):

(30) She is old enough that she can do some work.

which is of course no kind of reduction at all, since the *enough* remains;[22] but clearly, putting in 'so old that she can ...' would carry the implication, absent from (29), that the subject in question is old (as opposed to merely having some age or other—the neutral reading). In fact there is a second respect in which Quirk et al. (1985) do not defend what we are calling the *So/Such Reduction*s as reliable paraphrases, even setting aside

21. This may be connected with the oddity (noted in Meier 2003, p. 104) of 'Bertha is old enough to be self-identical', but since no analysis is attempted here of *because*, and since also we are accustomed to finding surprises with modally degenerate cases (here: a necessarily possessed property), I venture no confident conjecture. Meier, rather than explaining *too* and *enough* in terms of *so* (and *such*), gives a compositional semantic account of all these constructions, inspired by Angelika Kratzer's theory of conditionals. What we call the Scale Reversal Equivalences, she speaks of in terms of Duality (as also does Hacquard 2005*a*).

22. According to Huddleston and Pullum 2002, p. 969, sentences like (30) are not acceptable in British English, needing to be reformulated with *for–to* complementation. And on p. 396, they describe 'There was enough hot water that we could all have baths' as grammatical in American English.

this issue about markedness; they are not so specific as we have been in (26*b*) about the modal element entering here, and give several examples for which no modally complemented paraphrase is offered. We return to this issue in Section V.

III

Troubles for the Received Account? As we have sketched it, the Received Account appears to face difficulties on two fronts. The first is more a matter of our sketch—which simplified away the details of the modal or other material in the So/Such Reductions; we address this in Section V. The more serious difficulty arises over an internal conflict between the parts of the account: the Scale Reversal Equivalences on the one hand, and the So/Such Reductions on the other. According to the Scale Reversal Equivalences, (31) and (32) should amount to the same thing:

(31) Sam is not too young to join the police force.
(32) Sam is old enough to join the police force.

And according to the So/Such Reductions, these are respectively equivalent to (33) and (34), in the latter case understanding (31), as seems reasonable, as the negation of the sentence we get by removing 'not' from inside it:

(33) It is not the case that Sam is so young$_N$ that he cannot join the police force.
(34) Sam is so old$_N$ that he can join the police force.

It is a little hard to understand (33) and (34) because they are cast in a variant of English in which not only *old* but also *young* is understood as bearing a neutralized sense, which it is the point of the 'N' to indicate; that is, a scale is invoked (here, the age scale) but not one particular end of that scale. (While *old* is already the unmarked form of *young*/*old*, neutral in 'How Adj(?)' and 'Adj-er than' constructions, it is not neutral after *so*, explaining the resort to the subscript 'N' here.) But we can see anyway that they are not equivalent, as the Received Account requires them to be, because (34) entails, and (33) does not, that Sam can join the police force. (34) tells us that something makes Sam's joining the police force possible, while (33) merely tells us that something fails to make his joining impossible. To see the force of this abstract distinction in a concrete case, suppose that while Sam is above the minimum entry age he falls short of the minimum height requirements for joining the police: although old enough, he is not tall enough, to join. Since he is not tall enough to join, whatever his age might be, he can't join. So being old enough to join is simply not the same as being of such an age that one can join (as (34) says).

Three possible responses to the above difficulty come to mind. One reaction might be to deny that the difficulty exists. A second would be to acknowledge the difficulty and retract part of the Received Account—namely the claimed equivalence of (a) and (b) under (27): one half of the So/Such Reductions. One would then be able to retain the equivalence claim under (26)—the remaining So/Such Reduction principle, as well as the Scale Polarity paraphrases. And a third reaction, which can be found in the literature, would be to 'play down' the difficulty noted above in one way or another.[23]

Let us begin with the first response: deny the data. Here what is denied is the claim, troublesome for the Received Account, that (32) fails to entail that Sam can join the police force. At least—it will be said—this is not so straightforwardly and unequivocally false as we have taken it to be. The idea is that there is a sense in which it is true that anyone old enough to join the police force (to stick with our example) can join the police force, a sense we can bring out by saying something along the lines of (35):

(35) Sam can join the police *in so far as his age is concerned.*

A defender of this line of thought might cite with favour the following remarks from Lewis 1976:

23. A fourth reaction can be found in Meier 2003, which involves—adapting the case she discusses on p. 89—considering worlds in which Sam's age is as in the actual world (at the time of utterance) but his height is allowed to vary arbitrarily. In some of these Sam joins the police force, so we may say not so much that Sam *can* join as that he *could* join. (Compare Nelson 1980, p. 114, on 'Tom can vote' vs. 'Tom could vote'. In fact the current problem was, as we shall see below, was described by Nelson, but no recent writers seem to be aware of his paper and Meier instead thanks Delia Graff and Karina Wilkinson for bringing it to her attention.) As Meier notes, this requires that the property varied not be an essential property of its possessor. That gives one way of refuting the proposal: consider 'He's old enough to be your father.' (An appropriate 'necessity of origin' thesis is assumed here.)

> To say that something can happen is to say that its happening is compatible with certain facts. *Which* facts? That is determined, but sometimes not determined well enough, by context. An ape can't speak a human language—say, Finnish—but I can. Facts about the anatomy and operation of the ape's larynx and nervous system are not compossible with his speaking Finnish. The corresponding facts about my larynx and nervous system are compossible with my speaking Finnish. But don't take me along to Helsinki as your interpreter: I can't speak Finnish. My speaking Finnish is compossible with the facts considered so far, but not with further facts about my lack of training. What I can do, relative to one set of facts, I cannot do, relative to another, more inclusive set.[24]

The facts about Tom's age, this reply continues, are compatible with his joining the police force, making (35) correct, even as uttered without the italicized phrase, when the context makes this a suitable range of facts to which to understand a *can*-statement as relativized.

Lewis's example seems uncharacteristically unpersuasive: we simply wouldn't say that a person merely in virtue of working articulatory apparatus (to say nothing of the other prerequisites for speech in general) can speak Finnish—at best that such a person can learn to speak Finnish. As to whether a more plausible defence of the point concerned can be found—a point of interest to Lewis in defusing the 'Grandfather Paradox' argument against the logical possibility of backward time travel—let us not speculate here. If the point can be made out at all, it will certainly require supplementation by further considerations to bear on the case of *too* and *enough*, for the following reason. If *can*-statements exhibit the relativity claimed, then so do their negations. But if we know that Sam is too short to join the police force then we know that he can't join, and this is not something we shall have to revise in the presence of further information (concerning Sam as he now is, of course—which is not to deny the possibility of his growing taller or of the police entry regulations changing, in either of which eventualities it would now be true that he *will be* able to join the police force). So there is a contrast with the case of being old enough, for which case more information (or a more inclusive set of facts, as Lewis puts it) may of course force a new verdict on

24. This passage appears on p. 77 of the reproduction of Lewis 1976 in Lewis 1986.

Sam's present status as someone who 'can join' the police. The reply we have been considering does not respect the *too/enough* asymmetry here. While further considerations—perhaps such as those developed in Lewis 1979—may help with this, on the face of it, an alternative response seems worth exploring.

The obvious alternative is to take the position described above as the second reaction, jettisoning one half of one part of the two-part package we have been calling the Received Position. The package's two parts comprise the Scale Reversal Equivalences and the So/Such Reductions, and what we throw overboard is the So/Such Reduction for *enough* (that is, the claimed equivalence of (27*a*) and (27*b*)). What remains when that is discarded already suffices, after all, for a 'reduction' of *enough*-constructions, at least in the cases in which the adjective has an antonym so that the Scale Reversal Equivalences can be invoked. It's just that instead of saying that 'Margot was popular enough to be elected' amounts to 'Margot was so popular that she could have got elected', we now say this amounts—via the equivalence with 'Margot was not too unpopular to get elected'—to 'Margot was not so unpopular that she couldn't have got elected'. (In fact, of course, the Received Account was committed to both of these as paraphrases, and it was their non-equivalence with each other that was used to argue against the account.)

It would be nice to defend this second reaction against the third option listed above, which we described as consisting in 'playing down' the difficulty for the Received Account (the difficulty arising from the fact that being tall enough to join the police does not entail being able to join the police). For this more needs to be said about the exact nature of the downplaying, as it is to be found in particular in Nelson 1980:

> (131) a. Tom is old enough to vote.
>
> Sentences with enough and an infinitive complement are systematically ambiguous out of context and without intonation clues. With no special context, (131a) implies (131b).
>
> (131) b. Tom can vote.
>
> . . .
>
> (131a) does not, however, necessarily imply (131b); it may in fact, occur in a context which contradicts (131b):
>
> (131′) Tom is *old* enough to vote; he can't vote, though, because he's a convicted felon.

> (131′) is a marked reading in that it has a special intonation (contrastive stress on *old*) and is understood as it is only if it is placed in a special context. (pp. 113 f.)

Thus Nelson is saying that the supposed counterexample to what the Received Account says, in the So/Such reduction scheme for *enough*-sentences (the claim of equivalence for (27*a*, *b*)) simply shows that as well as the sense of *enough* captured in this account, which provides, as we may say, the default interpretation for such sentences, there is also another sense which comes into play when this default interpretation is not available, namely that sense predicted by the combination of the parts of the Received Account that survive the dropping, urged in the second reaction to the difficulty, of this equivalence claim. (Nelson does not actually defend the So/Such reductions, but puts matters in terms of making or not making things possible or impossible, as we shall see in the following section. This brings out what we called the '*because* aspect' of complemented *too* and *enough* constructions; as with *because*, this talk of *making* includes non-causal ways of making things the case.)

For a proponent of that second reaction this suggestion of ambiguity would be like suggesting that that there is an ambiguity in (36):

(36) I have no objection to your leaving the camp.

Imagine that (36) is addressed by person *b* to person *a*, who is only permitted to leave the camp if no one in authority—who let us suppose comprise persons *b*, *c*, and *d*—has an objection to the departure. If *b* knows that *c* or *d* has such an objection then the more helpful way of uttering (36) is with stress on the 'I' so as to suggest the possibility of a contrary situation in respect of at least of the other authorities. No such special emphasis would be in place if *b* knows that *a* has just been told by *c* and *d* that they do not object. It would be wrong to say that there was an ambiguity in (36) according as to whether it was used to announce the absence of one among several possible obstacles to the addressee's permissible departure, on the one hand, or to announce the absence of the only remaining such obstacle, thereby in the circumstances being sufficient (rather than merely necessary) for the permissibility of the projected departure. Similarly—one would like to be able to say—Nelson's (131a) is not ambiguous between a sense according to which only one of several necessary conditions for voting is being said to be met, on the one hand, and a sense according to which the only (in the circumstances) unmet such condition is being said to be met and thus a *de facto* sufficient condition satisfied.[25] Coming out with (36), with no stress on the 'I' may convey an impression of there being no further obstacles to be overcome, but the mechanism at work here is conversational implicature or something like it: the impression can be cancelled by further words, such as 'but of course that is not to deny that other considerations may rule out your going'. Indeed, the more specific version of such a cancelling rider, 'but others may have objections', would naturally induce a contrastive stress on the 'I', and the presence of such stress alone is already enough to suggest such a rider, even when it is not explicitly added. In the case of (131a) we can say, similarly, that the stress on 'old' works as it does to cancel an implicature ('Tom can vote') rather than to disambiguate an ambiguous sentence. There is no more an ambiguity in the present instance than there is over the word *some* in 'Some of the children are crossing the road', as between a some-but-not-all sense of *some*, and a more inclusive some-and-maybe-all sense.[26]

While it would be nice to be able to leave matters here there are some awkward points to note. One is that it seems implausibly complex to have 'Adj enough for–to S' always mean this roundabout thing: that S is not made impossible by the degree to which the subject is Adj. Postulating ambiguities in cases like this is also implausible, so one should decide where the greater implausibility lies. Another complication is raised by what Nelson goes on to say, immediately after the words 'only if it is placed in a special context' at the end of the passage quoted above, namely that '[t]he special context need not, however, rule out the *possibility* of Tom's voting, as (131″) shows', where (131″) is: 'Tom is old enough to vote; he just never does/prefers not to/always forgets' (Nelson 1980, p. 114). In a note (note 25) appended to this passage, Nelson mentions

25. Hacquard 2005*a* has some very interesting remarks about *enough* and necessary and sufficient conditions.

26. Grice's theory of conversational implicature has been the subject of intense criticism in recent years (as in Davis 1998), but I am hoping the minimal use made of the idea here is unobjectionable, requiring as it does little more than acknowledging that inferences drawn from the fact that something has been (all that is) said are to be distinguished from inferences from the content of what has been said.

Karttunen 1971, on p. 355 of which one finds (a) and (b):

(a) John was clever enough to leave early.
(b) John was clever enough to learn to read.

from the first of which, Karttunen writes 'one easily gets the impression that John left early' (and, he adds 'that this was in some way an advantageous course of action'[27]), by contrast with (b), in which '*clever enough* just seems to mean that John had sufficient mental capacity for learning to read'. The case of (a) analogous to the situation presented by what Karttunen calls implicative verbs, such as 'manage' and 'remember' in sentences like 'John managed/remembered to come', which imply (cancellably so in the latter case) that John came. Nelson observes that the sentential complement in (a) can still be taken to be 'John was able to leave early', because in the same situations in which (a) has the implicative interpretation, this sentence does too, so taken in conjunction with Karttunen's point, no further special story is required to take us from the 'unmarked' *enough* construction to the Karttunen *implicatum*. Karttunen also mentions what he considers a contrast parallel to (a)/(b), with *too*:

(c) John was too stupid to call the cops.
(d) John was too stupid to be a regent.

with the suggestion that (c) is negatively implicative (as with 'John forgot to lock his door'), implying that John didn't call the cops, by contrast with (d), assertible in a context in which all parties know that John is indeed a regent. In this case Nelson has a quite different treatment, since as we shall see in Section V, the complement sentences come in several different modal flavours, and in (d) the relevant modality is deontic: we are saying that because of his stupidity John shouldn't have been a regent, which is of course consistent with his in fact being one.[28] (More

27. Observe, however, that this latter impression is due to the *clever* and not to the favourably evaluative aspect of (certain occurrences of) *enough*, since we can equally well have (the similarly 'implicative') 'He was foolish enough to leave the door open'.
28. When Meier (2003, p. 95) discusses the Karttunen examples, she brings in, for (a), what she calls *ideal* worlds and says 'And suppose *ideally* that he had the money and the time to go to school instead of working every day of his childhood', etc.: terminology which suggests deontic modality—whereas in fact with (a) we are dealing with what in Section V we call dynatic modality.

accurately, Nelson's gloss is that it was *improper* that John was a regent.) In fact, (c) raises difficulties of its own for Nelson's account, as we shall at the end of Section V.

But why are the implicative cases of *enough* problematic for the proposed 'Grice's Razor' alternative to the ambiguity claim made by Nelson? Speaking of the Karttunen implicativity observations, and in particular of the suggestion that (a) in some way implies that John left, Hacquard (2005a, Section 1) writes: 'However, once we turn to the French counterpart of [*too* and *enough* constructions], we observe that this implication cannot just be pragmatic, as it is grammatically encoded.' In particular, she notes that translating (a) into French as (a′) or as (a″) gives different results:

(a′) Jean était assez rapide pour s'enfuir.
(a″) Jean a été assez rapide pour s'enfuir.

Of these, (a″) does, while (a′) does not, carry the implication that Jean/John escaped. Hacquard writes (with example labels adjusted) that 'English doesn't have an aspectual distinction in the past tense, hence (a) is ambiguous between a perfective and an imperfective reading, blurring the fact that implication and aspect are correlated and that, with the right aspect, the implication is not defeasible.'[29] This leads Hacquard to consider a novel approach, inspired by a treatment of the 'ability modal' developed by Rajesh Bhatt, on which the implicative *enough* construction is taken as basic and non-implicative readings 'are derived through a genericity operator, whose presence is reflected by imperfective morphology'. The details of that approach are not under consideration here—only the objection that the envisaged Gricean ('pragmatic') line against the ambiguity claim cannot be sustained, as the implicativity phenomenon is 'grammatically encoded'. Nor will this methodological principle itself be scrutinized here, where the point has simply been to note that all is not plain sailing for the Gricean response to this particular problem with the Received Account.

29. Perfectivity here has nothing to do with *perfect* aspect; when we turn to past-vs.-perfect it is (contemporary spoken) French that has the ambiguity and English that insists on its resolution ('went' vs. 'has gone', etc.); Section 5.1 of Hacquard 2005*a* goes into all this and its relation to the Karttunen implication.

IV

Eric Nelson's Proposals: Comparative Paraphrases. Nelson 1980, of which we have already had several glimpses, discusses the semantics of *too* and *enough* in two parts, one, a section entitled 'Comparative Paraphrases for *too* and *enough* sentences', and the other (pp. 110–22) divided over various sections, on the modal element in the complements of too and enough constructions. The latter forms the material for the following section. Under the former heading, with which we deal here, postponing the latter topic to the next section, the following passage may be found:

> When we hear a sentence such as *Tom is too young to vote*, we understand *Tom's age is less than age X*, where the value of *X* may be filled in by our knowledge of the world; specifically, by our knowledge of how old one has to be in order to vote. So we understand *Tom's age is less than 18*. (p. 108)

This is obviously false if taken literally, since there is no difficulty in understanding the first sentence mentioned in this quotation in the absence of knowledge of the minimum voting age, and no change in what is understood on acquiring that knowledge.[30] Evidently the problem is that Nelson is not quite sure how to deal with the variable *X* in the would-be paraphrase. (We address this issue below.) It remains in play with a suggested contrast, (113) vs. (114) in the passage below, which we can see as looking more closely at what happens around the point labelled 'min' in (10) above. This quotation from Nelson 1980 begins where that inset above finishes; the 'for P' is what we have been writing as 'for–to S':

> A statement with *too* is in this sense comparative. If Tom's age falls *far* short of 18, it might be said that he is *far too young to vote* or *much too young to vote*, but there is nothing incorrect about simply saying *Tom is too young to vote*.
>
> If Tom is eighteen years old, he is old enough to vote. He is also old enough if he is nineteen, twenty-three or ninety-seven. If he is *well* past the age of eighteen we might, to be informative, say he is

30. Appended to the passage quoted is an endnote reading, 'This is not to say that the italicized sentence is substitutable for the sentence with *too young*. The latter includes more information than just the comparison, as we shall see' (Nelson 1980, p. 130, n. 15). This is a retraction of what the quoted passage says.

> *more than old enough to vote*, but it is not inappropriate to use *old enough* without qualification. So *enough* indicates an age that *equals or exceeds age X*.
>
> In sum: (We abbreviate here, using mathematical symbols and substituting *for P* for the complement.)
>
> (113) a. Tom is too young for P. = b. Tom's age < age X.
>
> (114) a. Tom is old enough for P. = b. Tom's age ≥ age X.
>
> It should be clear from (113) why *too* cannot be modified by *more*. (Recall the sentence in (44): *Tom is more than too old to join the Cub Scouts.) *More* is ruled out with *too* on the same grounds as it is with an ordinary comparative adverb: **Tom is more than older than Bill*. *Enough* in contrast, allows modification by *more* (as well as *exactly*) because it has in interpretation in which is it expresses an equality relation.

Still keeping the status of the variable *X* unsettled, we can raise some doubts about these suggestions. First, is it correct to link *too* with the strict and *enough* with the weak inequalities in the way Nelson is proposing?[31] Somewhat artificially, let us define a real number to be *surgross* just in case it is strictly greater than 144.[32] There is no problem with understanding this definition, or with answering questions on the basis of it, such as: (i) Is 141 surgross? (ii) Is 145 surgross? (iii) Is 144.02 surgross? and (iv) Is 144 surgross? In expanding on the no, yes, yes, and no answers (respectively) to these questions, one would naturally say that the first and last numbers involved are too small to count as surgross, neither meeting the defining condition of being strictly greater than 144, while the second and third numbers are large enough, simply on the basis of the scale reversal equivalences and the fact that by contrast they are not too small to qualify. If this is right, then the 'min' point in (10) may have to be allowed not to represent the least point on a scale at which something is the case, but as an *external* greatest lower bound. What are we to make of the final sentence of the quotation from Nelson in this case? *Enough*, he tells us, allows modification by *more* (not how I would have described what is going on in the phrase

31. Meyer 2003, p. 92, has the same linkage, though she contrasts ≥ with > rather than with <, because of a scale reversal (on passage to the antonym).

32. Since this may no longer be common knowledge: a *gross* was a pre-metric, duodecimally based measure of quantity, usually applied in discrete cases (unlike that of the real numbers considered here—for which the rational numbers would do equally well, of course, as a domain of definition), amounting to 144 of whatever were being counted.

'more than enough', but let that pass) because it 'has an interpretation in which it expresses the equality relation', the latter presumably meaning that it has an interpretation (namely as $\geq$) which is compatible with the equality relation. In the case of being surgross, any number which is large enough to qualify as surgross is already more than large enough to count as such since we can find a smaller number which is surgross. (The fact that such examples do not occur naturally, or are at least rare, means that this need not make Nelson's hypothesis as to why there is a 'more than enough' construction untenable: indeed the mere existence of *some* cases in which the lower bound is included rather than excluded suffices for this.)

In the case of the 'surgross' example, as with the example being old enough/too young to vote, there is a minimum but no corresponding maximum point, like that indicated in (10) on the relevant scale. One can easily envisage alternative arrangements in which there is a maximum voting age, just as there are stretches of road in some countries subject to both a maximum and a minimum speed limit. In any case, we have familiar examples, in connection with which (10) was introduced in the first place, such as that already given of a police force admitting new recruits above a certain age provided the recruit is also below another age. We were imagining these ages set at 18 and 36. What if someone asked, concerning Nelson's 97-year-old voter (here assumed to be male), whether he was old enough to join the police force? If one answered *no*, one would be saying that the man was not old enough—and hence by the scale reversal equivalence, too young—to join the police force, which seems like a very bad thing to be saying: thus the answer must be *yes*, he is old enough. This would of course be a misleading thing to say to anyone—as indeed would be the earlier 'more than old enough'—but it would not, I take it, be false. One might think that this is because making an unqualified *enough*-statement would implicate the corresponding possibility (in this case, for the man in question to join the police force). Alternatively, one might think the reason is that, as we saw Nelson maintaining in the preceding section, the *enough*-sentence itself is ambiguous, and it is confusing to leave the possibility-implying sense still in the running. Recall from the end of that section that according to Nelson 'Tom is old enough to vote' ((131a) in the quotation) has two readings, which he calls the marked and unmarked readings. Now we can see how he cashes these out in terms of the inequalities ('comparative paraphrases'):

> The source of the difference between the marked and unmarked readings of (131a) is the shared assumptions we make use of in interpreting the sentence. When we interpret (131a) in the marked way, we assume the following about the relationship between voting and age:
>
> (132) If one's age $\geq$ *X* age, then one's age does not make it impossible for one to vote.
>
> (132) is consistent with a context in which something other than age prevents one from voting. When we interpret (131a) in the unmarked way, we assume:
>
> (133) If one's age $\geq$ *X* age, then one's age makes it possible for one to vote.
>
> (133) is not consistent with a context in which Tom *can't* vote. We assume, on the unmarked reading, that the other requirements for voting (besides age) are met.[33]

In fact our example of the person who is too old to join the police force, or of the imaginary case of someone too old to vote, shows that neither (132) nor (133) is assumed, since we have already seen that (to take the latter case) 97-year-old Tom is indeed old enough to vote, but Tom's *age* does make it impossible for him to vote—falsifying (132) and (133). This is therefore also a problem for anyone not sharing Nelson's ambiguity thesis. An account of what is going on here needs to be formulated in such a way that being old enough to vote is a matter of the one's low age (or the lowness of one's age) not precluding one's voting rather than one's great age not precluding this.

An incidental further complication is caused by the possibility of scales in which there are separated favourable intervals, where by a favourable interval I mean a stretch such as the middle segment of (10) in which something is neither not ADJ enough nor too ADJ (for–to S). One sometimes hears it said that squid (calamari) should be cooked for less than two minutes or more than twenty—anything in between and it will be unacceptably rubbery. Let us just assume that this is good advice. In the interests of plausibility, there should also be a lower bound (say, one

33. Nelson 1980, p. 114; I have inserted '$\geq$' into what appears as a blank in (133) of my copy of the paper on the assumption that that was what was intended.

minute) for the lower interval, giving an instance of the separated favourable intervals phenomenon. Now suppose that some squid has been cooked for ten minutes and then served. Has it been cooked too long, or not long enough?[34] The question is not settled by an insistence—the complete thought issue rears its head—that the *for–to* complement be specified, since it remains if this is supplied in the form of 'for a pleasantly textured meal to be produced'. In practice the choice of which remark to make, on the part of either an apologetic chef or a restaurant critic, may sometimes depend on the presumed intentions of the chef: whether to produce a quick stir-fry of calamari with chilli and garlic, or a slow-cooked seafood stew. But we may know perfectly well that, for instance, this particular reluctantly recruited camping ground cook had no intention more specific than that of converting whatever has just been brought to him into something edible for the family. The question seems to have no answer in such a case. The *too/enough* machinery has not evolved to cope with such cases, which of course make considerable trouble for Nelson's *X* variable proposal above, since it needs to take more than one value on the same scale.[35] Also under threat would be the argument form (6) from Section I: ten minutes is too long a time to leave squid cooking; thirty minutes is longer than ten minutes; therefore, thirty minutes is too long to leave squid cooking. In assuming the first premiss is true, the earlier unsettled question has been assumed to have the answer 'It's been cooked too long'. If on the other hand, we go for the negative answer, and say that it's not been cooked long enough, then we have trouble with (6′): ten minutes is not long enough to leave squid cooking; ten minutes is longer than one and half minutes; therefore one and a half minutes is not long enough to leave squid cooking. But as I say, the constructions with which we are concerned were not built to cope with these cases.

More interesting is a connection between, on the one hand, the argument forms (6) and (6′) from Section I, and on the other, the question of what to do with the mysterious variable *X* left

34. Strictly, since we are supposed to be considering adjectives, the example should ask whether the cooking time has been too long or too short.

35. Actually, on Nelson's own account for the standard cases, there are two relevant choices for *X*, distinguished using *min* and *max* below, so the present point would be more accurately put by saying that in the current case one would need four rather than two values.

inappropriately as a free variable in Nelson's paraphrases. One idea that comes to mind is that for sentences of the forms (37) and (38)—abstracting from the particular case of 'Tom is too young/old enough to vote'—

(37) NP_1 is too ADJ to VP.
(38) NP_1 is ADJ enough to VP.

we have something like (37′) and (38′) below, in which we write *deg*(NP_1, ADJ) for the degree to which NP_1 is ADJ, *min*(ADJ, VP) for the minimum degree to which something needs to be ADJ to VP, and *max*(ADJ, VP) for the maximum degree to which something can be ADJ to VP, and in which we have, for simplicity, reverted to Nelson's distribution of strict and weak inequalities (despite the issue raised by the surgross example):

(37′) $deg(NP_1, \text{ADJ}) > max(\text{ADJ}, \text{VP})$.
(38′) $deg(NP_1, \text{ADJ}) \geq min(\text{ADJ}, \text{VP})$.

To derive the Scale Reversal Equivalences we need the formal principles

(SR1) $min(NP_1, \text{ADJ}) = max(NP_1, \text{un-ADJ})$ *and*
$max(NP_1, \text{ADJ}) = min(NP_1, \text{un-ADJ})$,

which are equivalent to each other given the equivalence of un-(un-ADJ) and ADJ, as well as

(SR2) *For all x*, $deg(NP_1, \text{ADJ}) < x$ *if and only if*
$x < deg(NP_1, \text{un-ADJ})$.

(SR1) and (SR2) together encapsulate the idea that the scale for an adjective and its (scalar) antonym are mirror images of each other. Applying this to the case of

(i) Tom is too young to vote.
(ii) Tom is not old enough to vote.

we have the respective (37′)- and (38′)-style representations

(i′) $deg(\text{Tom}, \text{young}) > max(\text{young}, \text{vote})$.
(ii′) $\neg(deg(\text{Tom}, \text{old}) \geq min(\text{old}, \text{vote}))$.

By (SR1), (i′) is equivalent to

(i″) $deg(\text{Tom}, \text{young}) > min(\text{old}, \text{vote})$.

and thus by (SR2) to

(i‴) *min*(old, vote) > *deg*(Tom, old).

Since we are working with linear scales, (ii′) can be rewritten as (ii″)

(ii″) *deg*(Tom, old) < *min*(old, vote),

whose equivalence with (i‴) is now evident.[36]

Let us return to an example mentioned in Section I as being of the form (6′):

Chris is tall enough to join the police force.
Alf is taller than Chris.

∴ Alf is tall enough to join the police force.

If the first premiss tells us that Chris's height exceeds (or equals) what we are calling *min*(tall, join the police force), that is, the minimum height for joining the police force, then the second premiss secures this for Alf's height also, making the conclusion follow. But is the argument valid? I forgot to mention that the parties involved here, Christine and Alfred to give them their full forenames, live in a country where in the interests of gender balancing the police force, the height requirements are set at a lower level for female than for male entrants. Chris's height exceeds the female minimum while, though he is a little taller than she is, Alf's height falls short of the male minimum. I take this to show that the above argument is invalid, along with argument forms (6) and (6′), and that the suggested substitute for Nelson's '*X*', namely *min*(ADJ, VP) does not work.[37]

One could react in a similar way to the calamari case and say that the counterexample is not decisive, since for that the

36. A broadly similar pattern of explanation is to be found in Section 5 of Meier 2003.

37. After writing this I learnt from Meier 2003 that Kennedy (1999) considered the following pair of arguments. (a): Kim is too old to qualify for the children's fair; Sandy is older than Kim; therefore Sandy is too old to qualify for the children's fair. (b): The bottle of mild is too old to drink; the bottle of wine is older than the bottle of milk; therefore, the bottle of wine is too old to drink. Kennedy considered (a) to be valid and (b) invalid, and Meier concurs, though her explanation in the former case appeals to a background conversational assumption about the (age) rules being the same for everyone, so this disagreement with the verdict expressed above—according to which neither (a) nor (b) is valid—may be terminological: we can all agree that these arguments are not valid in virtue of having the form (6).

premisses would need to be true and the conclusion false in the envisaged situation, but in the situation as described the premiss 'Chris is tall enough to join the police force' is not clearly true, since there is no such thing as being tall enough to join the police force *tout court*—there is being tall enough for a man to join and there is being tall enough for a woman to join, so although there is no explicit definition description here, our premiss should go the way—whatever that is—of sentences with such descriptions when the associated uniqueness requirement is not satisfied. This reaction seems rather artificial, though, since even someone who knew about the gender-differentiated height-minima could still naturally ask Alf, for example, 'Are you tall enough to join the police force?', since what is at issue here is whether Alf reaches the height required *for Alf* to join the police force. What this suggests is that we use the whole of the *for–to* complement, and not just its VP, as the second argument of (reconceived) *min*.[38] The argument inset above would no longer be validated with this more discriminating *min* function in the background since the first premiss tells us that *deg* (Chris, tall) $\geq$ *min* (ADJ, Chris joins the police force) and the second that *deg* (Alf, tall) $>$ *deg* (Chris, tall), from which the conclusion follows that *deg* (Alf, tall) $\geq$ *min* (ADJ, Chris joins the police force), but not the conclusion that we need for the above argument, which is *deg* (Alf, tall) $\geq$ *min* (ADJ, Alf joins the police force). In fact, reflection on examples like (5) would already have alerted us to the need to use the whole of the complement S and not just the VP in this capacity.

V

Eric Nelson's Proposals: Complement Modality. As the passages quoted from Nelson 1980 in the preceding sections reveal, he thinks of something's being too ADJ for–to S as a matter of that thing's being ADJ to a degree which makes it impossible that S,

38. Cf. the following remark from Section 3 of Hacquard 2005*a*: 'Thus *too* and *enough* take three arguments: a proposition, a predicate of degrees and an individual (in 'Jean was quick enough to escape' the arguments are *that Jean escaped*, *quick*, and *Jean*).' This is not quite the same suggestion since a Noun Phrase needn't denote an individual. (For example, 'The children were close enough together to be able to communicate in whispers.') Nor is Hacquard's approach to the semantics of enough similar to anything being canvassed here.

and of something's being Adj enough for–to S as either its being Adj to a degree that makes it possible that S, or else as its not being Adj to a degree that makes it impossible (this disjunction recording the ambiguity claim). In fact this possibility vs. impossibility contrast is not the only modal flavour the complement sentence S can assume, and Nelson proposes a taxonomy which we will now examine. Quite how this is meant to be related to the discussion we have just been reviewing is not made clear by Nelson's own discussion. In our corrective reconstruction in the preceding section, the modality is hidden in the *min* notation used to replace Nelson's '*X*', which in the main cases reviewed amounted to the minimum degree one had to be Adj, below which something or other was impossible.

With examples (39) and (40),[39] however, Nelson reminds us—as we saw with (24) in Section II—that *too* does not always involve impossibility:

(39) Tom is too old to watch Captain Kangaroo.
(40) Tom is too sick to eat.

In the case of (39), nobody would interpret this as saying that Tom's age makes watching Captain Kangaroo impossible—or, that Tom is so old that he can't watch Captain Kangaroo, to use the *So/Such* reduction: instead, according to Nelson, the speaker is taken to be saying that it is 'not proper' for someone of Tom's age to be watching Captain Kangaroo.[40] In the case of (40), one might not know what was intended—perhaps surmising that Tom's illness does prevent him from eating, until (as Nelson, p. 119, suggests) one hears the follow-up, 'So tell him to quit eating', in which case one reinterprets (40) as claiming that eating was not the proper thing for Tom to be doing in his condition. (We return to this in Section VI.) The issue raised in Section III above as problematic for the Received View arises with the proper/improper modality as it does with possible/impossible. And Nelson again argues for an ambiguity, with a marked and an unmarked reading of (41) (Nelson's (134), p. 115):

39. These are respectively examples (129a) and (147) in Nelson 1980.
40. Captain Kangaroo was a US television program for young children, which expired in the mid-1980s after a 30-year run.

(41) Tom is old enough to babysit.

which is said to imply, in its unmarked reading, that it isn't/wouldn't be improper for Tom to babysit. To get the marked reading, stress 'old' and add (Nelson suggests) '... he shouldn't babysit, though (because he's too irresponsible)'. Let's not replay the alternatives to this ambiguity view here.[41] In fact in the present case it is somewhat worse, in that Nelson discerns a threefold ambiguity, best explained after the 'deontic operator' reformulation of the proper/improper contrast, introduced below.

The average philosopher encountering such examples will be put in mind of the systematic modal analogies expounded originally in the opening chapter of von Wright 1951, and much developed over subsequent years: we have alethic (possible/impossible) and deontic modality, except that in place of the familiar deontic contrast—permissible/impermissible—Nelson has formulated this as a 'proper'/'improper' contrast. One advantage in shifting to the usual deontic logical terminology arises over the formulation of the triple ambiguity claimed by Nelson for 'proper' *enough*:

> Some sentences with *enough*, unlike (134a) [Tom is young enough to watch Captain Kangaroo], imply not just the absence of improperness, but properness in a positive sense: a positive obligation. In such a sentence, the complement is understood like a sentence with *should*. In (136) we illustrate.
>
> (136) a. Tom is old enough to know better.
> b. It would be proper for Tom to know better.
> c. Tom should know better.
>
> To sum up, the modality PROPER may be understood in an enough complement in any of these three ways:
>
> (137) i. X does not make P improper. (But something else does.)
> ii. P is not improper. (the *need not not* interpretation)
> iii. P is proper (the should interpretation)
>
> (Nelson 1980, p. 115f.)

The new sense, then, over and above Nelson's distinction between not making something improper (not making it the case $\neg\Diamond P$)

41. There is of course an independent and uncontroversial ambiguity in (41), depending on whether we take 'Tom' as the understood subject (as presumed here) or the understood object of *babysit*.

and making it proper (making it the case that $\Diamond P$) is the stronger way of understanding 'making it proper', namely, as making it the case that $\neg\Diamond\neg P$ (alias $\Box P$). The word 'proper' is not conducive to clear-headed discussion for the same reason as the word 'right' is not: it obscures the issue as to whether the diamond notion or the box notion—permissibility or obligatoriness—is intended. (This is noted in Robinson 1971.) Two points that may deserve further thought arise here. First, it does seem that a word more in the vicinity of *proper* than of *ought*—namely the word *appropriate*—comes to mind more readily for the deontic-like complements. Secondly, whatever verbal formulation one opts for it would seem that the relevant deontic judgements are situational rather than agent-implicating.[42] The contrary is suggested by some of Nelson's formulations, as in talk[43] of Tom's acting properly or improperly in watching Captain Kangaroo. Consider Karttunen's example (d) at the end of Section III: just because John's low intelligence means he ought not to be a regent, one does not conclude that there is an obligation *on John* not to be a regent. (Cf. 'He was too young to die'.)

We can ask in passing whether, whatever we may think of the first alleged ambiguity, there is also this new 'obligatory' sense of *enough*. It would certainly be theoretically simpler if it did not exist, since it is in tension with the So/Such Reductions, according to which Nelson's (136a) should be paraphrasable by 'Tom is not too young to know better', and no claim of a special new sense is being suggested in the case of *too*. The example involves extraneous complications,[44] to avoid which we might consider replacing it with 'You are old enough to tie your own shoelaces', imagined as said by a mother to her son as he is getting dressed. A perfectly natural thing to say, and to say with the intention of conveying the idea that the boy should tie his own shoelaces. But it seems far from clear that the sentence just quoted has as its meaning, or one of its meanings, that the addressee should tie his own shoelaces. It may be more plausible that the mother intends the son to read into her utterance something along the lines of: 'The only reason I've been tying your shoelaces

42. This is terminology that may be found in Humberstone 1991, for instance.
43. Nelson 1980, p. 115, Example (134c′).
44. For one thing there is the idiomatic aspect of 'know better'; even setting aside this feature, the *know* itself creates problems (mentioned apropos of (57) below).

for you is that you were too young to do it yourself, and you're no longer too young.' There would accordingly be a two-stage implicature here, first the implicature whose acknowledgment was advised in Section III from 'you're not too young/you're old enough' to 'you can', and then a further implicature generated by the particular circumstances, which we can summarize by varying the familiar '*ought*-implies-*can*' dictum to: (in these circumstances) '*can*-implicates-*ought*'.

Following the usual expectation (consider the case of the modal auxiliaries) that where there are alethic and deontic parallels there will also be an epistemic parallel, we of course have epistemically interpreted *too* and *enough* statements. As Nelson observes, (39) could be the response to a question as to what Tom might be watching on TV: evidence of Tom's age is brought to bear negatively on the epistemic possibility that he's watching captain Kangaroo.[45] Likewise with Nelson's example

(42) Tom is mean enough to be the mugger.

Although noting the epistemic cases, Nelson doesn't quite treat them on all fours with the alethic and deontic cases, instead making a threefold 'root' modality division, two of the three parts are possible/impossible and proper/improper, and the third of which we will come to presently, and then tries to overlay an epistemic duplication over each of the three categories, so that we should end up with a two-by-three taxonomy. Finding it impossible to substantiate the root/epistemic distinctions in all but the possible/impossible case, wisely Nelson abandons this ambition.[46] So, roughly speaking, we are left with (i) something like alethic modality, (ii) deontic modality, (iii) epistemic modality, and (iv) a further category which may threaten to spoil things for those of us who would like to have had the von Wright tradition in modal logic provide all the systematic guidance we needed. Before getting to that further category, a couple of qualms should be aired about the terminology: first 'alethic' is perhaps not the right word if we are talking about

45. Nelson 1980, p. 118, at example (146a); the next example is from the same page, where it appears as (142a).
46. See Nelson 1980, pp. 118f. Nor will philosophers be impressed with Nelson's suggestion that it is epistemically possible that *p* just in case it is (non-epistemically) possible to believe that *p*.

the practical impossibilities and inabilities. 'Dynamic modal logic' was the label Kenny (1976) suggested for this area, but because that label has now gained currency for something quite different (the modal logic of programs), it is no longer available. A good alternative would be the cognate term *dynatic*. Also, there is a question as to what side of the deontic/dynatic divide to place the example of Tom's being too young to vote. Because one says that Tom can't vote, Nelson explicitly puts this case in the possible/impossible bag rather than with the proper/improper, noting that from (39) above, with the improper reading, it does not follow that Tom does not watch Captain Kangaroo, and claim that, by contrast, from 'Tom is too young to vote' it does follow that Tom doesn't vote. Really, though, isn't this just a matter of its not being legally possible—that is, legally permissible—for someone under 18 to vote? Many volunteer soldiers in World War I were too young to join the army in exactly the same sense as we are supposing Tom to be too young to vote, but, lying about their ages, they managed to join up all the same, this 'impossibility' notwithstanding. One would perhaps not want to call such things 'improper', but deontic modality is itself not monolithic (moral permissibility, legal permissibility, etc.), and perhaps Nelson has been misled by the mere fact that we say that children can't vote when we mean that according to the law they can't.

If this were the full story, there would be a pleasantly simple description to offer, in terms of the modal square of opposition (in its usual contemporary presentation, as, for instance on p. 86 of Kneale and Kneale 1962):[47] the modal notions in play in *too* and *enough* constructions are those located at respectively the lower and upper ends of the upward-sloping diagonal in the modal square of opposition for each of dynatic, doxastic, or epistemic modality—a diamond-like notion and a negated diamond-like notion, to recall the notation briefly introduced above. But this nice picture is threatened by a number of cases, two of which Nelson uses[48] to introduce the category of modal complement we have so far studiously avoided describing:

47. Humberstone 2005 is a recent 'square of opposition'-oriented survey of modal matters.
48. (42) and (43) are (130a) and (138a), respectively, in Nelson 1980.

(42) Tom is too lazy to help around the house.
(43) Tom is fair-minded enough to help around the house.

As with possible/possible (dynatic or epistemic) and proper/improper, Nelson offers a binary distinction, which he labels 'willing/refusal'. The latter term is potentially confusing since there need be no speech act of refusal involved (on the part of Tom as reported in (42)), so the contrast would appear to be that between *willing* and *unwilling*. Why does this seem a threat? Why not just add this modal opposition—boulomaic modality (Kenny's phrase, again)—to the others, as Nelson does? Under the same heading we might also classify the following examples, of which (45) is from Quirk et al. 1985, p. 1142—where they offer the so/such reduction, 'It was such a pleasant day that I didn't want to go to school'—as is (46); (47) is taken from Huddleston and Pullum 2002, p. 397, despite its containing an *enough* modifying an adverb (the invisible *much*):

(44) Who would be mad enough to wear a hat like that to a funeral?
(45) It was too pleasant a day to go to school.
(46) He's enough of a coward to do that.
(47) I don't like it enough to buy it at that price.

With these examples, there is some wavering between understanding them as involving, on the one hand, wanting or being willing to do something, and on the other, doing something willingly. But the element of willingness can be absent altogether, as in the following cases (the second of which is from Quirk et al. 1985, p. 1140):

(48) They ate enough to make themselves sick.
(49) They worked enough to be hungry.

Now, (49) may seem a little stilted as it stands, improving in this respect if spun out somewhat, say to 'They had already worked hard enough to become fairly hungry'. As for (48), we notice a 'make' in the complement, which is reminiscent of Nelson's favoured unmarked 'making possible' gloss on *enough* sentences, though here we have it in the *for–to* form itself rather than in the modal paraphrase, and there is no 'possible' either explicit or understood. The fact that a modal element is already there in the *for–to* construction is not unprecedented: one might say 'too sick to be able to get out of bed' just as one might say 'too sick to get out of bed'. Another such case is also given by Quirk et al. (loc. cit.):

(50) I had a bad enough headache to need two aspirins.

for which they offer the so/such reduction: 'I had such a bad headache that I needed two aspirins.' On the neat modal story, one would have expected here 'I had such a bad headache that I was able to need two aspirins', or '. . . that it was possible for me to need two aspirins', neither of which makes much sense (as goes also for their deontic or epistemic or boulomaic variants). Equally problematic for that simple modal complement account are the following:

(51) It was unusual enough to arouse suspicion.
(52) It was clear enough to need no further spelling out.
(53) These considerations are already enough to establish the result we were after.
(54) After reading the novel, I was sufficiently intrigued to want to get hold of the author's autobiography.
(55) The offence was serious enough to merit a prison sentence.
(56) The offence was too serious for a suspended sentence to be justified.
(57) Miss Foresight was feminine enough to feel that it was a little hard that so much concentration should be called for when talking to a member of her own sex.[49]
(58) We led a cowed, daunted existence, socially sophisticated enough to be conscious of our social inferiority.[50]
(59) He's been in politics long enough to know where all the bodies are buried.

49. This example is from Pym 1978, p. 16; the full context is as follows: 'Her expression as she listened to Miss Lydgate's plans for the writing up of her linguistic researches, was one of rather strained interest. Women must so often listen to men with just this expression on their faces, but Miss Foresight was feminine enough to feel that it was a little hard that so much concentration should be called for when talking to a member of her own sex.'
50. Eagleton 2001, p. 104.

(60) He knows me well enough to know that I would never do that.

The *know* in (59) and (60) for instance, does not sit well with the dynatic paraphrases 'so long/well that hc can know ...' or 'so long/well that it is possible for him to know ...'. We might also throw into the list the example labelled (c) in the discussion of Karttunen at the end of Section III: 'John was too stupid to call the cops.' One might thinking of subsuming this under the unwillingness rubric (or 'refusal', in Nelson's terms), but it would only be plausible for certain imagined scenarios—with John entertaining and rejecting the option of calling the cops. So the difficulty is made clearer by changing the example to 'John was too stupid to think of calling the cops'. (Though here again, one might revert to impossibility.)

We close inconclusively. Nelson made a laudably bold attempt to bring order into the semantics of *enough* and *too* sentences by giving a short list of candidate modal elaborations for the sentential complement. But are the problematic cases we have lately been airing simply marginal cases to be understood by analogy with (or by assimilation to) that taxonomy, or are they evidence that the apparent success of the taxonomy was due to a concentration on an unrepresentative set of examples?

VI

The Evaluativity and 'Complete thought' Questions. Why might the two topics featuring in the title of this question be discussed under one umbrella? Well, there is a precedent in the case of the verb *need*. According to enlightened wisdom in the 1970s (more specifically: White 1975, Chapter 8),[51] *need* statements which do not specify a goal for which the thing said to be needed is to be understood as needed for:

> 'Need' indicates a relation, namely that of a certain kind of necessity, between one of a number of alternatives, which is said to be what is needed, and a situation which consists of a set of circumstances and an end-state. *A* cannot in these circumstances reach the end-state without *V*-ing or without *X*. ... Because the

51. See note 11 of Wiggins 1987 for references to other writers taking the same line.

> end-state can be of many kinds, to say that *A* needs to *V* is elliptical for saying that *A* needs *V* in order to *F*. ... The need can be further qualified in regard to the aspect under which it is related to the end-state, as 'legally', 'logically', 'morally', 'psychologically', 'practically', 'ideally', 'in theory', 'according to the regulations', etc. (White 1975, p. 105)

I take the claim that *need*-statements which do not specify the end-state (the 'in order to *F*' part of the above schematic formulation) are *elliptical* for statements making this explicit to be the claim that no proposition has been expressed which can be evaluated for truth without the end-state being specified.[52] White says that this results in people talking at cross purposes when they express themselves in the elliptical manner. He suggests that this holds for ellipsis of the various adverbial qualifications at the end of the passage last quoted, as well as for ellipsis of the end-state specification:

> My daughter's claim that she needs another pair of shoes is made in the light of her wish to keep up with the latest fashions; while my insistence that she does not need them appeals to the ordinary requirements of daily use. There is no non-relative answer to the question 'Does she need them?', though one may legitimately suppose that the need to *V* in order to *F* is more important than the need to *V* [presumably a typo for '*V'*'—LH] in order to *G* because to *F* is more important than to *G*? (White, 1975, p. 106)

But one can readily imagine any reasons for claiming that *need*-statements are elliptical (or 'relative') will arise just as powerfully for making a similar claim in the case of statements about what is important—'important *for what*?' By the mid-1980s, those writing on this topic were pointing out that one natural continuation of the conversation described by White would be 'But do you really need to keep up with the dictates of fashion?', and as Wiggins (1987, p. 8), points out, White's daughter would be 'missing the point' if yet

52. For many linguists talk of ellipsis is only appropriate when the ellipsed material is recoverable from the intra-linguistic context, perhaps with various choices, giving rise to ambiguity, as in 'Jack loved his daughter more than his wife'. (See the second quotation from Bach below.) But no such restriction is intended in the use of the term *elliptical* by the philosophers under discussion here and their example is followed here. (An extensive range of cases that might be subsumed under the heading of ellipsis is reviewed in the editors' introduction to Elugardo and Stainton 2005.)

further purely adventitious project-dependent needs were cited in response. The term 'adventitious' here is from Braybrooke 1987, Chapter 2, where it is contrasted with *course-of-life* needs; the contrast is formulated by Wiggins, as well by Thomson (1987, Chapter 1), as being between instrumental and non-instrumental (or 'absolute') needs. All these philosophers are united in thinking that room must be made for a special non-instrumental sense giving a non-elliptical and indeed normative sense of *need*,[53] related to the instrumental sense by some such equivalence as the following: I need (absolute sense) to have *x* if and only if I need (instrumental sense) to have *x* if I am to avoid being harmed.[54] The interested reader can consult these sources to see a satisfactory explanation is given as to how the non-instrumental sense manages to acquire its normativity, where what the latter amounts to is something like this: to acknowledge that *a* needs such-and-such (in the current sense of 'need') is to acknowledge a prima facie moral obligation that *a* be provided with such-and-such.[55]

53. White (1975, p. 105) vigorously denies that there is any normative sense of *need*, but this raises tensions with other aspects of his discussion. Along with various good points about the relation between wanting and needing, White says (p.110) that whereas saying that one wants to *V* can *explain* one's actions, saying that one needs to *V* can serve to *justify* them. How so, if there is no normative element in *need*-statements? And on the following page he makes a very sensible point about another contrast between wanting and needing on p. 111 (last four lines), which can be summarized as 'Whether I need so-and-so partly depends on the characteristics of so-and-so ... but not at all on what I believe to be or believe of these characteristics'—whereas with wanting, there is such a dependence on believed characteristics. But what appears in the part I've blanked out with the '...' are the words (flanked by commas) 'whether or not these are desirable'. How on White's official, entirely non-normative account of needing, there can be any dependence on the desirability (a normative matter if anything is) of anything? (It is possible that I have misunderstood the 'whether or not', and they are not intended to indicate dependence on whether or not these are desirable, but simply to mean 'regardless of whether ...').

54. This follows the formulation of Wiggins 1987 (p. 10) with minor changes; elsewhere in the paper, Wiggins speaks of adverse effects on the needer's *vital interests*, of his or her life being 'blighted', and so on. Thomson 1987 (p. 6) has 'A needs (normative) if and only if A needs X (non-normative) in order to φ and φ-ing is vitally important.' It is not clear whether Thomson intends the right-hand side of this biconditional to be tacitly prefixed by 'for some φ'. The discussion in Braybrooke 1987 (pp. 30–3) is less formal. By contrast with White, all these writers are more interested in the political rhetoric of talk of *needs* talk than with the analysis of such talk for its own sake. A more succinct statement of Wiggins's position may be found in Wiggins and Dermen 1987.

55. Wiggins (1987, p. 26) writes in this connection of 'the prima facie compelling character of a true unexaggerated statement of need'.

The inevitable upshot of the position just reviewed (with considerable over-simplification, it must be said) is that a statement to the effect that someone needs this or that, without specification of what it is needed for, is ambiguous between an elliptical non-normative instrumental claim and a normative non-instrumental claim. Not only the latter but also the former is somewhat problematic, since a special story will have to be told as to how we manage to communicate by the uttering of sentences not expressing complete thoughts. One familiar way for this to happen is via the use of indexical or demonstrative expressions which exploit aspects of the context of utterance (including, for the latter, accompanying demonstrations) in order to complete the thought appropriately. So in the absence of an indexical expression, one may still hope for an account according to which the elliptical *needs*-claim is understood as instrumental 'relative to a contextually salient end state'. We return to this after looking at *too* and *enough*, and especially at *too*.

The remark in Section I that *too* and *enough* statements are heard as unfavourably and favourably evaluative needs considerable qualification. When anti-war protesters hold up placards on which all that is written is 'Enough!', we understand this as part of the protest rather than some incidental praise that a sufficient amount of something or other has been provided by the government. Compare the exasperated 'Enough is enough!', as well as the American English 'Enough already!' (variously claimed to be derived from Jewish American English or from Irish English). Or again:

(61) By that time, he'd had enough of her complaining.

All of these 'enough's are either on the verge of 'too much' or well into the latter's territory, and I shall have no more to say about them. The basic idea of favourable and unfavourable evaluation comes out if we hear the beginnings of utterances of either (62*a*) or (62*b*) but not the ends (which are accordingly suppressed here):

(62*a*) If you wait long enough, . . .
(62*b*) If you wait too long, . . .

I think we expect the missing consequents to report on the good consequences of waiting in (62*a*)—for instance 'She will realize you're the one for her'—and in the case of (62*b*) on the bad consequences of waiting—for instance, 'One of your rivals will propose to her and she will probably accept'.[56] Here the perspective from which the evaluation is made is that of the addressee, and perhaps also that of the speaker *qua* sympathetic advisor; with (63), said by a parent storming into a teenager's room:

(63) You're making way too much noise!

the unfavourable evaluation is evidently that of the speaker. This feature of *too* is what Mae West exploits to humorous effect (or at least with humorous intent) in

(64) Too much of a good thing is wonderful.

And it is this feature that makes it odd to issue (65) as an order, a piece of advice or a request:

(65) Take too many clothes with you.

The following excerpts from the editorial in a student magazine end with just such imperatives:

> Do you ever spend too much time reading about some byway of knowledge? Do you catch yourself starting out the window or giving inordinate attention to how you chop the garlic for your evening meal? Perhaps your excess is the lengthy shower in the morning or a chocolate bar at night. ... We feel guilty about these excesses. ... The problem with excess is that it is often very 'productive' in the long run. It is when we are wallowing in these moments of excess, spending time and energy beyond our means, that those precious moments light up corners of life. It is the scientist who spends months, if not years, excessively pursuing some inconsequential anomaly who makes the great breakthrough and transforms the field. It is when I spend far too long walking in Studley Park that an argument I am trying to work out becomes clear. It is when I spend too long with someone, wasting time waiting for a train maybe, that I fell I am finally getting to know them. ... So the little slogan to take away from these pages and write on the footpath with chalk is BE EXCESSIVE. Spend too much time, too much effort. ... (Spicer 2002)

56. The speaker may obtain a (mild) special effect by flouting this expectation, as in 'If you stand still in this area long enough, soldier ants will climb onto your shoes and up your legs.'

On reading this I wonder how many will share my reaction that all occurrences of 'too', 'excess' and 'excessive' are what Hare (1952) would call *inverted commas* uses of the words: alluding to an evaluative perspective which is not that of the user. The message after all is what might less strikingly if more honestly be expressed by saying that what *might appear (to others) to be* too much time or effort to spend on something often turns out not to be too much at all.

Variations on (65) where there is (at least some of) an explicit *for–to* complement make the oddity disappear, as in the following advice to a woman planning an escape:

(66) Wear too much make-up for anyone to recognize you.

As already mentioned in Section I, 'excessively', which is a passable substitute for the negatively evaluative *too*—though not for *too* in general (so the title of the present paper turns out not quite to summarize its subject matter)—does not sit well with *for–to* complements. Quirk et al. (1985, p. 1140) include what might seem to be a counterexample, in amongst some straightforward examples of *too* and *enough* with such complements:

(67) Your teacher was excessively generous to give you an A.

The contrast between (67) and the result of putting *too* for *excessively* in (67) is striking: the former suggests that the teacher gave the addressee an A, the latter that the teacher did not (but, say, an A+ instead). The *to* in (27) is not a fragment of the *for–to* complementizer but is instead just the *to* of 'You're very kind to say that.'

To return to the issue of whose perspective guides the unfavourable evaluations with (uncomplemented) *too*, the paradoxical effect of the subtitle of Hamilton and Deniss 2005, 'When Too Much is Never Enough', results from a mid-utterance perspectival shift: the *too much* is taken from the authors' anti-consumerist stance, while for the *never enough* ('always too little', by the Scale Reversal Equivalences) the perspective is that of the hapless consumers and profit-driven producers (as the authors see them).[57] In the following passage from p. 19 of Coetzee 1999, the two people concerned are at the early stages of a clandestine and potentially problematic sexual liaison; italics added:

> At the restaurant she has no appetite, stares out glumly over the sea.
> 'Is something the matter? Do you want to tell me?'
> She shakes her head.
> 'Are you worried about the two of us?'
> 'Maybe,' she says.
> 'No need. I'll take care. I won't let it go too far.'
> Too far. What is far, what is too far, in a matter like this? Is her *too far* the same as his *too far*?

Another kind of shift—not a shift between evaluative perspectives, but just as jarring—is evident in the following portion of dialogue in the 1944 MGM movie *National Velvet*, directed by Clarence Brown; the screenplay is by Helen Deutsch and Theodore Reeves.[58] The dialogue is between the characters Velvet Brown, who has the first line, and Mi Taylor (played respectively by Elizabeth Taylor and Mickey Rooney); the first line has the intonation it would have it the words had been 'Don't you just adore horses?';[59] the third line has stress on 'about':

> 'Don't you love horses?'
> 'I hate them.'
> 'You know too much about them.'
> 'That's when you really hate something—when you know too much about it.'

The sudden switch we see here can be described like this. Velvet's *too* is of the epistemically complemented variety: you know so much about horses that you must be someone who really loves them. But Mi's reply seems to shift to the unfavourably evaluative

57. There may even be an intrapersonal clash of perspectives, as in 'I love the pickled ginger, the spaghetti springs of cool white daikon, the little platters of soy and, most of all, the head rush of too much wasabi' (Terry Durack, writing in the May 22, 2005, *Good Weekend* magazine supplement to *The Age* 'Food for Thought' column, p. 41).
58. Though this is based on the book of the same name by Enid Bagnold, I was unable to find a corresponding passage in the book and presume accordingly that it was the work of the screenwriters.
59. As opposed to an intonation conveying that the speaker has just encountered evidence that, contrary to prior expectation, the addressee doesn't love horses.

too knowing too much is in this sense knowing more than it would be good to know about horses ('I've seen too much bloodshed').

One would perhaps expect the unfavourably evaluative use of *too* may be connected with the deontically complemented occurrences of *too*, but I will not speculate on such a connection here. The precedent set by *need*, reviewed above, seems promising. According to a popular view, a bare *needs* sentence—one not specifying what the thing said to be needed is needed for—is ambiguous between an elliptical version of a sentence with such a specification on the one hand, and a non-elliptical normative sentence on the other. This suggests the following hypothesis. A bare *too* sentence—one without an explicit *for–to* complement, that is—is ambiguous, either having an elliptical sense, the *for–to* complement being provided by the context, or else a non-elliptical (unfavourably) evaluative sense (roughly: 'NP is unacceptably ADJ').[60] The two senses are illustrated by the second contributions to these dialogues, respectively:

(68) 'Do you think John would be likely to fall for a scam like that?'
'(No,) he's too clever'.

(69) 'What do you think of John?'
'He's too clever.'

When Wallis Simpson uttered (70):

(70) You can never be too thin or too rich.[61]

she presumably meant that it wasn't possible to be thin or rich to an unacceptable degree, and was committed to denying that one

60. Heim (2001, p. 236) seems to combine or conflate these—as well as overlooking the possible/impossible and other modal complement flavours—in the following: 'For example, *too tall* roughly means "taller than is compatible with certain (contextually given) goals or desires". If John is too tall, he is taller than it is acceptable for him to be tall.' There is something to be said for this combination/conflation idea, I should concede. One does not expect to see a bare *too* construction in the title of a mathematical paper, but this is what happens in the case of Goralčik and V. Koubek 1982. Even someone fully conversant with the concept of subdirect irreducibility and of what it takes to be a rectangular band will not know what to make of the (sentential) title of this paper, but will, I think, expect the authors to outline—as indeed they do, in the opening paragraph—some desirable putative possibility which is excluded by the abundance of subdirectly irreducible rectangular bands. (So we have the combination: ellipsis + unfavourable evaluation.)

61. Different versions of this remark are attributed to Simpson in various places, conspicuously with 'One' or 'A woman' in place of the initial 'You'.

could be too rich to qualify for child support, or too thin to be amongst the top 10% of obese Americans. Similarly, you can enter a room and think out loud: 'It's too hot in here!' Imagine being overheard by someone maintaining—a position analogous to that defended in White 1975 for *need* statements—that in the absence of an explicit complement, we are always dealing with ellipsis, who then asks you 'Too hot for what?' If you can be bothered to answer this question, with a rather forced 'Too hot for me to be anything but very uncomfortable', perhaps, it would seem that you are simply trying to come as close as possible to filling out what you've said in the format requested, rather than spelling out the unexpressed part of the thought you just gave voice to. (Contrast the respondent in (68), who has no difficulty in answering someone entering the room halfway through and asking 'Too clever for what?') Such reliance on the phenomenology of the contents of thought is hardly the most respectable basis on which to decide the 'complete thought' issue, but rather than pursue this side of the hypothesis paralleling the view of Wiggins and others concerning *need*, I would like to turn to the other side of the story: the claimed ellipticality of the non-evaluative uses of *too* and *enough*. This position has recently come under criticism from Ernie Lepore and others, but we should begin with an advocate, Kent Bach.

According to Bach 1994, an unambiguous indexical-free declarative sentence can fail to express a proposition through being what he calls 'semantically underdeterminate' and illustrates with reference, *inter alia*, to the following examples (whence our interest in his formulation):

(71) Steel isn't strong enough.
(72) Strom is too old.

Such cases, he writes,[62]

> though syntactically well-formed, are semantically or conceptually incomplete in the sense that something must be added for the sentence to express a complete and determinate proposition (something capable of being true or false). With (71) we need to know *strong enough for what*. (Bach 1994, p. 127)

62. I have adjusted the example numbering in the quotation and italicized the last four words (not just for emphasis).

In the case of (72), Bach illustrates how with some additional words which provide what he calls a completion, in this case by way of example adding 'to be a good senator'. The completion makes explicit the proposition that might be merely implicit in an utterance of (72): it does not disambiguate an ambiguous (72), and in particular it does not disambiguate by restoring one of several possible deleted or ellipsed constituents as emphasized in the following passage:

> [T]here seems to be no syntactic reason why everything needed to deliver a complete proposition should correspond to something in the syntactic structure of the sentence. For this reason it would be misleading . . . to assimilate uses of semantically underdeterminate sentences to the category of elliptical utterances. Utterances are elliptical, strictly speaking, only if the suppressed material is recoverable, at least up to ambiguity, by grammatical means alone, as in tag questions and such reduced forms as conjunction reduction, VP-ellipsis, and gapping. (Bach 1994, p. 131)[63]

To this list, we might add cases like that of (3) from Section I above, which example remains, on each of the three disambiguations mentioned there, semantically underdeterminate according to this rather plausible view of Bach's. Thus in saying what a declarative indexical-free sentence means, or means on a given reading in the case of an ambiguous sentence, we are not specifying what proposition it expresses. 'The conventional meaning of the sentence determines not a full proposition but merely a *propositional radical*; a complete proposition,' Bach writes, 'would be expressed, a truth-condition determined, only if the sentence were elaborated somehow' (p. 127)—viz., with the specification of a (constituent) completion: but the phrase 'propositional radical', though appearing in italics, is actually nowhere defined.[64] How a complete proposition manages nevertheless to get communicated remains somewhat unclear, though Bach has some remarks on this in Section 8 of his paper, and also mentions that the kind

63. See also his note 8 on p. 132.

64. Perhaps Bach is thinking of something along the lines of the sentence radicals of Stenius 1967, in which case the terminology should have 'proposition', not 'propositional'; on the other hand perhaps he is expecting us to recall the chemical origin of Stenius's own usage. Since Bach operates with a conception of propositions according to which they have internal structure, a propositional radical may be like a proposition except that some of this structure is missing.

of semantic underdetermination with which we are currently concerned—constituent underdetermination, he calls it—amounts to the phenomenon isolated by John Perry with the terminology of 'unarticulated constituents' of a proposition, and Perry 1986 certainly gives clear examples illustrating how a complete proposition may be conveyed in these cases.[65]

There are obviously a number of different ways of spelling out the idea that in the absence of some kind of contextual indicator, bare *too* and *enough* sentences do not express complete thoughts, and recently the whole enterprise of discerning context-dependence beyond the narrow range of traditional indexicals (*I*, *here*, *now*, *this*, ...) has been subjected to trenchant criticism in Cappelen and Lepore 2005. (An overlapping discussion in the same vein is provided by Borg 2005.) These authors argue that any grounds for enlarging the traditional range rapidly mutate into grounds for saying that every sentence whatever is context-sensitive, and that a diversity amongst the kinds of situation in which a sentence is true, in particular, should not be taken to indicate a difference in the proposition expressed. Thus they argue that the fact that—another example considered by Bach—being ready for a doctor's appointment and being ready for a music exam, for instance, should not make us think that 'Joan is ready' expresses one proposition in a context when we are thinking of Joan as being ready for the one, and another when we are thinking of her as ready for the other. Rather, they argue, there is a perfectly good proposition which is expressed by 'Joan is ready' regardless of what project the context may suggest readiness with respect to, and this is just the proposition that Joan is ready, which is true if and only if Joan is ready *tout court*.[66] No incomplete thought here, then. Part of the reason:

65. Constituent underdetermination is contrasted in Bach 1994 with structural underdetermination, a more obscure phenomenon which does not concern us here. (Semantic underdetermination is itself in that paper just one of two ways in which the proposition communicated is not determined by the sentence uttered, namely the case in which no proposition is so determined; the other case, in which a proposition is thus determined by this is distinct from that communicated—what Bach calls 'sentence non-literality'—is again not of present concern.) Perry has also discussed unarticulated constituents in Perry 2001 (pp. 45ff.).

66. But what if Joan is dressing for a party and has been preparing for a law exam in two days and knowing that she is ready to go out but not ready for the exam I insist that I want to know whether or not she is ready *tout court*?

genuine context-sensitivity forces reformulations in indirect speech to adjust for changed context (Cappelen and Lepore, p. 91). Joan says 'I'm ready' and we reported her as having said that she was ready.[67] 'I' becomes 'she' to adjust for a changed contextual feature (namely the identity of the speaker), but there is no corresponding change in the 'ready', even though in the current context another project might be more salient as that for which one is ready.

As for *ready*, so for *enough*:

> Any utterance of 'Steel isn't strong enough' can be reported by 'She said that steel isn't strong enough' and any two such utterances can be reported by 'They both said that steel isn't strong enough.' (Cappelen and Lepore 2005, p. 95)

The case here seems little different from that of utterances of 'Steel is stronger', but whatever one's view of *enough* (or of *ready*), the view that sentences with bare comparatives (comparative adjectives with no *than* phrase) do not express complete thoughts seems enormously plausible, so we should perhaps be suspicious of this line of argument. Cappelen and Lepore explicitly press their case for complete propositions expressed by what *they* call comparative adjectives throughout—see the index of Cappelen and Lepore 2005, under 'comparative adjectives'—but for some reason (perhaps a confusion between *comparative* and *comparable*) use this phrase to refer to the positive rather than the comparative forms of gradable adjectives. This raises issues about vagueness it seems best to avoid, but something potentially surprising emerges from their discussion of these positive forms, and in particular with *tall*, of which they imagine an advocate of the incompleteness view remarking that there is no such thing as being tall *tout court* (and hence no truth-evaluable proposition that a given individual is tall): such an advocate is envisaged to maintain that there is only tallness relative to this or that comparison class, and so the role of context would be to select such a class when it is explicitly given. Cappelen and Lepore write that 'No one can deny that there such a thing as *being tall with respect to a privileged comparison class* or a

67. Actually for some reason Cappelen and Lepore always say 'said that she is ready' in cases like this, refusing to go through the usual 'sequence of tenses' procedure. The passage quoted next illustrates this.

contextually salient comparison class' (2005, p. 171). This is a surprising move, granting to the incompleteness theorist the idea that contextually salient class matters to what is said, but conceding this in such a way that far from showing no proposition to be expressed—by 'John is tall', say—in abstraction from a given context, it presents as the proposition thereby expressed the no-longer-context-dependent proposition that John is tall with respect to a contextually salient comparison class. The context no longer serves merely to fix on the comparison class so that the latter can figure in the proposition expressed: the concept of a contextually salient comparison class now enters the proposition itself under that description. Analogously for the case of *ready*, one could maintain that 'Joan is ready' expresses not one proposition in a context in which the salient project is Joan's getting dressed for dinner and another in a context in which the salient project is her taking her law exams, the propositions being that she is ready to go out for dinner and ready to sit her law exams, respectively, but, instead, that regardless of context the same proposition is expressed, and it is the proposition that Joan is ready for the contextually salient project. There is an obvious difficulty about this view, namely that the phrases 'the contextually salient comparison class' and 'the contextually salient project' are themselves context-sensitive. Nor is this exactly what Cappelen and Lepore were suggesting. Instead they were considering a metaphysical formulation of the hostility to a complete proposition's being expressed by such sentences as 'John is tall', 'Joan is ready', etc., which runs: there is no such property (or no such thing, as Cappelen and Lepore say) as being tall or being ready. The response to this objection is that there is indeed such a property as being tall/ready for the contextually salient comparison class/project. Accepting this offer, the incomplete thought theorist would say that the sentence 'John is tall' (to work with that example) is elliptical for

(73) John is tall for the contextually salient comparison class.

The fact that (73) contains a context-sensitive expression may seem now to run into trouble with the indirect quotation argument above, to the effect that for the paradigm cases of context-sensitivity, the standard indexicals and demonstratives, an indirect reporter must adjust for the reporter's context of utterance—something which does not, as already noted, apply in the case of the examples we are now considering. But as well as the standard indexicals, as Nunberg (1993) observes, there are also expressions which can retain the contexts they invoke even when embedded in constructions which might otherwise be expected to provide an overriding context.[68] Nunberg gives the following examples, imagined as uttered on a cross-country train:

(74) The landscape around here is getting prettier.
(75) The local landscape is getting prettier.

As Nunberg observes:

> In (74), around here can only denote the place surrounding the immediate point of utterance, and the utterance can only mean that that that very place is getting prettier (maybe the train has been stalled for a long time). But (75) can mean that the landscape around the point of utterance is prettier than the landscape the surrounded the place where the speaker was a half-hour ago. (Nunberg 1993, p. 36)

Suppose that a mother in England wants to warn her daughter that the street food in Bangalore, which the daughter is about to visit, is unsafe. She can do so, while both are still in England and travel plans are under discussion, by saying

(76) The local street food is not safe—please promise you'll stick to the hotel restaurant.

The daughter can write back after arrival:

(77) You were right—the local street food isn't safe, as I found to my cost last night.

And the mother can then report to others:

(78) My daughter confirmed that the local street food is indeed unsafe.

68. Cappelen and Lepore (1980, p. 1) mention *local* on a list of 'contextuals' and cite Nunberg 1992 *inter alia*; in a footnote they write: 'To be honest, we have our doubts about these so-called contextuals ... We will let you decide for yourself after reading the book.'

So the phrase 'the local street food' can be interpreted as 'the street food in the contextually salient location',[69] where one way of making a location salient is by speaking (or writing from) there, but another is by reporting on what someone there has said: embedding this in indirect quotation does not hijack the salient location automatically to that of the reporter. The contrast, as in Nunberg's examples, is with the case in which the daughter had written 'The street food here isn't safe', and the mother would have to have adjusted 'here' to 'there'. With such an understanding of local salience in mind, we can take (73) for *tall* and the corresponding formulation for *ready* as the 'incomplete thought' theorist's favoured explications of 'John is tall' and 'Joan is ready'. In the latter case, the explication in terms of readiness for some contextually salient project recognizes what we might loosely call the conceptual priority of relational notion of *being ready for* over any absolute notion of *being ready* even if—as the incomplete thought theorist was reluctant to—we were to concede the existence of the latter notion. The fact that 'any utterance of "Steel isn't strong enough" can be reported by "She said that steel isn't strong enough"' is likewise no objection to the claim that *strong enough* needs to be understood in terms of *strong enough for*, or the proposal—put here using the term *purpose* for the second relatum, though this would certainly not do in general—that 'strong enough' is elliptical for 'strong enough for the contextually salient purpose'. Having defended Bach's claim against Cappelen and Lepore's attacks,[70] I want

69. Well, 'the local street food' does not mean the same as 'the street food in the contextually salient location', since, while to understand the former one has be sensitive to the contextual salience of a location, one need not possess the concept 'contextually salient location'. A more accurate formulation would employ the notion of constitutive role, as in Peacocke 1983 (see index).

70. At more than one point in Cappelen and Lepore 2005—see notes 6 and 7 on pp. 167 and 169—the authors actually forget that Bach's question about what steel was wasn't strong enough *for* (i.e., the request was over supplying the *for–to* complement), and, in the first of these notes, consider 'a bunch of people who all have had enough. For example, one has had enough wine, one has had enough turkey, and one has had enough cocaine. All these people have something in common: *They have all had enough.*' The alternative choices of X for 'has had enough X' have no bearing on the issue under discussion, which is alternative choices of S for 'has had enough (±X) for–to S'. There are further distractions with this kind of example, of which two are the following. (1) The semi-idiomatic nature of the expression 'have enough of', which, as we have already had occasion to note, carries a connotation of being especially close to, if not on the wrong side of, the *too much* border. (2) The most

to close by returning to the main hero of our discussion, Eric Nelson, for the latter's position on the 'complete thought' question.

Nelson 1980 gives a two-stage account of the relation between bare *too* or *enough* sentences and fully explicit paraphrases, thereby locating two points at which an ellipsis might be held to occur. The first point is over the absence of the for–to complement. The second is over the particular modality of the modal complement Nelson proposes is always available as a fully explicit paraphrase. To illustrate the first point, Nelson uses the example

(79) This box is too big for Louise.

This example happens to illustrate more than just the first point, which would equally well be made by dropping the final 'for Louise'. Nelson writes that 'a complement such as the one in (79) looks like a sentential complement without the verb; but the verb is not recoverable in the way that a missing subject or object of an infinitive is, and the noun may be in any relation to the verb that is supplied by the context' (1980, p. 106). Nelson lists as possible specifications to follow 'This box is too big':

(80) ____ for Louise to lift; ____ for Louise to climb on top of; ____ to ship Louise to Alaska in; ____ to give to Louise.

And we might throw in, to underscore the point that the *for* in (79) need not be taken as the *for* of a *for–to* complementizer: ____ for us to ship Louise to Alaska in. While the remarks about recoverability indicate that Nelson is not proposing that we are dealing with a case of ellipsis in the narrow sense, it would seem from his talk of the noun being in 'any relation to the verb that is supplied by the context' that he does favour an elliptical account, understood in the loose sense that to specify the thought

conspicuous respect of variation in the cases listed by Cappelen and Lepore is over what constitutes *having*—they deliberately select products consumed in characteristically, though of course one uses the verb 'have' also when no kind of consumption is involved. This raises a question about whether there is 'such a thing as' having. One argument for a negative answer to this question was offered in Humberstone 1990 (p. 104). The question is closely related to a 'complete thought' issue involving possessives (touched on in Cappelen and Lepore 2005, pp. 35, 94, and elsewhere).

expressed, the missing material must be supplied with assistance from the context. But even with a full *for–to* complement available, there is still an issue of interpretation to be settled, as Nelson's discussion of 'Tom is too sick to eat' (already mentioned as (40) in Section V) makes clear. There is no missing *for–to* complement material here: we have (discarding an irrelevant cannibalistic meaning) S as 'Tom eats'. While (as noted in Section V) one hears this as implying that Tom can't eat, that is, one presumes the modal elaboration is of the dynatic kind, 'Our interpretation would be changed, however, if the sentence was followed by "So tell him to quit eating." '[71] I take this reference to changing interpretation to mean that in the absence of a specific modality, no specific proposition has been expressed. As we saw in Section V, however, Nelson may have overestimated the ubiquity of these modal elements.[72]

References

Bach, Kent 1994: 'Conversational Impliciture'. *Mind and Language*, 9, pp. 124–62.

Bolinger, Dwight 1972: *Degree Words*. The Hague: Mouton.

Borg, Emma 2005: 'Saying What You Mean: Unarticulated Constituents and Communication'. In Elugardo and Stainton 2005, pp. 237–62.

Braybrooke, David 1987: *Meeting Needs*. Princeton: Princeton University Press.

Cappelen, Herman and Ernie Lepore 2005: *Insensitive Semantics: A Defense of Semantic Minimalism and Speech Act Pluralism*. Oxford: Blackwell.

Coetzee, J. M. 1999: *Disgrace*. London: Secker and Warburg.

Cruse, D. A. 1992: 'Antonymy Revisited: Some Thoughts on the Relationship Between Words and Concepts'. In A. Lehrer and E. F. Kittay (eds), *Frames, Fields, and Contrasts*. Hillsdale, NJ: Lawrence Erlbaum, pp. 289–306.

Davis, Wayne 1998: *Implicature: Intention, Convention, and Principle in the Failure of Gricean Theory*, Cambridge: Cambridge University Press.

Eagleton, Terry 2001: *The Gatekeeper: A Memoir*. London: Allen Lane, The Penguin Press.

Elugardo, Reinaldo and Robert J. Stainton (eds) 2005: *Ellipsis and Nonsentential Speech*. Dordrecht: Springer.

Goralčik, P. and V. Koubek 1982: 'There are Too Many Subdirectly Irreducible Bands', *Algebra Universalis*, 15, pp. 187–94.

71. Nelson 1980, p. 119. There is a typo in this part of Nelson's discussion, since he numbers our (40) as (147) but then writes 'On hearing a sentence like (130), we are likely to infer *Tom can't eat*.' '(130)' should be '(147)'.

72. I learnt from Ernie Lepore (some years before the appearance of Cappelen and Lepore 2005) about Kent Bach's discussion of *enough*, and from Valentine Hacquard—who was kind enough to send me a copy of Hacquard 2005*a*—about recent work by linguists on *too* and *enough*. A producer for Radio National (ABC Australia), Suzanne Donisthorpe, kindly supplied me with the source of the quotation from National Velvet (which had been a radio quiz question). Thanks also to Monima Chadha for some helpful conversations on these matters.

Hacquard, Valentine 2005a: 'Aspects of *Too* and *Enough* Constructions'. In Effi Georgala and Jonathan Howell (eds), *Semantics and Linguistic Theory*, 15 (Proceedings *SALT* 15). Ithaca, NY: CLC Publications, Cornell.

——— 2005b: 'Aspect and Actuality Entailment: *Too* and *Enough* Constructions'. In E. Maier, C. Bary and J. Huitink (eds), *Proceedings of Sinn und Bedeutung*, 9, pp. 116–30. Available at www.ru.nl/ncs/sub9.

Hamilton, Clive and Richard Deniss 2005: *Affluenza: When Too Much is Never Enough*. Crows Nest, NSW: Allen and Unwin.

Hare, R. M. 1952: *The Language of Morals*. Oxford: Clarendon Press.

Heim, Irene 2001: 'Degree Operators and Scope'. In Caroline Féry and Wolfgang Sternefeld (eds), *Audiatur Vox Sapientiae: A Festschrift for Arnim von Stechow*. Berlin: Akademie. (Slightly modified version of a paper of the same name in Brendan Jackson and Tanya Matthews (eds), *SALT X* (*Proceedings of Semantics and Linguistic Theory*, 10). Ithaca, NY: CLC Publications, 2000, pp. 40–64.)

Horn, Lawrence R. 1989: *A Natural History of Negation*. Chicago: University of Chicago Press.

Huddleston, Rodney and Geoffrey K. Pullum (with other contributors) 2002: *The Cambridge Grammar of the English Language*. Cambridge: Cambridge University Press.

Humberstone, Lloyd 1990: 'Wanting, Getting, Having'. *Philosophical Papers*, 19, pp. 99–118.

——— 1991: 'Two Kinds of Agent-Relativity'. *Philosophical Quarterly*, 41, pp. 144–66.

——— 2005: 'Modality'. In Frank Jackson and Michael Smith (eds), *The Oxford Handbook of Contemporary Philosophy*. Oxford: Oxford University Press.

Jespersen, Otto 1924: *The Philosophy of Grammar*. Eighth impression, 1963. London: Allen and Unwin.

Kamp, Hans 1975: 'Two Theories About Adjectives'. In E. L. Keenan (ed.), *Formal Semantics of Natural Language*. Cambridge: Cambridge University Press, pp. 123–55.

Karttunen, Lauri 1971: 'Implicative Verbs'. *Language*, 47, pp. 340–58.

Kennedy, Christopher 1999: *Projecting the Adjective: The Syntax and Semantics of Gradability and Comparison*. New York: Garland.

Kenny, Anthony 1976: 'Human Ability and Dynamic Modalities'. In J. Manninen and R. Tuomela (eds), *Essays on Explanation and Understanding*. Dordrecht: Reidel, pp. 209–32.

Kneale, William and Martha Kneale 1962: *The Development of Logic*. Oxford: Clarendon Press.

Krifka, Manfred 1995: 'The Semantics and Pragmatics of Negative Polarity Items'. *Linguistic Analysis*, 25, pp. 209–57.

Lehrer, Adrienne 1985: 'Markedness and Antonymy'. *Journal of Linguistics*, 21, pp. 397–429.

——— and Keith Lehrer 1982: 'Antonymy'. *Linguistics and Philosophy*, 5, pp. 483–501.

Lewis, David 1976: 'The Paradoxes of Time Travel'. *American Philosophical Quarterly*, 13, pp. 145–52. Reprinted in Lewis 1986, pp. 67–80.

——— 1979: 'Scorekeeping in a Language Game'. *Journal of Philosophical Logic*, 8, pp. 339–59. Reprinted in Lewis 1983, pp. 233–49.

——— 1983: *Philosophical Papers, Volume I*. New York: Oxford University Press.

——— 1986: *Philosophical Papers, Volume II*. New York: Oxford University Press.

Meier, Cécile 2003: 'The Meaning of *too*, *enough* and *so … that*'. *Natural Language Semantics*, 11, pp. 69–107.

Natsopoulos, Dimitri 1985: 'A Verbal Illusion in Two Languages'. *Journal of Psycholinguistic Research*, 14, pp. 385–97.

Nelson, Eric S. 1980: '*Too* and *Enough*'. *Minnesota Papers in Linguistics and the Philosophy of Language*, 6, pp. 93–132.

Nunberg, Geoffrey 1993: 'Indexicality and Deixis'. *Linguistics and Philosophy*, 16, pp. 1–43.

Peacocke, Christopher 1983: *Sense and Content*. Oxford: Clarendon Press.
Perry, John 1986: 'Thought Without Representation'. *Aristotelian Society Supplementary Volume* 60, pp. 263–83. Reprinted with an 'Afterword' as Chapter 10 of Perry, *The Problem of the Essential Indexical and Other Essays*, Expanded Edition. Stanford, CA: CSLI Publications, 2000.
——— 2001: *Reference and Reflexivity*. Stanford, CA: CSLI Publications.
Puccetti, Roland 1964: 'Aristotle's Golden Tautology'. *Ratio*, 6, pp. 161–67.
Pym, Barbara 1978: *Less Than Angels*. London: Jonathan Cape. (Originally published 1955.)
Quirk, Randolph and S. Greenbaum 1973: *A University Grammar of English*. London: Longman.
——— ——— and G. Leech and J. Svartvik 1972: *A Grammar of Contemporary English*. London: Longman.
——— ——— ——— ——— 1985: *A Comprehensive Grammar of the English Language*. London: Longman.
Robinson, Richard 1971: 'Ought and Ought Not'. *Philosophy*, 46, pp. 193–202.
Rothstein, Susan 2001: *Predicates and Their Subjects*. Dordrecht: Kluwer.
Spicer, André 2002: 'An Excessive Editorial'. *Postgraduate Review*, University of Melbourne Postgraduate Association, July 2002, p. 2.
Stenius, Erik 1967: 'Mood and Language-Game'. *Synthese*, 17, pp. 254–74.
Thomson, Garrett 1987: *Needs*. London: Routledge and Kegan Paul.
Unger, Peter 1975: *Ignorance: A Case for Scepticism*. Oxford: Clarendon Press.
Urmson, J. O. 1973: 'Aristotle's Doctrine of the Mean'. *American Philosophical Quarterly*, 10, pp. 223–30.
von Wright, G. H. 1951: *An Essay in Modal Logic*. Amsterdam: North-Holland, Amsterdam.
Wason, Peter C. and S. R. Reich 1979: 'A Verbal Illusion'. *Quarterly Journal of Experimental Psychology*, 31, pp. 591–97.
White, Alan 1975: *Modal Thinking*. Oxford: Blackwell.
Wiggins, David 1987: 'Claims of Need'. In Wiggins, *Needs, Values, Truth*. Aristotelian Society Series, Vol. 6, Oxford: Blackwell, pp. 1–57. (Paper first published in essentially this form in 1985.)
——— and Sira Dermen 1987: 'Needs, Need, Needing'. *Journal of Medical Ethics*, 13, pp. 62–8.

NIETZSCHE ON FREE WILL, AUTONOMY AND THE SOVEREIGN INDIVIDUAL

by Ken Gemes and Christopher Janaway

I—Ken Gemes

ABSTRACT In some texts Nietzsche vehemently denies the possibility of free will; in others he seems to positively countenance its existence. This paper distinguishes two different notions of free will. Agency free will is intrinsically tied to the question of agency, what constitutes an action as opposed to a mere doing. Deserts free will is intrinsically tied to the question of desert, of who does and does not merit punishment and reward. It is shown that we can render Nietzsche's prima facie conflicting assertions regarding free will compatible by interpreting him as rejecting deserts free will while accepting the possibility of agency free will. It is argued that Nietzsche's advances an original form of compatibilism which takes agency free will to be a rare achievement rather than a natural endowment.

I

Introduction.[1] Regarding the free will debate it is helpful to distinguish two different approaches. According to the first approach the question of free will is intrinsically tied to the question of desert: of who does and does not merit punishment and reward. For simplicity of reference we might describe the notion of free will relevant to this approach as deserts free will. Writers who focus on deserts free will are typically exercised by such questions as whether determinism precludes free will, thereby undercutting all ascriptions of desert. Where deserts free will is at issue the question of whether having done such-and-such one could have done otherwise is typically seen as being crucial. The intuition here is that if one could not have

1. Quotations from, and references to, Nietzsche's works make use of the following abbreviations, '*UM*' for *Untimely Meditations*, '*GS*' for *The Gay Science*, '*TSZ*' for *Thus Spoke Zarathustra*, '*BGE*' for *Beyond Good and Evil*, '*GM*' for *On the Genealogy of Morals*, '*EH*' for *Ecce Homo*, '*A*' for *The Antichrist*, '*TI*' for *Twilight of the Idols*, '*WP*' for *The Will to Power*, '*KSA*' for *Sämtliche Werke: Kritische Studienausgabe*, '*D*' for *Daybreak*, and '*HAH*' for *Human, All Too Human*. Full bibliographic references for these works and other texts mentioned below are given at the end of this essay.

done otherwise then one should not be punished/rewarded for what one has done.[2] According to the second approach, the free will debate is intrinsically tied to the question of agency: what constitutes an action as opposed to a mere doing? For simplicity of reference we might describe the notion of free will relevant to this approach as agency free will. Writers who focus on agency free will are typically exercised by questions such as what makes for autonomy. Here the question of whether one could have done otherwise need not loom large.

The approaches can, of course, be tied together. For instance, one might claim that only a doing that involves free will, where one could have done otherwise, can constitute an action, and that one merits rewards and punishments only for one's actions. However, the two approaches need not merge. One might, for instance, deny that there is free will in the sense traditionally seen as needed for grounding questions of deserts while at the same time claiming that there is free will in the sense traditionally seen as needed for grounding the notion of agency and autonomy. It is the principal burden of this essay to argue that this is exactly Nietzsche's position: Nietzsche rejects deserts free will and affirms agency free will. Nietzsche wants to reject the notion that in doing such-and-such one might have done otherwise, yet he wants to affirm that genuine agency is possible, if only for a select few. It is this that explains why in some contexts he denies free will and in others he positively invokes free will. The denials are denials of deserts free will and the invocations are invocations of agency free will.

The notion of responsibility has long been tied to the notion of free will. Nearly all who write on free will take it that free will is a condition for responsibility. The not uncommon failure to separate deserts free will from agency free will is to some extent aided and abetted by an ambiguity in the term 'responsibility' (in German, '*Veranwortlichkeit*'[3]). To say that so-and-so is

2. Interestingly, while the intuition that one should not be punished for what one could not help doing is fairly strong, the intuition that one should not be rewarded for what one could not help doing is typically less strong.

3. Literally, 'answerability', a term which carries a similar ambiguity. One can be answerable for a result simply in the sense that the result was one's doing; alternatively, one can be answerable in the sense that one is deserving of punishment or reward for the doing in question.

responsible for such-and-such can mean that they deserve punishment/reward for it. On the other hand, to say that someone is responsible for such-and-such can simply means that it was their doing. The first kind of responsibility is that which is intrinsically linked to the question of deserts; the second kind of responsibility is intrinsically linked to the question of agency. It will be helpful then to separate deserts responsibility, the kind of responsibility which is a precondition of deserved punishment and rewards, and agency responsibility, the kind of responsibility that goes with being the effective agent behind a doing. We shall argue that while Nietzsche rejects deserts responsibility he leaves room for a positive account of agency responsibility.[4]

Now, it may immediately be objected that Nietzsche is constantly blaming people (Socrates, Jesus, Saint Paul, Wagner), and often praising others (Napoleon, Beethoven, Goethe, Wagner, Nietzsche), so it is hard to accept that he is not interested in questions of deserts. It is important here to separate the concept pair of punishment/reward from the concept pair blame/praise. It is natural to run these pairs together, since we tend to think of blame as a kind of punishment and praise as a kind of reward. This is to some extent true for our treatment of our contemporaries, and especially in our treatment of children: typically we reward children by praising them and punish them by blaming or scolding them. In order to separate these pairs of concepts it helps to focus on our attitude towards figures that have long been gone. For instance, those of us who admire Socrates may praise him, yet that praise hardly constitutes a reward—in some sense the dead are beyond rewards, though not beyond honours. Those who, like Nietzsche, take Socrates to be a (largely) baleful influence might blame him, yet not take that blame to be any kind of punishment. Ordinarily, punishing and rewarding is something we do to living beings, not those who have already passed away. Even in dealing with one's contemporaries one may be interested in praising and blaming them, yet not conceive of such praise and blame as a punishment or reward. Nietzsche, in fact, is full of praise and blame for figures who were his contemporaries and

4. The distinction between agency responsibility and deserts responsibility is in some ways similar to the distinction Gary Watson 1996 draws between the aretaic perspective and the moral accountability perspective.

figures who were long gone before his time. It is my contention that for Nietzsche such praise and blame is part of his taking them to be responsible for various effects, but only in the sense of being agency responsible, not in the sense of being deserts responsible. That Nietzsche does blame and praise does not show that he is committed to a positive account of deserts responsibility or deserts free will. In the course of this essay another dimension that will be seen as relevant to Nietzsche's use of praise and blame and his rejection of punishment and reward is the dimension of temporality: Nietzsche rejects the notion of punishment and reward partly because they are in a certain sense directed at the past, a matter of giving what has been earned; whereas, for Nietzsche, praising and blaming is fundamentally future directed. The objective behind Nietzsche's praising and blaming is to increase or decrease various influences. He blames such figures as Socrates, Jesus, Paul, and sometimes Wagner, not because he wants to give them their just deserts but because he wants to lessen their current and future influence. Similarly, he praises Beethoven, Goethe, Nietzsche, and sometimes Wagner, because he wants to increase their influence on us and the future, albeit if, at times, only as instructive exemplars.

II

Nietzsche's Rejection of Deserts Free Will. Some of Nietzsche's most trenchant dismissals of free will and responsibility occur in works of the middle period such as *Human, All Too Human.*

> *The fable of intelligible freedom*. ... Now one finally discovers that this nature [of man] cannot be responsible, since it is completely a necessary consequence and is assembled from the elements and influences of past and present things; consequently one is not responsible for anything, not for his nature, nor his motives, nor his actions, nor for his effects. Thereby one achieves the knowledge that the history of moral sensations is the history of an error, the error of responsibility which rests on the error of freedom of the will. (*HAH*, 39)

The principal target of this dismissal is Schopenhauer and, *inter alia*, Kant. Kant and Schopenhauer, while recognizing the necessity of all that happens in the phenomenal realm, notoriously allow for a freedom in the noumenal world. Nietzsche by the time of

Human, All Too Human has rejected his early Schopenhauerian endorsement of the idea of noumenal existence. The general aim of his rejection of free will and responsibility in *HAH* is to reject the notions of guilt and deserved punishment and reward;

> For he who is punished does not deserve punishment; he is merely being employed as the means of henceforth deterring others from certain action; likewise, he who is being rewarded does not deserve his reward: for he could not have acted otherwise than he did. (*HAH*, 105)

In the very next section Nietzsche gives what is probably his strongest endorsement of determinism: 'If one were all-knowing one would be able to calculate every individual action.'[5] The emphasis on determinism as an argument against free will and responsibility, and the rejection of the notions of desert in punishments and rewards, clearly indicate that what is a stake here is what we have called deserts free will and deserts responsibility.

In works from his later period, while there is less emphasis on determinism, there is a continued vehement rejection of the notion of free will. In *Twilight of the Idols* he simply refers to 'the error of free will' (*TI*, IV, 7). In the *Antichrist* he says:

> In Christianity . . . Nothing but imaginary causes ('God', 'soul', 'ego', 'spirit', 'free will'—or 'unfree will'). (*A*, 15)

In these and other passages where he disparages the notion of free will it is clear that what is at stake is the notion of a will autonomous from the causal order, an uncaused cause. It is free will in this 'superlative, metaphysical sense' (*BGE*, 21) that Nietzsche rejects. Again, contexts makes clear that it is deserts free will that is at stake here, the kind of free will seen as necessary to underwrite attributions of deserts responsibility, punishments and rewards.

III

Agency Free Will and the Sovereign Individual. In the second essay of *The Genealogy of Morals* Nietzsche introduces the striking figure of the sovereign individual, describing him as

5. In this passage, in a clear reference to Schopenhauer, he gives the analogy of a waterfall whose wild movements seem unconstrained but are in fact strictly governed by causal laws.

> ... autonomous ... the man who has his own independent, *protracted* will ... this *master of a free will*. (*GM*, II, 2; Nietzsche's italics)

This affirmative use of free will is in marked contrast to the dismissals of free will noted above. To get a better handle on what is at stake here it is best to return to the very beginning of the second essay, which reads:

> To breed an animal with the right to make promises—is this not the paradoxical task that nature has set itself in the case of man? is this not the real problem regarding man? (*GM*, II, 1)

The text might easily lead the unwary reader to think this is a task already accomplished, leading the reader into a sense of complacent satisfaction, though in fact the text says only that 'this problem has been solved to a high degree'. The sense that Nietzsche is talking of past events is heightened when, having first raised this question of nature's task, he concentrates on the prehistory of man, and man's first acquiring of deep memory—memory burnt in by punishment. The task of acquiring memory is one that has been clearly accomplished; it is something that his audience can proudly lay claim to. However, when a few pages later Nietzsche introduces 'the end of this tremendous process' as the 'sovereign individual', his audience should at least have a glimmering suspicion of whether they themselves are this proud, noble, sounding individual or the 'feeble windbags' he despises. Nietzsche describes the sovereign individual in hyperbolic tones clearly not applicable to ordinary individuals. He describes him as one

> who has his own protracted will and the right to make promises and in him a proud consciousness, quivering in every muscle, of what has at length been achieved and become flesh in him, a consciousness of his own power and freedom ... [and who] is bound to reserve a kick for the feeble windbags who promise without the right to do so. (*GM*, II, 2)

It is typical of Nietzsche's deliberately confusing caginess that it is not at first clear whether the sovereign individual is a creature already achieved or one yet to come. The very terms Nietzsche uses to describe the sovereign individual—'proud', 'quivering in every muscle', 'aware of his superiority', 'like only to himself', 'bound to honour his peers'—clearly hark back to the descriptions of the masters of the first essay. Since his audience are meant to identify themselves as the inheritors of slave morality, it is clear that they cannot be identified with this sovereign individual, who, unlike them, is 'autonomous and supermoral', a 'lord of the free will'. The implicit message to his audience is that you are not sufficiently whole to have the right to make promises; you have no free will, but are merely tossed about willy-nilly by a jumble of competing drives, and, hence, you cannot stand surety for what you promise. You can give no guarantee that the ascendant drive at the time of your making a promise will be effective when the time comes to honour that promise. The type of freedom Nietzsche is invoking here does not involve freedom from the causal order, nor is it bound to questions of deserts. Plainly it is tied to the question of what is it to have genuine agency.

IV

Nietzsche as a Compatibilist. One gets a sense of Nietzsche's positive account of free will, and its relation to the tradition, by contrasting it with that of David Hume. Hume, a compatibilist, famously argued that 'liberty of spontaneity' (free will) is consistent with the denial of 'liberty of indifference' (determinism).[6] On Hume's account, one acts freely where that action stems from one's character. Character for Hume is simply glossed as one's deeper dispositions. Here is not the place to canvass the various problems with Hume's notion of character. What is interesting for us is that Nietzsche may be seen as offering a similar naturalistic account of free will, with the very important difference that he gives a much more robust account of character.[7] To have a character is to have a stable, unified, and integrated, hierarchy of drives. This is a very demanding condition that most humans fail to meet:

> In the present age human beings have in their bodies the heritage of multiple origins, that is opposite and not merely opposite drives and value standards that fight each other and rarely permit each other any rest. Such human beings of late cultures and refracted lights will on the average be weaker human beings. (*BGE*, 200)

6. See *A Treatise of Human Nature*, Book II, Section 11.
7. An important difference between Nietzsche and Hume is that Hume's account of free will is an account of both agency and deserts free will, or at least an account of our attributions of agency and deserts free will; Nietzsche's account is only an account of agency free will.

In the *Nachlass* from the period of the *Genealogy* Nietzsche explicitly draws the conclusion that

> one should not at all assume that many humans are 'people' . . . the 'person' is a relatively isolated fact. (*KSA*, 12, 491, my translation)

The sovereign individual, who has a unified, independent, protracted will, counts as having a genuine character, being a person. Modern man, who is at the mercy of a menagerie of competing forces, internal and external, has no such character.[8]

Why after so much denigration of the terminology of free will and autonomy does Nietzsche in the *Genealogy* employ it in a positive fashion? Presumably as a subtle challenge to his readers. Rather than simply arousing his (libertarian) audiences' resistance with flat denials of free will and autonomy in the transcendent sense, or, in the case of (incombatiblist) naturalists, confirming their flat rejection of free will, Nietzsche uses that terminology in a positive, non-transcendent, manner in describing the sovereign individual. He then seeks to unsettle his audience with the uncanny idea that autonomy and free will are achievements of great difficulty, achievements which they themselves have by no means attained. While the thought that free will does not exist is disturbing, how much more so is the thought that free will does exist but one does not oneself possess it! What is at stake here is clearly the notion of agency free will and agency responsibility. It is these that are being attributed to the sovereign individual.

V

Agency Free Will versus Deserts Free Will. Those who take the key issue concerning free will to be the question of moral responsibility, deserts, the justification of punishments and rewards, will claim that this notion of agency free will relevant to the notion of the sovereign individual is no genuine notion of free will. For them, an action is free only if the agent could have done otherwise.[9]

8. For more on this, see Gemes 2001 and Chapter 1, Section 5 of the excellent Richardson 1996.

9. Leiter 2002 provides a well-argued and trenchant account of Nietzsche as a denier of free will. Leiter resists any compatibilist reading on the grounds that any genuine notion of free will must provide a basis for ascriptions of responsibility capable of grounding our practices of punishing and rewarding. Leiter is really insisting that free will can only be deserts free will and that the compatibilist agency free will we have ascribed to

But, as we have seen, there is another way of approaching the free will debate. This other way does not see the debate directly through the question of moral responsibility, but, rather, approaches it from the question of agency. Where one approach begins with the questions, 'For what acts is one morally responsible? For what acts can one be punished or rewarded?', the other begins with the arguably profounder question, 'What is it to act in the first place, what is it to be a self capable of acting?' Those who take the questions of moral responsibility and desert as paramount to the free will question tend to write as if we already have a notion of self and action more or less firmly in place and are only raising the question of whether such selves are ever to be held morally responsible for their actions. The other approach seeks to problematize the very notions of self and action. This is part of the import of the famous dictum from the *Genealogy* that 'the doer is merely a fiction added to the deed' (*GM*, I, 13). Nietzsche is here questioning our assumption that for every deed there is an individual agent who does the deed.[10] Now Nietzsche does, of course, want to question our practices of punishing and rewarding, our practices of assigning moral responsibility. This is part of his ongoing battle against the dominant Judaeo-Christian world-view in which moral responsibility, and, in particular, punishment and guilt are key notions. This aim does indeed account for many of his negative comments about free will. But ultimately the more profound Nietzsche wants to raise the question about what exactly it is to be a genuine self. Indeed, his whole attack on the Judaeo-Christian worldview is predicated on his belief that it is fundamentally inimical to the development of genuine selves. It is for this reason that for Nietzsche the problem of agency free will takes precedence over the problem of deserts free will:

Nietzsche is really a wholly revisionary concept of free will, divorced from the 'conventional meaning' of free will (see especially Leiter 2002, p. 99). This reading rests on a rather restricted reading of the history of philosophy. Putting it crudely, and oversimplifying, while the modern Anglo-Saxon tradition may have a convention of interpreting the question of free will largely through the narrow prism of the question of moral responsibility and deserts, the German tradition, including Kant, Hegel, Fichte and Schelling, has a convention of interpreting the question of free will as much, if not more, through the prism of the question of agency and autonomy.

10. For some deeds, in which individual humans are involved, what is behind the deed is merely the will of the herd.

those who take the deserts free will problem as central typically complacently assume that we have a coherent notion of self and agency already in hand.[11]

To interpret Nietzsche as an opponent of deserts free will because he rejects *causa sui* free will, deserts free will, is to emphasize a purely negative aspect, his hostility to Judaeo-Christian notions of responsibility and punishment. This undoubtedly is an important and oft-repeated theme in Nietzsche's work. To interpret Nietzsche as giving a positive, naturalist account of agency free will is to emphasize a positive and original aspect, his notion that under the right conditions genuine agency, a truly great achievement, is possible, albeit only for a special few. Furthermore, this interpretation helps us to properly appreciate the famous passage in *Gay Science*, 125, where Nietzsche's 'madman' tells us that we must ourselves become Gods to be worthy of the deed of killing God. To become Gods is to be autonomous, self-legislators who are not subservient to some external authority, be it a God, the *summum bonum*, or an (allegedly) universal moral law.

VI

Neither Free nor Unfree, but Strong or Weak Wills. In some prominent places where Nietzsche disparages the notion of free will he also takes care to disparage the notion of unfree will, as we saw in the quotation above from *The Antichrist*. In the famous passage from *Beyond Good and Evil* where he rejects free will in the 'superlative metaphysical sense', he concludes:

> Suppose someone were thus to see through the boorish simplicity of this celebrated concept of 'free will' and put it out of his head altogether, I beg of him to carry his 'enlightenment' a step further, and also put out of his head the contrary of this monstrous conception of 'free will': I mean 'unfree will', which amounts to a misuse of cause and effect. (*BGE*, 21)

11. It is important to realize that this criticism is not directed specifically against philosophers, but rather against what in the *Genealogy* Nietzsche calls 'we moderns' who are unknowingly 'strangers to ourselves'. For more on this see Gemes 2006. That some philosophers, for instance Kant, Hegel, Fichte and Schelling, were clearly aware of the problematic nature of autonomy and agency—even granting that Nietzsche rejects their accounts of these notions—is beside the point.

Why does Nietzsche do this? Clearly a central reason why Nietzsche rejects the traditional notion of free will is that it typically functions to instil guilt, thereby fostering a passive attitude to the world (the rule of the 'Thou shall not's). But he is also aware that the new modern notion of unfree will, by fostering a fatalistic pessimism, what in *Beyond Good and Evil* he calls 'a fatalism of the weak willed', can also be inimical to active worldly engagement. For Nietzsche, 'unfree will is mythology, in real life it is only a matter of strong and weak wills' (*BGE*, 21).[12] It is when a strong will takes command, orders and organizes lesser drives that a genuine self can emerge. This is implicit in his accounts of Wagner's development.

> The dramatic element in Wagner's development is quite unmistakable from the moment when his ruling passion became aware of itself and took his nature in its charge: from that time on there was an end to fumbling, straying, to the proliferation of secondary shoots, and within the most convoluted courses and often daring trajectories assumed by his artistic plans there rules a single inner law, a will by which they can be explained. (*UM*, III, 2)[13]

The story of Wagner's achievement of a higher unity borne from some master drive is, of course, the story Nietzsche would repeat about himself in the dramatic section of *Ecce Homo* where Nietzsche elaborates the subtitle of that work 'How One Becomes What One Is':

> To become what one is, one must not have the slightest notion of what one is ... The whole surface of consciousness—consciousness is a surface—must be kept clear of all great imperatives ... Meanwhile the organizing 'idea' that is destined to rule keeps growing deep down—it begins to command; slowly it leads us back from side roads and wrong roads; it prepares single qualities

12. Gudren von Tevenar has pointed out that, given that talk of strong and weak wills suggests the notion of a sliding strength scale of wills, perhaps a more nuanced version of Nietzsche's account of autonomy and agency free will would allow that these also come in degrees. The point is well taken; however, Nietzsche's strong concern with the question of how to awaken his audience from their complacent assumptions militated in favour of the more rhetorically effective presentation in terms of agency free will as something either wholly present (for instance, in the sovereign individual) or wholly absent (for instance, in modern windbags).

13. Of course, Nietzsche would later take a less favourable view of Wagner.

> and fitnesses that will one day prove to be indispensable as a means towards the whole—one by one, it trains all subservient capacities before giving any hint of the dominant task, 'goal', 'aim', or 'meaning'. (*EH*, 'Why I Am So Clever', 9)

Nietzsche, as we shall soon see, often gives similar accounts with respect to Goethe's achievement of self-creation.

A helpful picture: According to Nietzsche, most humans, being merely members of the herd, are merely passive conduits for various disparate forces already existing and operating around them. Some individuals, due perhaps to conscious design, but more likely due to fortuitous circumstances, actively collect, intensify, and order some of those disparate forces, and create a new direction for them, thereby, in fortuitous circumstances, reorienting, to some degree, the whole field of forces in which we all exist. It is these individuals, according to Nietzsche, who deserve the honorific 'person', who by imposing their strong will exercise a form of free will and genuine agency.

In an interesting passage in *Beyond Good and Evil* Nietzsche characterizes the generation of his day as having

> inherited in its blood diverse standards and values, everything is unrest, disturbance, doubt, attempt, the very virtues do not allow each other to grow and become strong; balance, a centre of gravity, and perpendicular poise are lacking in body and soul. But what becomes sickest and degenerates most in such hybrids is the will: they no longer know independence of decisions and the intrepid sense of pleasure in willing—they doubt the 'freedom of the will' even in their dreams. (*BGE*, 208)

The implication here is that strong individuals who have a 'centre of gravity' would not doubt that they have freedom of the will. On this picture, having free will is not a matter of being free of necessity, but rather acting from a kind of inner necessity stemming from this centre of gravity. It is just this type of necessity that prompted Luther to famously say, 'Here I stand, I cannot do otherwise.'[14]

Nietzsche's positive account of free will and agency finds its echo in his many positive pronouncements about responsibility in *Ecce Homo*, and especially in *Beyond Good and Evil*. Typically

14. Sue James suggested this nice illustration of the point.

these positive pronouncements are forward-looking: they involve responsibility towards the future. In the *Ecce Homo* passages they evince a near megalomaniacal sense of possible influence on the future. Thus in *Ecce Homo*, 'Why I Am So Clever', Nietzsche speaks of having a 'responsibility for all millennia after me', and in the same work, in the section 'The Case of Wagner', he says, 'an indescribable responsibility lies upon me ... in that I bear the destiny of mankind on my shoulders'. These hyperbolic pronouncements find a more toned-down expression in his general pronouncements about responsibility in *Beyond Good and Evil*, where he continually emphasizes the duty of the philosopher to take responsibility for the future, for it is '[t]he philosopher as *we* understand him, we free spirits—as the man of the most comprehensive responsibility who has the conscience for the overall development of man' (*BGE*, 60). For Nietzsche the greatness of the ideal philosopher lies in his 'range and multiplicity, in his wholeness in manifoldness'; such a philosopher 'would determine rank in accordance with how much and how many things one could bear and take upon himself, how far one could extend his responsibility' (*BGE*, 212). The idea of holding a multiplicity of aspects within a single coherent manifold is, we have seen, the core of Nietzsche's account of what it is to be a person, a sovereign individual capable of exercising free will and responsibility. The idea that Nietzsche's ideal philosopher exhibits both free will and responsibility gets its clearest formulation at the end of Section 10 of the third essay of the *Genealogy*:

> Is there already enough pride, daring, bravery, self-assuredness in existence today, enough will of spirit, will to responsibility, *freedom of the will* so that henceforth on earth 'the philosopher' is truly—possible? ...

VII

Nietzsche's Revisionary Naturalistic Metaphysics of the Soul. That Nietzsche is open to notions of agency free will and agency responsibility that genuinely promote active engagement is further suggested by the analogy with his attitude to the related notion of soul. Generally he is extremely disparaging of the notion of the soul because of its Christian baggage. In his notebooks he tells us:

> To indulge the fable of 'unity', 'soul', 'person', this we have forbidden: with such hypotheses one only covers up the problem. (*KSA*, 11:577, June–July 1885)

Forbidding the use of these notions fits in easily enough with his general rejection of them. But in the same place he immediately goes on to say 'with such hypotheses one only covers up the problem'.

But why does he talk here of covering up a problem? What is the problem if all such things are simply irredeemable fictions? The problem being covered up is that unity, soul, personhood are not pre-given existences but rare achievements to be gained by hard effort. The fable is in the notion that these have already been achieved, that we as mere humans already have unity, are persons.

In *Beyond Good and Evil*, 12, Nietzsche hints that his more perceptive reader will see beyond the clumsy naturalists' simple rejection of the soul with its associated notion of superlative metaphysical free will and realize that an imminent notion of soul is now available:

> Between ourselves, it is not at all necessary to get rid of 'the soul' at the same time, and thus to renounce one of the most ancient and venerable hypotheses—as happens frequently to clumsy naturalists who can hardly touch on 'the soul' without immediately losing it. But the way is now open for new versions of the soul-hypothesis; and such conceptions as 'mortal souls' and 'soul as subjective multiplicity' and 'soul as social structure of the drives and affects' are henceforth to have citizen rights in science.

Now, one might be tempted to simply treat this suggestion of a new notion of soul, and the characterization of the sovereign individual as a being with agency free will, as isolated incidents in Nietzsche's wider corpus. But against this it is first worth noting that there are other places where Nietzsche uses free will in just this positive way. In *The Gay Science* he writes:

> Once a human being reaches the fundamental conviction that he must be commanded, he becomes a 'believer'. Conversely one could conceive of such a pleasure and power of self-determination, such a freedom of the will that the spirit would take leave of all faith and every wish for certainty, being practised in maintaining himself on insubstantial ropes and possibilities and dancing ever near abysses. Such a spirit would be the free spirit par excellence. (*GS*, 348)

Indeed the idea of freedom though self-determination is central to his characterization of his greatest hero, Goethe:

> What he wanted was totality . . . he disciplined himself to wholeness, he created himself . . . Goethe conceived of a person, strong, highly educated, accomplished in all corporeal matters, self-controlled, self-respecting, who can dare to allow himself the whole range and richness of naturalness, who is strong enough for this freedom . . . Such a spirit who has become free stands with a happy and trusting fatalism in the midst of the universe. (*TI*, 49, my translation)

This notion of freedom is echoed in some *Nachlass* passages, for instance,

> The freest act is that in which our own most strongest most finely practised nature springs forth, and in such a way that at the same time our intellect shows its directing hand. (*KSA*, 10:258, Spring–Summer 1883)

Nietzsche, then, should not be seen simply as one who rejects received metaphysical notions of free will, autonomy, agency, personhood and soul, but as one who replaces them with immanent naturalist accounts. Moreover, these accounts serve distinctly normative ends: they aim to replace a passive stance and engender a genuinely active creative engagement with the world. Nietzsche aims to change his preferred readers from being mere conduit points of a vast array of conflicting inherited drives into genuinely unified beings. As Nietzsche's Zarathustra puts it,

> And when my eyes flee from the present to the past, it always discovers the same thing: fragments and limbs and dreadful chances—but no men! . . . I walk among men as among fragments of the future: of the future which I scan. And it is my art and aim, to compose into one and bring together what is fragment and riddle and dreadful chance. (*TSZ*, II, 21)[15]

15. As Chris Sykes has pointed out to me, the theme that in modern times—or more specifically in modern Germany, as Nietzsche emphasizes in the second of the *Untimely Meditations*—there are no men, but only fragments of men is clearly a deliberate echo of the same charge that occurs in Hölderlin's *Hyperion*:

> I can think of no people more at odds with themselves than the Germans. You see artisans, but no men, thinkers, but no men . . . Is this not like a battlefield on which hacked-off hands and arms and every other limb lie scattered about? (Hölderlin 1952, p. 420, my translation)

VIII

Nietzsche and the Modern Tradition on the Self. This interpretation allows us to see a Nietzsche who has come to grips with a central problem of modern philosophy in a way that many of his predecessors, contemporaries, and even successors, have failed to do. If we take part of the central trajectory of modern philosophy to be the move from a religious to a secular world-view, we (should) see that giving up the metaphysics of God and soul raises a crucial problem about exactly what we are. The modern tradition offers a number of answers: we are in essence reasoners (Descartes, Kant);[16] we are bundles of sensations (Hume). None of these answers is particularly satisfactory. Nietzsche offers an interesting and rather original alternative. He claims that in a sense we do not exist.[17] This is not a version of that kind of academic, philosophic scepticism that brings philosophy into deserved disrepute. The existence of human bodies, like the existence of the so-called external world, is not something Nietzsche would ever dream of really denying. What Nietzsche questions is whether there are genuine selves inhabiting these bodies. In place of empiricist or rationalist accounts of the self, Nietzsche offers what might be called a naturalist-aestheticist account: to have a genuine self is to have an enduring co-ordinated hierarchy of drives. Most humans fail to have such a hierarchy; hence they are not sovereign individuals. Rather, they are a jumble of drives with no coherent order. Hence they are not genuine individuals or, we might say, selves. As Nietzsche says with particular reference to modern scholars,

> Whatever still remains in him of a 'person' strikes him as accidental, often arbitrary, still more disturbing; to such an extent he has become a passageway and reflection of strange forms and events even to himself. (*BGE*, 207)

16. Of course, Descartes and Kant were theists. Nevertheless, the intellectual trajectory of their work, whether intended or not, was inevitably towards a secular world-view.

17. The Hume of the Appendix to his *Treatise* concedes that the account of the self given in the *Treatise* rendered the self non-existent (see Hume 1978, pp. 635–6). However, this for Hume was an unintended and unacceptable consequence of his philosophy. For Nietzsche our general failure to achieve genuine selfhood, and the possibility, for at least a select few, of overcoming that failure is the very point of much of his philosophy.

Nietzsche's various attacks on the Kantian notions of autonomy and free will have multiple objectives. The negative objectives are to show that the notion of a will that transcends the causal order is intellectually unacceptable, and to attack the notion of deserts—objectives hardly unique to Nietzsche. The positive, and more profound and original, objective is to offer his readers the challenging notion that agency free will, genuine autonomy, and hence existence as an individual and self, is possible for some. This challenge should awaken his readers to the profoundly disturbing possibility that they themselves are not yet persons.

IX

The Normative Dimension to Nietzsche's Account of Agency Free Will. Now, one might object that the concept of agency free will that we have ascribed to Nietzsche lacks a normative dimension that is intrinsic to any notion of free will. Acts involving deserts free will are typically seen as those which should be punished/ rewarded. But acts involving agency free will, especially for those who deny deserts free will, might be seen as carrying no normative dimension. The worry here is that the terminology of agency free will amounts to a clever re-description that fails to capture the normative dimension that is essential to any free will debate. But this merely fails to identify the locus of the normativity relevant to agency free will. Proponents of deserts free will say that one must have acted with free will if one's action is to merit punishment or reward, so the normative dimension flows from, among other things, the fact that the act involved deserts free will. In the case of agency free will the normativitity is in the actual imperative to exercise agency free will, to be an agent rather than a mere cog in the causal network. One could, of course, endorse the possibility of agency free will and be indifferent as to whether anyone ever achieved agency free will. But in fact those, like Kant and Nietzsche, who endorse agency free will typically see it as something valuable. Indeed, if Nietzsche's account is correct, in the first-person case it is hard to see how one can be indifferent to whether one has free will, since that is tantamount to being indifferent as to whether one really exists. That Nietzsche wishes to promote the development of genuine individuals, that, like

Kant, Nietzsche sets autonomy as a goal, clearly indicates that he endorses agency free will as an aspiration.[18]

References

Gemes, K. 2001: 'Post-Modernism's Use and Abuse of Nietzsche'. *Philosophy and Phenomenological Research*, 62, pp. 337–60.

——— 2006: 'We Remain of Necessity Strangers to Ourselves: The Key Message of Nietzsche's *Genealogy*'. Forthcoming in Christa Acampora (ed.), *Nietzsche's Genealogy of Morals: Critical Essays*. Lanham, MD: Rowman and Littlefield.

Hölderlin, F. 1952: *Dichtungen und Briefe*. Munich: Winkler-Verlag.

Hume, D. 1978: *A Treatise on Human Nature*. Edited with an analytical index by L. A. Selby-Bigge. Oxford: Clarendon Press.

Leiter, B. 2003: *Nietzsche on Morality*. London: Routledge.

Nietzsche, F. 1966: *Beyond Good and Evil*. Trans. W. Kaufmannn. New York: Vintage.

——— 1968a: *The Antichrist*. In *Twilight of the Idols and The Antichrist*. Trans. R. J. Hollingdale. Harmondsworth: Penguin.

——— 1968b: *Twilight of the Idols*. In *Twilight of the Idols and The Antichrist*. Trans. R. J. Hollingdale. Harmondsworth: Penguin.

——— 1968c: *The Will to Power*. Trans. W. Kaufmann and R. J. Hollingdale, ed. W. Kaufmann. New York: Vintage.

——— 1969a: *Ecce Homo*. In *On the Genealogy of Morals and Ecce Homo*. Trans. W. Kaufmannn and R. J. Hollingdale. New York: Vintage.

——— 1969b: *On the Genealogy of Morals*. In *On the Genealogy of Morals and Ecce Homo*. Trans. W. Kaufmannn and R. J. Hollingdale. New York: Vintage.

——— 1974: *The Gay Science*. Trans. W. Kaufmann. New York: Vintage.

——— 1975: *Thus Spoke Zarathustra*. Trans. R. J. Hollingdale. Harmondsworth: Penguin.

——— 1982: *Daybreak*. Trans. R. J. Hollingdale. Cambridge: Cambridge University Press.

——— 1983: *Untimely Meditations*. Trans. R. J. Hollingdale. Cambridge: Cambridge University Press.

——— 1986: *Human, All Too Human*. Trans. R. J. Hollingdale. Cambridge: Cambridge University Press.

——— 1988: *Sämtliche Werke: Kritische Studienausgabe in 15 Einzelbänden*. Ed. G. Colli and M. Montinari. Berlin: de Gruyter.

——— 1993: *The Birth of Tragedy out of the Spirit of Music*. Trans. Shaun Whiteside, ed. Michael Tanner. London: Penguin.

Richardson, J. 1996: *Nietzsche's System*. Oxford: Oxford University Press.

Watson, G. 1996: 'Two Faces of Responsibility'. *Philosophical Topics*, 24, pp. 227–48.

18. Thanks are due to Chris Janaway and Sebastian Gardner and participants of the Gemes/Leiter Nietzsche Seminar held at the University of London in the autumn term of 2005–6 for helpful discussions on this topic.

NIETZSCHE ON FREE WILL, AUTONOMY AND THE SOVEREIGN INDIVIDUAL

by Ken Gemes and Christopher Janaway

II—Christopher Janaway

ABSTRACT This paper aims to distinguish a conception of 'free will' that Nietzsche opposes (that of the pure agent unaffected by contingencies of character and circumstance) and one that he supports. In *Human, All Too Human* Nietzsche propounds the 'total unfreedom' of the will. But by the time of *Beyond Good and Evil* and the *Genealogy* he is more concerned (a) to trace the affective psychological states underlying beliefs in both free will and 'unfree will', (b) to suggest that the will might become free in certain individuals, a matter of having a consistent strong character, self-knowledge, and ability to create values. The paper explores the kind of autonomy required in agents who would 'revalue' existing values.

Nietzsche talks of free will towards the end of the First Treatise of *On the Genealogy of Morality* and towards the beginning of the Second, and may appear to contradict himself within the space of a few pages. He describes as nonsensical and false the belief in a 'neutral "subject" with free choice'[1] standing behind an individual's actions; yet he says there has existed or may exist a type of individual who 'has become free' and is a 'lord of the *free* will'.[2] Any reading of the *Genealogy* ought to address this apparent tension. Whatever else the mysterious 'sovereign individual' is, he is not supposed to be a nonsense or a falsehood. Nietzsche must regard the sovereign individual's achievement of freedom as something other than his becoming a neutral subject with free choice. Ken Gemes's distinction between deserts free will and agency free will is an appealing way of resolving the tension. Here I want to complement Gemes's treatment by addressing two chief topics. First, I document a change in Nietzsche's writing about free will between the earlier *Human, All Too Human* and the period of the *Genealogy* and *Beyond Good and Evil*, a change which, I shall argue, corresponds

1. *GM*, I, 13.
2. *GM*, II, 2.

with the development of his genealogical method.[3] Second, I shall argue that Nietzsche should attribute a kind of autonomy to those of his readers whom he imagines being cured of their attachment to morality and creating their own values.

I

Acting Otherwise. In the Preface to the *Genealogy* Nietzsche names as his opponents two thinkers who had previously exerted positive influences on him: Schopenhauer and Paul Rée. Both thinkers deny free will in a specific sense: they claim that for any particular action *A* of any human individual, if the individual's character and all the circumstances in which he or she acts are assumed unchanged, then no action other than *A* is possible for that individual. No one could have done otherwise on some occasion than they in fact did on that occasion. For both, the notion of responsibility for human actions becomes unsustainable as a result.

Schopenhauer's argument for determinism is clear and effective: a free will would be a will from which all necessity is absent, but nothing that occurs in the empirical world is without a cause that makes it necessary (one instance of the principle of sufficient reason). Human actions are events in the empirical world, and are caused by the interaction of the individual's character and the motives or mental representations that occur to him or her. So it is an error to think that 'contrary to all laws of the understanding and of nature, the will determines itself without sufficient reasons, and that under given circumstances its decisions could turn out thus or even in the opposite way in the case of the same human being.'[4] Nowhere does anything determine itself, nor act without sufficient reason. We do not understand all the causal connections between our character and experiences and the actions that issue from them, because they are of greater complexity than other observable connections in nature, and because the effects can be remote and heterogeneous from their causes. We rightly believe in many instances that *if* we will to do *A*, we can do it. But that does not make it true that we control whether it is *A* that we will

3. See Owen 2003 for an account of the development of the genealogical method.
4. Schopenhauer, *Prize Essay on the Freedom of the Will*, p. 36.

rather than *B*.[5] Schopenhauer imagines a man deliberating:

> 'It is six o'clock; the day's work is over. I can now go for a walk, or go to the club; I can also climb the tower to see the sun set; I can also go to the theater; I can also visit this or that friend; in fact I can also run out by the city gate into the wide world and never come back. All that is entirely up to me; I have complete freedom; however, I do none of them, but just as voluntarily go home to my wife.' This is just as if water were to say: 'I can form high waves (as in a storm at sea); I can rush down a hill (as in the bed of a torrent); I can dash down foaming and splashing (as in the waterfall); I can rise freely as a jet into the air (as in a fountain); finally, I can even boil away and disappear (as at 212 degrees Fahrenheit); however, I do none of these things now, but voluntarily remain calm and clear in the mirroring pond.' Just as water can do all those things only when the determining causes enter for one or the other, so is the condition just the same for the man with respect to what he imagines he can do. Until the causes enter, it is impossible for him to do anything; but then he *must* do it, just as water must act as soon as it is placed in the respective circumstances.[6]

Nevertheless, Schopenhauer believes that there is moral responsibility. We feel guilt, and have an irremovable sense that 'we ourselves are *the doers of our deeds*'.[7] Schopenhauer argues that since we feel responsible, but cannot be genuinely responsible for our actions, we must be feeling a deeper responsibility for our very character, for what we are, our being (*esse*). A person realizes that the action that issued from him was not absolutely necessary; it was necessary relative to the circumstances and to his character, but it might not have occurred 'if only he had been another person'.[8] Schopenhauer's idea is that we truly feel guilty for being that out of which a harmful action emanates, despite the fact that we could not have acted otherwise. From this notion of responsibility for our being he argues, questionably, to the conclusion that there must be a kind of freedom residing in our character. Using the Kantian distinction between empirical and intelligible characters, the latter supposedly what I am in myself

5. Ibid., pp. 16–17.
6. Ibid., pp. 36–7.
7. Ibid., p. 83.
8. Ibid., p. 84.

beyond the forms of space, time and causality,[9] he suggests that my moral freedom is transcendental and lies in my non-empirical essence. The suggestion is hard to grasp. The intelligible character could be a locus of responsibility only if there is some sense in which it involves a free act, or a choice to have such-and-such character (as Schopenhauer sometimes claims[10]). But how I could have chosen my own innate, unchanging non-empirical character by some kind of act lying outside of time is never explained.

Rée dismisses this notion of intelligible freedom: 'We have received our innate character not through any fault of our own; our remorse is not a feeling of regret over the fact that, by virtue of this intelligible freedom, we have chosen just this character and not some better one.'[11] With Schopenhauer's only refuge for responsibility and freedom thus blocked, Rée holds that we have neither, and the rest of his discussion of free will could be described as a thoroughly naturalized version of Schopenhauer's. 'I could have acted differently' is true only if it means 'The capacity for acting differently was also in my nature at that time, and my nature could have been swayed by it under other circumstances (that is, if a thought or sensation had been different).'[12] I could have acted differently only under different causal input, just like any animal. Responsibility falls immediately:

> We hold others responsible for particular blameworthy actions they have committed, although they were able, as we suppose, to have acted differently.
>
> Holding others responsible is thus based ... on the error of supposing that the human will is free.
>
> In contrast, when we have understood that every person is born with certain characteristics, and that certain thoughts and feelings necessarily emerge from the conjunction of these two factors, which in turn necessarily give rise to certain actions—when we have understood the necessity of all human actions, we will no longer hold anyone responsible.[13]

9. Ibid., p. 86.
10. See *Prize Essay*, p. 87: 'the whole being and essence ... of the human being himself ... must be conceived as his free act'; and *World as Will and Representation* I, 289: 'the intelligible character of every man is to be regarded as an act of will outside time.'
11. Rée 2003, 108.
12. Rée 2003, 106.
13. Rée 2003, 111.

Responsibility is a plain illusion for Rée, though people do not often acknowledge it as such because they fear 'that those they have punished might say: Why are you punishing me? I had to act in that way', and 'are afraid of the conclusions of the mob: if everything is necessary, then, giving in to our instincts, we will steal, pillage, and murder.' This fear, which Rée says is 'often perhaps well-founded', leads philosophers to hide from the truth that there is no free will.[14]

Earlier in his career Nietzsche's thinking on free will was largely in step with Rée's and not especially original. In *Human, All Too Human* he consistently describes the belief in free will as an error[15] and refers to the *unfreedom* of the will as 'total' and 'unconditional'.[16] Human beings are no more free than animals,[17] or indeed than a waterfall in which we may 'think we see ... capriciousness and freedom of will'.[18] In a section entitled 'The fable of intelligible freedom' (*HA* I, 39) he elegantly recaps the argument for determinism and Rée's rejection of Schopenhauer's attempt to save responsibility from it. The fable culminates in Schopenhauer's inference that because we feel guilt we must be responsible and must have freedom in some sense; but the inference is faulty, argues Nietzsche in clearly Rée-inspired mode:

> It is because man *regards* himself as free, not because he is free, that he feels remorse and pangs of conscience.—This feeling is, moreover, something one can disaccustom oneself to. [...] No one is accountable for his deeds, no one for his nature; to judge is the same thing as to be unjust. This also applies when the individual judges himself. The proposition is as clear as daylight, and yet here everyone prefers to retreat back into the shadows and untruth: from fear of the consequences.

However, I shall claim that a decade later, in the *Genealogy*, Nietzsche attaches little thematic importance to the question whether there is free will in the 'acting otherwise' sense and offers no arguments against it.

14. Rée 2003, 107.
15. See *HAH*, I, 18, 39, 99, 102, 106; *HAH*, II/2, 12.
16. *HAH*, II/1, 50, 33.
17. *HAH*, I, 102.
18. *HAH*, I, 106.

II

The Doer and the Deed. In the opening of *GM* I, 13 Nietzsche's rhetoric, as often in the *Genealogy*, aims to tease out fundamental inclinations and aversions in the reader, probing thosc habitual affects which, for Nietzsche, are the bedrock of our attachment to the values of morality.[19] Our instinctive reaction to the mini-parable in which lambs feel anger at birds of prey, but the birds of prey love lambs, may be to sympathize with both affective standpoints in quick succession, revealing how readily we understand the morality of *ressentiment* from within, and how absurd we can also find its radical conception of freedom as unconstrained by causal factors. Nietzsche suggests that language may provide a kind of passive platform for all sorts of reification, and hence for the construction of the fiction that the agent, the 'doer', is some thing distinct from the sum total of his or her actions or doings. But his explanation here includes a more precisely motivated element, namely the will to power of the weak, whose affects actively exploit the tendency to believe in metaphysical 'subjects' in order to gain a kind of mastery over the naturally strong by persuading them that to exercise their strength is evil, and to refrain from exercising it good:

> Small wonder if the suppressed, hiddenly glowing affects of revenge and hate exploit this belief and basically even uphold no other belief more ardently than this one, that *the strong one is free* to be weak, and the bird of prey to be a lamb—they thereby gain for themselves the right to hold the bird of prey *accountable* for being a bird of prey ... When out of the vengeful cunning of powerlessness the oppressed, downtrodden, violated say to themselves: 'Let us be different from the evil ones, namely good! And good is what everyone is who does not do violence, who injures no one, who doesn't attack, who doesn't retaliate [...]' as if the very weakness of the weak [...] were a voluntary achievement, something willed, something chosen, a *deed*, a *merit*. This kind of human needs the belief in a neutral 'subject' with free choice, out of an instinct of self-preservation, self-affirmation, in which every lie tends to hallow itself.[20]

19. On the role of affects in genealogical explanation see Janaway 2003 and Janaway 2006.
20. *GM*, I, 13.

Nietzsche's thought is that prior to the invention of the idea that our essence resides elsewhere than in the sum of our actual behaviour and underlying drives, we could not have believed in accountability or blame in the manner required to maintain the moral practice of judging actions good and evil. The notion of a radically free subject of action is required in order to make human beings controllable, answerable, equal, and in particular to re-describe inaction as a virtue of which all are capable and dominant self-assertion as a wrong for which all are culpable. Note the role of feelings in Nietzsche's explanation. It is the reactive affects of the weak, described as 'hiddenly glowing', that drive the need to assign blame and call to account. This accords with a wider tendency of Nietzsche's genealogical explanations to trace moral beliefs and conceptual distinctions back to more basic feelings. Present-day adherents of morality have inherited affective habits because of the prevalence of the system of evaluative concepts good, evil, blame, guilt, and so on, and that system of concepts came to exist because of feelings such as *ressentiment*, hatred, revenge, fear, joy in inflicting cruelty, at earlier historical stages.

Bernard Williams provides a convincing discussion of Nietzsche's analysis of free will here. We have the metaphysical idea of the 'pure will', or of the wholly free or indifferent 'doer' that lies somewhere behind the deed, detached from all contingencies that could push it one way or the other, and Nietzsche's question is: What might have motivated this way of thinking about actions? His answer is (in Williams's phrase) that there needed to be a target for blame. Injured parties had (as I would suggest) a *felt need*, closely associated with the feeling of *ressentiment*, to locate an absolute responsibility in the other, who could then be conceived as having freedom to bring about a radically different course of events that resulted in no injury. Williams describes this as

> a fantasy of inserting into the [other] agent an acknowledgement of me, to take the place of exactly the act that harmed me ... The idea has to be ... that I, now, might change the agent from one who did not acknowledge me to one who did. This fantasized, magical change ... requires simply the idea of the agent at the moment of the action, all isolated from the network of circumstances in which his action was actually embedded.[21]

21. Williams 1994, p. 245.

The salient point is that the re-description of the agent as existing in isolation from the pressures of nature, culture, and circumstance is *already a moralized description*, one you would make only if you already thought in terms of moral goodness and responsibility, and hence sought a target for blame. The human being naturalistically described, as the product of actual physical and cultural forces, does not provide a proper target for blame, so we have to resort to metaphysics. This reinforces Nietzsche's idea, expressed so clearly at the beginning of *Beyond Good and Evil*, that no metaphysics is morally neutral.[22]

One difference between this treatment of free will and the earlier discussion influenced by Rée is that the conception of the radically free agent is assigned a genesis firmly within the slavish morality of the weak who are afflicted by *ressentiment*. The needs of a specific psychological type in a specific set of power relations motivate the invention of the metaphysical concept of free agency. It is just '*this kind* of human' who needs the belief in a neutral 'subject' with free choice—a more pointed explanation of its genesis than Rée's idea that humans think there is free will because of generalized habits of association and error. But note also a second difference. Nietzsche is now focusing on 'could have acted otherwise' in a different sense. What concerns him is whether the strong could have acted other than strongly, other than in their own character. The question is not whether a Homeric warrior could have done action *B* rather than action *A* in a particular circumstance—spared an enemy with aristocratic magnanimity, say, rather than killing him with aristocratic disdain or enslaving him with aristocratic contempt—but whether the hero was 'free' to run away whimpering like a weakling, or to shrug off all concern for honour and victory and opt for an easy life. In order to blame the strong for failing to behave weakly, the weak need to believe in these latter possibilities, which Nietzsche claims are merely invented or fantasized. True, once you believe in the radical metaphysical conception of the free, neutral subject, you will become like Schopenhauer's man deliberating at six o'clock, and hold that for any individual limitless actions are possible other than what they actually do. But it would be a fallacy to infer

22. See *BGE*, 6.

from the falsity of the radical metaphysical conception to the falsity of 'I could have done otherwise'. Nietzsche's position in this passage need be read, therefore, only as embodying the claim that our repertoire as agents is circumscribed by our character, not the claim that particular actions are necessitated. The passage leaves it open that Achilles could have refrained, in character, from killing Hector.

Against this, however, it might be argued that there can be no free will at all unless there is a radically indifferent subject of the kind Nietzsche rejects. Schopenhauer takes this line, saying that unless we define free will as the classical *liberum arbitrium indifferentiae*, or free choice determined by nothing at all, we give up 'the only clearly determined, firm, and settled concept' of freedom of the will, and fall into 'vague and hazy explanations behind which lurks a hesitant insufficiency'.[23] If this is the only proper sense of free will, and if in this sense there is no free will, then there is no free will at all. Brian Leiter also subscribes to what is effectively this line,[24] and attributes it to Nietzsche: 'Nietzsche argues that an autonomous agent would have to be *causa sui* (i.e. self-caused, or the cause of itself); but since nothing can be *causa sui*, no one could be an autonomous agent.'[25] But does Nietzsche argue that there is no free will at all from the premisses that free will entails being *causa sui* and that being *causa sui* is a contradiction? In *Beyond Good and Evil*, 21, he unequivocally states that the notion of being self-caused is a contradiction. However, that passage contains no premise that resembles 'there can be free will only if there is a *causa sui*'. Here Nietzsche is not even pursuing the question whether there is or is not free will. Rather he is at his usual genealogical business: flushing out an underlying affective state—'*the longing for* "freedom of the will" in the superlative metaphysical sense'—and hypothesizing an explanation for its genesis and persistence. How do we come to have a thirst for this extremity of metaphysics, and why is it lodged so firmly in the modern consciousness? Nietzsche's answer here is that we cannot stomach any sense that we are not *wholly* in control of ourselves. Nietzsche is not doing metaphysics,

23. *Prize Essay*, p. 8.
24. See Leiter 2002, pp. 88, 90.
25. Leiter 2002, p. 87.

rather unearthing the valuations of ourselves that underlie our inclining to a certain metaphysical position.

So far this is, admittedly, compatible with Nietzsche's rejecting free will altogether. However, the remainder of *Beyond Good and Evil*, 21 signals a radical change from the *Human, All Too Human* passages discussed above. There Nietzsche harped on about the total unfreedom of the will and the illusoriness of responsibility; now he asks his reader 'to rid his mind of the reversal of this misconceived concept of "free will": I mean the "un-free will" [. . .] The "un-free will" is mythology.' There is reason to believe, Nietzsche now argues, that in nature itself there is no 'causal association', 'necessity' or 'psychological un-freedom'; we merely project such notions on to reality. When he asks why we make this projection, he is again seeking psychological explanations for some feelings (vanity, self-contempt) that lie beneath our thoughts:

> It is almost always a symptom of what is lacking in a thinker when he senses some compulsion, need, having-to-follow, pressure, un-freedom in every 'causal connection' and 'psychological necessity'. It is very telling to feel this way—the person tells on himself. And in general, if I have observed correctly, 'un-freedom of the will' is regarded as a problem by two completely opposed parties, but always in a profoundly *personal* manner. The one party would never dream of relinquishing their 'responsibility', a belief in *themselves*, a personal right to *their own* merit (the vain races belong to this group —). Those in the other party, on the contrary, do not want to be responsible for anything or to be guilty of anything; driven by an inner self-contempt, they long to be able to *shift the blame* for themselves to something else.[26]

Nietzsche does not direct these diagnostic and condemnatory words towards Rée and his former self, who asserted the total unfreedom of the will and the illusoriness of responsibility, though he could well ask himself what affects that episode in his career had been symptomatic of, or what had been lacking in himself. The Nietzsche of this text, Nietzsche the genealogist, asks instead what affective psychological states explain the origination of these extreme metaphysical pictures of ourselves. Similarly in *Genealogy* I, 13, he asks for the psychological origins of belief in the indifferent subject unconstrained by nature and

26. *BGE*, 21.

circumstances, and finds the answer in *ressentiment* and its outgrowth, the felt need for a target for blame.

III

The Free Will of the Sovereign Individual. Sections 2–3 of the Second Treatise introduce the 'sovereign individual' as 'autonomous' and 'lord of the *free* will'; but the text leaves us uncertain as to who this individual is, was, or might be. He or she is described as an end-product of the conformist 'morality of custom', a mode of evaluation prior to the Christian morality Nietzsche is out to re-evaluate in the *Genealogy*.[27] But are 'sovereign individuals' supposed to have existed after the age of the morality of custom was over or during its later stages? And are they supposed to have existed once and then faded away into history, or are there sovereign individuals around today? Or have they never existed? The tone suggests that Nietzsche may be describing an ideal type, giving us what Aaron Ridley has called 'a sort of foretaste of the (enlightened) conscience of the future'.[28] It has been claimed that being a sovereign individual is for Nietzsche constitutive of being truly human.[29] But this is difficult to support. For although Nietzsche attributes to the sovereign individual a 'feeling of the completion of man himself',[30] he emphasizes the distinction and superiority of the sovereign individual over other types of human individuals who lack power, pride and autonomy.[31] So, to reiterate a central point in Gemes's paper, in the sense of free will at issue here not every human being will have free will, or at least not to the same degree. Nietzsche again ignores the global, metaphysical question whether absence of necessity is possible in human agency, and poses a cultural and psychological question about qualities and conditions that mark out certain human beings as peculiarly admirable or valuable. Free will in this sense is a variably realizable condition, not a universal one. It is an achievement, or a blessing, of the few, and can occur

27. Nietzsche introduces the 'morality of custom' (*Sittlichkeit der Sitte*) in *D*, 9.
28. Ridley 1998, p. 18.
29. See Havas 2000, pp. 94–5.
30. *GM*, II, 2.
31. The point is made in reply to Havas by Ridley 2000, pp. 106–7.

only in some cultural circumstances with people of certain character types.

A further pointer in this direction appears right at the end of the Second Treatise, where Nietzsche envisages a rare and exceptionally strong 'human of the future', a 'bell-stroke of noon and of the great decision, that makes the will free again, that gives back to the earth its goal and to man his hope.'[32] Such talk of making the will free *again* suggests a fall and redemption pattern: at some time in the past, as a product of the harshly repressive 'morality of custom', there became possible sovereign individuals with a free will. Since that time the post-Christian morality of selflessness has been victorious, positing the desirability of guilt and self-suppression and the conception of the non-self-suppressing individual as blameworthy for not making the supposedly available choice to be harmless. In some future we might cast off this conception of morality, and the will could be free again.

The individual with free will contrasts starkly with the morality of custom (*die Sittlichkeit der Sitte*) because, as Nietzsche mischievously puts it, ' "autonomous" and "moral" are mutually exclusive'.[33] For there to be values at all, Nietzsche suggests, there had to be a long prehistory in which simple conformity to tradition determined what was good, departure from tradition what was bad and fit to be curbed. Civilization begins with the proposition 'any custom is better than no custom', and tradition is a 'higher authority which one obeys [. . .] because it *commands*'.[34] Yet the end-product or 'fruit' of this whole constraining process is an individual 'resembling only himself', having the capacity to be 'free again from the morality of custom'. Nietzsche says much in a short space here, perhaps grasping for a vocabulary that will capture his insights. The sovereign individual's will is 'free', 'his own', 'independent', 'long', and 'unbreakable'; and in virtue of this will the sovereign individual is permitted to promise, has 'mastery over himself', has his own standard of value, is permitted to say 'yes' to himself,[35] and has a consciousness of his 'superiority'

32. *GM*, II, 24.
33. *GM*, II, 2.
34. *D*, 16, 9.
35. *GM*, II, 3. All immediately surrounding quotations and paraphrases are from *GM*, II, 2.

and 'completion'. To be *permitted* to make promises, one must not only be minimally capable of promising but have the power to fulfil one's promises and the integrity to promise only what one genuinely has the will to do. This suggests a kind of self-knowledge in which one is properly conscious of what it is that one wills, and confident of the consistency with which one's will is going to maintain itself intact until the moment at which it can be delivered upon. The sovereign individual can count upon himself to act consistently, to be the same in the future when the time comes to produce what he promised in the past. Understanding oneself in this way, one will presumably attain a justified sense of satisfaction in one's power and integrity, and value others according to their manifestation of the kind of power and integrity one recognizes in oneself.

This positive conception of free will, then, involves acting fully within one's character, knowing its limits and capabilities and valuing oneself for what one is rather than for one's conformity to an external standard or to what one ought to be. In the later *Twilight of the Idols* Nietzsche eulogizes Goethe as 'a spirit *become free* [*freigewordner*]', who 'dares to allow himself the whole compass and wealth of naturalness, who is strong enough for this freedom' and 'stands in the midst of the universe with a joyful and trusting fatalism'.[36] In another passage about artistic creativity Nietzsche emphasizes how much the right kind of freedom stems from submitting to constraints rather than escaping them: 'Every artist knows how far removed this feeling of letting go is from his "most natural" state, the free ordering, placing, disposing and shaping in the moment of "inspiration"—he knows how strictly and subtly he obeys thousands of laws at this very moment.'[37]

These are among the harder parts of Nietzsche's philosophy to feel one has understood or re-expressed faithfully. There is a vagueness in Nietzsche's evocations of what future values and future individuals will be once they have liberated themselves from moral self-descriptions. We may excuse the vagueness to some extent: Nietzsche is writing of an aspiration that he thinks

36. *TI*, 'Expeditions of an Untimely Man', 49. My translation of *freigewordner*, in preference to Hollingdale's 'emancipated'.
37. *BGE*, 188.

has rarely, if ever, been realized, writing in the midst of a moralized vocabulary that by his own lights is all-pervasive, and *ex hypothesi* cannot give a general or formulaic account of the values of his future individuals because of their very individuality, their intensely personal, self-legislating nature that must resist universalization. But we might be able to conceive of something like the following as an approximation to Nietzsche's sovereign individual: someone who is conscious of the strength and consistency of his or her own character over time; who creatively affirms and embraces as valuable the entirety of his or her self, and who values his or her actions because of the degree to which they are in character; who welcomes the limitation and discipline of internal and external nature as the true conditions of action and creation, and whose evaluations arise from a sense of who he or she is, rather than from conformity to some external or generic code of values. This is a glimpse of the sense in which free will might be attained, or re-gained for Nietzsche. But to gain even this glimpse we must step outside our learned moralistic preoccupation with blame and the neutral subject of action, and look beyond the dichotomy between radical independence from nature and the 'total unfreedom' of Rée's naturalism: a dichotomy between two myths, as Nietzsche has warned us, myths that prevail because they are driven by differing affective impulses within us.

IV

Autonomy and the Achievement of New Values. Nietzsche is hoping for a re-valuation of values: he wants some of us at least to change our allegiance away from the values of selflessness as he has diagnosed them, to regard them as symptoms of sickness and decline which we will do our best to distance ourselves from in future. But what is this change in allegiance, and how might it occur?

An important aspect to re-valuation is the claiming of values as one's own. Rather than adhering to values which are received, traditional, generic, universal, one is to discover one's own personal values. For example, Nietzsche says:

> Let us [. . .] *limit* ourselves to the purification of our opinions and value judgements and to the *creation of tables of what is good that are new and all our own*: let us stop brooding over the 'moral

> value of our actions'! Yes, my friends, it is time to feel nauseous about some people's moral chatter about others. Sitting in moral judgement should offend our taste.[38]

Discovering truths about the psychological origins of our evaluations does not as such re-value them, but, as Nietzsche says in a notebook entry,[39] only 'brings with it a *feeling* of diminution in value ... and prepares the way to a critical mood and attitude' towards them. He also puts this by saying, 'Your insight into *how such things as moral judgements could ever have come into existence* would spoil these emotional words [such as 'duty' and 'conscience'] for you.'[40] The effect, I take it, could also be described as a loss of one's more or less automatic emotional alignment with received values, a suspension of the single-dimensional 'pro and contra' inherited from the Christian culture of Nietzsche's most typical readers. This suspension allows a space for a new evaluation and a shift or reversal in values, which Nietzsche often describes in ways which seem to presuppose agency, judgement, and choice.

A relevant example comes at the end of the *Genealogy*'s Second Treatise. Here Nietzsche takes himself to have shown that guilt came to be regarded as a good in the Christian world-view because the conception of our natural instincts as an ultimate transgression against God allowed us the most powerful guarantee of being able to vent our in-built drive towards cruelty upon ourselves. Nietzsche evaluates this state of self-torture as 'the most terrible sickness that has thus far raged in man'.[41] But then he offers us the healthy alternative, 'a reverse attempt ... namely to wed to bad conscience the *unnatural* inclinations, all those aspirations to the beyond, to that which is contrary to the senses, contrary to the instincts, contrary to nature'[42]—though he doubts that any but that most exceptional human being of the future, the redeeming, creative spirit of great health, will be able to accomplish this.

How to characterize the change of allegiance in values that Nietzsche here imagines someone undergoing? We start with the

38. *GS*, 335.
39. From 1885–6, published as *WP*, 254.
40. *GS*, 335.
41. *GM*, II, 22.
42. *GM*, II, 24.

observation that people feel guilt and regard life lived with an enduring guilty conscience as having positive value. We offer to explain these phenomena in terms of historical psychological states: in brief, a instinctual drive to inflict cruelty, internalization of aggressive instincts that were originally outward-directed, and rationalization of the resultant self-cruelty by the invention of a theistic metaphysics. We judge this psychological complex a sickness, allowing ourselves, as Nietzsche says, to feel horrified and unnerved by the sadness of it.[43] Although we are the inheritors of Christian attitudes of disapproval towards what is labelled as egoistic, we can take a step back from our accustomed valuations, and then—if strong enough—try to feel negatively towards ourselves if we feel tempted to despise our natural instincts and inclinations, or to hope for a higher, otherworldly order of values. The process of reversal Nietzsche envisages is cognitive at many stages. One *comes to believe* a certain explanation as true, one *judges* a set of psychological states as unhealthy, one *tries* to feel a new set of affects, and *identifies oneself with* specific critical second-order attitudes regarding certain of one's feelings.

In *Daybreak* Nietzsche describes the change in valuation he seeks with the phrase 'we have to *learn to think differently*'—that is, outside the moral evaluative oppositions of good and evil, egoistic and selfless—'in order at last, perhaps very late on, to attain even more: *to feel differently*.'[44] Also in *Daybreak* Nietzsche adumbrates a kind of liberation of the individual's thinking, not from feelings *per se*, which for him would be impossible and undesirable,[45] but from feelings which are not original or appropriate to the individual. Instead of carrying around 'valuations of things that originate in the passions and loves of former centuries'[46] and figuratively giving 'obedience to one's grandfather and grandmother and their grandparents', one is to honour what he strikingly calls 'the gods which are in *us*:

43. *GM*, II, 24
44. *D*, 103.
45. As witness the famous passage in *GM*, III, 12, where Nietzsche urges that 'there is ... *only* a perspectival "knowing", and the more affects we allow to speak about a matter ... that much more complete will our "concept" of this matter, our "objectivity" be. But to eliminate the will altogether, to disconnect the affects one and all, supposing that we were capable of this: what? would that not be to *castrate* the intellect?'
46. *GS*, 57.

our reason and our experience'.[47] Other passages suggest that a re-valuation of values will be an act of placing trust in values that are authentically one's own, an autonomous decision taken in the light of self-understanding.

> It is selfish to consider one's own judgement a universal law, and this selfishness is blind, petty and simple because it shows that *you haven't yet discovered yourself or created for yourself an ideal of your very own* [my emphasis] [...] No one who judges 'in this case everyone would have to act like this' has yet taken five steps towards self-knowledge. [...] We, however, want to *become who we are*—human beings who are new, unique, incomparable, who give themselves laws, who create themselves! To that end we must become the best students and discoverers of everything lawful and necessary in the world.[48]

Nietzsche here predicates both self-knowledge and autonomy of those who would successfully follow him. Against this one may range any number of places in which Nietzsche asserts that self and will are illusions, that there is no internal 'helmsman' controlling one's actions, no unitary subject of thought or action known to oneself by privileged access, only a subterranean multiplicity of competing or hierarchically organized drives, of which one's knowledge will always be incomplete. But the difficulty and incompleteness of self-knowledge is not the same as its impossibility. Self-knowledge, and indeed selfhood as such (as Gemes shows), is a matter of degree for Nietzsche, rare among human beings, a task set for a few of us rather than a given. He imagines that by examining our own deep-seated attitudes of inclination and aversion, by accepting hypotheses about their origin in past psychological configurations such as those of the ancient masters and slaves, by reflecting on which values we feel as most congenial to our characters, we may attach ourselves to a new set of values. The latter step of becoming free from the inherited values of morality requires, I argue, the conception of oneself as deciding, choosing and trying as a genuine agent with autonomy. Such genuine agency does not require that one be a neutral subject of free will that has unlimited possibility of action unconstrained by character and the causal

47. *D*, 35.
48. *GS*, 335.

order—in that sense there is no free will. But that we have the capacity to change our values and make something new of ourselves does require, as Nietzsche says, that we rid ourselves of the other myth, that of the total unfreedom of the will. To those who incline to think that Nietzsche's denial of radical *causa sui* free will leaves him no room for such autonomous, transformational choice of values, his own words may perhaps be addressed:

> In human beings, *creature* and *creator* are combined: in humans there is material, fragments, abundance, clay, dirt, nonsense, chaos; but in humans there is also creator, maker, hammer-hardness, spectator-divinity and seventh day:—do you understand this contrast?[49,50]

References

Works by Nietzsche

BGE *Beyond Good and Evil*. Trans. Judith Norman. Cambridge: Cambridge University Press, 2002.

D *Daybreak*. Trans. R. J. Hollingdale. Cambridge: Cambridge University Press, 1982.

HAH *Human, All Too Human*. Trans. R. J. Hollingdale. Cambridge: Cambridge University Press, 1986.

GM *On the Genealogy of Morality*. Trans. Maudemarie Clark and Alan J. Swensen. Indianapolis: Hackett, 1998.

GS *The Gay Science*. Trans. Josephine Nauckhoff. Cambridge: Cambridge University Press, 2001.

TI *Twilight of the Idols*. Trans. R. J. Hollingdale. Harmondsworth: Penguin, 1990.

WP *The Will to Power*. Ed. Walter Kaufmann, trans. Walter Kaufmann and R. J. Hollingdale. New York: Vintage, 1968.

Other Works

Havas, Randall 2000: 'Nietzsche's Idealism'. *Journal of Nietzsche Studies*, 20, pp. 90–9.

Janaway, Christopher 2003: 'Nietzsche's Artistic Revaluation'. In S. Gardner and J. L. Bermúdez (eds), *Art and Morality*. London: Routledge, pp. 260–76.

——— 2006: 'Naturalism and Genealogy'. In Keith Ansell-Pearson (ed.), *The Blackwell Companion to Nietzsche*. Oxford: Blackwell, pp. 337–52.

Leiter, Brian 2002: *Nietzsche on Morality*. London: Routledge.

Owen, David 2003: 'Nietzsche, Re-evaluation and the Turn to Genealogy'. *European Journal of Philosophy*, 11, pp. 249–72.

——— and Aaron Ridley 2003: 'On Fate'. *International Studies in Philosophy*, 35, pp. 63–78.

Rée, Paul 2003: *Basic Writings*. Ed. and trans. Robin Small. Urbana, IL and Chicago: University of Illinois Press.

49. *BGE*, 225.
50. This paper owes much to Ken Gemes's paper above, to Owen and Ridley 2003, and to conversations with the authors.

Ridley, Aaron 1998: *Nietzsche's Conscience*. Ithaca, NY and London: Cornell University Press.

——— 2000: 'Ancillary Thoughts on an Ancillary Text'. *Journal of Nietzsche Studies*, 20, pp. 100–8.

Schopenhauer, Arthur 1969: *The World as Will and Representation*. Trans. E. F. J. Payne. 2 vols. New York: Dover.

——— 1999: *Prize Essay on the Freedom of the Will*. Trans. E. F. J. Payne. Cambridge: Cambridge University Press.

Williams, Bernard 1994: 'Nietzsche's Minimalist Moral Psychology'. In Richard Schacht (ed.), *Nietzsche, Genealogy, Morality*. London and Berkeley: University of California Press, pp. 214–36.